FLUCTUATIONS IN AMERICAN BUSINESS
1790-1860

FLUCTUATIONS IN AMERICAN BUSINESS

1790-1860

BY

Walter Buckingham Smith

Sometime Orrin Sage Professor of Economics
Williams College

AND

Arthur Harrison Cole

Professor of Business Economics, Emeritus
Harvard University

NEW YORK / RUSSELL & RUSSELL

HARVARD ECONOMIC STUDIES
VOLUME L

ACKNOWLEDGEMENTS

Professor Smith wishes to acknowledge his appreciation of the advice and help of Professor Warren M. Persons and the late Professor Allyn A. Young — but for whom this study would not have been begun. To Miss Ruth Crandall he is indebted for many helpful suggestions and criticisms.

Professor Cole wishes to make appreciative acknowledgement particularly to Dr. Edwin Frickey, whose collaboration in the study of stock prices, 1825–66, was most helpful; to Mr. C. L. Bullion, Chief Accountant of the Public Land Office, Washington, D. C., whose courteous assistance made possible the collection of the data on public land sales; to Mrs. Lora S. Weston and Miss Ruth Crandall for invaluable aid in the preparation of statistical material and in the task of seeing the book through the press; to Dr. Warren M. Persons, Dr. Homer B. Vanderblue, and the Harvard Economic Society for encouragement and advice in the development of constituent sections of this volume; and to the Milton Fund for Research and the Harvard University Committee on Economic Research (now the Committee on Research in the Social Sciences) for financial aid in the collection and treatment of statistical material.

TABLE OF CONTENTS

CONTENTS

APPENDICES

LIST OF TABLES

SECTION I

BUSINESS FLUCTUATIONS, 1792–1820

SECTION II

BUSINESS FLUCTUATIONS, 1815–1845

SECTION III

BUSINESS FLUCTUATIONS, 1843–1862

APPENDIX A

COMMODITY PRICES, MONTHLY, 1792–1862

APPENDIX B

DOMESTIC AND FOREIGN COMMODITY PRICES, QUARTERLY, 1825–1862

APPENDIX C

SECURITY PRICES, MONTHLY, 1795–1862

APPENDIX D

PUBLIC LAND SALES, QUARTERLY AND ANNUALLY, 1796–1860

APPENDIX E

FINANCIAL DATA, MONTHLY, 1795–1862

LIST OF CHARTS

PREFACE

SECTION I

BUSINESS FLUCTUATIONS, 1792–1820

SECTION II

BUSINESS FLUCTUATIONS, 1815–1845

SECTION III

BUSINESS FLUCTUATIONS, 1843–1861

FLUCTUATIONS IN AMERICAN BUSINESS
1790-1860

PREFACE

Research sometimes seems to proceed backward from the less to the more fundamental aspects of a problem. The restriction period of English economic history long has been of interest to historians both political and economic; and yet until Dr. Silberling's investigation a decade ago no one had plumbed the depths of the controversy between the bullionists and their opponents. The structure of the American railroad rate system has unquestionably been an outstanding fact in American economic development; and yet we still lack an adequate treatment of this portion of our transportation history. Similarly, the fluctuations in American business life during the pre-Civil-War period have been touched upon by innumerable writers dealing with one phase or another of our political, social or economic history; and yet hitherto no attempt has been made to gather together the available facts regarding this fundamental aspect of our economic experience.

Lack of adequate data upon these earlier business fluctuations has led to two particularly grievous types of error. Until quite recently historians have tended to treat of such episodes as the downturn of business after 1818, or the so-called "panic" of 1837, as isolated, inexplicable blows of fortune occasioned by such external events as the "dumping" of English goods, or the issuance of the Specie Circular. Again, ignorance of the duration and intensity of early business depressions has permitted numerous inaccurate and unwarranted comparisons with disasters of more recent date. To a rectification of such conditions, the present research has been in part devoted.

Obviously, however, an inquiry into the ups and downs of general business in the decades before 1860 should serve still larger purposes. Material gathered from divers geographical areas should throw some light upon the political sectionalism of the country at particular times. Time-series pertaining to banking, exchange or speculation should contribute to knowledge of the evolution of American business institutions; while the extension backward from our pre-existing data on wholesale commodity-price or stock-price movements cannot fail to result in a greater understanding of current business cycles. Particularly would the present authors emphasize that in looking to the past, they have attempted to do so in the light of the present. Despite the fact that their inquiry terminates with the Civil War, and despite their own realization that economic forces change in influence relative to one another over any considerable period of time, they believe that at least a modicum of their findings can be utilized in the analysis of current problems.

The first purpose of the present volume, as already intimated, is to make generally available a number of important time-series which reflect changes in American business conditions over the decades between 1790 and 1860. These time-series refer to all the significant aspects of American business for which monthly or quarterly data can be gathered: commodity prices, stock prices, sales of public lands, interest rates, and the like. Least adequately represented are series relating to the volume of trade, since material on this point is woefully lacking in original sources. At most, certain annual indices upon the physical quantum of trade have been attempted. As to the terminal years, it may be suggested that here again availability of data has been the determining influence. We begin at the point when, after a lapse in the Revolutionary and early post-Revolutionary periods, newspapers again commenced to present regular tabulations of prices current, and when also regular data on other phases of business can be secured. We close at the Civil War, since, for later decades, statistical series relating to many of the business phenomena which we were investigating now become available, thanks to the research of such scholars as Professor Mitchell or Professor Snider.

The authors have drawn the greater part of their material from original sources, especially the newspapers of the decades studied. At times when printed sources failed, as in the case of quarterly data on the sales of public lands, they have resorted to manuscript material. Probably further series other than those now offered may be extracted from unexplored manuscript sources. Supplementary findings would be particularly valuable in the fields of interest rates, employment, wages, and real estate values. Again, it should be remarked that the attention of the present investigators has been primarily directed to the northeastern section of the country. Of course, in the decades covered, while the area north of Maryland and east of the Alleghenies still held undoubted primacy in the commercial and industrial activities of the nation, the authors have not hesitated to include material relating to other sections of the country when such material was readily available; yet it is obvious that regional investigations would greatly extend the scope of the narrative here attempted. In some measure this lack is already, or will shortly, be supplied as far as commodity price movements are concerned, through inquiries fostered by the International Scientific Committee on Price History.[1] Unfortunately, however, no corresponding prospects relate to the phases of stock prices, wages or interest rates.

With respect to the series actually collected, the further warning may be advanced that for the most part the authors have not indulged in extended statistical manipulation. Many of the series are presented in unadjusted form: trends have not been eliminated, seasonal variation has not been extracted, nor have the cycles been measured by any method of computation. In some cases, the omission of statistical treatment was due to an appreciation of the inherent crudity of the original material. In others, it has flowed from a preference for the exposition of

[1] See, for example, Dr. George R. Taylor's articles, "Wholesale Commodity Prices at Charleston, S. C., 1732–91" in the *Journal of Economic and Business History*, vol. 4 (1932), pp. 356–77, and "Wholesale Commodity Prices at Charleston, S.C., 1796–1861" in the same *Journal* as a Supplement to vol. 4 (1932), pp. 848–68, with statistical appendix.

See, also, the studies of Professors G. F. Warren and F. A. Pearson, "Wholesale Prices in the United States for 135 Years, 1797–1932" (pp. 1–200), and Dr. H. M. Stoker's "Wholesale Prices at New York City, 1720 to 1800" (pp. 201–222), published as *Memoir 142* by the Agricultural Experiment Station of Cornell University (1932), under the title of "Wholesale Prices for 213 Years, 1720 to 1932."

"raw data,"—a preference which, in turn, has been due to a belief that such data are more generally useful to economists with their varying interests and requirements. Unmodified material can be easily corrected or adjusted to suit the special needs and purposes of the individual student. Moreover, such material may be treated by the particular statistical method that satisfies the specific object of the study undertaken. Where convenient, of course, the writers have not hesitated to employ indices, but they have been of simple construction—in large part dictated by the character or paucity of data—and always effort has been made, as in the case of partial indices for commodity prices, to lessen the weight that otherwise might be given to the various general indices here presented.

The historian of political or social change in the decades before the Civil War will perhaps find greatest interest in the material relating to commodity prices given in detail below. Divergent movement in the price of domestically-produced and imported commodities during the troubled period before 1815—so divergent, in fact, that a single index embracing all commodity prices appears inappropriate—supplies new information that aids in the interpretation of governmental policy during these years. Likewise, the difference in price movement of agricultural and industrial commodities during the latter 'thirties or middle 'fifties—and particularly the persistence of high prices for the former group for two years after the so-called "panic" of 1837—gives a significant suggestion respecting the incidence of the various crises for several sections of the country. Such historians also will find interest in the changing situs of extreme speculation in public lands. Here, as in other phenomena of the period, one can detect a striking westward movement.

Not foreign to the considerations of the political historian, and surely of equal significance to his colleagues in the economic or social fields, is the obvious lesson from the data elsewhere exhibited that throughout the decades here under review, foreign influence continued to play an important, if not a predominant rôle. This situation is apparent not only in the vicissitudes of commodity-price movements in the early decades (to which reference has just been made) but in the correlation of commodity-price movements here and in England during the rest of the period. The Peace of Amiens, or the impediments to foreign trade after 1807, are matched in later decades by the indirect influence on American markets of the Anglo-South American crisis of 1825 or the occurrences of the Crimean War. The persistence of foreign lending into 1839, or the curtailment of such loans in the 'forties, likewise has varying consequences for the American business situation, not only in the case of commodity prices but also probably in the level of interest rates. Nor should it be ignored that although foreign business fluctuations created corresponding movements in the domestic area, not infrequently aid from England, either in the form of commercial credits or even by large shipments of gold, came to place an end to depressions. Before the Civil War our bankers had learned that same dependence upon foreign, older banking systems which they were disposed or compelled to employ in our post-Civil-War crises. To be sure, the student of commercial history will not be surprised at any such conclusions. While the United States continued largely a producer of surplus raw materials and foodstuffs, events in the foreign area could not fail to have repercussions upon American business conditions. Perhaps, however, the demonstration here offered will set at rest the notion still occasionally voiced that international crises are a phenomenon of distinctly recent experience.

Data upon movements in foreign and domestic exchange, and data upon changes in the domestic banking situation likewise display the influence of foreign factors; yet other features of this material are worthy of comment. The episode of New England's distaste for the War of 1812 presents a striking case of inter-regional trade and shifting financial balances. Perhaps the variant fortunes of the West and East in the years 1837–39 can be interpreted along similar lines. Again, events relating to certain portions of the country indicate the rising significance of deposit currency and the definite checking, at least in New York City, on the expansion of bank notes; while incidentally the changing effectiveness of banks as creators of credit is suggested. Alteration of banking practice, however, is obviously insufficient to explain the varying intensity of commercial crises. No progression

in such intensities is apparent. Almost in the middle of our period occurs the prolonged rise of values and the prolonged decline that marked the years from 1830 to 1843—a rise and fall which finds no equal until the years after the World War.

Speculation and the media for speculation likewise occupy much attention in the ensuing pages. To anyone who has read the absorbing story of William Duer[2] or recalls the early history of the New York Stock Exchange, there is no surprise in the price movements of United States "stock" in the years after 1795, or the existence of regular quotations for bank stocks in the corresponding years. Yet the particular month-to-month or year-to-year movements of these securities form a valuable, hitherto unavailable adjunct to the study of business in this eventful period. Dovetailing with such early data on stock-exchange action are those revealing the movements in the sale of public lands. Here the three striking peaks of land sales, occurring in 1818, 1836, and 1854–55, respectively, display the characteristic mode by which lands passed from the hands of the Government to those of private citizens. In view of certain later observations regarding the divergent character of certain price series, it is also worth comment that in nearly all these cases the peak of movement with respect to the price of speculative media, whether Government "stock," public lands or railroad securities, was reached earlier than that of commodity prices or interest rates. One is tempted to conclude that much of the opprobrium heaped in recent years upon the stock market is in a sense unjust. The speculative spirit of American citizens showed itself at an early date, manifested itself in various guises, and perhaps may be itself declared responsible for the creation of that instrumentality by means of which stocks and bonds are now passed from hand to hand.

Finally, the authors reveal no secret if they indicate that in their hoped-for audience they trust to find the student specializing in business cycles. In a certain sense all the data presented are grist for his mill. To him there is no need to point out the special features of such material;

[2] Davis, Joseph S., *Essays in the Earlier History of American Corporations* (1917), vol. 1, pp. 339–45.

and yet as every craftsman has a modicum of preference for one or another element in his product, the writers take occasion to indicate certain phenomena. Peculiarly striking in these decades under review were the long swings in commodity values. The recession which reached the first point of support in 1821 may, in fact, be looked upon as having been merely a part of a long up-and-down movement which started as early as 1808 or, when allowance is made for political factors, possibly in 1802 or even in 1792, and continued until 1830. The second long swing extends from 1830 to 1843, and the third from 1848 to 1861. While these may be cast aside by followers of Kondratieff or Simiand as mere fragments of longer "waves,"[3] the authors are inclined to find some significance in them. Again the experience of the seventy years under examination provides ammunition for those who would combat the significance of war or any other particular external event as the cause of a major movement of values. Wars, whether that of 1812 or the Civil War, are, of course, not without influence; but it is significant that the striking rise and fall in 1830–43 was not accompanied by important political disturbances of this character. The "starters" or "impulses" —in the terminology of Fisher or Pigou—are here found not in political events, but perhaps in the introduction of the railroad (1830), the influx of specie from abroad (1843), and probably the discovery of gold in California (1848). Thirdly, though without exhausting the catalog of features useful to the cycle student—for instance, the longer period for the establishment of possible periodicity—the intensity of pre-Civil-War downturns and depressions relative to corresponding episodes in later decades, deserves elaboration. The task of providing comparable data for the measurement of cyclical change over any considerable period is by no means a simple one. To do so adequately would entail a much more elaborate statistical analysis than the present authors have had opportunity to carry through. Moreover, in this particular case, limitation of material reflecting business fluctuations in pre-Civil-War decades restricts the

possibilities of comparison between earlier and later events. As already suggested, little can be said respecting changes before 1860 in that important element, the volume of trade. Data on banking and interest rates are also scanty for these earlier decades. Such considerations have led us to confine attention here (Charts 1 and 2) to a comparison of downward movements of business—depressions, recessions, and the like— as shown by indices of stock and commodity prices.

Even in this narrowed field, the difficulties of comparison are by no means small. We have, to be sure, indices of both stock and commodity prices running back to the latter part of the eighteenth century, but the question of internal comparability among the several indices is a particularly important one. They were constructed in varying manner, some being geometric and others arithmetic, some weighted and others unweighted, and scarcely any two related to the same base. Thus an unweighted geometric index of commodity prices on the base of 1802 may be offered for comparison with a weighted arithmetic average on the base of 1848–58, or with an unweighted arithmetic index on the base of 1926. Furthermore, one is confronted with the yet more significant difficulty that these several indices are variant in their internal composition. The degree of selection exercised and the basis of choice have differed in the construction of one index and another. This, to be sure, is of comparatively small consequence in the case of stock prices. Almost all of the indices presented are selective in character— the only exception being that of our early bank-stock prices, for which paucity of continuous series restricted appreciably freedom of choice. In regard to commodity-price indices, however, the variety is quite great. While those for 1801–02 and 1818–20 are fairly general—partly by reason of limitation of choice—those for the latter 'thirties and 'fifties must be classified as selective, since "insensitive" and irregular price series were eliminated. For the post-Civil-War period, one has to deal either with a peculiarly responsive index such as the "ten-commodity" and "sensitive" indices of the Harvard Economic Society, or with indices compounded of a large number of series and therefore less selective in quality, such as Miss Bacon's index for the

[3] Kondratieff, N. D., "Die langen Wellen der Konjunktur," *Archiv für Sozialwissenschaft und Sozialpolitik*, 56. Band, 3. Heft (1926), pp. 573–609; and Simiand, F., *Les Fluctuations Economiques à Longue Période et la Crise Mondiale*, 1932.

CHART I. — RECESSIONS IN STOCK PRICES: MONTHLY, 1802–1934

(Uniform vertical logarithmic scale)

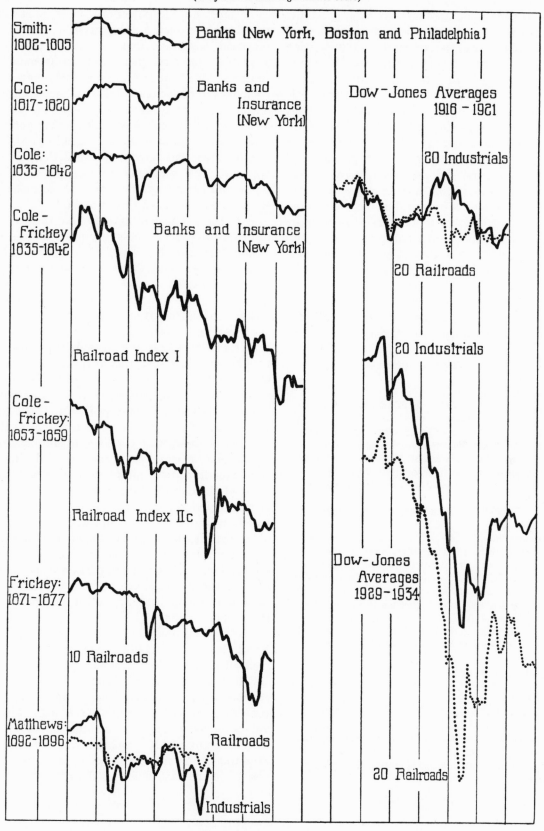

middle 'nineties, or the Bureau of Labor Statistics index for the period since 1920.[4]

A quandary of another sort relates to the periods in the various price movements since 1795, which shall be selected as representing "downward movements of business." Sometimes, to be sure, the problem is simple, e.g., in 1801–02 or even the middle 'nineties. Again it is possible to rely upon the analysis of previous investigators to exclude particular periods from consideration, as when, for instance, Professor Snider states that "during 1866–78, [commodity] prices in general did not move in a cyclical fashion. There is just a trace of a cyclical movement with the peak in 1872, but the characteristic movements down to January 1879 were irregular fluctuations with a rather sharp downward trend."[5] In a number of cases, however, the point at which to begin the picture of "downward movements" is not self-evident. Is the decline in stock prices in the year 1857 separable from the fall which began with 1853; and is the decline of commodity prices during 1925–29 to be

distinguished from that which followed the break of stock-market values in the latter year?

To meet all the objections which might be raised against such a comparison as that now proposed, would be impossible with the data available. On the other hand, an attempt to construct long-time indices on a single form and compounded of a single category of series may in itself be subject to much suspicion. Nicety of measurement in dealing with prices over periods a hundred years or more in length is probably unattainable; and perhaps the most that can be hoped for is a rough measure of movement in representative periods relative to a normal position or base for such time-intervals.

With these considerations in mind, the decline in stock-price and commodity-price indices at various significant periods over the decades since 1795 have been charted on the same scale (or, more exactly, the same scale for each group of indices), and are presented herewith as indications of the relative intensity and duration of the several declines (Charts 1 and 2).

As far as stock-market values are concerned, it may be remarked, first, that as revealed by these several indices no decline of the post-Civil-War period up to 1929 compared in severity with some of those which preceded 1860. The decline from 1871–77—the most extreme in the decades of the former period—probably should be set aside, as was done in the case of the index of commodity-prices for these same years, because of the influence of paper-money deflation. If this period is left out of the comparison, the case is even clearer. For duration and intensity of movement, the decline in the middle 'nineties does not compare with the fall subsequent to 1835. If one is making a comparison of spectacular and sharp recessions, the fall of values in 1873 and that in 1920–21 are less notable than the débâcle of 1857.

The extraordinary decline in stock prices which began in August 1929 and probably reached its nadir in the summer of 1932, possessed a severity unexampled in our previous experience as far as amplitude of movement is concerned or the precipitousness with which values melted away. On the other hand, if the extreme point in this outstanding decline was indeed touched in the summer of 1932, there were periods in the past which for duration of down-

[4] The indices employed for the period subsequent to 1860 are as follows:

Stock prices

    1871–77: that compiled by Dr. Edwin Frickey in an article on "Business and Financial Conditions Following the Civil War in the United States" in the *Review of Economic Statistics*, Preliminary Volume 2 (1920), Supplement 2, p. 33.

    1892–96: that of Miss Ada M. Matthews, in her study of "New York Bank Clearings and Stock Prices, 1866–1914" in the *Review of Economic Statistics*, vol. 8 (1926), pp. 191 and 194.

    1916–21 and 1929–34: the Dow-Jones industrial and railroad averages.

Commodity Prices

    1893–97: that published by Miss Dorothy C. Bacon in "A Monthly Index of Commodity Prices, 1890–1900," *Review of Economic Statistics*, vol. 8 (1926), p. 182; "Ten-commodity" index of the Harvard Economic Society, published in the *Review of Economic Statistics*, Preliminary Volume 3 (1921), p. 368; index of the U. S. Bureau of Labor Statistics.

    1920–22: index of the U. S. Bureau of Labor Statistics; "Ten-commodity" index of the Harvard Economic Society, *op. cit.*

    1925–34: index of the U. S. Bureau of Labor Statistics; "Sensitive" index of the Harvard Economic Society (not published).

[5] Snider, J. L., "Wholesale Prices in the United States, 1866–91" in the *Review of Economic Statistics*, vol. 6 (1924), p. 115. It should be noted that the decline in commodity prices immediately after the War of 1812 had already been excluded from comparisons here attempted, because of its relationship to paper-money deflation.

CHART 2. — RECESSIONS IN WHOLESALE COMMODITY PRICES: MONTHLY, 1801–1934
(*Uniform vertical logarithmic scale*)

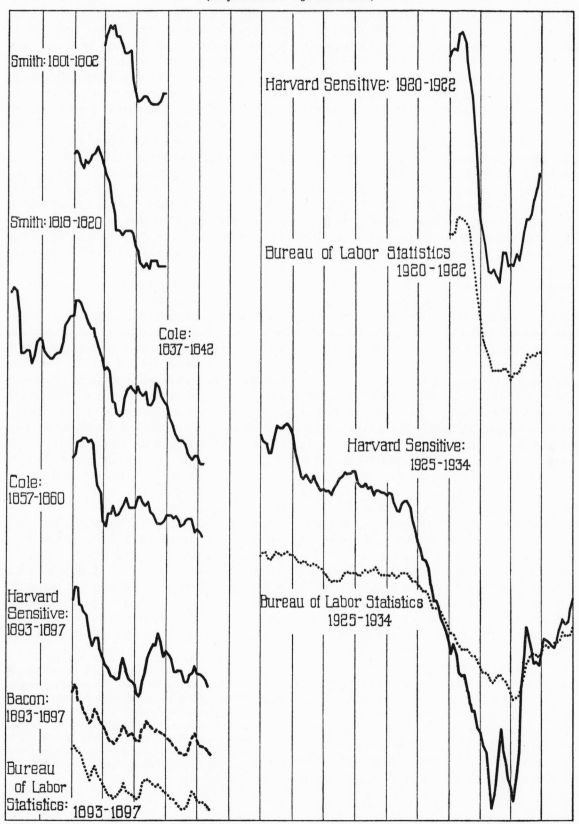

Smith: 1801-1802

Smith: 1818-1820

Cole:
1837-1842

Cole:
1857-1860

Harvard
Sensitive:
1893-1897

Bacon:
1893-1897

Bureau
of Labor
Statistics: 1893-1897

Harvard Sensitive: 1920-1922

Bureau of Labor Statistics
1920-1922

Harvard Sensitive:
1925-1934

Bureau of Labor Statistics
1925-1934

ward course exceeded measurably that of our most recent history. While the latter extended less than three years, the downward movement of the 1870's persisted six, that of the 1850's five, and the longest on record, that which began in the forepart of 1835, nearly seven. Perhaps an index of crisis severity might be constructed in which degree of movement was weighted by its duration. If this were done, one result certainly would be difficult to explain, namely, that the decline which in severity most nearly equaled (or perhaps exceeded) that of the 1930's occurred nearly a hundred years previously.

Turning to a consideration of commodity prices, one may note that the declines prior to 1860 are quite comparable with those of the post-Civil-War period up to the time when the last decade or so is reached. It is apparent that the decline following 1818 must take its place with those of 1837–43 and 1857–58 as equaling or exceeding in severity the recession of the middle 'nineties—the recession which, up to 1920, is the only post-Civil-War decline worth comparing with the earlier movements—and which has, in fact, been frequently spoken of in recent decades as a reaction of unusual proportions.

The crisis of 1920 involved commodity values in a special degree, but the duration of downward movement was exceeded in divers earlier periods. Indeed, if the index covering the early period, 1801–02, be considered of such a character as to fall somewhere between the "general" and "highly selective" indices for 1920–21, this first major decline included in the present survey would appear to equal in duration that of 1920–21. On the other hand, if all the pre-Civil-War indices be considered as falling somewhere between "insensitive" and "sensitive" in character, the degree and rapidity of decline in the crisis of 1920 exceeded that of any pre-Civil-War period.

A comparison of the most recent downward movement with those which preceded it is rendered difficult by the slow contraction of value from 1925 to 1929. It is somewhat doubtful whether this slow recession should be included in determining the starting point of the cyclical down-turn of most recent date. If these years of gradual contraction be excluded, the movement which began in the late months of 1929 and probably reached its low point in the summer of 1932, or the opening of 1933, exceeded

in degree of amplitude, of course, anything of which we have knowledge in our previous experience. To be sure, the decline in 1920–21 was more precipitous, as indeed was also that in 1857. Moreover, the duration of decline was substantially greater in the period of devolution that began in 1837. Even if one attempts to take into account both amplitude and duration, it is probable that the decline of most recent occurrence was not equaled in the past. In the comparison here presented (Chart 2), the highly insensitive index of the Bureau of Labor Statistics for 1929–34 may be compared with the somewhat selective index of 1837–43; and while the conclusion is not without a modicum of doubt, it seems sufficiently clear that even the prolonged decline of the latter 1830's and early 1840's does not exceed in what might be called aggregate severity that of our most recent experience.[6]

In closing this Preface, the authors wish to forestall certain possible sources of disappointment on the part of their professional audience. Economic historians and advanced students of the business cycle may both be dissatisfied with the present volume, though not for the same reasons. The former will note failure to weave always the phenomena of business fluctuations intimately into the background of economic development in these pre-Civil-War decades. Particularly is this true of the period subsequent to 1820. This failure we readily admit; but we would urge that to do so was far from our intention. An adequate interweaving of fluctuation with the economic background would have entailed in reality the drafting of a general economic history of the United States. All we have attempted for these later decades is to present, in chapters introductory to each section, a sketch of economic development during the particular period under survey sufficient merely to guide the less professional reader in an understanding of the setting to the events therein portrayed.

[6] The authors would call attention to the fact that they are using the concept of "severity" here and in connection with stock prices above, in a special sense. Severity of a depression is not, of course, to be measured merely by degree of price change. Certain additional indices of such "severity"—volume of unemployment or that of business failures—we should have gladly presented, had data for them been available. Others, such as the curtailment of governmental operations or the postponement of potential enjoyments, are not subject to statistical measurement.

Fuller utilization of our statistical material in the "interweaving" task just mentioned may be left to other writers.

The special student of business cycles, on the other hand, will miss any substantial attempt at explanation of the phenomena exhibited in the various indices or other data, except perhaps as movements may be interpreted in terms of their immediate circumstances. No answer is proposed to the persisting puzzle of the genesis of business cycles in general, or to the allied question of varying intensities of the several cycles of which we have knowledge. This task, however, also lies beyond the original intentions of the authors. Obviously, any consideration of these problems would soon have led us beyond the time-period of 1795–1860 as well as beyond the confines of the United States—and any unity that the present volume may possess would have been immediately lost. The above-mentioned students of these matters will, we trust, find food for thought in the data which we offer; and neither of the present authors waives his rights to utilize his own or his colleague's material in some future attempt at theoretical analysis. Such, however, is not our present purpose.

Such, then, are the more general weaknesses or deficiencies of the following pages. The discovery of others—and possibly the unearthing of a few redeeming qualities—we leave to those with temerity enough to penetrate beyond this Preface.

SECTION I

BUSINESS FLUCTUATIONS, 1790–1820
WALTER BUCKINGHAM SMITH

SECTION I

CHAPTER I

INTRODUCTION

VARIATIONS in business in the United States between 1790 and 1820 are comparable in many ways with the changes which occurred more than a century later between 1914 and 1933. In the early phase of both periods we observe the shipping industry on this side of the Atlantic prospering during years of benevolent American neutrality, while Europe is torn by war. We perceive a rapid development in New England and the Middle States of industries suddenly freed, because of these wars, from the competition of English producers. Disorganized currencies were accompanied by fluctuating exchange rates. In the second phase of this period, as in the twentieth century, the United States declared war on a European power and, to finance the war, borrowed heavily from the commercial banks, and ultimately brought about a suspension of specie payments. A further parallel is the inflation of the currency, the effects of which may be studied in Charts 3, 4 and 7. Another interesting parallel is the inevitable post-war contraction of economic activities which had been artificially stimulated by the abnormal demands of war. Manufacturing in the earlier period and agriculture in the contemporary period responded to the stimulus of war in a measure which compelled later and painful readjustments with the resumption of peace. In both periods the level of real incomes rose sharply. Great European conflicts, to which our relation is either that of spectator or participator, have a way of making America "come of age."

To clarify the statistical history of the period from 1790-1820, a sketch of accompanying economic developments is suggested in the following chapter. The intelligent interpretation of statistical materials requires a general picture of economic institutions in the period discussed, a critical examination of sources of data, and a statement of the methods used in statistical computations. In the present case, it is necessary to add a narrative of the significant events in the markets for commodities, stocks and bonds, money, and foreign exchange. Such a commentary must finally attempt to identify the forces at work which produced the great upswing in prices from 1790 to 1814-18, the downswing from 1818 to 1820, and the minor movements within these main tendencies.

CHAPTER II

THE ECONOMIC SETTING

AMERICANS in this period, 1790-1820, exploited two of their great natural resources. Gifted with an abundance of land, challenged by relatively small supplies of capital and labor, American enterprise turned to the soil and the forests. The South produced cotton, tobacco, and rice. The Middle States produced flour, meat, tar, and turpentine. The New England States produced pot and pearl ashes, and lumber, and engaged extensively in whaling and fishing. The British Isles and the West Indies were important foreign customers for these American products.

Any quantitative description of agricultural production during this period is unavailable. The press of the day concerned itself with the weather and the prospects for crops. Exports supply our one channel of information. Since we have no knowledge of how much the farmer produced, it is difficult to gauge precisely the effects of price changes upon the money incomes of farmers.

One point of distinction between the period under discussion and our own cannot be over-emphasized by the student. We are dealing with business experiences not only agricultural, but pioneering. The pioneer farmer could control his production situation and his costs in a measure that the twentieth-century farmer cannot. The economy of the early days did not contain the vast machinery of relatively fixed interest charges and wage scales with which the contemporary producer is familiar. The individualistic experience of the early American entrepreneur, with initiative and natural resources as the two chief factors in his situation, emphatically does not parallel the experience of the American entrepreneur today.

For the most part, American imports in the late 18th and early 19th centuries consisted of manufactures and of tropical and Far Eastern products. From England came textiles, iron and steel products. From Russia came flax and sail cloth. France and Spain contributed wines. The Far East supplied us with silk and tea. The West Indies shipped sugar, molasses, rum, and coffee. Cotton textiles came from India, some iron and steel from Scandinavia. Even after 1815, when as the result of European disturbances America had developed some manufactures of her own, such goods continued to be imported in large quantities into this country.

The importance of this foreign trade is one reason for the strikingly large proportion of foreign news printed in the press of the day. Letters from distant parts of the world were reprinted and read with interest by American merchants dependent on the foreign market. Price-Currents, weekly newspapers publishing wholesale commodity prices, were issued in Boston, New York, Philadelphia, Baltimore, and elsewhere. These with minor exceptions related to exported and imported goods. Any picture of the economic life of the people on the Atlantic seacoast must include statistics indicating price levels of imports and exports.

Turning to domestic trade between the cities of the Atlantic seacoast we find a well-organized trade in commodities. Frequent sailings brought the cotton of the South and the flour of the Middle States to New England. Boston and Salem coasting vessels carried tea, silks, and various Oriental imports to other Atlantic seacoast cities.

Information as well as commodities flowed readily from market to market. In Boston, New York, Philadelphia, Baltimore, Charleston, and other cities each week were published the prices of one to three hundred commodities. Business journals were widely distributed and quotations were printed again and again. Ample knowledge of prices and market conditions together with good facilities for transport made of the Atlantic seacoast a unified trading area. The Embargo on foreign trade under President Jefferson in 1808 and the War of 1812 were the only occasions when the flow of information and of commodities between the larger market centers was seriously interrupted.

Two factors sharply stimulated domestic

American manufactures between 1808 and 1815. The first of these was diffusion of knowledge as to the technical processes necessary to produce commodities as excellent in quality as those received from Europe. Even philosophical societies in centers such as Philadelphia were concerned with mechanical techniques, inventions, and processes. Leaders as divergent as Jefferson and Hamilton interested themselves actively in what we should now call applied science.

The second and more challenging factor, already referred to, was the cutting off of imports of manufactured goods. Reinforced by the quickened demands created by the War of 1812, there resulted an intensive and rapid development of American manufacture in textiles, flour, rum, glass, leather, paper, iron and steel, staves, etc.[1] One line of American production which these interruptions in foreign trade did not favor was that of the construction and operation of ocean vessels. Statistics of clearance at the port of Salem, statistics of shipbuilding at such places as Medford, Massachusetts, observations in the press of the day concerning the numbers of unemployed mechanics and seamen, all point to the fact that activity in shipping and its derivative industries fluctuated with the play of foreign demand. However there remained the construction of vessels for coastwise shipping and for the use of the whaling industry as an important part of the business of American shipbuilders.

Turning to the currency which facilitated all this commercial development we find that Spanish silver dollars from the mints of Mexico were the most widely used type of metallic currency. These were universally acceptable in America, in the West Indies, in the Orient, and in Europe. The minting of silver and gold coins of our own had commenced with the inception of our government under the Constitution, and issues of United States metal currency slowly assumed importance, but up to 1820 the honors were divided between the Spanish and American dollars.

Paper currency took the form of notes issued by privately owned state banks and by the First and Second Banks of the United States. Issues of better known institutions such as the Massachusetts Bank and the Bank of the Manhattan

Company of New York normally circulated a considerable distance from their home city without great depreciation. Occasionally, however, even in Massachusetts, banknote issues caused commercial embarrassment. Small institutions over-issued, and their notes depreciated in value. For example, in 1814 New England merchants found themselves possessed of notes issued by banks in New York and to the south which were worth twenty per cent less than par in terms of silver. Banknote depreciation occurred at the time of the stoppage of specie payment in New York, Philadelphia, and elsewhere; and from 1814 to 1817 depreciated paper currency was the principal medium of exchange in the middle and southern States.

In 1795 there were twenty-one banking institutions; by 1812 this number had increased to one hundred and nineteen.[2] In the year 1814 forty-one new banks were chartered in the State of Pennsylvania alone. These banking corporations made loans to their borrowers in the form of their own note issues. They also carried on deposit banking as we know it today to a surprising extent. Contrary to our present general impression, the check was widely used in the United States in the first decade of the nineteenth century. The large numbers of canceled checks still extant support the opinion of contemporaries[3] to the effect that the American people carried the use of the check to greater length than any other nation.

The national checkbook habit is not the only feature of early nineteenth century banking which is anticipatory of twentieth century procedures. Banks lent money to private individuals whose promissory notes either were secured by the endorsement of responsible members of the community, or were supported by collateral in the form of government securities or mortgages. Then as now boards of directors met to decide upon such loans and to establish "lines of credit" for individuals.[4]

These striking similarities must not blind us to

[1] Hope's Philadelphia Price-Current, Mar. 4, 1811.

[2] Gouge, W. M., A Short History of Paper Money and Banking (1833), Part II, pp. 42-44.
[3] Raguet, C., A Treatise on Currency and Banking (1840), p. 185; and Minutes of Meetings of the Directors of the Massachusetts Bank, May 25, 1807 and December 8, 1807. (Mss.)
[4] Minutes of Directors Meetings of the Newark Banking and Insurance Company, Jan. 29, 1808. (Mss.)

the fact that the banking system of the earlier period was from our point of view almost completely decentralized. No clearing house associations existed even in the cities of New York and Boston. Even such national institutions as the First and Second Banks of the United States were by no means bankers' banks. In addition to receiving and paying out public funds, these organizations concerned themselves with the machinery of remittance from one part of the country to another and with such surveillance over private banks as would improve the redeemability of their notes. They did not act in any way as a source of strength to banks in difficulty. Prior to 1820 every bank held its own reserves and in times of stress could rely only upon its own resources and connections.

Another sharp contrast with present day banking is the relative inflexibility of interest rates in the early period. There was no such mechanism as our present-day call-loan market. A bank loan was then exclusively an individual and "over-the-counter" affair. Personal banking, at best inflexible, was made even more rigid by the restrictions imposed by the usury laws. Instead of attempting to meet their difficulties by charging high interest rates bankers attempted in 1818, for instance, to curtail their loans by the awkward process of rationing — a principle which is still under discussion.

Turning to the mechanism for making foreign payments, we observe well-developed foreign exchanges. Thirty-, sixty-, and ninety-day bills on London were bought and sold by merchants like Alexander Brown of Baltimore and John Hancock of Boston. At times the rates of exchange on Paris, Amsterdam, Bremen, and Hamburg were quoted. The supply of these bills rose out of the direct shipment of commodities to England and the Continent and from shipments to the West Indies. The captains of trading vessels frequently returned bringing bills drawn on London in payment for commodities delivered in the West Indies.[5] Foreign drafts drawn in one American city were readily marketable in other centers.

Individual merchants and mercantile houses rather than banks dominated the foreign-exchange market. Keenly aware of changes in the commodity markets, the prices paid by these merchants for foreign bills might well be expected to reflect commodity-price movements.[6] At few times have conditions been so ripe for working out the purchasing-power parity theory as from 1790 to 1808 and from 1815 to 1820. The correlation between commodity-price levels, however, and foreign-exchange rates did not occur. Among the factors concerned was the enormous increase in American exports of highly priced commodities. This led to a flooding of the foreign-exchange market with foreign bills. The flooding of the market, of course, held the quotations below the purchasing-power parity rate.

Foreign investment did not influence foreign exchanges very greatly at this period. The security issues of the United States Government were held in fairly large quantities abroad, and from time to time additional issues were exported — the Louisiana stock, for example, put out to pay for the territory ceded by France. Stock of the First and Second Banks of the United States was held in London in substantial amounts. Judging from the public press, some Englishmen even had the hardihood to invest in American land,[7] and private bank and turnpike stocks.[8] There is little evidence to show that the flotation of large security issues abroad had much effect on foreign exchanges. That interest charges were of some importance in the balance of payments became clearly apparent when American exports were cut off. At those times the foreign-exchange market, devoid of the customary supply of commodity bills, felt acutely the demand for exchange with which to make interest payments.

Short-term borrowing by Americans took the form of credit to American importers. "Many men, who, eight, ten, or fifteen years since, were always heavily indebted to their European correspondents, now almost constantly pay in advance for their importations," wrote Matthew

---

[5] *Lawrason and Fowle Letter Book, 1806–08:* Letter dated Mar. 4, 1807. (Mss.)

[6] Stocks were sometimes substituted for bills of exchange as is seen from the following: "Six per cent stock of the United States, a Boston paper says, is now remitted to London in lieu of Bills of Exchange." The (Philadelphia) *General Advertiser*, Nov. 10, 1791.

[7] The *Columbian Centinel*, May 28, 1794.

[8] *New York Evening Post*, Oct. 3, 1807; The *New Jersey Journal*, Apr. 26, 1797.

Carey in 1810.[9] This was an optimistic statement of the situation for that time or for later days. Of some slight effect upon the exchanges was the custom for certain merchants to hold large bank balances in England. Short-term indebtedness of both sorts affected the foreign-exchange markets to a noticeable extent in the periods when the commodity trade failed to furnish the needed supply of exchange.

Turning from the money and foreign-exchange markets to that imponderable but important factor, speculation, we note a number of points of contrast between the earlier situation and the present. First, speculation was accustomed to concern itself mainly with commodities and land, and only in a minor degree with stocks and government issues.[10] Second, the machinery of speculation was not highly organized. Not until 1817 was the New York Stock and Exchange Board founded. Most of the trading in stocks took place in brokers' offices — in the offices of such well-known brokers as Nathaniel Prime and Romulus Riggs of New York. Speculators used borrowed money and in that sense traded on margin. Occasionally we read in the daily press that there have been forced sales of goods because of pressure from the banks. Such a statement at least implies something remotely like margin trading already existing at the period. Although the speculative technique seems antiquated, popular beliefs on the subject were the same as now. The *Columbian Centinel* of 1791 quoted the statement that "In all countries it is in the power of *Bulls* or *Bears* to lower or raise the public paper several per cent."[11] In 1820, a questionnaire put out in Pennsylvania elicited answers from many to the effect that speculation had had a sensible effect in diminishing the number of productive laborers, and that thus, whilst the nominal prices of commodities were raised, the real quantity of the products of industry was diminished.[12]

[9] Carey, M., *Desultory Reflections* (3rd ed., 1810), p. 21.

[10] See the *Columbian Mirror and Alexandrian Gazette*, Mar. 5, 1796, for an elaborate description of speculation as it appeared in that year.

[11] The *Columbian Centinel*, Jan. 19, 1791.

[12] Hazard's *Register of Pennsylvania*, vol. 4 (1829), p. 145 ff.

CHAPTER III

ANALYSIS OF PRICE STATISTICS, 1790–1820

BECAUSE American business conditions were largely a reflection of the state of international trade, we have divided our commodity-price statistics into two groups: (1) domestically produced goods which were exported and (2) imported goods; and from these we have constructed index numbers of prices of American produced exportables and of imports into the United States. The utility of this classification is apparent in a year like 1808, when the Embargo caused a great scarcity of foreign goods and a plethora of domestic goods. An all-inclusive index number would convey an impression of price stability, because the increased price of foreign goods would tend to cancel out the low price of American products — a general impression which clearly would be in error. Again, in the years 1815-16, our two sets of index numbers appear to be more serviceable in depicting the situation in the United States than would have been a single general index. At the close of the war, the price of European products in our markets fell to a very low point; while American agricultural products, after a precipitate drop, recovered almost to the level that they had attained during the war. This disparity in the import and the export price levels provides the clew to the understanding of the years from 1815 to 1818. Experience in the handling of statistics as well as the theoretical considerations of international trade leads us to emphasize index numbers of prices of import and of export commodities rather than a single all-inclusive index.[1]

The index number for domestically produced goods[2] (Index A) is a weighted "aggregative" index of sixteen wholesale commodity prices with 1802 as the base year. The original series were transcribed from the *Boston Price Current and Marine Intelligencer, Russell's Gazette*, the *Boston Gazette*, and the *American Apollo* for dates near the middle of the month, and refer to the Boston wholesale market. Quotations were often given in the form of a high and low for an interval of time, and when this was the case the arithmetic mean of these two quotations was used as the representative price. In Table 1 will be found a description of the commodity-price series and the weights.

For purposes of determining the different degrees of depreciation of the American currency between August 1812 and February 1817, a set of supplementary index numbers of domestically produced goods is included for New York, Philadelphia, and Baltimore as well as Boston.[3] Owing to the suspension of specie payments by the banks of New York and to the south, business was carried on in terms of irredeemable banknotes. The fluctuation of prices of commodities and the depreciation of the inconvertible banknote currency are indicated by the index numbers in Chart 3.[4]

CHART 3. — UNWEIGHTED REGIONAL INDICES OF WHOLESALE DOMESTIC COMMODITY PRICES IN BOSTON, NEW YORK, PHILADELPHIA, AND BALTIMORE: MONTHLY, 1812–17
(*Base: 1810. Arithmetic scale*)

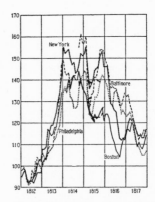

---

[1] In order to have an index comparable with those constructed for the later periods, 1815-45 and 1843-62, an all-inclusive index was constructed to cover the years 1792-1820. This index is to be found in Table 36, Appendix A.

[2] Marketed at home and abroad.

[3] For a continuation of these indices back through 1810 and on through 1819, see Smith, W. B., "Wholesale Commodity Prices in the United States, 1795-1824," in the *Review of Economic Statistics*, vol. 9 (1927), pp. 171-184.

[4] For the index numbers, see Table 39, Appendix A.

TABLE 1. — SERIES AND WEIGHTS USED IN THE CONSTRUCTION OF THE BOSTON WHOLESALE DOMESTIC
COMMODITY-PRICE INDEX (A), 1795–1820[1]

Weight	Commodity	Unit	Period Covered
1	Ashes, pearl............................	ton	Sep. 1795–Dec. 1825
10	Beef, 1st quality.......................	bbl.	Sep. 1795–Feb. 1797
	Beef, ship stores......................	bbl.	Mar. 1797–Dec. 1800
	Beef, mess (200 lb)....................	bbl.	Jan. 1801–Dec. 1824
100	Candles, American tallow, moulded.......	lb.	Sep. 1795–Dec. 1825
200	Cheese, American......................	lb.	Sep. 1795–Aug. 1816
	Cheese, new milk.....................	lb.	Sep. 1816–Dec. 1825
100	Corn, Indian..........................	bu.	Sep. 1795–Dec. 1825
1000	Cotton, American......................	lb.	Sep. 1795–Dec. 1800
	Cotton, Georgia, upland...............	lb.	Jan. 1801–Dec. 1825
20	Fish, alewives.........................	bbl.	Sep. 1795–Dec. 1807
			Mar. 1809–Dec. 1825
	Fish, shop............................	cwt.	Dec. 1807–Feb. 1809
40	Flour, superfine.......................	bbl.	Sep. 1795–Dec. 1825
100	Leather, sole..........................	lb.	Sep. 1795–Sep. 1817
	Leather, slaughter, dry hides.............	lb.	Oct. 1817–Dec. 1825
1	Lumber, boards, clear..................	M ft.	Sep. 1795–Dec. 1802
	Lumber, Ken. and Mach. clear[2].........	M ft.	Jan. 1803–Mar. 1809
	Lumber, Quad. and Mach...............	M ft.	Apr. 1809–Dec. 1825
10	Pork, one hog.........................	bbl.	Sep. 1795–Apr. 1802
	Pork, cargo, No. 1.....................	bbl.	May 1802–Dec. 1825
30	Rice, good............................	cwt.	Sep. 1795–Dec. 1820
2	Staves, white oak, hhd..................	1200	Sep. 1795–Feb. 1796
	Staves, white oak, ca..................	1000	Mar. 1796–Aug. 1797
	Staves, white oak, hhd.................	1000	Sep. 1797–Dec. 1825
30	Tar..................................	bbl.	Sep. 1795–Dec. 1815
	Tar, Wilmington......................	bbl.	Jan. 1816–Dec. 1825
30	Tobacco, Georgia, Kentucky, and North Carolina............................	cwt.	Sep. 1795–Dec. 1820
100	Whale oil, common....................	ton	Sep. 1795–Apr. 1803
	Whale oil, common....................	gal.	May 1803–Dec. 1825

[1] For index numbers, see Table 37, Appendix A.
[2] Probably from Kennebunk and Machias.

The wholesale commodity-price index numbers for the four cities were made from price quotations for an identical list of commodities as quoted in each market. The commodities were about the same as those used in making the general domestic commodity-price index and listed in Table 1. The unweighted geometric mean was the type used and the price relatives were on an 1810 base. Both formula and base are different from the formula and base of the 1795-1820 domestic commodity-price index numbers.

Seventeen series of prices of imported commodities (Index B) were welded into the index number of import prices. Like its companion, the imports index is of the "aggregative" type, with the year 1802 as its base, and refers to the Boston market. In some respects, this index number is less homogeneous than the domestic index, for the constituent series of which it was made were subject to diverse influences. The supplies of hemp from Riga and of coffee from the West Indies were obviously controlled by very different conditions of trade — a fact which makes the index number ambiguous at times. In Table 2 is a statement of the commodity-price series and the weights used in making this second computation.

Subsequent to the construction of the domestic and imported commodity indices for the period 1795–1820, it was found possible to extend them back to 1792 through the use of the *American Apollo*. The series which were transcribed and the periods covered are listed below.

TABLE 2. — SERIES AND WEIGHTS USED IN THE CONSTRUCTION OF THE BOSTON WHOLESALE IMPORTED COMMODITY-PRICE INDEX (B), 1795–1820[1]

Weight	Commodity[2]	Unit	Period Covered
3	Alum.......................	cwt.	Sep. 1795–Jun. 1813
	Alum, Swedish.......................	cwt.	Jul. 1813–Dec. 1816
			Sep. 1823–Dec. 1825
	Alum, English.......................	cwt.	Jan. 1817–Aug. 1823
40	Brandy, French.......................	gal.	Sep. 1795–Dec. 1800
	Brandy, French, 4th pf.................	gal.	Jan. 1801–Aug. 1820
	Brandy, Roch., 4th pf.................	gal.	Sep. 1820–Dec. 1825
4	Brimstone, roll.......................	cwt.	Jan. 1801–Dec. 1807
			Apr. 1809–Dec. 1825
3	Coal, foreign.......................	chal.	Sep. 1795–Dec. 1815
	Coal, Liverpool..	chal.	Jan. 1816–Dec. 1825
400	Coffee	lb.	Sep. 1795–May 1797
	Coffee, green.......................	lb.	Jun. 1797–Dec. 1800
	Coffee, West India, middling	lb.	Jan. 1801–May 1806
	Coffee, West India, ordinary............	lb.	Jun. 1806–Dec. 1825
70	Copper, in sheets.......................	lb.	Sep. 1795–Jun. 1803
	Copper, English sheathing..............	lb.	Jul. 1803–Dec. 1807
			Mar. 1809–Dec. 1825
3	Duck, Russia.......................	bolt	Sep. 1795–Dec. 1802
	Duck, Russia, 2nd qual.	bolt	Jan. 1803–Dec. 1807
			Mar. 1809–Dec. 1825
3	Glass, 8 x 10.......................	100 ft.	Sep. 1795–Feb. 1796
	Glass, foreign, 8 x 10....................	100 ft.	Mar. 1796–Dec. 1797
	Glass, Bristol, crown, 8 x 10...	box	Jan. 1798–Nov. 1823
.2	Hemp	ton	Sep. 1795–Dec. 1807
			Jul. 1808–Dec. 1825
.4	Iron, Swedish, assorted	ton	Sep. 1795–Dec. 1825
5	Lead, white, dry	cwt.	Sep. 1795–May 1823
	Lead, white, English....................	cwt.	Jun. 1823–Dec. 1825
30	Nails, 10 d, wrought...................	M	Sep. 1795–Dec. 1825
15	Salt, Liverpool.......................	8 bu.	Sep. 1795–Dec. 1825
200	Steel, blistered.......................	lb.	Sep. 1795–Dec. 1807
			Apr. 1809–Dec. 1815
	Steel, English blistered best (O. L.).......	lb.	Jan. 1816–Dec. 1825
10	Sugar, brown.......................	cwt.	Sep. 1795–Aug. 1798
	Sugar, Havana, brown.................	cwt.	Sep. 1798–Dec. 1807
			Jul. 1808–Dec. 1825
50	Tea, Hyson	lb.	Sep. 1795–Dec. 1825
2	Tin, in sheets.......................	box	Sep. 1795–Feb. 1798
			Jan. 1801–Dec. 1801
2	Tin plates, No. 1, 3 d x	box	Jan. 1803–Dec. 1825

[1] For index numbers, see Appendix A, Table 38.
[2] For a description of these commodities, see Kauffman, C. H., *The Dictionary of Merchandise and Nomenclature*, (1805).

TABLE 3. — SERIES AND WEIGHTS USED IN THE CONSTRUCTION OF THE BOSTON WHOLESALE DOMESTIC COMMODITY-PRICE INDEX (A), 1792–1794[1]

Weights	Commodity	Unit	Period Covered
1	Ashes, pearl	ton	Oct. 1792–Dec. 1794
10	Beef	bbl.	Oct. 1792–Dec. 1794
100	Candles, tallow	lb.	Oct. 1792–Dec. 1794
100	Cheese, American	lb.	Feb. 1794–Dec. 1794
100	Corn, Indian	bu.	Oct. 1792–Dec. 1794
1000	Cotton	lb.	Oct. 1792–Dec. 1794
40	Flour, superfine	bbl.	Oct. 1792–Dec. 1794
10	Pork, mess	bbl.	Oct. 1792–Dec. 1793
	Pork, 1 hog.	bbl.	Jan. 1794–Dec. 1794
30	Rice, good	cwt.	Oct. 1792–Dec. 1794
1 2/3	Staves, white oak hhd.	1200	Oct. 1792–Dec. 1794
30	Tar	bbl.	Oct. 1792–Dec. 1794
30	Tobacco, Georgia	cwt.	Oct. 1792–Dec. 1794
.386	Whale oil, common	ton	Oct. 1792–Dec. 1794

[1] For index numbers, see Table 37, Appendix A.

TABLE 4. — SERIES AND WEIGHTS USED IN THE CONSTRUCTION OF THE BOSTON WHOLESALE IMPORTED COMMODITY-PRICE INDEX (B), 1792–1794[1]

Weights	Commodity	Unit	Period Covered
40	Brandy	gal.	Oct. 1792–Dec. 1794
400	Coffee	lb.	Oct. 1792–Dec. 1794
3	Duck, Russia	bolt	Dec. 1792–Dec. 1794
.2	Hemp	ton	Oct. 1792–Dec. 1794
.4	Iron, Swedes, bar	ton	Oct. 1792–Dec. 1794
15	Salt, Liverpool	bu.	Oct. 1792–Dec. 1794
10	Sugar, brown	cwt.	Oct. 1792–Dec. 1794
50	Tea, Hyson	lb.	Oct. 1792–Dec. 1794

[1] For index numbers, see Table 38, Appendix A.

CHAPTER IV

COMMENT ON COMMODITY PRICES, 1790–1820

ONE of the principal effects of the American Revolution was to change the character of the regulations governing foreign trade. Released from their colonial status, the American merchants were at liberty to trade unrestrained by British commercial regulations. However, independence brought with it one serious trading loss. It meant that the British West Indies were closed to American products as they had not been at an earlier date.

Hamilton's program of paying off government debts was highly acceptable to the responsible merchant class. Differential tonnage duties protected American shipping interests by charging foreign vessels a fifty cent port duty per ton while American vessels paid only six cents a ton. The successful establishment of a new and independent government gradually spread assurance of national unity and internal peace. Transactions formerly taken care of by London offices (insurance, for example,) were now handled by new American companies and organizations, which developed rapidly in the new nation. Europe, entangled in warfare, made an excellent customer for a people newly and favorably embarked upon rapidly developing commercial enterprises. The prosperous march of these years was accompanied by speculation in government securities and in land, leading to mild financial panics in 1792 and again in 1797. The business outlook was temporarily dimmed by the prospects of a war with France in 1798. Happily, President Adams managed our affairs so that the war with France was averted, and an important European customer was saved for us. This period as a whole was one of increasing prosperity.

Turning to a more detailed description, let us consider the events of the minor cycle which lasted from 1790 to 1792. The public reaction to the prosperous business situation in America in 1790 is well described by the following quotations:

The United States . . . are by the dispensations of Providence placed at a goodly distance from all these scenes of tumult and misery — peace reigns triumphant through our country — arts, agriculture, manufactures and commerce, under the fostering hand of the federal government, are pursued with pleasure, profit and security — the seasons shed their mildest and most benignant influences on our labors — our land yields its increase — the exuberance of our fields are transported to distant regions — while produce of every clime is wafted to our shores — every man enjoys in security the fruits of his industry — nor is there any one to annoy, or make us afraid.[1]

The Commerce of the United States is rapidly recovering from the injuries it received from partial laws, impolitick restrictions, and selfish regulations. Its basis now rests on extensive and equal principles; and while our enterprising merchants and hardy navigators are exploring every region between the Poles, for new marts of commerce; the products of our country are increasing in demand, and appreciating in value.

The Manufactures of our country, too, rapidly increase in extent and reputation. Many articles, for the supply of which we have heretofore depended on foreign countries, we have ceased to import, and a spirit to encourage home manufactures prevails.[2]

In 1790 there was under way a boom which developed during 1791 and came to an end in the spring of 1792. Conditions were ripe for a speculative craze. Many men had made a good deal of money through speculative purchases of the government debts which had been greatly enhanced in value by Hamilton's arrangements for funding and for assuming the debts of the States. In 1790 there were large exports of grain to Spain where it was much in demand.[3] France offered a bounty on grain imports which made trade with her profitable. Generally speaking the harvest of 1790 was a good one. Shipping and shipbuilding revived.[4] A business revival was well under way in 1790.

[1] The (Philadelphia) *General Advertiser*, Oct. 15, 1790.

[2] The *Columbian Centinel*, Nov. 3, 1790.

[3] The *Columbian Centinel*, June 30, 1790; (Philadelphia) *General Advertiser*, Oct. 19, 1790.

[4] The *Massachusetts Centinel*, Apr. 10, 1790.

Stimulated by the gains which accrued to the fortunate holders of the government debt and encouraged by the optimistic commercial outlook, speculators turned their attention to bank stocks[5] and to land.[6] "Public funds have rose amazingly," wrote William Taylor on August 15, 1791, "and immense fortunes have been realized by individuals in consequence of the establishment of the National Bank. The crops in Europe are plentiful the last year and all expectation of a war in Europe has subsided. We then may expect a low price for our provisions."[7] And a Philadelphia newspaper remarked: "All disinterested and thinking men seem to agree that the spirit of speculation, which has lately shown itself, is an evil, but many appear to think it will work its own cure."[8]

In the spring of 1792 the "rage for speculation" collapsed. Bank stocks, which had been speculative favorites, tumbled in price; securities issued by the United States declined 15 per cent in price between March and May; and speculation in both urban and agricultural land came to a stop. Banks which had lent their support to these speculative operations the year before now reversed their policy. In New York and Philadelphia, short-time money rates were as high as 1 per cent per day to individuals pressed to "make good their engagements to the different banks."[9] In Boston, it was said that "the total stop of discounts at the bank . . . will greatly distress that part of the community for which it was said the bank was instituted."[10] A dramatic incident in this financial panic was the ruin of the famous speculator, William Duer. He had been the leader in the bull market of 1791. When he failed to meet his financial obligations he carried many others down to ruin with him.

"Here was a typical stock market and financial panic," says Davis. "Violent over-speculation and over-extension of credit; failures of a few entailing failures of many and severe losses to more; a shock to business confidence affecting seriously mercantile activities themselves entirely unconnected with speculation; a tumble of prices not only of securities, but also of real estate and commodities; thoroughgoing confusion, uncertainty of mind on the part of the abler business men, and excitement and irritation on the part of the crowd; a temporary stoppage of building, improvements, and even of more essential economic activities, — a temporary derangement of the whole economic machinery."[11]

The commodity trade in the early months of 1792 by no means warranted this speculative exuberance. It seemed unlikely that American produce would continue to be sold on exceptionally favorable terms. News came from Britain[12] that the 1791 crop was excellent and from Lisbon[13] that the produce market was glutted. On the other hand, there was the fact that American merchants had contracted for the purchase of exceptionally large quantities of English merchandise.

> Late accounts from England inform us that the demands for British manufactures, owing in a great measure to the extravagance of the Americans, is so great, that goods of most kinds will come charged much higher than usual. It is not to our credit to have all our solid circulating cash drained from us to foreign gewgaws. . . . This is one of the effects of speculation. It has introduced pride and foppery, and kicked industry and economy out of doors; but we shall soon find that a flood of paper money will not fill an hungry belly.[14]

Following the collapse of speculation in stocks and land in 1792, there came a revival of business which lasted until 1797–98, a revival more solidly based than the previous boom for the reason that it was founded on an increasingly profitable foreign trade in commodities and on an expanding carrying rate. The war which broke out between England and France in 1793 meant not only better markets in Europe but also the opening up of the French West Indies to American trade. The war offered to American navigators not only gains from carrying goods to war-torn Europe but also a profit peculiarly theirs as

[5] The *Columbian Centinel*, Aug. 13, 1791; Feb. 4, 1792; Mar. 28, 1792.

[6] The (Philadelphia) *General Advertiser*, Jan. 23, 1792.

[7] *William Taylor Papers, 1775-1794.* (Mss.)

[8] The (Philadelphia) *General Advertiser*, Aug. 22, 1791.

[9] Rush, *Memorial*, p. 136, quoted in Davis, J. S., *Essays in the Earlier History of American Corporations* (1917), vol. 1, p. 297.

[10] The (Philadelphia) *General Advertiser*, Mar. 21, 1792.

[11] Davis, J. S., *op. cit.*, vol. 1, pp. 307–308.

[12] The (Philadelphia) *General Advertiser*, Jan. 26, 1792.

[13] *Ibid.*, Feb. 8, 1792.

[14] *Ibid.*, May 5, 1792.

neutrals for transporting goods from the French West Indies to the United States and thence to the rest of the world.

While the war was responsible for immediate prosperity, it was also responsible for the temporary set-backs that occurred. Business in 1794 was hurt by the prospects of an American war with Great Britain. In 1796 rumors of peace on the other side of the Atlantic caused commodity prices to decline in the late summer; while the eventual collapse of business in 1797–98 is definitely traceable to our disputes with France. Thus in the years 1793–97 American prosperity was both accelerated and threatened by the war between France and Great Britain.

To merchants dealing in commodities, the year 1793 was full of uncertainties. France went to war against England and against most of the other European nations. From customers in England came news of the failure of merchants and of financial strain. Thus a correspondent from Manchester characterized England as "undoubtedly, the most wretched country in the universe." The war had caused great scarcity of money, destroyed confidence completely, occasioned immense numbers of bankruptcies, and thrown hundreds of thousands out of employment, while cash was not to be had at any premium.[15] By the end of the year apprehension was expressed lest war arise between the United States and Great Britain.[16] Almost as important a disturbing factor during this year was the growing chaos in San Domingo. In that most important of the French West Indies there was widespread revolt among the negroes — a revolt which reduced the supply of sugar and cut down our profitable trade in lumber, flour, fish, and other provisions.[17] The commodity price situation was chaotic. Russian hemp, duck, and iron; Swedish iron; cordage, tar, turpentine, and pitch rose in price with the news of declaration of the European war. In the United States there were many complaints of profiteering in foodstuffs.[18] The price situation was well summed up by William Taylor in a letter as follows:

> In the present situation of things I did not expect or wish credit. . . . The critical situation of ye times with the rise of goods would deter me from going in debt was it in my power, except I had the most certain prospect of payment. Those who have had goods on hand for some time would have a capital advantage over a purchaser now, if goods have rose as I have heard.[19]

The year of 1793 was an anxious one for traders in commodities with markets that were dull and precarious.

In spite of the rumors of war with Great Britain, merchants must have found 1794 a more favorable year for business than 1793. The harvests were abundant and brought good prices.[20] At the close of the year the index number of prices of exportable goods began its rise — a large one when compared with imports. Gains in business activity came too to the merchants in the re-export trade. While in the previous year re-exports had amounted to $1,769,000 only, in 1794 they were $6,500,000. Shipping and shipbuilding prospered.

> It can be demonstrated that the quantity of shipping owned in this town [Boston] has increased more than double within the last eighteen months. Another indication that our Federal Rulers have not "impoverished" the country.[21]

In spite of rumors of war, of rising insurance rates, of the capture of American vessels by privateers, the return of prosperity to the United States was clearly apparent in 1794.[22]

The boom came to a peak in 1795 and '96. In the first of these years there was heavy buying of American produce by the French.[23] Further, the re-export trade netted large gains for Americans. "Prior to the war," wrote Thomas MacDonogh of Boston, "there was no great surplus of these articles, but for some time past much of the exports from Boston consisted of Sugar,

[15] The *American Apollo*, July 12, 1793. See also the *Columbian Centinel*, June 15, 1793.
[16] The *Columbian Centinel*, Nov. 30, 1793.
[17] The *American Apollo*, Feb. 1, 1793. See also *Wetmore Papers:* Letter from Sam Lawton to Christopher Champlin, Feb. 15, 1793. (Mss.)
[18] The *American Apollo*, Mar. 1, 1793.

[19] *William Taylor Papers, 1775-1794.* Oct. 12, 1793. (Mss.)
[20] The *Columbian Centinel*, Oct. 1, 1794.
[21] *Ibid.*, June 21, 1794.
[22] See Chart 4 and Tables 37 and 38, Appendix A.
[23] F. O. 5 (11), *American Consuls' Letters and Papers, 1795:* Letters from I. Hamilton to Lord Grenville, Feb. 21, 1795; July 28, 1795. (Mss.)

CHART 4. — WEIGHTED INDICES OF WHOLESALE DOMESTIC (A) AND IMPORTED (B)
COMMODITY PRICES IN BOSTON: MONTHLY, 1792–1820
(*Base: 1802. Vertical logarithmic scale*)

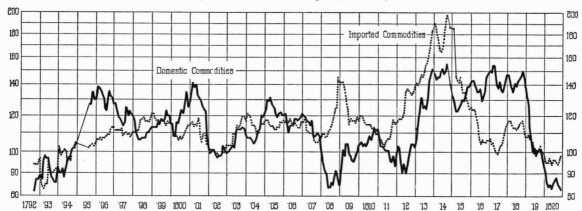

Coffee, Cotton and other West India Produce, brought from Calcutta, Bourbon and the West Indies. These have been sent at considerable advantage to Holland, France, Ostend and Hamburg."[24] America was favored by bumper crops in this year while those of Great Britain were reported to be under normal.[25] Stimulated by this favorable trade in commodities, many new sailing vessels were constructed.[26] It was reported that in June 1795 there were fifty-two vessels under construction between Newburyport and Haverhill, Massachusetts. "The affairs of Europe are certainly of less and less consequence to us in a political point of view; in a commercial, they rain riches upon us; and it is as much as we can do to find dishes to catch the golden shower."[27] The golden shower was more than a figure of speech. "Such is the astonishing abundance of money at present in this city [Boston] that it is difficult to get good bills to discount at four per cent."[28] The prevailing business optimism of 1795 was well founded.

The year 1795 and the bulk of 1796 constituted a high, sustained level of prosperity. The latter year, however, saw the abatement of this in a very different way from the modern sharp decline with which we are familiar. With rumors of peace in the latter part of the summer of 1796, prices began to fall. Criticism was voiced to the effect that Americans were speculating in their own produce and that prices were rising above the European and British level — a procedure naturally tending to decrease the profits of exporters. At the close of 1796, however, prospects of peace had faded out, and prices once more revived. In November, the *Columbian Centinel* wrote:

> In the course of one week, in the past month, the arrivals in the United States, from foreign parts, exceeded three hundred. Business never was brisker: — the truckmen can scarce find horses to do this business — the labourer has full employment, and pay — every branch of mechanicks is benefited; and the history of the world can scarcely exhibit a parallel to our prosperity.[29]

The next two years — 1797 and 1798 — were years of declining prosperity. Commerce was insecure and insurance rates were high, because of the captures of American vessels by privateers. Increasingly it looked as if the United States might go to war with France. In February 1797, Mr. Pickering, our diplomatic representative in France, departed from that country. Later in the year, three commissioners sent by the United States made an unsuccessful attempt to come to some sort of agreement with France. Finding it impossible to deal with Talleyrand, these men left with nothing settled, and returned to the United States. In April 1798 the "X.Y.Z." papers were published. These documents con-

[24] *Ibid.*: Letter from Thomas MacDonogh, Boston, to J. B. Burges, Esq., July 2, 1795.

[25] The *Columbian Centinel*, Sept. 30, 1795.

[26] The *Philadelphia Gazette and Universal Daily Advertiser*, June 24, 1795.

[27] The *Columbian Centinel*, May 9, 1795.

[28] The *Boston Price Current and Marine Intelligencer*, Nov. 16, 1795.

[29] The *Columbian Centinel*, Nov. 5, 1796.

vinced many that war with France was inevitable. The army was enlarged and reorganized, new fighting vessels were added to the navy, and Congress passed in all over twenty Acts designed to improve the national defence. Not until December was there any assurance that diplomatic relations would not be severed. In 1799 and 1800, however, relations improved; and on September 30, 1800 a treaty was concluded in which France agreed that "free ships make free goods."

The commodity trade situation in 1797 was well described in the following communication from New York City:

> The situation of the American merchants must at this period be exceedingly embarrassed; and it is but justice that the most efficacious and early measures should be adopted for their relief. The capture of our vessels by France and Great Britain has rendered our commerce so precarious, that insurances when effected, must have made the profits of trade extremely trifling indeed.—The merchants, however, are not the only sufferers — the evil has extended itself to every class of citizens. The premium of insurance is eventually paid by the consumer, and every insolvency that happens is sure to involve many in its misfortunes.[30]

The commodity trade was further unsettled by rumors of peace between France and England that were circulated in the middle of the year. Trade with the West Indies was dull.[31] To add to the pessimism, news of the suspension of specie payments by the Bank of England reached the United States in April 1797; and predictions were freely made "that the paper of this great depot of English wealth was upon a par with the assignats of France, or with the late continental currency with ourselves."[32] The abandonment of a specie standard in England must have caused some alarm in America at a time when the banks here were regarded with suspicion. "The speculations in hand," wrote the *Boston Price-Current*, "are among the most fruitful sources of embarrassment. They have given rise

to a system of credit, which involves inextricable difficulties and misfortunes. The multitude of banks in this country destined originally to aid the merchants solely, have contributed much to augment the present calamities of business; — they have been too much used to support speculating projects, by granting enormous credits."[33]

The depression in the market for American exports reached its low point in the middle and latter part of 1798. The papers were full of talk about the inevitable war with France. Insurance rates were as high as 15 per cent at one time, and some merchants even found it impossible to effect insurance on ocean-going vessels. The trade conditions of the year were well summed up in a letter to William Taylor as follows: "I am sorry to inform you that times are very dull, people are alarmed about a war, and hold up their hard money."[34]

Import prices rose to a high point in the first quarter of 1799 and then declined. This movement was the inverse of the movement of export prices and is to be explained by the same causes, notably the depredations of privateers and the likelihood of war. With unfavorable trade prospects, Index B changed less violently than Index A, owing, perhaps, to the fact that our import trade with the West Indies and the Orient was never seriously endangered. Moreover, threats to our foreign commerce depressed the prices of some re-exportable goods such as tea and sugar. High prices of coffee in Amsterdam were not sufficient to induce a speculative purchase of that commodity in America.

During 1800 and 1802 the commodity trade went through the phases of revival, prosperity, and collapse. In February 1800, Mr. Bond of Philadelphia wrote, "In the present deranged state of mercantile credit, here, it is much to be doubted, whether any cargoes of grain or flour, will be shipped from hence to Europe upon speculation."[35] By December the situation had changed. Flour and grain prices were very high, partly because of the wet autumn which

[30] The (Baltimore) *City Gazette and Daily Telegraph*, Apr. 10, 1797.

[31] The *Boston Price-Current and Marine Intelligencer*, Feb. 6, 1797; Mar. 6, 1797; Mar. 20, 1797; Apr. 27, 1797; July 10, 1797; Aug. 14, 1797.

[32] The (Baltimore) *City Gazette and Daily Telegraph*, Apr. 12, 1797.

[33] The *Boston Price-Current and Marine Intelligencer*, Jan. 5, 1797.

[34] *William Taylor Papers, 1775-1794*. Letter from John Kelly of Charlottesville, dated June 24, 1798. (Mss.)

[35] F. O. 5 (30), *American Consuls' Letters and Papers, 1800*: Letter from P. Bond of Philadelphia to Lord Grenville, Feb. 5, 1800. (Mss.)

made threshing difficult, and partly because of the flourishing export trade with the West Indies. The export trade to Great Britain was light in spite of the fact that merchants had made satisfactory gains on flour and grain sent there earlier in the season. "The prevailing opinion, now, is, that if peace should take place, grain will fall considerably in Great Britain."[36]

In the early part of 1801 the export trade was very active. Grain was scarce in Europe.[37] "There is, undoubtedly, my Lord, a prodigious quantity of Grain in this country — but it has risen to a monstrous price," said one observer in January 1801. The limiting factor on exports in the early spring months was the "want of shipping to convey it away."[38] At this time, the West Indies, deprived of produce from Europe, were an especially attractive market for the American merchant. Exports moved in such volume abroad that the foreign-exchange rate was much depressed by the large supply of sterling bills arising from this trade. Observers remarked the "low rate of exchange . . . a circumstance which always happens when there is a great demand for American produce in Europe."[39]

Accompanying this vigorous export trade was an increase of trade in imported British merchandise. "America has become a great channel for the disposal of British manufactures," wrote Thomas MacDonogh of Boston.[40] Through America, British goods were sold to the colonial dominions of other European powers, and America herself took increasing quantities of such goods.[41]

November and December of 1801 saw the end of this brief boom in commodities. The news of peace demoralized the Boston markets where a spirit of "caution and timidity" depressed "the spirit of speculation."[42] "The immediate conse-quences of the Peace in Europe, so far as relates to this city," wrote the *Aurora* of Philadelphia, "are of a stupendous nature. It is calculated that the failures already amount to Fifteen Hundred Thousand dollars."[43]

The worst depression in business thus far encountered took place between the end of 1801 and the spring of 1803. This was an interval of peace in Europe — the peace of Amiens — and of business readjustment in the United States.[44] Prices both of imports and exports fell sharply with the news of peace. Business failures were numerous, sailing vessels lay idle in the docks from Salem to New Orleans.[45] There was much unemployment.

Underlying the depression was the reduced demand by foreigners for American exports. The English harvests of 1801 and 1802 were abundant.[46] The resumption of English trade with the Baltic ports following the death of Emperor Paul of Russia made alternative supplies of grain available to Great Britain. Naval stores fell in price because of the "great surplussage of shipping." At the same time imported goods, such as copper, salt, hemp, duck, Swedish iron, cocoa, coffee, and sugar were declining. Prices seem to have fallen the world over. In England there was a mild commercial crisis which may have caused forced sales of some of these commodities in America.[47]

American business not only reflected the changed state of the markets for commodities, but also felt severely the decline in the demand for the services of her shippers. Europeans were once more able to do some of their own carrying. Certain European powers laid on duties which tended to "prohibit the carrying thither our own produce in our own vessels."[48] The indirect carrying trade between the West Indies and Europe languished, in part at least, because of

[36] *Ibid.*: Letter from P. Bond of Philadelphia to Lord Grenville, Dec. 5, 1800.

[37] The *Boston Gazette*, Feb. 5, 1801. Letter from Lisbon, Nov. 14, 1800.

[38] F. O. 5 (33), *American Consuls' Letters and Papers, 1801:* Letter from P. Bond of Philadelphia, Feb. 10, 1801. (Mss.)

[39] *Ibid.*: Letter from P. Bond of Philadelphia to Lord Grenville, Feb. 10, 1801. Also letters to Lord Hawksbury, June 5, 1801 and July 13, 1801.

[40] *Ibid.*: Letter from Thomas MacDonogh of Boston to Lord Hawksbury, July 27, 1801.

[41] The *Boston Gazette*, Sept. 17, 1801.

[42] *Ibid.*, Nov. 23, 1801.

[43] The *Aurora* quoted in the *Boston Gazette*, Dec. 31, 1801.

[44] Preliminaries of the Peace of Amiens were signed October 1, 1801 and the definitive treaty was signed March 27, 1802. War was resumed with a declaration of war by England, May 18, 1803.

[45] The *National Intelligencer*, April 27, 1803.

[46] Galpin, W. F., *The Grain Supply of England During the Napoleonic Period* (1925), p. 33.

[47] The *Boston Gazette*, Dec. 30, 1802.

[48] Jefferson's second message to Congress in Richardson's *Messages and Papers of the Presidents* (1900), vol. 1, p. 342.

hostile regulations directed against the American shipping industry.[49]

The cycle of revival, prosperity, and depression was repeated between 1803 and 1808. The outbreak of hostilities between France and England brought into operation all of the forces which had brought trade gains to Americans in the earlier periods. While the revival of the export trade and the shipping industry was slow, by 1805 and 1806 the United States was in the flood tide of prosperity again. There was a ready market for commodities, the trade in tropical products was lucrative, and American shipping presented an "astonishing spectacle." The rise in domestic commodity prices in 1805 was enhanced by the fact that crops generally were scanty.[50] Specie flowed to this country, and was deposited with the banks in large quantities. In later years, this period was spoken of as the golden age. American farmers, merchants, and ship owners were not to see again such prosperous times until 1816-18.[51]

Shortly, however, American trade was jeopardized by the *Essex* decision, the British Orders in Council, Napoleon's decrees regulating commerce, and finally by Jefferson's Embargo. In the case of the *Essex*, the English courts reversed an earlier ruling and held that the payment of customs duties in an American port did not prove the neutrality of the goods. Cargoes of sugar from the French West Indies were therefore liable to capture by British privateers even after they had been entered in a port of the United States and paid duty. In 1806, a series of Orders in Council by the British government restrained neutral trade with the continent of Europe: many ports in the north of France were declared under blockade, and in November 1807, neutrals were forbidden to trade with the French until they had first called at an English port and paid duty. Napoleon responded to these English orders by issuing a series of decrees authorizing the seizure of vessels which obeyed the British regulations. By the end of 1807, therefore, compliance with British orders rendered neutral

carriers subject to capture and condemnation by the French, and non-compliance with British orders made American ships liable to attack by the English.

The state of commerce became so precarious in 1807 that President Jefferson asked Congress to pass an embargo law, forbidding trade between the United States and the rest of the world. From December 1807 to March 1809, American products, such as cotton, flour, and naval stores accumulated in our warehouses; and imports from Europe became more and more scarce. Domestic commodity prices fell to a very low point in the third quarter of 1808, and imported-goods prices reached a higher point at the close of the year than ever before. Shipbuilding continued on a greatly reduced scale, and there was a falling off in the number of registered seamen.[52] The "almost universal stagnation of business" which existed in the latter part of 1807 was followed by many business failures.[53] Even the western frontier felt the blighting hand of the prohibitions on trade. "It cannot be denied," wrote Governor Huntington of Ohio in 1808, "that the privations and embarrassments arising out of the present state of our foreign relations, so sensibly felt by the people of the Atlantic states, are in a degree experienced by a respectable portion of our own citizens."[54]

From the first quarter of 1809 to the middle of 1812, the United States went through a mild revival in business which turned into a depression in 1811 and the first half of 1812.[55] When the

---

[49] *Israel Thorndike Papers:* Letter from Capt. Tarbox Moulton from San Domingo, Apr. 30, 1802. (Mss.)

[50] F. O. 5 (46), *American Consuls' Letters and Papers, 1805:* Letter from P. Bond of Philadelphia to Lord Mulgrave, Sept. 27, 1805. (Mss.)

[51] See Chart 4 above, and Tables 37 and 38, Appendix A.

[52] *Essex Institute Historical Collections*, vols. 39-42.

[53] *The Diary of William Bentley* (1911), vol. 3, p. 309; the *Boston Gazette*, Jan. 4, 1808; King, C. R. (Editor), *Life and Correspondence of Rufus King* (1898), vol. 5, p. 50.

[54] *Journal of the House of Representatives of Ohio*, 1808-09, p. 41.

[55] The condition of business probably was made the more serious by the tightness of the money market following the closing of the First Bank of the United States. Typical of the business apprehensions aroused is the following: "We did hope the dismal consequences that will attend the non-renewal of the United States Bank charter would be principally confined to places where they have a Branch. We now fear it will be more extensive in its calamities. The curtailing of the Branch here has for some time rendered the press for money very great. . . . Notices have been sent to all customers that they are compelled to reduce their accommodations." *Alexander Brown and Sons Letter Book*, December 1810–May 1814: Letter to Mr. Romulus Riggs, Jan. 21, 1811. (Mss.)

Embargo was removed, the export market revived, and to the close of 1810 the course of values of America's domestic products was generally upward. Imported goods were declining in price and reached a low point in the second quarter of 1811.

A reversal of the trends of our two index numbers accompanied the passing of a Non-Intercourse Act against Great Britain. Napoleon — in his letter to Cadore — promised not to molest American commerce, and to withdraw his decrees restraining our trade. Under the terms of a statute known as Macon's Bill No. 2, the American government could do nothing but revive the Non-Intercourse Act against Great Britain. Thus with February 1811, we were cut off from direct trade with England; and all signs pointed to war between that country and the United States. American export products sagged in price, while quotations of imported goods climbed steadily from the early part of 1811 to the declaration of war.

Hostilities between England and America lasted from June 1812 to the first quarter of 1815. Both commodity-price indices rose rapidly during these years; in Boston many domestic commodity prices were enhanced because of the blockade of our coast by the British fleet, which made it almost impossible to get cotton and flour to New England by water. Although there was much smuggling, imported goods continued to increase in price. Scarcity of such goods as salt, copper, hemp, and iron arising out of the war Embargo Act and the enemy blockade is one obvious explanation of the price rise which took place. Prices were enhanced by speculation in the latter part of 1813; but when, in the middle of 1814, it looked as if the United States and England would make peace early in 1815, a temporary speculative decline occurred in the quotations of many foreign articles.

There was a remarkable similarity in the upward movement of commodity prices in Boston, New York, Philadelphia, and Baltimore from the middle of 1812 to the beginning of 1814. A priori one would not have expected to find the congruence of the lines given in Chart 3, for communication between markets was difficult in war time. It is true that overland transportation developed rapidly during 1813, but the cost of such transportation was high. Throughout

1814, the index numbers diverged — the New York index number stood from ten to twenty points higher than the similarly constructed index of prices in Boston. The divergence was especially great after August 1814, when the banks of the middle and southern States suspended specie payments, and prices were quoted in irredeemable banknotes. By the close of the war, prices had reached the highest point that they attained in the thirty years previous to 1820.

Enhanced prices in the United States during the War of 1812 did not mean prosperity to the country in general. Unlike the earlier and apparently boom times (1795–1796, 1800–1801, 1805) the war period was one in which the prices of domestic commodities did not rise so fast as those of imports. American producers of cotton and flour in the South and West were at a disadvantage even when they exchanged their commodities for New England manufactures as well as for imported goods. The price-index charts show that the prosperous years were those in which Index A (domestic goods) is above Index B (imports).[56]

New England had a measure of business prosperity in spite of the fact that the War of 1812 temporarily ruined the shipping industry. Gains of a sort were made by New Englanders through evasion of the prohibitions on foreign trade that existed during most of the war, and some New England merchants even profited handsomely by sale of supplies to the enemy; but a far more significant source of gain was the newly created manufacturing interests of New England. With competition of foreign products practically eliminated, domestic manufacturers found a ready market for their wares. The Quartermaster's Department of the United States Army was making large purchases. In July 1814, came the following item from Middletown, Connecticut:

> The people of New England have one consolation in the war; that they can endure the privations much longer and with less inconvenience than the Southern States can. This by no means reconciles us to the war, for it is to us as well as to them a very great calamity. But it does not bear on all parts of our population

[56] See Chart 4.

with the same severity as it does on theirs. Merchants who had large capitals invested in foreign commerce, and in shipping, sailors, whose rights the war falsely professes to vindicate, mechanics connected with navigation, and those who live on fixed incomes, are great sufferers. But [New England] farmers and manufacturers, who form the great body of our population, are growing rich faster than they ever were in a time of peace. The surplus produce of the farmer meets a ready market and commands an extravagantly high price. The manufactures of New England sell quite well. They amount in the whole to fifteen or twenty millions annually, and not more than half of that amount are consumed in the Northern States, the residue enters into our Southern trade; and produce a balance in favor of New England and against the Southern States, of at least six millions of dollars annually. This balance is paid in specie. Hence the large and continued draughts that are made on the southern banks.[57]

News of the signing of the treaty which ended the American war with Britain reached the United States early in February 1815; and internal and foreign trade were resumed at once. Merchants discovered to their dismay that they were trading with a new Europe — a Europe at peace (save for the brief Napoleonic interlude that ended at Waterloo), a Europe that had the whole world in which to buy supplies, a Europe that was able to do much of its own ocean carrying, and an England that had new and well-developed manufactures. It soon became apparent that American traders could not for long sell on such favorable terms as they had in the past. In the early months of 1815, prices of both imports and exports fell drastically.

Partly because crop failures on the other side of the Atlantic improved the demand for flour, mess pork, mess beef, and corn, and partly because cotton and tobacco prices were enhanced by speculation abroad, the business depression under way in the early part of 1815 soon was turned into a period of prosperity. An important economic group in the United States that suffered hard times between 1815 and the close of 1818 were the manufacturers. Many American establishments were driven out of business by the competition of cheap English wares in

our markets, and now came the demand for a protective tariff. The prevailing impression that the years following the War of 1812 were years of hard times is derived from the complaints of our domestic manufacturers — a small percentage of the population. For the great body of American income receivers the years 1816, 1817, and 1818 were moderately prosperous. Domestic products were sold abroad once more, and sold on favorable terms. American ships, while less in demand than they were before the war, were nevertheless able to secure cargoes and bring some gains to the owners. The lamentations of manufacturers, whose newly created factories could not meet the competition of British products, should not obscure the fact that by and large this was a period of prosperity.

Turning from the foreign trade picture to the relations between prices for different parts of the United States we note that price indices for domestic goods in the four big Atlantic seacoast markets came into coincidence in the second quarter of 1817.[58] At this time there was a general resumption of specie payments by the banks of the middle and southern States, the depreciation of the domestic exchanges became negligible, and prices in the four markets differed by amounts mainly determined by the cost of carriage. The Atlantic seacoast was once more a unified market for staple products.

The crisis that overtook American business at the close of 1818 was largely due to a shift in the world's demand for American staples. Within a space of nine months, cotton fell from thirty-three cents a pound to twenty cents; flour from ten dollars a barrel to seven; and rice from seven and three-quarters to four and a quarter dollars a hundredweight. These price declines meant serious losses to merchants who had speculated in commodities; they portended decreased money incomes to the American farmer; and they precipitated the first major banking crisis of our period. Banks with extended loans to speculators were now confronted with a demand for specie — much of which was needed for export. Contraction of discounts at this time became a necessity, and the curtailment of bank loans made the position of the American merchant even more difficult. On October 19, 1818, the

---

[57] The *New England Palladium*, July 15, 1814.

[58] See Chart 3, page 8.

[Philadelphia] *Aurora* described the situation in the following language:

> A great crisis approaches — slow in its march, but deadly and relentless as the yellow fever which desolated your cities — and like it compounded of foreign contagion acting upon internal predisposition.

"Foreign contagion," the collapse of the European markets for American export products, and "internal predisposition," the over-extended condition of bank and mercantile credit, became indeed disastrous. Throughout 1819 the newspapers were full of accounts of the failures of merchants and banks, of unemployment, of idle ships, and of generally depressed business. According to Condy Raguet, commercial distress took the form of "ruinous sacrifices of landed property at sheriff's sales," "forced sales of merchandise," "numerous bankruptcies," "a general scarcity of money," unemployment, "an almost entire cessation of the usual circulation of commodities . . . limited to the mere purchase and sale of the necessaries of life," closed factories, "usurious extortions, overflowing debtors' prisons, law suits, depreciation of bank notes," and "a general inability of the community to meet with punctuality the payment of their debts."[59]

We shall close our study of commodity prices and trade from 1790 to 1820 by pointing out once more the vital connection between European disaster or confusion and American business. America, in 1819-20 as in 1920, presented the picture of a nation intensely disturbed by the inevitable difficulties and adjustments of a Europe emerging from prolonged warfare. Similarly then, as happened a century later, when Europe resumed production and again entered the world's markets, American business went through painful "readjustments."

On the basis of the present study, any picture of an isolated America generating booms and depressions in a vacuum lacks conviction. More accurate was the diagnosis in 1821 of Lord Liverpool, who forcefully told the House of Lords:

> Great as the distress is in every country in Europe (and certainly it prevails more or less in every country in Europe) it is, nevertheless, at the present moment greater in the United States of America than it is in any country in Europe. . . . There is no *mystery* in the cause of the existing distress in the United States of America. That distress cannot proceed from any war in which the United States have been engaged; for, during the last thirty-five years, America has been at war only during two years. Nevertheless, she has felt the effect of the wars which during the greatest part of that period have raged in every other quarter of the globe.
>
> But how has she felt it? During the whole of the late war America was the principal neutral power. . . . She enjoyed the most extensive carrying trade. She supplied this country, and she supplied other countries, with many articles which neither this country or other countries could at the time obtain elsewhere. What was the natural consequence? That America increased in *wealth*, in *commerce*, in *arts*, in *population*, in *strength* more rapidly than any nation ever before increased in the history of the world. . . . But now all the world is at peace. . . . Every country is at leisure to attend to its own condition, is diligently cultivating its domestic arts and industry. The state of America, my lords, at this moment is not so much the effect of present positive distress, as of extraordinary past prosperity. She must retrograde to a certain point. It is the result of former advantages which America exclusively enjoyed, which she must now reimburse, (if I may use the expression) until she has returned to that which is her natural condition.[60]

---

[59] Raguet, C., *A Treatise on Currency and Banking* (1840), pp. 290-292.

[60] *Niles' Weekly Register*, vol. 19 (1821), pp. 353-55.

CHAPTER V

SECURITY PRICES, 1795–1820

Trade in securities was unimportant in the United States from 1795 to 1820 — unimportant quantitatively, and without much significance as a means of forecasting the state of business. In 1795, only one bank stock was quoted in the *Boston Gazette* — and this at a time when hundreds of commodity prices were listed every week. In the days of Jefferson the security market played a minor rôle in business life.

United States Government three per cent stocks. The bank-stock index number is an unweighted aggregative index of eight bank-stock prices with 1802 as the base. The series composing the index are three of the oldest Boston banks, two of the oldest New York banks, and three Philadelphia banks. The price of United States three per cent stocks is probably the best single indicator of government credit. At the beginning of

CHART 5. — ACTUAL PRICES OF UNITED STATES 3 PER CENT STOCK IN BOSTON: MONTHLY, 1795–1820
(*Unit: dollars per share. Arithmetic scale*)

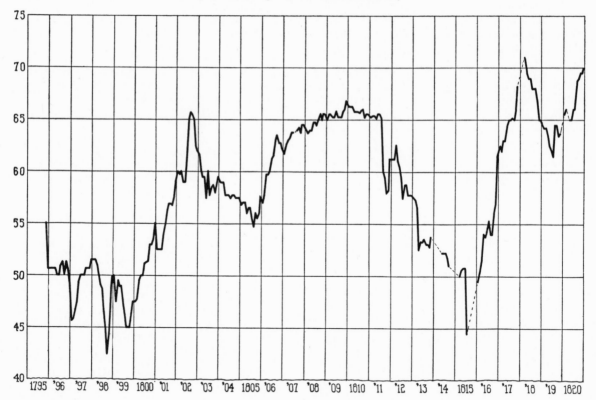

During the thirty-year period under consideration, however, there was a steady growth in importance of the corporation as a vehicle of business activity, so that by 1820 the commercial papers published lists of bank, insurance, turnpike, and bridge stocks.

Two series are presented here as indicative of the movement of security values: (1) the index number of bank-stock prices and (2) the price of

1802, the value of this issue at par was about $19,000,000, and comprised roughly one-fourth of the government debt. For our purposes, United States three per cent stock is superior to other issues partly because it was held in the hands of the public throughout the three decades, and partly because it was of itself an important security.

The newspapers of the day did not deign to

[22]

discuss the causes underlying movements of security prices, and a present day explanation of these fluctuations is largely guesswork. A few comments on the variations of prices can be made with reasonable assurance, however. First, it is obvious that the general trend of the bank-stock index number was downward, while, over the period as a whole, the trend of three per cent United States stock was upward. The growth of many new and unsound institutions, the opening up of new types of investment, and the impairment of bank credit which accompanied the War and the crisis of 1818–19, all were important elements in explaining the downward trend of the stock-price index number.[1]

A second statistical fact is noteworthy. There is a close resemblance between the "cycles" of bank-stock prices and of United States Government securities. For one thing, bank stocks and Government issues were regarded as alternative forms of investment. Another factor, which came into play with the occurrence of the War of

assets, a considerable part of which was made up of war stocks of the United States.

Thirdly, the statistics of bank-stock prices reveal a noticeable difference from those of domestic-commodity prices in violence of movement. For example, in the year 1813 the latter index rose 50 per cent at a time when the bank-stock price index remained almost unchanged. The day of speculation in stocks had not yet arrived.

Fourthly, prices of bank stocks previous to 1820 cannot be considered significant as a means of forecasting price movements in other fields of enterprise. Whatever may be true at a later date, in the first quarter of the nineteenth century stock prices did not anticipate the movement of commodity prices. Such fluctuations as occurred seem to have been due to special circumstances affecting banks. Bank-stock prices declined in 1803, when banks were losing specie through shipment abroad; in 1811-12, when it appeared that the United States would go to war with England; in the latter part of 1814, when

CHART 6. — INDEX OF BANK-STOCK PRICES: MONTHLY, 1802–20
(Base: 1802. Vertical logarithmic scale)

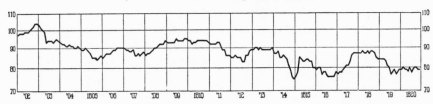

1812 and which made for similarity of movement between the two types of series, was the circumstance that most of the banks of the United States — outside of New England — were heavy purchasers of United States issues. The value of bank stocks fluctuated with the value of their

the banks of the middle and southern States had suspended specie payments; in 1816, when many banks were preparing for the resumption of specie payments; and finally, during the period of crisis and depression in 1818 and 1819, bank-stock series moved with, not in anticipation of, commodity prices. Variation in bank-stock prices clearly did not serve as a business barometer.

[1] See Tables 59 and 61, Appendix C.

CHAPTER VI

FOREIGN AND DOMESTIC EXCHANGE, 1795–1820

FOREIGN- and domestic-exchange statistics are inferior to our commodity price index numbers but superior to bank-stock prices as a guide to business history in the United States from 1790 to 1820. The fluctuations of foreign-exchange rates show only the effects of variations in foreign trade, disordered currencies, and the payment of principal and interest on the foreign debt.

There are three important differences between the early foreign-exchange market and that of the present. (1) Much of the foreign-exchange business of the early period was done by merchants. For example, Alexander Brown of Baltimore dealt in exchange as well as in linen. Americans desiring bills on England were able to purchase drafts from Brown drawn upon his correspondents on the other side. (2) Neither long- nor short-term lending and borrowing was of particular importance at the turn of the century, although there is some evidence that merchants occasionally accumulated foreign balances, and to that extent invested in foreign currencies. In 1811, Stephen Girard of Philadelphia made strenuous efforts to bring back to America the large balances that he had accumulated abroad. On the whole, however, in comparison with the practice of the present day, it appears that there was then little short-time lending and borrowing through the exchanges. (3) A very considerable amount of trade was carried on by barter. It was customary for ships to depart for the West Indies, sell flour or fish, and return with a cargo of sugar or molasses.

To return, however, to the data on exchange, rates on London varied by large amounts from month to month. For example, between February and March 1801, a 3 per cent discount on 60-day bills changed to a discount of 6–6½ per cent. Such a month-to-month variability was due in part to the smallness of the bill market. Had there been more dealers in exchange, and had there been more willingness on the part of American merchants to invest in foreign drafts, undoubtedly the rate would have been more

steady. A small market for bills of exchange had to absorb a greatly fluctuating supply of bills arising from a commodity trade in which there were wide swings. The situation was complicated further by the fact that Spanish dollars — the metallic currency most commonly exported by Americans in settlement of balances in international indebtedness — had a fluctuating gold value; that insurance rates fluctuated; and that the cost of transport (for specie) was high. Moreover, from 1797 to 1820, the sterling drafts which were bought and sold, were drafts redeemable in paper pounds. It was to be expected, therefore, that when the exchange market was small, when the supply of bills fluctuated sharply and when the currency of the world was in a state of chaos, the price of foreign bills would show a high degree of variability.[1]

As to the longer swings in the course of exchange rates, we note that the first serious depreciation occurred in 1799 — a decline in the value of the pound that is surprising in view of the upward movement from a 2–3 per cent discount to 1–2 ½ per cent premium between February and April 1797. Suspension of specie payments by the Bank of England did not seriously affect exchange on London in 1797. Although America had been virtually in a state of war with France in 1798, the rate of exchange recorded this fact by no marked change from what had held during the two previous years. In 1799, apparently the fall in the price of bills on London was due to an excessive supply in the American market of foreign bills which traders were unwilling to take except at a low price. The year was one of rising commodity prices — a period when America was sending accumulated stocks of goods abroad. In 1801, again in 1805 to 1807, and in 1816–1818, there were similar depressions in the rate of exchange; and in each of these periods, America sold large quantities of goods to Europe on very favorable terms, so that the result was a large volume of bills brought to market.

[1] See Chart 7 and Table 73, Appendix E.

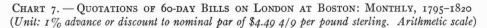

CHART 7. — QUOTATIONS OF 60-DAY BILLS ON LONDON AT BOSTON: MONTHLY, 1795–1820
(*Unit: 1% advance or discount to nominal par of $4.49 4/9 per pound sterling. Arithmetic scale*)

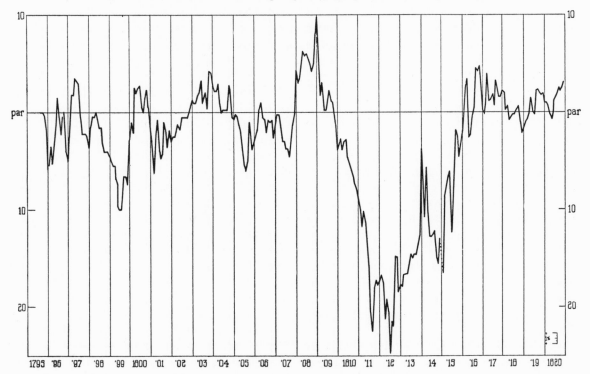

A long period of depreciation in sterling bills accompanied the War of 1812. For more than a year before the outbreak of hostilities, merchants had been expecting a state of war in the near future and were beginning to withdraw their foreign balances. The Non-Importation Act — forbidding direct trade between the United States and Great Britain — well may have lessened the willingness of buyers to take such bills on London as came on the market. In addition, the period was one of great depreciation of the pound in terms of all currencies — in terms of the Spanish silver dollar and of commodities. It should be noted in connection with this period of extreme depreciation that the rate began to rise almost as soon as America declared war. The rise is explicable along the lines which apply to the year 1808, that is, the necessity for making interest payments on long-time security issues held abroad. In 1808 and again in 1812–15, the demand for bills with which to make interest payments continued, while the supply arising from commodity exports almost entirely ceased. The sharp decline in the latter part of 1814 was due partly to the reaction following

the speculative boom of the late months in 1813 and partly to the sale of bills on the British Treasury for specie. Wagon loads of silver dollars were finding their way to Canada, in return for the British Treasury bills sold in all our Atlantic seacoast cities.

Two upward movements in the price of the pound ought to be noted — those in 1808 and 1820. The first of these was undoubtedly due to the demand for bills with which to pay interest charges and for earlier purchases made on credit. The embargo shut off the flow of exports, but it did not eliminate the necessity for the payment of foreign debts. The second rise in exchange rates on London occurred in the latter part of 1820, and continued steadily on through 1821. During these years, Great Britain was returning to a metallic standard — the gold standard — and under the circumstances American merchants were willing to pay higher prices for pounds sterling than they had during the period of restriction by the Bank of England. We see in the American market a steady rise in value of the gold doubloon at the time that the London exchanges were appreciating.

The student of monetary theory may ask if there may not be some unifying explanation back of all of these variations in foreign exchange. Computations based upon the index numbers presented here and upon Dr. Silberling's index numbers of commodity prices in Great Britain convince us that purchasing power parities do not supply the needed clue to the general level of foreign exchange rates.[2] A second basis of explanation possibly might be found in the notion that the rate of exchange on London was closely related to the price of Spanish dollars in London. This is true only in a very rough way. The immediate causes of fluctuations in rates seem to have been: (1) variations in the supply of foreign bills — depending both on physical volume of exports and the foreign prices of American products; (2) American demand for bills — a demand influenced by commodity imports and by the amount of other indebtedness to be met abroad; and (3) the willingness of American merchants to hold foreign balances.

Domestic exchange rates exhibited significant variations only between the years of 1814 and 1817. In the latter part of August 1814, the banks of the middle and southern States suspended specie payments; and at once the rates on New York, Philadelphia, and Baltimore depreciated about 20 per cent. The termination of the War of 1812 — the news reaching the United States in February 1815 — brought a rise in rates. This was due to the expectation that the banks would soon redeem their currency, and that bills would be as good as silver. This expectation was not realized; and in the latter part of 1815, exchange declined again. In 1816, Congress and the United States Treasury indi-

cated a determination to force resumption of specie payments; and, with one minor dip, the movement of rates was upward. In February 1817, with the actual return of a convertible currency, rates came back to the normal discount — a fraction of one per cent under par. Domestic-commodity prices were higher in New York, Philadelphia, and Baltimore than they were in Boston, but these price differences did not bear a close relationship to the depreciation in domestic-exchange rates. The closest relationship between commodity prices and domestic exchanges occurred in 1816–1817, when the approach of resumption was accompanied by a narrowing gap between commodity prices in Boston, New York, Philadelphia, and Baltimore. The differences between prices of bills on London at Boston, New York, Philadelphia, and Baltimore showed a high correlation with the depreciation of domestic exchanges. When bills on New York in Boston were to be had at a discount, bills on London sold for a higher price in New York than in Boston. The ease with which foreign bills were sent from one American city to another and the keenness with which the price of these bills was watched, probably accounted for the closeness of the adjustment in the relative prices of London exchange and the rates of domestic exchange.

Throughout the period from September 1814 to February 1817, we conclude that prices of domestic exchange were greatly influenced by speculative activities which hinged upon the prospect of redemption of currency in silver. The relative levels of the prices of foreign bills seem to have been subject to the same influences — a fact not at all strange, since the same dealers traded in both foreign and domestic bills. The variation in levels of prices of domestic goods seems to have lagged behind the movement in the quotations of domestic bills.

[2] Silberling, N. J., "British Prices and Business Cycles, 1779-1850," in the *Review of Economic Statistics*, vol. 5 (1923), pp. 219-62.

CHAPTER VII

BANKS AND BANKING, 1790–1820

THE records of banking are statistically unsatisfactory and economically without much significance. The data are fragmentary, because most States required reports neither from the chartered institutions nor from the numerous unchartered banks. In this period government control of banking, which in later years has provided us with such voluminous records of financial operations, had hardly begun. Moreover, such statistics as are available are not homogeneous. State legislatures changed their requirements from time to time, so that even for Massachusetts — where the data are most abundant — the reports do not form a homogeneous series. Accounting practice was unstandardized, with the result that the reports for banks — in Pennsylvania, for example — cannot be combined into a time series of much value. For a study of business conditions in the United States between 1790 and 1820, the statistics of banking are of much less utility than general observations concerning the state of the currency to be found in the files of newspapers and in the letters of merchants.

The records of the First and Second Banks of the United States are well known, and need not be cited here. State banking — always of greater significance than national banking — has left us only one satisfactory statistical record for the period — the semi-annual returns of the Massachusetts banks. These records are valuable as straws indicating the state of banking in those days under conservative management, and of banking in a particular area, New England; but they tell little concerning banking conditions in the country at large. Following 1809, there are annual records for the State of Rhode Island. Statistics for Pennsylvania and the District of Columbia have some meaning after the close of the War of 1812. For Virginia, New York, and New Jersey, there are a few records of the business of individual banks. Any attempt to use the statistics — except those of Massachusetts — until after the close of the War seems hopeless.

Banking by unchartered organizations was not uncommon in many States. These associations issued notes, accepted deposits, and did a general banking business. Certain of the currency difficulties of the period were due more to excessive note issues by unincorporated banks than to the mistakes of the chartered banks; but concerning these private institutions there are, of course, no statistics.

Between 1790 and 1820, there was an enormous growth in the number of banks and the volume of business which they were transacting. At the beginning of the period, a bank was a rarity — one or two were to be found in each of the large Atlantic seacoast towns, and almost none in the interior.[1] By the end of the period, banks were scattered all over the country. Even the Ohio valley, which in 1790 was a wilderness, was blessed, or cursed, with many of these institutions. The bank note, almost unknown beyond the Alleghenies in 1790, was all too common a medium of exchange by 1820. The rapid growth of American banking was accompanied by and partly caused by the expansion of American trade and commerce.

On two occasions during the period covered by this chapter, the banking system of the United States was subjected to very great strain — during and immediately following the War of 1812 and during the crisis of 1818–19.[2] The surprising thing is that there were not more banking crises. Banks were unintelligently regulated — in fact they were hardly regulated at all; the principles of commercial banking were not well understood; and banks were expected to bear the strain of war finance and to adjust themselves to rapid overturns in the state of international trade. It is little wonder that there was a general suspension of specie payments through the middle and southern States in September 1814, and that there were many bank failures in 1818 and 1819.

[1] Gouge, W. M., *A Short History of Paper Money and Banking in the United States* (1833), Part II, pp. 42-44.

[2] The dissolution of the First Bank of the United States in 1811 caused a tightness in the money market. It did not cause wide-spread business failures.

Of course, the suspension of specie payments by the banks of New York and to the south and west, in the latter part of August 1814, was due to the war. After 1811, State institutions sprang up in large numbers; for in that year the charter of the First Bank of the United States had been allowed to expire. During the war with England the United States Government borrowed heavily through the sale of bonds and short-term notes. These government issues were bought by individuals and banks in the middle and southern States. New England would have none of them. Opposition to the War was so strong in that quarter, that the *Boston Gazette* urged its readers not to purchase war stocks. On the other hand State banks in New York and to the south bought heavily of these government obligations, paying for them by crediting the Federal Treasury with the right to draw drafts, and by the issue of banknotes. Throughout the War a great expansion of currency took place — the government sold bonds, the banks gave the government the right to draw, drafts were honored by means of payment with the banks' own notes.

The banks might have weathered the storm of the War without suspension of specie payments had it not been for two circumstances: (1) the unwillingness of New England to cooperate financially, and (2) the drain of silver to Canada. Throughout the War, New Englanders sold goods to the Federal Government — goods which New England produced and goods which she imported. These commodities were paid for by means of drafts and banknotes redeemable by the banks in the middle and southern States. Especially in 1814, therefore, we observe a growth in the specie holdings of New England banks; while outside of New England came loud complaints that the banks were losing their cash reserves. New England banks not only were unwilling to lend money to the Government but also they were unwilling to hold balances in New York City, Philadelphia, or other financial centers friendly to the national cause. Notes of banks outside of New England were sent to the issuing institutions for redemption in specie. The inter-regional balance of trade was in New England's favor, and the balance due was demanded in cash. This situation is depicted in the following table.

TABLE 5.— SPECIE RESERVES OF THE MASSACHUSETTS, THE BOSTON, AND THE UNION BANKS (BOSTON): SEMI-ANNUALLY, 1810–1820*

Date	Specie
Jan. 1810	.........$ 558,701.64
Jun. 1810	.... 700,606.68
Jan. 1811	.... 508,094.20
Jun. 1811	.... 830,829.45
Jan. 1812	.... 1,805,505.03
Jun. 1812	.... 2,284,624.26
Jan. 1813	.... 3,500,202.07
Jun. 1813	.... 3,837,275.71
Jan. 1814	.... 3,954,531.87
Jun. 1814	.... 3,866,926.15
Jan. 1815	.... 1,658,197.71
Jun. 1815	.... 1,831,102.99
Jan. 1816	.... 859,601.05
Jun. 1816	.... 562,085.25
Jan. 1817	.... 694,256.30
Jun. 1817	.... 313,864.19
Jan. 1818	.... 363,069.30
Jun. 1818	.... 287,724.24
Jan. 1819	.... 258,934.05
Jun. 1819	.... 299,889.74
Jan. 1820	.... 376,845.51
Jun. 1820	.... 435,308.22

* Source: *Bank Returns* (a manuscript in the Archives of the Commonwealth of Massachusetts).

A minor circumstance which may have contributed to the suspension of specie payments was the sale of British government bills in 1814. If newspaper accounts are to be believed, these foreign drafts were sold in large quantities in all of the Atlantic-coast cities, and the silver received for these bills taken to Canada. How important this external drain of silver was, we shall never know; but certain it is that the knowledge that specie was leaving the country did contribute to the alarm over the state of bank reserves in 1814.

When the British invaded Maryland and captured Washington, the banks outside of New England availed themselves of this pretext to suspend specie payments. The invasion was, of course, merely the pretext for the suspension; the main cause was the redistribution of the specie of the country, which gave New England an embarrassingly large share, while a minor cause was the drain of silver to Canada.

There was a close relationship between banking and the state of trade between 1815 and 1819. As we have seen elsewhere, banks during 1815 and 1816 did not resume specie payments. We observe that domestic-exchange rates depreciated, and that both commodity prices and the quotations of foreign bills were higher in New York, Philadelphia, and Baltimore than in Boston. As the date of resumption approached, there was some complaint that banks were contracting their loans — thereby reducing their demand liabilities. Business was not very seriously embarrassed at this time, however, for foreign demand for American produce was strong. Resumption of specie payments in February 1817 was accompanied by no embarrassing outflow of precious metals.

In 1817 and 1818, we find that the State banks, as well as the Second Bank of the United States, greatly expanded their note issues and their advances to borrowers. Quantitatively this bank expansion was large, and qualitatively the loans were poor. Without question, the speculation in land and in commodities that occurred in 1818 was enhanced by the liberality with which credit was granted. This speculative boom collapsed in the latter part of 1818 and the first half of 1819, when commodity prices fell, land values declined, banks and merchants went into bankruptcy, and unemployment was worse than it had been for many years.

As has been suggested the most important circumstance that brought about a readjustment in business at this time was a decline in the prices of our exports. European harvests were better than they had been for two years previous to 1818. Foodstuffs no longer brought famine prices, for Europe and England were able to a large extent to supply their own needs. The market for cotton became less favorable, as was shown by the collapse of the speculative boom in Liverpool. The banks of the United States were faced with a demand for specie with which to pay the balance of foreign indebtedness — a demand that no longer could be met easily through the purchase of bills arising from the export of high-priced agricultural staples. The strain on our bank reserves was increased by two other circumstances: by the export of large amounts of specie to the Orient at this time, and by the demand for specie in Europe and elsewhere. Not only in England, but also in Russia and Austria, preparations were being made for a return to metallic currency, with the result that American ship captains were glad to take consignments of Spanish dollars to the Continent and dispose of them on favorable terms.

Owing largely to the circumstances mentioned in the preceding paragraph, American bank reserves were greatly reduced. Throughout the latter part of 1818, there were constant complaints concerning a scarcity of money — complaints that specie was hard to get, that the banks were contracting their loans, and that by their niggardly loan policy they were ruining the merchants of America. Without question, the period from 1818 to 1820 was the most acute financial crisis that America had seen since the introduction of commercial banking into this country.

CHAPTER VIII

GENERAL OBSERVATIONS ON THE PERIOD, 1790–1820

1. THROUGHOUT the years from 1790 to 1820, there was a rapid development of American business institutions and a great increase of wealth in the country. The United States became a great ocean carrier; our international trade in commodities expanded; banks and banking developed; the corporation as an institution began to play a part in our economic life; the market for securities — for those issued by private enterprise as well as for those issued by governments — broadened; and manufactures of such things as textiles, and iron and steel products, grew rapidly in New England and the middle States. The disturbances on the other side of the Atlantic which were inaugurated by the political revolution in France brought about an economic revolution in America. Generally speaking, the secular drift of real incomes was upward, while the economic organization of the country as a whole was becoming more and more complex as the years passed.[1]

2. From the point of view of the student of economic history a consideration of statistical material covering a thirty-year period of time gives rise to many questions. Is the concept of "long waves" applicable to the interval under consideration? Did a long wave begin in 1790–91, and, reaching its highest point in 1814, then begin to subside? For the building of a long-continued upward trend, were there any economic factors which had not completely spent themselves by 1814? Was the buoyant effect of such possible factors the cause of the short duration of the depressions that occurred between 1790 and 1814? Was the depression of 1819–20 particularly severe, because it came when the long wave was on the downward side? Such questions can be answered at least partially by the data studied.

The price indices constructed for this study do not clearly warrant calling the years from 1790 to 1814 a rising phase in a long wave. Between 1795 and 1812, certainly the domestic commodity-price index did not show a consistent upward trend. Domestic commodity prices were high in 1813–1814 and again in 1816–1818. Following 1818, domestic goods moved lower in value until well into the 'forties. At least for domestic goods the analogy of the long wave does not hold. More in accord with this theory were the price movements of imported goods. These showed a general drift upwards to a maximum in 1814, following which year they fell in a series of wave-like declines. Generally speaking, the analogy of a long wave for commodity prices as a whole is not close.

Other economic phenomena such as the volume of agricultural production, the volume of manufactures, the volume of foreign trade, and the amount of per capita real income, did show an upward drift. Economic phenomena of this type, however, developed along progressively upward lines from 1790 to 1860 and later years except for interruptions in periods of depression that were minor relative to the growth factor. The scanty evidence available indicates that the analogy of the long wave cannot be applied to many factors in American economic life during the expansive decades of 1790 to 1820.

The analogy of the long wave is of doubtful usefulness, apparently, from the standpoint of studying the working of economic forces. Indeed, it seems to be not only not useful, but often even misleading when applied to the period between 1790 and 1820. For the sake of argument to grant that such a suggested pattern of economic phenomena were correct, we should be faced with the formulation of a law explaining the generation of the long-wave pattern. Behind the disturbances of this early period, however, our researches lead us primarily to a perception of the economic phenomena as the result of a series of political events. It is difficult if not impossible to reconcile the idea of long waves with the facts.

3. Turning from a consideration of "long waves" to those shorter fluctuations which we now call "cycles," we see that our three decades

---

[1] *Niles' Register*, vol. 19 (1820), Sept. 16, pp. 38-39.

were punctuated by depressions in 1792, 1798, 1802, 1808, 1815, and 1818–19. Business boomed in 1795–96, 1800–01, and 1805. In 1810, 1812–14, and 1816–18 a state of mixed prosperity and depression existed. Perhaps if we had more accurate data on business activity, all booms would be described as those of mixed prosperity. Certainly the famous period of Coolidge prosperity was "mixed," for even then farmers were feeling the effects of the relative overexpansion of agriculture. We have sufficient data to show that the prosperity of 1816–18 was limited by the fact that foreign competition forced manufacturers to take heavy losses. Yet, because, on the whole, farmers and merchants made money during 1816–18, and because of the numerical importance of these classes of the community, prosperity was widespread.

The starting points of fluctuations in business in the United States from 1790 to 1820 appear to have arisen mainly from changes in international trade. These changing states of trade in turn were partly brought about by foreign wars and international diplomacy. Our exports expanded and trade flourished because of the war between England and France. When England turned to the United States for supplies of food, the direct consequence was a booming trade in agricultural staples in 1796, 1800, and 1803–05. Ship-builders and ship-owners called the years before 1806 the golden age, for it was then that America was the great neutral shipper for the world. Military and political events abroad were responsible also for the fluctuations in the volume of manufactured goods coming to this country. In the years before 1808, shut out from trade with the continent of Europe, British manufacturers poured their products into the United States. In 1815 and the following years vast stores of goods, accumulated during the previous war period, were shipped across the Atlantic; and North America, rather than South America, became the recipient of these commodities because of the closing of Latin-American markets by numerous political revolutions. And lastly, a direct and crude severance of economic relations between America and the rest of the world was the cause of certain other American depressions — witness the years 1798, 1808, and 1812–15. During the years that we are studying, we conclude, therefore, that the

impulses that disturbed the business of America came from abroad; and that fluctuations in foreign demand and supply are attributable directly to the state of war and politics.

A second foreign circumstance of considerable importance for American prosperity was the state of European crops. For example, the comparative prosperity of this country in 1816 and 1817 was due to the fact that crop failures abroad gave a favorable market to the American producer of foodstuffs. And not the least significant factor in the overturn of business and the depletion of our bank reserves was the collapse of this favorable market with the improved European harvest in 1818.

Our findings indicate that the organization of production and the nature of the marketing process were such as to make for business stability between 1790 and 1820. Agricultural production was by far the most important type of production. A decline in agricultural prices in those days brought with it decreased money incomes to the farm owner, but it did not lead to a general discharge of farm employees nor to a complete stoppage of income for the farm workers; for the status of farming as an industry was that of the household type. Relatively few employees were on a wage basis; and although prices declined, the work of the farm went on. In the three decades under review, the agricultural population was accustomed to accept such incomes as were returned to it by the current prices for its products and to continue producing goods. The cost structure was flexible and for agriculture at least declining prices did not entail a lesser volume of production.

A second structural aspect of the economic system in the years under review may have made for stability. To a less degree than at present, merchants were influenced by rumors, by trumped-up alarms, and by bullish talk. Moreover, there were no commodity markets so organized as to encourage speculation on margin. Throughout the period we see no signs of the phenomenon so characteristic of recent years — that of a price decline augmented and finally turned into a débâcle by the selling out of weak holders with narrow margins. The market, to be sure, was considerably affected by psychological influences, but the effect of these influences was not augmented by the very character of the machinery by which the exchange of produce was consummated.

Against this stabilizing factor in the economic life of the day must be balanced the weakness of the banking system. Here the defects were so great that often the result for the business community was increased instability. The absence of a central bank with power to put on the brakes at times of business expansion, or to come to the aid of member banks in periods of distress, was partly responsible for the large number of bank failures during the early crises — in 1819, for instance. Moreover, the absence of banking experience, and the ignorance of the principles of banking or even of danger signals, added to the economic confusion of the day. Commercial banks did not keep their loans so liquid as they later learned to do, and many banks exercised little caution in the volume of their note issue. The restraints on the loan policy of banks, which have gradually been evolved and which now are embodied in a tradition of "sound banking," were not generally operative during the first three decades of our history as an independent nation. During the period from 1790 to 1820, apparently the banking practices of the times tended to accentuate and not to minimize the effect of a fluctuating international trade upon the American business system.

4. Before going on to a description of the relation of the banking situation to the fluctuations of wholesale commodity prices in the period 1792–1820, it might be well to devote a paragraph to our devices for measuring these changes. Early in the study of the statistical material available to us, it became evident that an all-inclusive wholesale price index would be by no means such a serviceable statistical device as would separate index numbers for prices of imports and of exports. And, in point of fact, the index numbers of "secondary price levels" proved to be reasonably free from ambiguity. For example, for the years 1816–1818, Indices "A" and "B" each give significant information; since, at that time, the prices of imports were falling rapidly while those of export goods, because of sustained foreign buying, were almost at war-time levels. The year 1808 offers a second example. Here, again, the prices of imports were rising, while those of domestic commodities

were falling to a very low level. For each of these periods an all-inclusive index number would have masked the true situation so significant to American business; would have averaged out the differences and conveyed an erroneous impression of stability, even during the Embargo. The present study bears out Mr. Keynes when he says, "The notion of there being a variety of price-levels, which fluctuate relatively to one another just as the prices of individual commodities fluctuate relatively to one another, is very helpful to an understanding of Monetary Theory."[2]

5. When considering the expansion and contraction of banking and the fluctuations of wholesale prices in the United States from 1792 to 1820 we notice at once that the inflow and outflow of specie seems to have depended almost solely upon the balance of international trade and upon one other item — the earnings of our ocean carriers. Apparently, in those days, capital movements played a negligible part in the flow of specie. For example, the excellent terms under which we carried on our foreign trade in 1794–95, in 1804–05, and in 1816–17 were largely responsible for the big imports of specie. In 1818, the year when prices broke, there occurred a large outflow of specie — an outflow caused in some measure by the desire of Americans to acquire far eastern products the payment for which was made in Spanish dollars, much to the sorrow of American banks.

6. Returning, however, to periods of specie inflow, of expansion in banknote issues and of rising prices, can we find in our data any evidence as to the relative level of American prices when compared with the world level? Generally speaking there was a fair degree of correlation between prices on this side of the Atlantic and those in England. On a few occasions it was charged that American commodity prices had been driven so high by speculation that exports were thereby discouraged. To such speculations the activities of the banks were no more than contributing factors; for, on the whole, the cause of the outflow of specie from the United States was not that domestic-commodity prices were out of line with foreign prices, but that the buying of foreign goods by

[2] Keynes, J. M., *Treatise on Money*, vol. 1 (1930), p. 54.

Americans was over-rapid. A simplified and generalized picture of the relation between prices and specie movements for the period 1790 to 1820 apparently is as follows: (1) high prices for American produce, (2) specie inflow, (3) expanding money incomes in America, (4) expanding banknote issues, (5) increased purchases of foreign goods by Americans, and (6) a stoppage and perhaps reversal of the specie movement.

7. The final question of foreign-exchange rates as a reflection of price levels in America and England still remains to be considered. As we mentioned earlier, the evidence offered by Index A — if Index A can be taken to represent the American price level — seems to show that exchange rates and purchasing-power parities were negatively, rather than positively, correlated; for high prices for American products led to a flooding of the American foreign-exchange market with foreign bills. At such times, the price of bills declined, while the purchasing-power parity rate rose. When Index B is used as the source of evidence, however, the correlation between the theoretical purchasing-power parity rates and the market quotations for sterling bills is closer.

SECTION II

BUSINESS FLUCTUATIONS, 1820–45
ARTHUR HARRISON COLE

SECTION II

CHAPTER IX

INTRODUCTION

FOR the purpose of presentation, it is convenient and, in a certain sense, necessary to divide history — even a history of business fluctuations — into chronological periods. These periods should be long enough to ensure proper perspective, and yet not so large as to prove unwieldy. In conformity with this view fixed upon early in our joint inquiry, an attempt will be made in the pages immediately following to analyze the years between 1820 and 1845. Roughly speaking, these twenty-six years extend from the close of one major crisis to the conclusion of another, namely, from the nadir following the crisis of 1819 to the beginnings of revival after the long-continued difficulties of 1836–43. To be sure, a shorter period, dated 1820–34, might have been chosen with some propriety, but benefit seems to be derived from comparing the lesser movements of these years with the broader swing of the subsequent decade. Less reason, on the other hand, could be found for prolonging the period beyond 1845. Evidence is adequate that a revival was in process at that time from a low point of depression in the spring of 1843; and the later 'forties may most advantageously be treated as a period of relative calm, comparable to the 'twenties and early 'thirties and preceding another major movement — that which surrounded the crisis of 1857.

Economic historians have occasionally proposed to designate the War of 1812 as in reality the closing act of our Colonial period or, in somewhat more accurate terms, as the first stage in the economic development of the United States. In many ways, the economic life of the country between the Revolution and the second conflict with Great Britain was merely a continuation of the modes of activity and of the relationship between the new and the old Worlds which had obtained in the period when this country was politically a colony. If such a view be maintained, the further step of making 1820 the somewhat mythical dividing point between significant periods of economic change is fairly defensible; for economic events between the Peace of Ghent and this latter year were mainly connected with readjustments after the War of 1812. With considerable validity, then, one may contend that 1820 marks the beginning of a new era in the economic evolution of the United States.[1]

To draw with any considerable detail the delineaments of this new era, and to point out the differences of this time-period from that which preceded it or followed after, would entail the elaboration of what would in effect be a broad economic history of the country for these several decades. As already suggested, such an aim lies far beyond the purposes of the present volume. It must suffice here to sketch those phases of the new period which are essential or useful in the interpretation of such statistical series as the present research has devised or made available. Limiting ourselves for the moment, then, to the period embraced in the present section of this study, namely, 1820–45, we had best confine attention to those aspects of American economic development which relate most closely to the fluctuations in general business conditions. These aspects include particularly the increased division of labor, with its consequent enhancement of interdependence among the several geographical sections and various economic groups of the country, and the manifold relationships between certain events occurring in the United States and contemporary events abroad.

The feature of economic development, as well as the element of political evolution, that is commonly picked out as differentiating these

[1] However, much of the data is carried back to 1815.

Of course the bases for making 1820 a dividing line relate mainly to the domestic developments of manufacture and transportation. As will be pointed out frequently hereinafter, commercial dependence on Europe continued to form an important element in the American situation.

[37]

present decades from the Colonial or post-Colonial periods, is the suddenly enhanced interest of the nation in its own internal problems and in its own tremendous growth. In metaphorical language, it has been sometimes said that the country now for the first time turned its face away from Europe and pointed it westward. To be sure, this *volte-face* did not occur in a single year or even in a single decade, yet undoubtedly the direction of American economic (and political) life in 1830, for instance, was distinctly different from that of 1790 or even 1810. Europe had in fact receded somewhat from our economic (and political) horizons, and the West had arisen to a position of compelling significance.

This change was not reflected merely in increased population although numbers in the nation did not fall in fact far short of doubling during the two decades between 1820 and 1840. It is to be observed not merely in the rapid westward advance of population although by 1840 that mythical, statistical point of the "center of population" in the United States had made several steps in its westward journey — a journey as yet not terminated.

Those features, to be sure, were not without potent influence, especially that of the growth of population in the trans-Appalachian area. This latter change meant expansion of the domestic market — a market, moreover, peculiar in the fact that its demands for manufactured goods were particularly of a character to coincide with the productive capacities of American factories. The shift was of importance also in providing the possibility of an inter-regional trade upon which, in turn, greater national division of labor could be based. For our purposes, however, this trans-Appalachian settlement has yet another significant angle. The westward trend of population gave occasion for a recurrence from time to time of speculation in western lands. Already the Government had ceased to view its public lands as a treasure trove from which to secure the maximum of advantage to national finances; and by various devices it had sought to facilitate the transfer of these public lands into the control of *bona fide* settlers. But this transference, even with low prices per acre, was not accomplished without the intrusion of various unforeseen evils — among them, occa-

sional excited competitions for the acquisition of government lands — such as those which occurred in 1815–18 and again in the middle 'thirties. These events could not fail to influence both directly in creating an impression of prosperity, and indirectly, through its effects upon government finance, the course of business conditions in the eastern areas.

The westward trend of population was in some measure facilitated by, and to some extent the occasion of, improvement in the means of communication and the inter-regional flow of goods. The construction of improved highways, including turnpikes, had made an appreciable advance prior to 1820, and work had also been started towards building a great national highway which should ultimately reach the Northwest. Yet the period after 1820 marks in a particular degree the launching and development of projects designed to tie together distant sections of the Union and to make possible in ever-increasing volume the intersectional exchange of commodities. As against the essentially local Middlesex Canal or the improvement of navigation on the Potomac, the period of the 1830's launched and completed that extraordinary engineering feat which tied the Hudson River to the Great Lakes. Consequent upon the success of the Erie Canal came the development of railways and canals all along the Atlantic coast — railways and canals reaching out in many cases toward the Ohio valley. The movement of railway construction merged and overlapped with that of canal building; and each year after the launching of the Baltimore and Ohio saw an increasing mileage of railway line in operation. By the end of the period now under review (1845) more than 4600 miles of railway were in use and many hundreds more were on the way to completion. While much of this mileage was as yet ancillary to waterways or was distinctly local in character, other portions of it provided means of transportation distinctly inter-regional in character.

In the meantime, canal construction had improved communication in various parts of the old Northwest, while the introduction of steamboats on the Mississippi had brought this latter area much closer to New Orleans than had been dreamed of in the years before the War of 1812. At the same time, the older means of transportation, both highways and ocean shipping, had not declined. The tonnage of domestic (chiefly coastwise) shipping had, in fact, more than doubled between 1820 and 1845, and that concerned with foreign trade had increased by sixty-five per cent.[2] Yet both highways and, to some extent, coastwise and river shipping had become integral parts of that enlarged and expanding intra-continental commerce which reflected the growing disposition of the nation to turn its face away from Europe.

The same economic forces which produced this significantly enhanced domestic commerce were responsible in large measure also for the development in the East of those particular manufacturing industries, the products of which formed an important element in inter-regional trade. Here, to be sure, an additional factor must be reckoned with — namely, the introduction, especially after the War of 1812, of increased protection to domestic manufactures. The fabrication of goods ready for consumption was, of course, nothing altogether new to the decades following the Peace of Ghent but reached back into the period when the country was politically, as well as economically, dependent upon Great Britain. Factory production in various important American industries — such as those using cotton, wool, or iron — had also had its beginning prior to 1820. To a significant degree, however, the period now under discussion was one of marked expansion in the manufacturing activities of New England and north-Atlantic States. Although the country in 1843 was still predominantly agricultural, and although its prosperity was still largely dependent upon the exportation of agricultural and other extractive commodities, nevertheless the map of commercial relationships had strikingly changed; and an important element in the new arrangement was a growing number of manufacturing establishments which fed sheetings and nails, kerseys and machinery to the stream of goods which moved over the new canals and railways into western and southwestern areas.

Coincident with these changing conditions of trade and industry, and in some measure contributing thereto, was a rapid development of commercial banking in the country. Here again, naturally enough, the roots of development lie back in the period prior to 1820; but after that date came an expansion of banking facilities and an increase in total banking resources which made this phenomenon one of the characteristic features of the decades now under consideration. The essentials of this development are presented in the following tabulation in which dates have been chosen that permit allowance for cyclical changes.

TABLE 6. — CONDITION OF THE AGGREGATE BANKS OF THE UNITED STATES: ANNUALLY, 1820–45[†]

(*Unit: $1,000,000*)

Year (Nearest to January 1st)	No. of Banks and Branches	Loans and Discounts	Deposits	Circulation
1820........	308*	.....	36.0	44.9
1830........	330*	200.5	55.6	61.3
1834........	506	324.1	75.7	94.8
1837........	788	525.1	127.4	149.2
1840........	901	462.9	75.7	107.0
1843........	691	254.5	56.2	58.6
1845........	707	288.6	88.0	89.6

† "Condition of Banks" in 28th Cong., 1st Sess., House Executive Document No. 15, p. 984 and 30th Cong., 1st Sess., House Executive Document No. 107, pp. 336–7. As suggested below (p. 74), these data are lacking in desirable accuracy. However, they serve the present purpose of giving a general picture.

* Branches not enumerated before 1835.

Throughout the greater part of this period the banking life of the country was dominated by the existence of the Second Bank of the United States, under either Federal or Pennsylvania charter. It is not here necessary, however, to go into the history of this institution, beyond noting that the withdrawal of Federal deposits in the late fall of 1833 and the distribution thereof to State banks was undoubtedly an influence of major proportions in determining general business conditions in the last year or two prior to the "crisis of 1837," and that the vicissitudes of this bank until its final, disastrous closing in 1840 constituted a factor which tended to prolong the devolution of business conditions after the initial crash. The prestige which Biddle and his bank enjoyed and the efforts which they jointly made in the support of the

[2] Tonnage.—

	Coasting Trade	Foreign Trade
1820	588	584
1845	1223	904

English cotton market, were surely contributing factors to the second peak of prices and of business activity in 1839.

In addition to the organization and operation of individual commercial banks, attention should also be given to certain allied phenomena. In spite of the great influence exerted by the Second Bank of the United States, the banking community of New York City had been enjoying a steadily increasing importance in the financial affairs of the country. The evolution of a network of domestic exchange with its most important center in New York City; the increasing prominence of that community in the financing of cotton and other export activities; and the rapid growth of New York both in population and banking capital — all contributed to the creation of such a situation that fluctuations in conditions in the New York money market were of significance to large parts, if not to the whole, of the nation. In 1846, it was said in Pittsburgh, "Our market, as everyone knows, is more or less affected by the financial movements eastward. What is said and done there is felt, sooner or later, here and elsewhere in the West."[3] Philadelphia still played a large rôle in this "eastward" money market, but New York was coming more and more to the fore.

Secondly, note may be made of the development of investment banking. Here, to be sure, by reason of the paucity of information along these lines, we are treading on quite uncertain ground; yet there is some reason to believe that in the decades following the War of 1812, exchange dealers and note-brokers added traffic in securities to their other operations until something like a commerce in securities was established. With this period, moreover, came a substantial advance in the size and prominence of the New York stock exchange. Arising as an amorphous group of traders in the latter years of the eighteenth century, it took on more definite form in 1816 and steadily expanded the scope of its influence. To be sure, many securities were still dealt in locally — Baltimore securities sold usually on the small Baltimore exchange, for instance — but it is symptomatic

of the waxing position of the New York exchange that in years of major speculative activity, such as 1835–37, quotations on the New York market were reproduced in the local journals of Boston, Baltimore, and other cities of the East.

In sum, then, one may observe on the financial side an increasing prominence of banking and finance as a distinct element in the national division of labor combined with a considerable development of inter-relationships between the various parts of the country, centering particularly in New York City; so that conditions in one area could not fail to exert increasing influence over other sections. Local independence and self-determination in business affairs — though, of course, almost always qualified in various ways since the settlement of the country — were steadily losing what potency they had once possessed.

Before turning to the final group of elements which must be mentioned in this brief survey — namely, the various foreign influences — a further, semi-independent factor in domestic conditions must be considered; for the varying circumstances and dispositions of Government finance were of real significance in these decades. In connection with the influence of the Second Bank of the United States, this subject already has been touched upon above. The withdrawal of Government deposits from that institution had a particular significance; because at that time, the Government was enjoying a sizable and even somewhat embarrassing surplus. Generally good business; tariffs which had been raised in 1828 and 1832, and which had become politically stabilized by the "compromise tariff" of the succeeding year; plus the considerable and growing revenue from the sale of public lands; all these conspired to pour funds into the Federal Treasury in substantially greater volume than were needed for the current expenses of the Government under Jacksonian principles. The world saw the curious phenomenon of a nation paying off completely its public debt — a phenomenon not without its influence on foreign loans to this country — and money still was rolling in. Accordingly, the transfer of Government deposits from the responsible United States Bank to the less responsible State institutions meant a transfer of funds, which not only were unlikely to be withdrawn but which would pre-

[3] *Pittsburgh Gazette*, May 21, 1846, quoted in L. C. Hunter's "Financial Problems of the Early Pittsburgh Iron Manufacturers" in the *Journal of Economic and Business History*, vol. 2 (1930), p. 540, footnote 9.

sumably increase in volume over an indefinite period ahead. Money loaned by these State banks to facilitate the purchase of Government lands would, in due time, return to the same banking institutions as additional Federal deposits and form the basis for further loans. Not until the release of the so-called Specie Circular of 1836, in which the Government refused longer to receive State bank notes in payment for public lands, and until the attempt was made during 1836 and 1837 to distribute the Government surplus to the several States in accordance (roughly) with their population (a very considerable shift from the existing distribution of Government funds) was this halcyon period brought to its end. In fact, as noted elsewhere, these latter changes in the management of Government funds were the important immediate occasion for the reversal of that speculative movement which had characterized American business in the early and middle 'thirties.

Of less significance but yet worth mention are two later developments: first, the necessity of the Government borrowing through the issue of Treasury notes when Government deficits replaced the extraordinary surpluses; and, second, the institution for a brief period of the Independent Treasury. Treasury notes were first issued in October 1837, reached their maximum in February 1843, and were not fully retired until after 1845. At a time when business was floundering in a sea of financial difficulties, here was the needy Government making demands upon a straightened money market.

The Independent Treasury, on the other hand, was an institution which owed its origin largely to the situation in which the commercial banks of the country found themselves after the onset of crisis conditions in 1837 and again in 1839. Instituted in 1840, the Independent Treasury was supposed to provide, as its name implies, an independent and safe depository for all Government moneys. Government finance was to be divorced from the untrustworthy banking institutions of the nation. With Government finances in the condition existing at that time, it is improbable that the withdrawal of Government funds for safe-keeping in the coffers of this new institution was for the moment of much significance to the money markets. Moreover, the institution did not long survive. It was soon

disestablished when, after the political success of the Whig party in 1840, Clay and his followers held the belief that a Third United States Bank could be erected. An act was passed in 1841 disestablishing the Independent Treasury, and Government funds were again entrusted to the State banks until the re-inauguration of the Independent Treasury system — to last for many years — in 1846.

Contacts of the United States with foreign countries and especially with England, of course, were manifold in the period 1820–45. Any selection among such relationships, however, to include those most important from the point of view of their effect upon American business conditions, would undoubtedly place first the position of England and continental Europe as the chief market for American staple exports. Our cotton, tobacco, wheat, and naval stores — items which formed the great bulk of our domestic exports — were shipped to European ports in such quantity that their principal market was to be found abroad rather than within the United States. Again, a large part of the carrying trade performed by American vessels consisted of the transportation to Europe of these bulky American products. Consequently, directly and indirectly, factors influencing the demand for American staples abroad set the tune for American business. One may legitimately think of American business activity during this period as having one foot in Europe. Accordingly, steady progress was impossible if the situation across the water was unfavorable.

Europe, however, was more than a large-scale consumer of American goods. Another bond of connection was more specifically financial in character; for much of the American export trade, probably the greater part, was financed ultimately in the London money market. British merchants also facilitated the import of goods into this country either by the extension of substantial credits directly to American import merchants or, through action of their own agents, to wholesalers in the distributive system of the United States. In the field of short-time credit, therefore, London offered a peculiarly important avenue of supply; and no appreciable variation in the affairs of the London money market failed to have reactions upon the American financial and commercial situation.

Very similar was the case of capital funds. England was the principal source of loans to American enterprise, both directly, as, for example, through the purchase by Englishmen of stock in American banks or railways, as well as indirectly through the purchase by English investors of American State bonds, the proceeds of which in large measure were employed in the furtherance of "internal improvements." In the 'twenties and 'thirties, particularly in the period between 1825 and 1839, large quantities of foreign and especially British capital came to this country, thereby giving support to the prosperity which was generally enjoyed in those years. The year 1825 marks the time when England's early enthusiasm for South American investments encountered disillusionment in the wake of the commercial and financial crisis in England of that year; and 1839 may be taken as the date when once more renewed banking difficulties of "the States," followed by threatened or actual repudiation of their obligations by several American State governments, cooled the ardor of English investors towards the commitment of funds to this country. The prolonged and severe decline in prices and in volume of trade for the years after 1839 was indubitably connected with the withdrawal of that foreign support which inflowing new capital had previously given to American financial and commercial enterprise. Not without much essential truth was the allegation of the period that "the barometer of the American money market hangs up at the Stock Exchange in London;" — and, of course, whatever affected the American money market was bound to have influence on American business in general.[4]

A third significant relationship between the Old World and the New lies in the field of immigration. From a low level of about eight thousand immigrants in the early 'twenties, the stream of new arrivals had swollen to approximately three-fold that figure in 1828-30, and to proportions previously undreamed (nearly sixty-five thousand per annum) in the years of maximum general prosperity from 1832 through 1837. Moreover, inspection of these data for the whole period suggests a substantial correlation between the inflow of immigrants and changes in the business situation of the country. The numbers of new arrivals rose and fell with the tides of general business. Yet, looked at from another point of view, the inflow of new residents served as a stimulus to prosperity. To a country such as the United States of the 'twenties and 'thirties, whose complement of productive factors was deficient in the quantity of labor and capital, the acquisition of more hands to work meant a really substantial improvement in its powers of production. It is by no means strange that a fair degree of correlation may be found between an inflow of immigrants, an increase in the sale of public lands, and a rise in the volume of trade.

For these several reasons, no study of the fluctuations in American business during the decades now under consideration would be complete without investigation of concurrent changes in the general business situation of European countries, especially England. Such material as we now possess[5] demonstrates the marked susceptibility of American business, commerce, and industry to alterations in the course of English enterprise. It may be noted, for example, that in the middle 'twenties England experienced a brief though striking rise and fall of commodity prices, all encompassed within the years 1824 and 1826; and American prices showed a similar episode. English commodity prices generally rose from 1830 onward, broke sharply in 1836-37, recovered and held their ground fairly well until the spring of 1841, after which they declined pretty steadily until the middle of 1843; and American prices displayed somewhat similar movements. As elsewhere suggested, the degree and sharpness of movement as measured by Silberling's index is by no means so great as that suggested by the index of commodity prices herewith presented, yet one cannot observe the similarity in general contour of the two curves and mark their relative timing without an appreciation of the degree of influence which English affairs continued to have throughout this period over business conditions in the United States.[6]

---

[4] *Financial Register*, vol. 1 (1837), p. 83. The remark is ascribed to Mr. Gorham in Congress.

[5] Silberling, N. J., "British Prices and Business Cycles, 1779-1850" in the *Review of Economic Statistics*, Preliminary Volume V (1923) Supplement 2, pp. 219-61; Thorp, W. L., *Business Annals* (1926), pp. 156-61.

[6] For fuller discussion of these matters, see pp. 66-69.

Such was the character of the country which must be held in mind when viewing the statistical material now presented. The United States was young but rapidly growing. Although its coherence was still affected by the plenitude of vacant lands available at low prices from Government holdings, the country was beginning to take on both industrially and financially some of its more modern characteristics. Furthermore, as a young though growing nation, its own economy was peculiarly sensitive to changes in the economic and business situations of older areas — especially to those in Great Britain with which its commercial, financial, and indeed all its economic contacts were closest.

CHAPTER X

STOCK PRICES AND PUBLIC LAND SALES

ONE feature of this volume has already become obvious, namely, that an attempt is being made to give as far as possible equal weight to all the elements in the business situation: commodity prices, stock prices, the banking situation, and the like. In the preceding period, few data were available on certain aspects of business conditions, as, for example, finance and the volume of trade; and accordingly, perforce rather than by choice, little consideration could be given these elements. With the decades now under review, information becomes more abundant: data on public land speculation; some information on money rates; and a few figures on the volume of trade. The possibility is open to begin the discussion with any one of various factors. With certain arbitrariness, however, the data on speculation have been chosen for presentation first. If reason is to be found for this choice, it would lie in the manner in which a speculative movement generally anticipates the course of commodity prices, although equally plausible reasons might very well be advanced for other arrangements. Subsequent to this discussion of speculative movements in stocks and public lands, material will be offered pertaining to commodity prices, to the volume of trade, and to banking and exchange.

PRICES OF COMMON STOCKS, 1815–45

Data upon the changing values of common stocks become increasingly numerous as well as increasingly satisfactory with the passing of the decades. In the years around 1820, quotations relative to bank and insurance stocks alone are available. Subsequently, figures pertaining to the stocks of canals and gas-light companies appear, while by the 'thirties data on railroad stocks come to swell the growing stream. On the whole, too, there is a quite considerable change in quality of quotations. While for the earlier years one must be content for the most part with quotations indicating the "spread" of values (high and low points) on particular days

as reported to and published in contemporary news-sheets, by the close of the period now under discussion, figures became obtainable, especially those relating to railroad stocks, which indicate the prices at which actual purchases and sales were made.

Despite the difficulties in selecting data which may be accepted to represent fairly the course of speculation in company securities throughout the whole twenty-six year period, 1820–45, and despite the somewhat dubious character of quotations in the earlier years thereof, it has been thought desirable to present such indices as the material warrants, in the belief that these indices would show the changes in direction of general values, even though they might fail to measure the degree of such changes with the maximum accuracy desirable. Two major indices are, in fact, offered. The first is based upon the prices of the stocks of banks and insurance companies, and extends throughout the period of years now under consideration. The index has in fact been extended back through 1815 in order that this series might adequately overlap the index presented in the preceding Section. The second major index — covering the twelve years from 1834 through 1845 — was constructed by utilization of railroad stocks alone, and obviously cannot be pushed back before the early 1830's. Of course, these two indices might have been combined for the common period, 1834–45; but a comparison of the courses pursued during these years by the two groups of stock values seems to confirm the view that here two indices are better than one. In this particular case, light from two angles seems more illuminating than one more general beam; and therefore, they have not been thrown together.

A total of 96 series upon stock values in the period 1815–45 was transcribed. Of these, 69 pertained to banks, insurance companies, canal projects, gas-light companies, and a few additional, miscellaneous enterprises, while the other 27 related to railroad companies. All in all, these series, upon which additional information is elsewhere presented (Appendix C, Table 63), are believed to supply a sufficient cross-section of the security markets for a study of the years in which we are now interested. Other series might have been secured relating to market areas, such as Philadelphia or Baltimore, which are not well represented on the present list; but doubt is reasonably entertained whether the use of supplementary information would add appreciably to the picture as revealed by the series examined, since such series as were acquired from these other markets showed no consistent variation in movement from the New York values.[1]

The first index, as already stated, was constructed upon prices of the stocks of banks and insurance companies. More specifically, the process of its derivation was as follows: quotations from contemporary newspapers were transcribed relative to the common stocks of various American enterprises operating in these decades. At first attention was confined to enterprises whose stocks were bought and sold in the central-Atlantic markets of New York, Philadelphia, and Baltimore, inasmuch as the commodity-price index for this period (which had already been developed) was constructed chiefly from New York prices. Subsequently — as will be indicated shortly — a special investigation was made of stock prices in the Boston area.

The greater number of these stocks pertained to banking institutions, but a substantial proportion related to insurance companies, canals, gas-light producers, and miscellaneous enterprises. Some of these series — of which, as already suggested, the details are presented elsewhere (Appendix C, Table 63) — covered the three decades, 1815–45, in which we are now interested; but many were defective as far as the continuity of quotation was concerned, either because they lacked evidence on the earlier or the later years, or because they revealed a breakdown in the middle. For example, quotations for the stock of the New York Gas Light Company become available only with 1825, and for

the Equitable Insurance Company with 1824. Acceptable data on the stock of the Second Bank of the United States, of course, ceased with the failure of that institution in 1840, although curiously enough this stock continued to be rather actively traded in for two or three years thereafter; while the Morris Canal and Banking Company, as well as the Lehigh Coal and Navigation Company, suffered inconvenient disasters of one sort or another in the important period, 1839–44. Moreover, a few, such as the Union Manufacturing Company of Maryland, were set aside because they displayed movements distinctly peculiar to themselves, as compared with the main group of series persisting over these decades; or because the quotations at times became infrequent and apparently nominal, as in the case of the Aetna Fire Insurance stock.

All of these series were, of course, separately charted on translucent paper and were compared by super-position of their respective charts, one upon another, over a light table. Study conducted in this manner finally brought the conclusion that an index based upon a selected group of these series would bring out the characteristic movements of the whole body of such data. Moreover, this procedure would avoid the statistical difficulty of attempting to splice together into an all-inclusive index the series which began late, ended early, or had serious gaps in the midriff. The development of a selective index involved, to be sure, reliance upon the judgment of the investigator, but in this particular case, with relatively moderate movements of nearly all the acceptable series, such reliance was not an important element. Furthermore, the representative movements of common stock values secured by this procedure is in many ways preferable to the *potpourri* which would result from a utilization of any and all series for which quotations were obtainable in the period covered.[2]

---

[1] Note should also be made of difference in statistical method employed for the construction of the miscellaneous and the railroad stock indices (see Appendix C). The former is an arithmetic index, while the latter is geometric. Both employ the base 1834–42.

[2] The question might very well be raised whether under such circumstances the investigator, even though he exerts every effort to make an absolutely fair selection, may not unconsciously be affected by a personal bias as to the kind of series which ought to be included, or by a preconceived notion as to the kind of result he ought to obtain. This possibility unquestionably represents a real danger. However, it does not appear that in the present case, taking account of the scantiness of the

At all events, the index to cover the entire present period was compounded of the seven following series.

City Bank
Bank of the Manhattan Company
Bank of New York
Mechanics' Bank
Merchants' Bank
Union Bank
New York Marine Insurance Company

(Charts 8 and 9); but it has been extended to cover the subsequent decade, 1834-45, for purposes of comparison with the railroad-stock index.

The course of common stock values over the three decades subsequent to 1815 as revealed by this "index of bank-stock prices" is noteworthy for three elements: the appreciable rise and fall around 1818; the long and gentle swing of values through the years 1819-29; and the even longer, though more eventful advance and decline which

CHART 8. — INDEX OF BANK- AND INSURANCE-STOCK PRICES: MONTHLY, 1815-29

(Base: 1834-42. Vertical logarithmic scale)

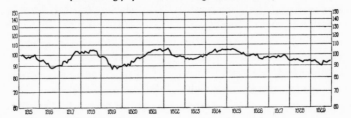

This index, of which the base is the average monthly quotations for the period 1834-42 — the same period as that employed for the commodity-price index of these decades — constitutes the principal evidence that we have on the movement of stock prices in the period 1815-33

extended from 1829 to 1842. The first phenomenon has been adequately described in the preceding Section, and need concern us no further here. The second and third are notable for their extraordinary duration. If to these could be added the subsequent long-continuing move-

CHART 9. — INDEX OF BANK- AND INSURANCE-STOCK PRICES; ALL-INCLUSIVE RAILROAD-STOCK INDEX; AND SPECIAL RAILROAD-STOCK INDEX I: MONTHLY, 1829-45

(Base: for bank-stock index, 1834-42; for railroad indices, 1853 adjusted to average 1834-42. Vertical logarithmic scale)

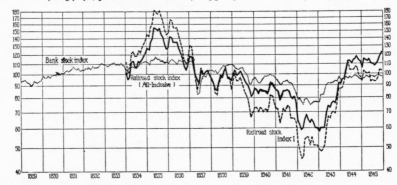

available data and the mixed nature of these data, there was available a more satisfactory method for selecting a typical group of series than the process which was employed, or that such selection could possibly have been made without exercising discretionary judgment. In fact, it may be said that in general the application of statistical methods to any practical

economic problem of necessity always involves at some point the use of discretionary judgment; and the most that the research worker in economics can do is to make the fairest and most accurate decisions possible, taking into account all of the available facts, and then, as a matter of scientific candor, state clearly and fully the bases upon which his decisions were made.

ment of railroad-stock prices lasting from 1843 to 1857, it is obvious that we have in this pre-Civil-War period phenomena of peculiar quality. Here are long-run "cycles" quite unlike the less sustained movements with which we are familiar in the post-Civil-War decades.

Each of these long-continued movements, however, contains interesting features. With respect to the earlier, its marked moderation may be noted. Its course throughout the decade of the 'twenties is comprehended within the values of 90 and 106 relative to the base chosen. (Admittedly the inclusion of two highly "insensitive" stocks — the shares of the Bank of the Manhattan Company and of the Bank of New York — imparted some stability to this index; yet such insensitive series were not of sufficient number to dominate the entire group.) However, its interest is upheld by the character of the picture presented (Chart 8): the rather rapid advance in 1819–22; the revival in 1823–24; and the long devolution from April 1825 to July 1829.

The second extended movement is noteworthy for the appreciable though protracted advance of values from the middle of 1829 to the closing months of 1833; for the sharp, though brief reaction which set in with November 1833; and the revival which lasted until the more exciting years of the later 'thirties and early 'forties. The appearance of broader movements in these latter years is of interest by reason of the long period of moderate activity which had preceded. Like a canoe pushing out from the riverbank that suddenly feels the compelling force of the main river current, this group of bank stocks apparently became caught by the middle 'thirties in a convulsion of economic forces such as they had not encountered over many decades — not even in the rise and fall of 1816–19. As inspection of the accompanying diagram (Chart 9) indicates, this group of securities moved upward rather sharply in 1834–35 to reach a high point in the summer of the latter year. Recession ensued but did not become marked until the precipitate decline in the spring of 1837. Recovery and a subsequent halting decline marked the succeeding half-decade until bottom was reached in 1842. The average low level attained in this year, it will be noted, fell below any point of recession registered by this index in the whole period subsequent to 1815.

With a point of view provided by this bank-stock index over the long period 1815–45, it is possible to take cognizance of additional information regarding stock-market activities at various points of these decades — information provided by a study of stock prices in the Boston area, by the movement of canal stocks as a special group, and by indices based on railroad-stock prices in the years 1834–45. The examination of bank and insurance stocks in the Boston area was confined to the periods 1815–24 and 1834–43.[3] The motive in this inquiry was to discover whether or not the course of stock prices in New England varied in character from that of corresponding stocks in the central-Atlantic states; and an interesting difference in fact did appear. Boston securities passed through the relatively troubled times of 1816–19 with hardly a tremor, and they coursed through the yet even more active period of the late 'thirties and early 'forties with much less movement than the index of New York bank stocks reveals. Oscillations from month to month and year to year are evident even in the earlier period, and there is admittedly a slight "cyclical" movement between 1834 and 1838; but, by and large, one is forced to conclude that Boston securities were strikingly insulated from forces which were active in other parts of the country, and which, as we shall see, were producing wide swings in the leading phases of speculation — railroad stocks and public land sales.

The lessons to be drawn from examination of canal stocks may be briefly stated. From inspection of the course described by the four leading stocks in this group (Chart 10), it is apparent (a) that the speculative movement which culminated in the middle 'thirties began earlier than 1834 — perhaps as early as the date indicated by the New York bank-stock index — namely, 1829; (b) that a recession of moment occurred in 1834; and (c) that there were stocks — for example, those of the Schuylkill Navigation and the Lehigh Coal and Navigation — which passed through the "panic" of 1837 without perceptible effect. As far as this last point is concerned, it may also be noted that the other two stocks charted — those of the Delaware and Hudson Canal and of the Morris Canal

---

[3] The Boston bank and insurance stocks transcribed and examined are listed in Appendix C, Table 63.

and Banking Company — described movements in timing not unlike those of the "bank-stock index." The accompanying diagram (Chart 10), in which the curves have been extended somewhat beyond the limit (1845) of the present period, reveals the difficulties of including such stocks in the construction of a general index to cover the present decades. The sharp break in the Lehigh Coal and Navigation Company prices is due primarily not to economic forces, but to a disastrous flood affecting its property, which occurred in 1839; a lengthy hiatus appears in 1841–44 in quotations of the Morris Canal stock; while the prices for the Schuylkill Navigation stock show such a persistent downward course even to 1850 that one is led to believe some unusual factor is here operating, possibly potent railroad competition. Only the prices of Dela-

CHART 10. — ACTUAL PRICES OF FOUR CANAL STOCKS:
FIRST MONTH OF EACH QUARTER, 1825–50
(*Unit: dollars per share. Uniform logarithmic vertical scale*)

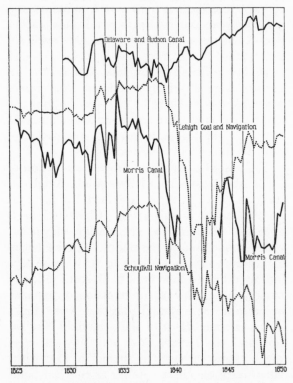

ware and Hudson Canal stock conform with what appears the general movement, and these, as a matter of fact, were taken into account in the investigation of stock prices for the period which they covered.

Of more general significance, however, than either Boston bank and insurance stocks or canal securities are the prices of railroad shares, the series of which become sufficiently numerous by 1834 to warrant the construction of indices. As already intimated, railroad stocks appear with public lands to have been the main vehicle of speculation in the years subsequent to 1830. The analysis which, accordingly, they so well deserve, led to the development of two indices. The first, which for convenience may be called "Index I" (Chart 9), indicates the average movement of eight stocks selected from the total of 11 stocks for which prices were available over the greater part or whole of the period 1834–45.[4] The basis for the selection of these eight stocks was their representative performance. In some cases, such as the Boston and Providence or the Utica and Schenectady, the series were discarded because they showed little movement at all, continuing on an even level when the typical movement was one of appreciable "cyclical" quality. In others, such as the New York and Erie, the movement was erratic — bearing no close relationship to the general swings as indicated by most of the series. The eight series ultimately secured were the following.

TABLE 8. — SERIES USED IN THE CONSTRUCTION OF
RAILROAD-STOCK-PRICE INDEX I, 1834–53

> Baltimore & Ohio
> Camden & Amboy
> Long Island
> Mohawk & Hudson
> New York & Harlem
> Paterson
> Providence & Stonington
> Philadelphia & Reading[5]

[4] A complete statement of this selection process would indicate that the railroad-stock indices used hereunder were devised with the time-period 1834-66 in mind (see the article by Cole, Arthur H., and Edwin Frickey, "The Course of Stock Prices, 1825-66" in the *Review of Economic Statistics*, vol. 10 (1928), pp. 117-39). The basis for selecting the railroad stocks for Index I was really their availability over the period prior to 1853. A detailed discussion of the methods and construction of this and of the other stock indices is to be found in Appendix C, pp. 174-84.

[5] Quotations for the Philadelphia and Reading stock become available only with 1839. This series was added for January of that year. Previous to that date logarithms were extrapolated using as the basis the stocks included in the rest of the group. (For 1844-53, see also footnote 4, p. 178.)

In addition to this selective index, one was devised utilizing all the series for which data were available for any significant part of the period 1834–45. While it was believed that this further index would not be materially divergent from the story conveyed by the selective one, and would be in fact less accurate as a description of the representative railroad-stock movements, it was undertaken for the purpose of providing a definitive check to the one which involved the use of discretionary choice. In each case, the base employed was the average monthly value for the years 1834–42; and accordingly the movements of these indices (in Chart 9) may be compared directly with those of the bank-stock index already described.[6]

The indices for railroad-stock values start in the year 1834 — a circumstance which is in some ways unfortunate. The few railroad series which antedate that point, the series pertaining to other stocks, the movement in sales of public lands, and that in commodity prices, suggest that the year 1834 embraced the low point of an intermediate reaction in a larger upward movement which had been proceeding at least since 1830. Martin reports, probably with exaggeration, that the year was one of "panic," with a decline in stocks so great that, as quotations became nominal, the *Boston Daily Advertiser* omitted them from its columns. The reaction must have been brief, however, for stocks, he says, generally advanced in the latter half of the year.[7]

After this reaction, if such a reaction may be assumed, the upward movement continued until the middle of 1835, and Index I shows a value of 181 for August.[8] Thereupon a downward

movement set in, broken early in 1836 and again early in 1837, which reached bottom in June of the latter year. No appreciable recovery followed, however; but an uneven sidewise movement occurred until May 1839, when again the average turned downward. After another brief period of relative stability and another decline, the index reached its lowest point in March 1842, when it stood at 45.

There is some doubt at this point as to whether Index I gives a full story. It would suggest a recovery after March 1842, lasting for a few months, and succeeded by another sinking spell to February 1843. The all-inclusive index, on the other hand, indicates that the low point of this downward movement came early in 1843 rather than in the spring of the preceding year — although confirming the indication that there was some minor recovery in the intervening months. The difference between the low points in either index is not considerable; and it is best to consider the two periods on a parity, with the spring of 1843 as the real turning point of the reaction which began in 1835. The movement thereafter, at least, is persistently in the upward direction.

Particularly noteworthy, then, with respect to both Index I and the "all-inclusive" index, are the attainment of the highest peak as early as 1835; the relatively inconsiderable, though sharp, decline which appeared in the crisis of 1837; and the long-continued, broken, downward tendency of the years 1835–43. The picture thus revealed contrasts markedly with that usually given by non-statistical accounts of this period. The "catastrophe" of 1837 is almost lost in a greater movement. A summer's fever is seen to be but a minor part of an eight-year sickness.

In the investigation which accompanied the construction of the two general railroad indices just described, it was observed that railroads in New England were for the most part a group to themselves, failing to manifest movements typical of railroad stocks in the country as a whole. Accordingly, it appeared advantageous to devise two supplementary indices — one compounded

---

[6] For additional data on the statistical methods employed in the construction of these railroad-stock indices, see Appendix C, pp. 177–84.

This "all-inclusive" railroad-stock index was, in fact, constructed prior to the development of the bank-stock index for the earlier decades. The meagre advantage of having two indices (as will appear shortly) — and the logical necessity of an index conveying *representative* movements — led to the decision (noted above) not to construct an all-inclusive bank, insurance company, canal, and miscellaneous index for the years 1815–45.

[7] Martin, J. G., *One Hundred Years' History of the Boston Stock and Money Markets* (1898 ed.), p. 28.

[8] The value for May was fractionally higher, and the figures for June and July were slightly lower. For figures in detail of this index, see Appendix C, Table 64.

The base here employed is the average value for the period

1834–42. The original index on the base of 1853 values (see an article on "The Course of Stock Prices, 1825–66" by Cole, Arthur H., and Edwin Frickey in the *Review of Economic Statistics*, vol. 10 (1928), p. 129) was converted to that of 1834–42 by dividing through by 0.67.

of railroad stocks in New England and the other of corresponding securities in the central-Atlantic States.[9]

The results are interesting (Chart 11). Like the bank and insurance stocks of Boston to which reference has already been made, the values of New England railroad securities showed extraordinarily little response to the economic forces which, in the period 1834–45, were producing wide fluctuations in the values of stocks in the central-Atlantic group. To be sure, there was an appreciable rise and fall between 1834 and 1837 not far different from that contemporaneously described by the stocks of the central-Atlantic roads. Thereafter the values of New England stocks for the most part moved at variance with those of the other group, reaching 1843 with a low point scarcely 20 per cent below the peak attained in 1835; while values

CHART 11. — GEOGRAPHICAL INDICES OF RAILROAD-STOCK PRICES, QUARTERLY, 1834–45: NEW ENGLAND AND CENTRAL-ATLANTIC

(*Base: 1853. Logarithmic vertical scale*)

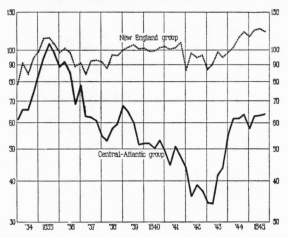

[9] Series used in the construction of the New England index:
    Boston & Lowell
    Boston & Providence
    Boston & Worcester
    Eastern of Massachusetts
    Western of Massachusetts

Series in the central-Atlantic index:
    Baltimore & Ohio
    Camden & Amboy
    Philadelphia & Reading
    Mohawk & Hudson
    Paterson

in the central-Atlantic stocks had fallen to scarcely a third of their former level.

The reasons for such a wide sectional difference are not easily ascertainable, with so limited an amount of information as yet collected upon investment banking in this period, upon the early financing of American railroads, and upon the inter-regional flow of capital in these decades. Some basis for the relative inflexibility of the railroad stocks in New England may perhaps be found in the attitude early adopted by the State of Massachusetts towards railway earnings. While the roads were permitted to fix their own rates, the legislature reserved the right to lower such charges if the net income of the company exceeded 10 per cent per year of the cost of the property. The legislature, also, reserved the right to purchase the railroads for the State at the end of twenty years from the date of their completion.[10] Such a threatening attitude might well curb speculative enthusiasm for the shares of railroads incorporated in Massachusetts.

Force is added to this consideration by the circumstances surrounding the case of Utica and Schenectady stock. Here is a security which almost alone among the non-Boston series moved lethargically over practically the entire period for which we have data. Here also, the railroad was burdened by restrictions which — although they did not prevent a fair measure of prosperity — seemed to curtail the potential earning power of the company. At first — up to 1844 — the road was forbidden to carry freight of any sort, and subsequently — until 1847 — it was limited in its carriage of freight to those seasons when the Erie Canal was not navigable. Throughout these years and indeed until 1851, tolls equivalent to those charged upon goods moving upon the Erie Canal were imposed upon all freight carried by the railroad.[11] Hence, up to the time when a prospective combination of railroads into the New York Central system began to have influence upon the value of Utica and Schenectady stock, the potentialities of profit were limited by restrictions of one sort or another. Apparently for

[10] Meyer, B. H., *Transportation in the United States before 1860* (1917), p. 320.
[11] Stevens, F. W., *Beginnings of the New York Central Railroad* (1926), pp. 268–73.

this reason, the stock moved in a sluggish manner throughout the interval 1834–51.

In addition to State restrictions, the New England situation was influenced by the character of the region served and possibly by a greater conservatism among stock purchasers there than elsewhere. When railroads were proposed radiating from Boston, the region was already more adequately settled than many other parts of the country; industries were already launched; and considerable data existed for the forecast of future traffic. Thus, when the Boston and Lowell was constructed, the Middlesex Canal had been serving the Merrimac Valley for over thirty years; mills were active in Lowell itself; and the potentialities of business on the railroad could be estimated without immoderate enthusiasm. By the same token, the more reckless speculators among the moneyed men of New England would be inclined to direct their purchases into stocks of other areas where the possibility of profits seemed distinctly greater. Again, the securities of the New England railroads may well have been closely held — as later were the stocks of many mills: we do not know. Possibly, their acquisition had been dictated as much by the desire for an income-yielding investment as by an itching for marked appreciation in values. Surely, it is more than a coincidence that the two groups of stocks covering both Boston bank and insurance companies and the railroads operating (and probably financed) in New England should each manifest much less considerable fluctuations than corresponding groups of securities tied more closely to the central-Atlantic states.

In conclusion one might summarize the evidence upon the course of stock prices in the period from 1820 to 1845 in some such fashion as follows:

(a) After the crisis of 1818, a considerable period of relative quiet supervened, with no marked general movements in stock values approximating in magnitude those of subsequent decades. At most, the rise in 1819–22 and the second advance in 1823–25 are to be noted.

(b) Beginning in 1829, greater activity appeared — perhaps not unconnected with the incipient railroad development. The advance in values between 1829 and 1833 was of considerable proportions when canal and railroad stocks, as well as bank and insurance shares, are taken into account. A recession of real significance occurred in 1833–34, but the upward movement thereafter became accelerated, especially in the case of the newer railroad securities. The peak was reached in the middle of 1835. Thereafter for several years, a sharp though irregular downward tendency ruled until 1842, or even the spring of 1843. This prodigious movement which began in 1829 may be considered to have closed only in the year last mentioned, the year when recovery became dominant in the closing months which complete the present period of investigation.

(c) Divergencies in the course of stock values are apparent both as between groups of stocks and between regions. The older and more seasoned varieties of stocks, such as those of bank and insurance companies, moved over a narrower range than did the securities of canal enterprises, and were far more restricted in movement than were the stocks of railroad companies in the period for which comparable data are available. Moreover, values in the Boston region were much more stable than those of the New York and central-Atlantic markets. Accordingly, description of the general movement must be qualified by recognition of these various exceptional cases. The movement of bank stocks in the Boston area and that of railroad securities in New York or Philadelphia are birds of quite different plumage, although both types belong to the picture of business fluctuations in this early period of American development.

PUBLIC LAND SALES

Let us turn to the sale of public lands. Here new data drawn from previously neglected files of the General Land Office enable us to see more clearly than has been possible heretofore the course of public land sales — data sufficiently detailed to present a comparison with the stock values just discussed. Studies that have been made upon the land sales of the National Government in the pre-Civil-War period — among others the volumes of Donaldson, Treat, and most recently that of Hibbard — have presented the general course of the movement.[12] Such

[12] Donaldson, Thomas, *The Public Domain* (1884); Treat, P. J., *The National Land System* (1910); Hibbard, B. H., *A History of the Public Land Policies* (1924).

For a statement of the annual figures on volume of land sales, 1796-1860, see Appendix D, Table 71.

statistics as these writers have advanced indicate that there were three occasions when the volume of sales reached particularly great heights. These occasions were the years preceding the crises of 1818, 1837, and 1857. At these several times, speculation was rampant, and the rush of purchasers to the local governmental agencies was so great that feverish activity of any sort came thereafter to be commonly described as "doing a land-office business." But these accounts of land sales fail in several respects to give as full a picture of this important phenomenon as could be wished. Based on annual data, they cannot show the timing of the speculative movements with an accuracy desirable for a study of business cycles. Moreover, since previous studies have presented time series only for the country as a whole, little can be learned about the variation of sales in the several sections of the country — especially as to what particular areas in the nation were most affected at the different periods of speculative buying.

Fortunately there exists in the records of the General Land Office material which makes possible a more thorough-going study. Quarterly data on the moneys received and deposited in the Treasury by the numerous local land offices, is shown in the accounts submitted by them every three months to the General Land Office in Washington. Although these data extend as far back as 1806, they are not sufficiently complete to serve our purpose — except for special areas — previous to 1816; since it was only then that these reports were submitted with consistent regularity. However, the 45-year interval, 1816-60, embraces the occasions of the chief speculative activities in public land sales, and also, indeed, the important periods of general speculation in the decades before the Civil War. These financial items, it may be observed, can be supplemented and tested by statistics of the quantity of land sold — data which appeared in the annual reports of the Commissioner. The latter series apply also to the several land offices, and were presented first — 1820 to 1845 — merely as annual data but later — after 1845 — in half-yearly periods. Using these two sets of figures, one can ascertain not only the significance in money terms of total land sales over the relatively short periods of quarter-years, but also receipts in each land office for similarly brief

periods as well as the acreage sold, office by office, each year or half-year. For the interpretation of cyclical movements in the sale of public lands and for the determination of the sectional variation in these sales, such detailed statistics are invaluable.[13]

In the analysis here made of this mass of new data, some simplification of the material has been thought advantageous; and this has been accomplished, first, by grouping together the statistics relating to the land offices located in each of the several States and, secondly, by employing only the summations of moneys received or acreage sold in each group of offices for the various time periods. Since the boundaries of land districts (in each of which a single land office had control) usually did not extend over State lines, this method of operation serves merely to divide the country into conveniently sized areas for descriptive purposes, i.e., States. In the use of this material, moreover, chief reliance has been placed upon the data on moneys taken in. This for two reasons: first, these figures are available by quarterly periods, whereas those of acreage sold appear only for annual or at best semi-annual intervals; and, secondly, they extend back in time somewhat further than do the statistics of acreage. For most of the period under consideration — the decades preceding 1860 — it is a matter of indifference for the purposes of this study which set of annual aggregates is used. Public land was sold under regulations of certain minimum prices per acre; the minimum prices (as we know) usually formed the actual purchase price; and so the two series move together. Indeed, if the two sets of annual figures on the sale of public lands for the country as a whole be plotted on a logarithmic scale, no significant variation between the curves will be found to appear up to the last few years of the period. With the passage of the "graduation" scheme in 1854, a divergence does appear — to which reference subsequently will be made.

Let us first confine our attention to the period prior to 1845 and to the series for quarterly data on receipts from land sales, using first the statistics for the country as a whole. Inspection of these aggregate figures indicates that there were

[13] For a statement of the quarterly receipts from land sales, 1815-1860, see Appendix D, Table 72.

CHART 12. — PUBLIC LAND SALES: RECEIPTS BY THE UNITED STATES: QUARTERLY, 1816–45

(Unit: $1,000. Vertical logarithmic scale)

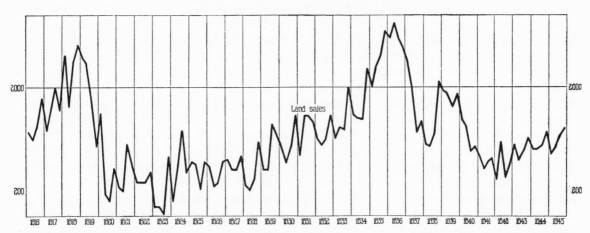

two major periods of land speculation, and two minor ones (see Chart 12). The major movements reached their highest points in the fourth quarter of 1818 and the second quarter of 1836, respectively; and they stand out with marked prominence on the accompanying diagram. The lesser movements, however, which reached peaks in the third quarter of 1824 and the fourth quarter of 1838, are not without significance.[14]

Such movements have a character in some ways more striking than those of the stock-market indices just discussed; and yet the configuration of the curve itself seems to warrant the deduction that here, as in stock prices, the speculative spirit entered largely into the phenomenon which the curve describes. Before plumbing immediately such a thesis, however, it may be well to consider other hypotheses. For example, it may be of moment to relate the course of immigration to that of public land sales. The immigration movement we know was not regular; and perhaps its variations synchronized with those of land distribution. To test this hypothesis, the annual movement of immigration — annual figures alone being available — was compared with the annual data on land sales from the time when immigration statistics first began to be collected (1820). It became apparent from this

comparison that in the years preceding 1839 there was some correlation — especially if one allows a lag of a year or two of sales behind the flow of immigrants — and such a lag would not be incompatible with the circumstances of the problem.[15] But the correlation is by no means close. Land sales reached a peak in 1836, not fairly warranted by the course of immigration; the fall thereafter was more precipitate than the decline of immigrant flow; and in the 'forties and 'fifties the relationship became even more divergent.

A second element which might be held accountable for changes in land sales is the progress of "internal improvements." While, since the landing of the Pilgrims, there has been no time when the means of transportation were not under betterment, the advance along this line has not been without periods of boom nor without times when particularly significant developments came suddenly to fruition. Possibly, then, the course of improvement in roads, canals, and railways had something to contribute in explanation of the movement of land sales. And upon reflection

[14] The relative importance of the several peaks spoken of above may be seen in the following figures of the receipts at the maximum quarters in these movements:

4th quarter of 1818	$4,967,000
3rd quarter of 1824	726,000
2nd quarter of 1836	8,423,000
4th quarter of 1838	2,239,000

[15] Something of the relationship between the movements of immigration and of land sales is apparent in the following tabulation of relatives based on the first low points in the two curves after 1820, i.e., 1823. With the exception of 1836 regular five-year intervals have been used after this last date. The acreage figures for land sales have been employed; as for this purpose the feature of land settlement is particularly important, not the financial element.

	1823	1828	1833	1836	1838	1843	1848
Immigration	100	386	862	1121	572	1062	3629
Land Sales	100	148	590	3072	522	246	288

such, indeed, seems to have been the case. For example, the years preceding 1818 were years of conspicuous activity in the improvement of transportation facilities — improvement engendered in part by the military difficulties experienced in the War of 1812. Particularly important from our point of view was the gradual extension of the Cumberland Road westward until in this same year, 1818, the highway was opened to traffic as far as Wheeling on the Ohio River; and, again, the appearance of the steamboat. The former gave a direct through route to the West, affording to prospective settlers an easy access into southern Ohio and southern Indiana. The steamboat, soon introduced upon the Great Lakes and the Mississippi, similarly offered to would-be settlers of the West a better means of maintaining contact with the outside world than that area had previously possessed.

In the years just preceding 1836, also, the extension of "internal improvements" was even more notable than it had been twenty years earlier. General communication with the West had been established with the completion of the Erie Canal in 1825. In the next decade, the construction of the canal and the portage-railway between Philadelphia and Pittsburg, and the digging of canals in the "Northwest" States gave added inducements to those who contemplated moving into Ohio, Indiana, and Illinois. Further improvement of steamboat service upon the Mississippi and Ohio rivers and on the Great Lakes might also be taken into consideration as affecting the movement of immigrants into other parts of the West.

Obviously, a fairly strong case may be built up on the influence of transportation development over the course of land sales. And yet it is not convincing. Not only was the continuity of transportation improvement the predominant feature of the period — despite some irregularities of movement — but the influence of each betterment would continue to be felt after it was accomplished. Accordingly, while the increasing efficiency of the means of communication was undoubtedly a stimulus to land sales, there seems to be no constituent peculiar to this factor which would explain the sharp declines in sales that always followed a boom period. On the basis solely of changes in transportation facilities, one would rather expect a continually mounting volume of land sales, though such an increase might not proceed at a regular rate. Nor could "internal improvements" be offered as an adequate reason for such a brief expansion of land sales as occurred in 1838-39, or for the particular timing of the breaking-points in the upward trends of sales before 1818 or 1836. Perhaps then we may view this element as a prerequisite to the characteristic movement in the disposition of public lands but, like immigration, not a sufficient cause for the intensity of that movement. We must look further for this.

The third force, that of speculative fever, is suggested by the marked irregularity — to which reference has already been made — in the configuration of the curve of land transfers, and by the very special manner in which usually the course of land sales is associated with the general cyclical movements of these decades. As the latter point will be touched upon again shortly, it will suffice here to indicate that the peaks in the sale of public lands uniformly preceded the outbreaks of the several crises — at least, in so far as the latter is indicated by the movement of commodity prices — and frequently recovery in the volume of land sales preceded that of general business. To be sure, the issuance of the famous Specie Circular in July 1836 may be held accountable in large part for the break of land sales in that year; but the phenomenon referred to is to be seen also in the attainment of a high point in 1824 preceding the minor crisis of the succeeding year, and in the occurrence of a peak at the end of 1838; whereas commodity prices continue to move upward until February of 1839.[16] Of which, more later.

[16] Even in 1818 when the decline in land sales and the break in commodity prices seemed to have occurred at about the same time, appearances are in some measure deceptive. In the older public-land States, such as Ohio and Indiana, the volume of sales tended downward from the end of 1817. The high level of sales in 1818-19 is to be attributed almost wholly to the course of activity in the newer areas — especially in Alabama — where sales mounted in such fashion as to countervail and conceal the movement in the other regions.

In addition to attaining their peaks earlier, the commencement of an upward movement in aggregate sales after a period of depression seems also to have come first in land sales: e.g., the lift of sales in 1828, 1838, and 1842.

The amounts of purchase money turned in by the land offices in Alabama during the years 1816-20 were as follows:

1816	$398,000
1817	1,718,000
1818	8,676,000
1819	4,148,000
1820	1,067,000

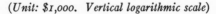

CHART 13. — PUBLIC LAND SALES: RECEIPTS BY THE UNITED STATES AS A WHOLE AND BY
OHIO, ILLINOIS, AND INDIANA: ANNUALLY, 1814–60

(*Unit: $1,000. Vertical logarithmic scale*)

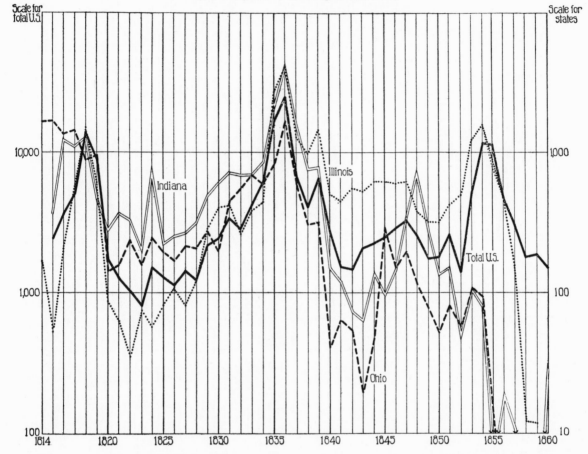

Let us turn to an examination of the receipts grouped according to the several States. Here it is advantageous to use annual figures, since those on the quarter-year basis display such irregular movements as to be difficult to follow. We are now chiefly interested, moreover, in the part played by the various States in the several speculative activities, and not in the exact timing of the movements State by State with relation to other events of the period.

Inspection of the accompanying graphs (Charts 13-16), in which the course of land sales by calendar years in the several States is compared with that of the country as a whole, yields many significant facts. Particularly it shows that the degree in which the States shared in the boom movements varied markedly one State from another, and that not infrequently there were special movements for individual States

which do not fit in with the analysis of speculative activity above presented for the country as a whole.

As to the first point, one may note the following:

(a) In the speculative movement which culminated in 1818, Alabama — as already indicated — was affected in a particularly large measure, while only in a somewhat smaller degree were Illinois and Mississippi. On the other hand, the volume of sales in Ohio does not appear to have followed the general course. Although, to be sure, sales in this area fell sharply with those of other States, they seem to have been proceeding for some time previously upon a high level. Missouri, too, presents an exception. Presumably on account of the recent opening of a land office in that area, the quantity of sales did not reach its peak until 1819.

CHART 14. — PUBLIC LAND SALES: RECEIPTS BY THE UNITED STATES AS A WHOLE AND BY
MICHIGAN, WISCONSIN, MINNESOTA, AND IOWA: ANNUALLY, 1816–60

(Unit: $1,000. Vertical logarithmic scale)

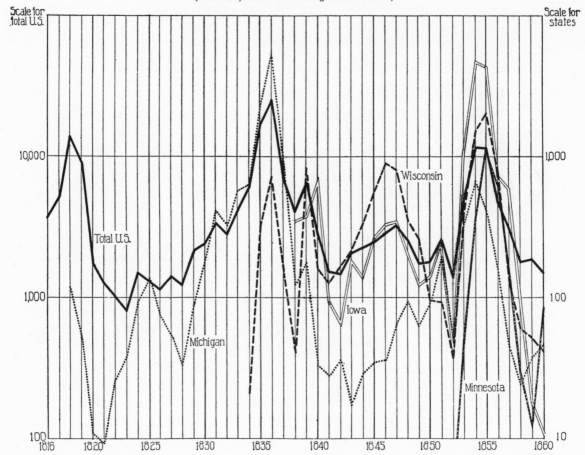

(b) The special activity in land sales culminating in 1824 was much less general than the above. Indiana shows an upward thrust for the single year 1824; Mississippi exhibits a rising volume of sales in the years immediately preceding but shows no considerable downward trend thereafter; and Michigan alone reveals a pronounced rise and fall around that date.[17] Ohio, Illinois, Alabama, and Missouri are little affected, if indeed they show any effect at all.

(c) The breadth of speculative movement was particularly great in the years preceding 1836. All States were drawn in upon a greater or lesser scale. The intensity of the movement, however, differed appreciably among the several States. In some cases, e.g., Ohio or Alabama, there was a gradual enhancement of sales extending over six or eight years. For Indiana and Illinois, indeed, the volume swells with only minor recessions over the whole period 1822–36. On the other hand, the rise and fall are peculiarly rapid and extreme in the cases of Michigan, Mississippi, and Arkansas. In those newer areas, speculation seems to have played particular havoc.[18]

(d) Various States manifested in a minor way the secondary movement which culminated for the country as a whole in 1839 — for example, Ohio and Michigan, although those especially concerned were Louisiana, Wisconsin, and Missouri.

(e) The recovery after 1842 again was irregu-

[17] In fact, the culminating point for Michigan lies in 1825, not 1824, the movement being prolonged perhaps by peculiar, local factors.

[18] Sales in Florida seem to have followed a largely independent course, especially in so far as they reach a peak later than the sales in the other States.

CHART 15. — PUBLIC LAND SALES: RECEIPTS BY THE UNITED STATES AS A WHOLE AND BY
MISSOURI, ARKANSAS, AND LOUISIANA: ANNUALLY, 1816–60

(Unit: $1,000. Vertical logarithmic scale)

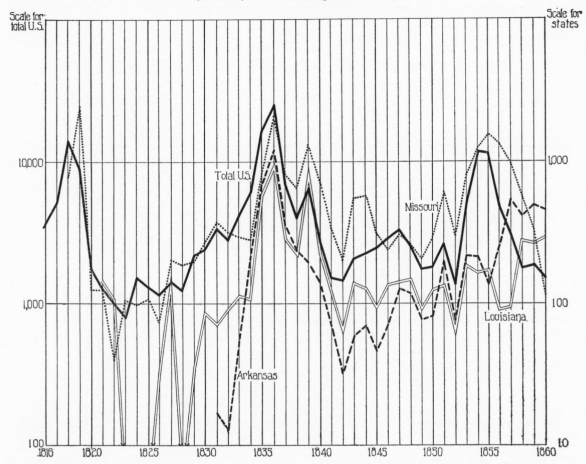

lar, being generally more marked in the North-west than in the South or Southwest. Ohio, Indiana, Wisconsin, and Iowa moved up fairly sharply, whereas Alabama, Mississippi, Louisiana, and Arkansas lagged behind.

The second feature above mentioned, special movements in the case of individual States, is apparent at a casual inspection of the charts. Although those occurring in the 'forties are particularly numerous, similar features had appeared earlier. One may note the frequent slumps in land sales of particular areas after the first year or two when data are available — for example, in Louisiana, Florida, and Iowa, and the occasional odd movement such as that in Louisiana sales in 1826-27. The former were due presumably to the fact that prior to the opening of land offices, people who had already come into

the region and who had occupied public lands as "squatters" rushed to the new bureaus to purchase the land that they had staked out for themselves. In the other cases, changes in transportation facilities or the opening up of Indian lands seem usually to have occasioned the particular events.

In sum, there seems reason to conclude that the course of land sales over this period was one of fairly consistent timing and, therefore, an element which can properly be included as a normal feature of business fluctuations in these decades. Moreover, the characteristic relationship in time of this movement of land sales with that of commodity prices seems clearly to place the former in the same general category with the course of stock prices — with which, indeed, it is included in this chapter. To be sure, there are differences

CHART 16. — PUBLIC LAND SALES: RECEIPTS BY THE UNITED STATES AS A WHOLE AND BY
ALABAMA, MISSISSIPPI, AND FLORIDA: ANNUALLY, 1814–60

(*Unit: $1,000. Vertical logarithmic scale*)

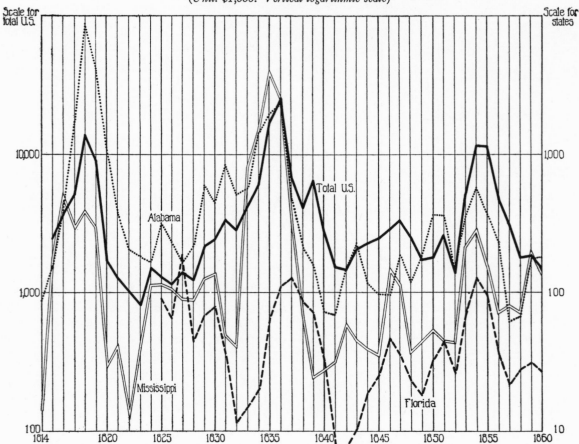

in the intensity of movement in land sales and in stock prices — to which reference will be made later.[19] Yet both these items were subject in these years to waves of popularity and disfavor; and the two tended to move together.

Secondly, as regards land sales, it may be concluded that the incidence of speculation in the sale of public lands displayed a westward movement. The areas most affected in 1818 were, generally speaking, passed over in the excitement of the middle 'thirties, and interest was

concentrated more largely in the States farther west; while the similar speculative movements of the 'forties and 'fifties — if we may anticipate our story a bit — involved a range of States still more remote from the eastern seaboard. Even as, in the case of common stocks, securities of new types in some measure came to displace interest in those previously favored by each new generation of stock-market speculators and of investors in common stocks, so new areas of public lands attracted the enthusiasm of each successive generation of land speculators.

[19] See below, p. 81.

CHAPTER XI

COMMODITY PRICES

IN no manner is the paucity of information relative to the pre-Civil-War period in the United States made more evident than by indication of the fact that hitherto we have lacked a monthly index of commodity prices.[1] Faulkner and Hansen have given us annual indices which reflect general price movements of the period, but such indices obviously lack the detail which is invaluable for close investigation into business conditions, and for the adequate treatment of the economic development in these decades.[2]

Scarcity of data has not been the chief obstacle in this highly desirable inquiry. Many series of prices were collected and published in the Report of the Secretary of the Treasury for 1863. Many others necessary to supplement this "Finance Report" are available in contemporary newspapers, such as the *New York Shipping List* or the *Boston Daily Advertiser*. Indeed, as appears elsewhere (see Appendix A), these were, in fact, the sources utilized in the collection of the material for the present study. Out of these records we acquired some 90 series of commodity prices covering the whole or part of the three decades, 1815-45. These series were charted, examined, and tested. From the total number, 38 were selected as providing a satisfactory foundation in the construction of index numbers which would mirror the characteristic movements of commodity values in the decades now subject to examination.[3]

Two general indices were in fact devised: first, an unweighted index covering the period 1825-45; and, subsequently, a weighted index covering the years 1815-45, when it seemed advantageous to test the adequacy of the unweighted type and when it became desirable to push this form of measurement back to overlap with indices which had been developed for the years prior to 1821.[4] Details of the construction of the indices presented in this study are to be found elsewhere (Appendix A); but with such details, we have now no need to concern ourselves. Herewith (Table 9) is presented a list of the commodity series employed in the development of the weighted index, together with a diagram (Chart 17) presenting the two indices — weighted and unweighted — over the periods which they respectively cover. Beyond this, there remains to remark only: (a) that the two indices contain substantially the same list of series; and (b) that the weights given the various constituent items in the weighted index — which weights, of course, for lack of reliable statistical data, had to be estimated — were intended to reflect the significance of the several commodities in determin-

---

[1] The above was written before the appearance of Dr. George R. Taylor's study of Charleston prices (*op. cit.*) and the publication of a corresponding inquiry into New York prices by Professors G. F. Warren and F. A. Pearson (*op. cit.*), and before Dr. Taylor had completed an investigation of commodity prices in New Orleans of the period before 1860 (as yet unpublished). In fact, the manuscript of this volume was all but ready for the printer in the fall of 1931. Press of other work prevented its appearance earlier than now, as it also prevents the recasting of the text to take into account these significant contributions to American economic history. A first examination of these later studies, however, suggests that the major conclusions stated herein, related to particular aspects of price history, would not be changed materially by attention to the new data. But it should be mentioned that when further studies now in progress into the course of commodity prices in Philadelphia and the Ohio River Valley are added to those already available, we shall be in a position to learn much concerning comparative movements in regional prices in the pre-Civil-War period; and such comparisons will naturally enrich, if they do not call for the recasting of, this volume.

[2] Roland P. Faulkner prepared a series of annual index numbers for the Aldrich Report, covering the period 1840-91, with 1860 as the base (52nd Cong., 2nd Sess. (1893), Senate Report 1394, pt. I, pp. 27-111). Alvin H. Hansen pushed this annual index back to 1801, using data from Boston newspapers for the period 1801-25, and those from the Report of the Secretary of the Treasury for 1863 for the period 1825-40. *American Statistical Association Journal*, vol. 14 (1915), pp. 804-12.

[3] While 38 commodities were used in the unweighted index, but 35 were used in the weighted index (Tables 9 and 42).

[4] The unweighted index was presented in an article entitled "Wholesale Prices in the United States, 1825-45" by Arthur H. Cole, published in the *Review of Economic Statistics*, vol. 8 (1926), pp. 69-84; and the indices for the years preceding 1821 were those devised by Walter B. Smith in his doctoral dissertation and subsequently published in the same *Review*, vol. 9 (1927), pp. 171-83, "Wholesale Commodity Prices in the United States, 1795-1824."

CHART 17. — WEIGHTED AND UNWEIGHTED INDICES OF WHOLESALE COMMODITY PRICES: MONTHLY, 1820–45

(Base: 1834–42. Arithmetic scale)

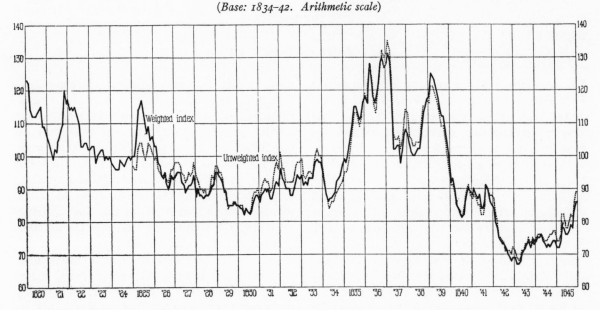

ing the character of business conditions in eastern market areas of the 'thirties and early 'forties. The first point is of present importance in

TABLE 9. — SERIES USED IN THE CONSTRUCTION OF
WEIGHTED WHOLESALE COMMODITY-PRICE
INDEX, 1815–45

Ashes, pearl	Nails, assorted
Beef, prime	Oats, northern
Butter, western dairy	Olive oil
Candles, sperm	Pork, mess
Coal, Liverpool	Rice, ordinary
Coffee, Brazil	Rosin, common
Corn, northern	Rum, New England
Cotton, upland	Rye, northern
Cotton yarn, 5–10	Salt, Liverpool, fine
Fish, bank cod	Spirits of turpentine
Iron, British bar	Staves, white oak, hhd.
Lard	Sugar, New Orleans
Lead, pig	Tallow, American
Leather, hemlock sole	Tobacco, Kentucky
Linseed oil	Whale oil
Molasses, Havana	Wheat flour, superior
Molasses, New Orleans	Whiskey, domestic
	Wool, merino

that by reason of the close identity of movement in the two indices (as revealed by Chart 17), we are able to utilize with general indifference either the weighted or unweighted index. The second point is of moment in that it would tend to restrict the use which advisedly could be made of the weighted form of index. This particular measuring device is not intended to mirror busi-

ness conditions in the West or South, nor is it pretended to be a measurement of changing costs of living. As just indicated, it is an index constructed primarily for the present purpose; namely, the investigation of changing business conditions in the eastern section of the country.

Two major elements are noteworthy in the course of prices between 1820 and 1845 as shown by these general indices; namely, the secular trend, and the movements which, for lack of a better term, may be called "cyclical." The former is relatively simple of description. As a casual inspection of the graph suggests, there is a slight downward trend through the entire period, amounting, in fact, to little more than one-half of one per cent per annum from 1821 to 1843, two years which embrace low points subsequent to "cyclical" declines.[5] This result is in accord

[5] A straight line fitted to the index and centered gave ordinates as follows: 1821, 102.21; 1832, 96.40; and 1843, 90.59. The secular trend of this general index is somewhat greater than that evident in Hansen's annual index. A straight line fitted to his index shows a declination of .0047 per annum, as compared with .528 for our index. The discrepancy between these two cases may be explained by the inclusion in Hansen's index of a number of price series which evidenced an insensitive character and which on that account were discarded in the construction of the present index.

Admittedly there is the probability of a downward bias in the index here presented as far as the first decade in the period under consideration is concerned. The base of this arithmetic index is the average values for the years 1834-42.

with the general belief that for several decades prior to 1850 the tendency of prices in this country as well as the world over was in a downward direction.

The fluctuations in these indices about the line of trend — the "cyclical" movements, if you will — offer greater novelty. Following the sharp decline of prices which set in with the closing months of 1818 and lasted until April 1821, a series of up-and-down movements ensued, brief at first but more sustained as the years advanced. The latter months of 1821 were marked by a rather sharp upward tendency; but this petered out in November, and prices moved irregularly downward in the next year or year and a half. Again, in 1825, especially as indicated by the weighted index, there came a sharp rise, also of brief career, followed by a year or so of reaction. With the middle of 1830 a more gradual but more persistent upward tendency ensued, which in fact maintained itself until the opening months of 1834. The reaction of this year was probably connected in a direct manner, as Martin asserts, with the removal of governmental deposits from the Bank of the United States, and with the curtailment of loans which was carried on during 1833-34 by that institution.[6] Moreover, good harvests in England during these years may have had some influence.[7] The movement as a whole, however, seems in character to approximate closely the "business cycle" which we have come to recognize for later decades. To be sure, the amplitude of this "cyclical" swing was much less than that of the somewhat similar movement which began with the year 1834. But the configuration of the price curve during these years suggests that, for prices at least, the break in the latter year was more than an intermediate reaction in a general movement lasting from 1830 through 1842.

After the price decline in 1833-34, a rise and fall over an unusually protracted term of years put in an appearance — a rise and fall which may be conceived to extend nearly a decade.

Activity in business returned with the late spring of 1834 — if the recovery of prices can be taken to indicate the general trend of business. Prices rose rapidly and decisively in 1835-36 and reached a peak in February 1837. The break became marked in the second quarter of the year; and thereafter followed a long period of readjustment. Indeed, outstanding features in the price movements in 1837-39 are: first, the inconclusive though sharp decrease in the general level which occurred soon after the peak of high prices had been attained in 1837; secondly, the minor recovery in the autumn of that year; and thirdly, the major upturn (especially as measured by the weighted index) which carried the general level to a point but little short of that attained in the earlier upward thrust. Even in 1840-41, prices again steadied after a severe decline from this second peak of February 1839. In fact they again reacted temporarily to somewhat higher levels than had ruled in the middle of 1840 or thereafter in 1842. The year, 1841, says Sumner, "was considered comparatively a year of prosperity;"[8] but the reaction could not be maintained, and again values slumped drastically. Not until the close of 1842, or indeed the first part of 1843, was the true bottom of the price movement finally reached.[9] Thereafter the trend was more definitely upward, and a new tendency may be said to have been initiated. The course of prices, in fact, continued to move almost steadily higher until 1845.

How shall one characterize this peculiar movement from 1834 to 1842 or 1843; and with what general description shall one cover the halting liquidation that followed the crisis in 1837? Was there a single crisis — 1837 — or were there several — 1837, 1839, and 1841? Nothing more is necessary than a study of this single price movement to show the difficulty of generalizing in any narrow way about the cyclical course of business — especially of positing any regularity or simplicity in the swings of general business conditions. The fairly regular and brief movement of 1830-34 was succeeded by the long and highly involved swing of 1834-42. However, let us not pause at this point longer than to note

---

[6] Martin, *op. cit.*, p. 28. Cf. McGrane, R. C., *The Panic of 1837* (1924), pp. 3-5. McGrane, like all writers who have noted the depression in business in 1834, speaks of the lapse as but a hesitation in the upswing of activity after 1830 which culminated in 1837.

[7] Tugan-Baranowsky, Michael von, *Theorie und Geschichte der Handelskrisen in England* (1901), p. 85.

[8] Sumner, W. G., *History of American Currency* (1874), p. 153.

[9] Sumner (*op. cit.*) speaks of the year 1843 as "one of the gloomiest in our industrial history."

this general moral in the story. Study into special features of the whole movement will give certain additional information necessary for any broad conclusions. Tentatively we may regard the course of prices as rising to a culmination in 1837 and as experiencing divers intermediate reactions in its downward phase.[10]

With this broad picture in mind, we may examine particular features of the movement more carefully.[11] The first situation which calls for attention is that which obtained in the years 1825-30. The picture revealed by the general unweighted index, as already indicated, is one of relatively sharp rise in the first half of 1825 followed (after October) by a slower decline in the next year or so. Thereupon, one may add, followed an irregular series of brief up-and-down movements, with a general downward trend, lasting to the middle of 1830. While this picture is undoubtedly a fair representation of the general course of prices, one should note that on the whole there was then less general agreement among the various price series than at any other time of the 20-year period now under consideration. Some series exhibited little activity for the whole six years, although subsequently they became much more sensitive to changes in general business conditions. Other series were experiencing a movement quite dissimilar to that displayed by the general index. Of these a group of 14 has been made, and index numbers constructed in the same manner and with the same base as the general index. This group is made up of the following series.

TABLE 10. — SERIES USED IN THE CONSTRUCTION OF SUPPLEMENTARY WHOLESALE COMMODITY-PRICE INDEX A, 1825-34

Butter, western dairy	Rum, New England
Corn, northern	Rye, northern
Corn meal, northern	Rye flour, fine
Fish, bank cod	Spirits of turpentine
Molasses, Havana	Wheat, Pennsylvania
Oats, northern	Wheat flour, superior
Rice, ordinary	Whiskey, domestic

[10] It is of interest to note that McGrane (*op. cit.*) finds it necessary at times to speak of more than one crisis. He recognized at least two crises, one in 1837 (his "panic") and one in 1839 (p. 110). In his treatment, he is generally following that of Juglar, Clément, *Des Crises Commerciales* (1862), pp. 459-67 and Tugan-Baranowsky (*op. cit.*, pp. 85-103), who distinguish crises in 1837 and 1839.

The index secured by the employment of these series alone is brought into comparison with the general index in the accompanying chart (Chart 18). Obviously, the supplementary index (hereinafter spoken of as Supplementary Index A) describes a "cyclical" swing in the period 1825 to 1830, whereas the general index is moving slowly downwards.[12]

CHART 18. — UNWEIGHTED INDEX OF GENERAL WHOLESALE COMMODITY PRICES AND SUPPLEMENTARY WHOLESALE COMMODITY-PRICE INDEX A: MONTHLY, 1825–34

(Base: 1834–42. Arithmetic scale)

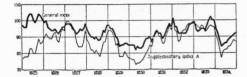

Some explanation of this diversity might be attempted through a comparison of the composition of the two indices. The series that went into the construction of the Supplementary Index A are, it appears, largely agricultural in character; while the general index covers a mixture of agricultural and industrial series. To be sure, not all the agricultural series of the general index are to be found in the group which went to form the supplementary one: not all agricultural commodities were affected in the same manner as the 14 articles above listed. Yet there is considerable evidence that the course of agricultural prices was in fact different from that in industrial lines. The deduction would then be warranted that 1825 was not a crisis year in domestic agriculture, although it may have been in other branches of the business world.

An examination into the question of what branches of business were in fact affected in the advance and decline of prices around 1825 brings to light another explanation of the divergence

[11] The unweighted index will be employed in the discussion of the next few pages, inasmuch as this happened to be the device employed when this analysis was originally undertaken. See the article on "Wholesale Prices in the United States, 1825-45" in the *Review of Economic Statistics*, vol. 8 (1926), pp. 77-83. Incidentally, some of the features encountered in this analysis were partly responsible for the later computation of an index in the weighted form.

[12] The indices are presented for a few years beyond 1830 to indicate the subsequent general similarity of movement.

above noted of these two indices. It will be noted, for example, that among the items included in the general index but missing in this special supplementary one are ashes, cotton, lard, linseed oil, and certain other goods — all of which would be specially subject to changing business conditions abroad, particularly in England. Commodities such as English bar iron and Liverpool salt are also omitted from the supplementary index. Apparently the conclusion from this and collateral evidence is justified: that in so far as domestic agriculture was primarily dependent upon domestic markets, it escaped the rise and fall in prices which culminated in 1825; and in so far as it was tied closely to foreign markets, it tended to feel the speculative movement around 1825, which was in origin predominantly external to the United States.

Another somewhat similar situation pertains to the turning-point in the course of the general index — the crisis year of 1837. Inspection of the individual price series indicated that there were several among them which manifested little or no break at that time. Such, for example, were beef and wheat. With these were combined certain other series which, although exhibiting a decline in the crisis year, reacted with particular celerity and, on the whole, showed high quotations throughout the period 1837–39. These were set apart as a group. Included in it were the following series.

TABLE 11. — SERIES USED IN THE CONSTRUCTION OF SUPPLEMENTARY WHOLESALE COMMODITY-PRICE INDEX B, 1834–45

Beef, mess	Pork, mess
Beef, prime	Rye, northern
Butter, western dairy	Rye flour, fine
Candles, sperm	Tallow, American
Fish, bank cod	Wheat, Pennsylvania
Fish, mackerel	Wheat flour, superior
Molasses, Havana	Whiskey, domestic

An index of prices for this group (Supplementary Index B), covering the period 1834–45, and constructed in the same manner as the general index, may be brought into contrast with the latter (Chart 19).

It is apparent that the decline in prices in 1837, while notable, was by no means as definitive in the case of this Supplementary Index B as in that of the general one; and that the height reached by the former in 1839 was nearly that which it attained two years earlier. If one were not looking for a real break in prices during 1837, he would be inclined to say that for the group of commodities included in this second supplementary index, there was a broad upswing of price from 1834 to 1839 with a brief and temporary reaction in 1837. The later year, 1839, was unquestionably the true turning-point in the general course of this movement.

CHART 19. — UNWEIGHTED INDEX OF GENERAL WHOLESALE COMMODITY PRICES AND SUPPLEMENTARY WHOLESALE COMMODITY-PRICE INDEX B: MONTHLY, 1834–45

(*Base: 1834–42. Arithmetic scale*)

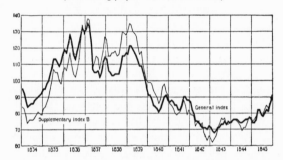

Since this index is compounded largely of agricultural series, the presumption arises here, as in the case of Supplementary Index A in 1825–30, that prices of foodstuffs followed a somewhat independent course during these years; and that the crisis of 1837 was of lesser influence as far as such commodities were concerned. Specific evidence of business conditions in the areas primarily agricultural tends to give some color to this presumption.[13] "Contrary to the generally accepted opinion," writes McGrane of the year 1837, "the pressure in the West in no way compared with that of the East and South until after the collapse of 1839," — although, he adds, the difficulties of the latter year "more than equalled the distress of other sections."[14] In short, the

[13] The cotton-producing section is an exception to this statement, and the absence of the cotton series from the above group is noteworthy.

[14] McGrane, *op. cit.*, p. 123. See also Sumner, W. G., *History of Banking in the United States* (1896), vol. 1, p. 308: "The year 1839 opened with a gloomy outlook in the southwest, especially at New Orleans. In the spring there was great distress in Mississippi. A great deal of property was changing hands. The state of things was far worse than in 1837."

reaction of prices in 1839, though it was in part but a revulsion bred of the incomplete liquidation after 1837, would seem also to have a certain character of its own.

The causes underlying the buoyancy of prices during 1838–39 remain yet to be fully ascertained. However, certain suggestions may be made. Faith in the all-sufficiency of the United States Bank and of Biddle, still widespread, may have had a considerable influence on business; for there seems much validity in Sumner's remark that "the real collapse" of the speculative movement did not come until 1839 with the first closing of the big bank.[15] However, there may have been a force of equal significance: the continuation of loans by Europe — especially England — to this country through 1838 and into 1839. Possibly here is a case similar to that discovered by Professor Williams,[16] when things ran smoothly while loans were still flowing into the country but soon became tangled as lending ceased. Moreover, it is indicative of the influence of foreign factors that among the series included in the general index but omitted from this second supplementary one were those relating to ashes, cotton, lard, English goods, etc., — indeed, much the same group that failed to find place in the first supplementary index, and that has the common characteristic of being especially sensitive to conditions in foreign countries.

A third divergence by a sizable group of commodities from the general course pertains to the brief period 1840–42 (Chart 20). The general index suggests a cessation of price decline in 1840, followed by a minor recovery. This reaction brought prices to a somewhat higher level than that which had prevailed early in 1840 or that which came after the final break of October 1841. However, the rebound of prices as shown in the general index for 1840 and 1841 was rather unstable — note the relapse to June 1841 — and distinctly moderate in degree. An annual average of prices or even a smoothed curve would indicate little more than a stabilization of prices during these two years.

For a number of commodities, on the other hand, the inspection of their respective price

15 Sumner, *op. cit.*, p. 308.
16 Williams, J. H., *Argentine International Trade under Inconvertible Paper Money: 1880–1900* (1920).

charts showed that the downward movement of prices had in fact reached its nadir by 1840. Thereafter came a substantial and well-sustained reaction of prices — a reaction that seems to have been a false start toward prosperity — only to be followed by a slump in 1842. For these commodities, prices reached another low point at the close of the latter year and in the first months of 1843 — a point, however, little if any lower than that experienced in the middle of 1840. Subsequently, as in the case of the general index, appeared the more persistent upward trend of 1843–45.

CHART 20. — UNWEIGHTED INDEX OF GENERAL WHOLESALE COMMODITY PRICES AND SUPPLEMENTARY WHOLESALE COMMODITY-PRICE INDEX C: MONTHLY, 1837–45

(*Base: 1834–42. Arithmetic scale*)

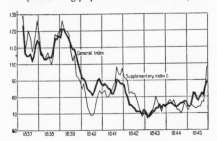

The price series which reveal this distinctive movement after 1840 were segregated; a third index (Supplementary Index C) was constructed in the same manner as in the other cases; and finally it was brought into comparison with the general index (Chart 20). The constituent price series are listed below.

TABLE 12. — SERIES USED IN THE CONSTRUCTION OF SUPPLEMENTARY WHOLESALE COMMODITY-PRICE INDEX C, 1837–45

Corn, northern	Olive oil
Corn meal, northern	Rye, northern
Cotton, upland	Rye flour, fine
Fish, bank cod	Wheat, Pennsylvania
Oats, northern	Wheat flour, superior

Again it is apparent that the chief constituents of this index are price series of agricultural commodities. For these articles, price conditions became no worse after 1840, and the downward movement, begun in 1837 or 1839, might be held to have ceased in that year.

The possibility of a general contrast between agricultural and industrial price movements became so apparent in the study of special periods that for purposes of testing the hypothesis of divergence due to this difference in type of commodity, indices for agricultural commodities as a whole and for industrial commodities as a whole were prepared to cover the full 20-year period. These are now presented (Chart 21). The price series that went into the construction of the general agricultural index — chosen without reference to previous analyses — are given here.

Obviously the term "agricultural" is here employed in a sense which may occasion criticism. Cotton and wool might be regarded quite as agricultural as corn or pork. Again, tallow or linseed oil may be regarded as in no sense more advanced manufactured materials than butter or wheat flour. Division of the series was made, in fact, more from the point of view of use than of origin. The employment of cotton and wool as raw materials in industrial activity placed them in the "industrial" group, while similar considerations rule the decision respecting tallow or lin-

CHART 21. — UNWEIGHTED INDICES OF AGRICULTURAL AND INDUSTRIAL WHOLESALE
COMMODITY PRICES: MONTHLY, 1825–45

(*Base: 1834–42. Arithmetic scale*)

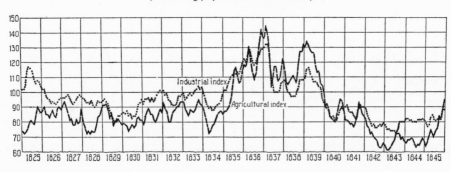

TABLE 13. — SERIES USED IN THE CONSTRUCTION OF
THE UNWEIGHTED AGRICULTURAL WHOLESALE
COMMODITY-PRICE INDEX, 1825–45

Beef, prime	Rice, ordinary
Butter, western dairy	Rye, northern
Corn, northern	Rye flour, fine
Corn meal, northern	Sugar, New Orleans
Lard	Tobacco, Kentucky
Oats, northern	Wheat, Pennsylvania
Pork, prime	Wheat flour, west canal

The series comprising the industrial index — similarly chosen — appear below.

TABLE 14. — SERIES USED IN THE CONSTRUCTION OF
THE UNWEIGHTED INDUSTRIAL WHOLESALE
COMMODITY-PRICE INDEX, 1825–45

Ashes, pearl	Molasses, New Orleans
Coal, Schuylkill	Rum, New England
Cotton, upland	Spirits of turpentine
Cotton yarn, 5–10	Staves, white oak
Iron, British pig	Tallow, American
Lead, pig	Whale oil
Leather, hemlock sole	Whiskey, domestic
Linseed oil	Wool, American, full-blood

seed oil. Perhaps a better title for the "agricultural" group or "agricultural" index would be the "foodstuffs" group or index — although this also would be inexact since tobacco would hardly be included in the latter category. No difficulty, however, is anticipated if we keep this differentiation in mind.

The course of the two indices is in considerable measure such as one would anticipate from the foregoing discussion. For particular periods, especially 1825–30 and 1837–42, there are substantial divergences in movement — divergences which coincide in part with those revealed by comparisons of the various supplementary indices with the general commodity index. The divergences between the agricultural and industrial indices, however, are somewhat less in amplitude and sometimes less in distinctiveness. These differences in relative movement may readily be attributed to the fact that in both the agricultural and industrial groups there are price series which move in greater or less disagreement with the broad trend of their respective associates. Yet it is significant that something like a cyclical swing between 1825 and 1830 is preserved in the agricultural index, whereas in the industrial index the period shows a persistent downward tendency. Likewise, the delay in culmination until 1839 of a later cyclical movement, as above posited for certain series (see Supplementary Index B in Chart 19 above), is reflected in the present index for agricultural commodities by a second high peak of prices early in 1839 — in comparison with a less important upturn at that time in the industrial in-

form, and the tool which probably better reflects the general course of business conditions. The peak of prices indicated for 1825 by the "industrial" is, of course, closely similar to that indicated by the general (weighted) index for that year. On the other hand, movements of the general index in 1837–39 seem to resemble those of the "agricultural" (foodstuffs) more closely than those of the "industrial" over the same years; while prior and subsequent to this three-year interval, the general index appears to follow a course intermediate between the two partial in-

CHART 22. — WEIGHTED INDEX OF GENERAL WHOLESALE COMMODITY PRICES (MONTHLY) AND SILBERLING'S INDEX OF WHOLESALE COMMODITY PRICES IN GREAT BRITAIN (QUARTERLY), 1820–45

(Base: 1834–42. Arithmetic scale)

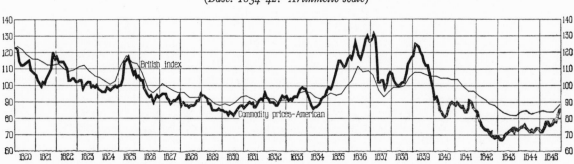

dex.[17] A new difference of some significance between agricultural and industrial price movements is made evident in the failure of the industrial index to fall as low in 1834 as did the agricultural, relative to the levels reached in 1829–30. On the whole, too, it should be observed, the extremes in fluctuation of the agricultural index during the long period, 1830–42, are substantially greater than are those of the industrial.

It may be noted, finally, that neither the industrial nor the agricultural (foodstuffs) index moves throughout the period 1825–45 consistently in agreement with the weighted general index — the tool of measurement fashioned subsequent to this analysis based on the unweighted

dices. Perhaps this lack of partisanship evidenced by the general index may be indicative of fairly satisfactory weighting in the scheme devised for the development of this index.

PRICES OF FOREIGN AND DOMESTIC COMMODITIES

Examination and analysis of the commodity price data in the period now under review would fall short of adequacy if regarded merely from the standpoint of the domestic situation. Contact with foreign affairs is in fact possible by two substantially different procedures. One pertains to relative price movements in foreign and domestic areas, while the other traces the impact of certain forces for the most part external to the United States upon price conditions in the domestic market. First, comparison may be made of the general (weighted) price index, as herein developed, with the index of 35 commodities for the same decades constructed for Great Britain by Professor Silberling.[18] To be sure, Professor

[17] The sharpness of the break for the agricultural index in 1837 and the duration of the lower prices in 1837-38 are greater than had been expected when, after the comparisons already presented had been made, the analyses of agricultural prices as a whole and industrial prices as a whole was undertaken. Conditions in certain agricultural markets — notably sugar, tobacco, oats, and lard — may be held chiefly responsible for these differences from the anticipated movement.

[18] Silberling, op. cit., pp. 232-3.

Silberling's index is of the quarterly type and uses the year 1790 as the base; but comparison is here made as close as possible by converting his index to the base used for our general index, 1834–42,[19] and by centering the quarterly figures for the middle month of each quarterly period. The results thus secured are brought into comparison with our general index number in the accompanying chart (Chart 22).

A casual inspection of this diagram suggests that there were significant differences in the two movements. In some measure, to be sure, the differences are due to varying methods in the construction of the two indices. The greater moderation in the course of British prices apparently is accountable on this score, since Silberling seems not to have excluded "insensitive" series, as was done in the case of the American index. When the speculative movement was especially keener in Great Britain than in the United States, as in the middle 'twenties, the British index does rise above the American; but otherwise not. Perhaps the same reason explains the seeming indecision in the course of British prices through 1834, and the less considerable decline of the British index in the latter year relative to the American index; though perhaps this difference in movements is real. And possibly the composition of the British index may explain the much more gradual retrogression of British commodity prices after the secondary high point had been reached early in 1839.

Other differences — those of timing rather than magnitude of movement — are no less significant, though from another point of view. Almost without exception, the rise and fall of British prices anticipate corresponding movements of American. Obviously this is true of the peak in 1825 — and, by virtue of the predominantly British character of this "crisis," the relationship between the two curves was doubtless to be expected. But it is notable that a similar situation obtained in 1836–37. Almost a year before the definite turn came in the American cycle, March 1837, British prices were beginning to move rather rapidly downward. The earlier culmination of the British speculative movement is undoubtedly connected with the failure of

British banks in November 1836, and the contingent embarrassments of the "three W's"— the cotton-importing houses of Wilkes, Wilde, and Wiggin.[20] Again, it may be noted that the British prices displayed a revival of strength after the decline in 1836–37, which began somewhat earlier than our own, and seems to have carried our prices along with it. In 1833–34, to be sure, this relationship seems to have been reversed — when possibly the movement of American origin may indeed have had effect on British conditions. Likewise, and more importantly, the American curve unquestionably turned upward at the close of this whole episode — 1843 — in advance of the British curve. Here one is permitted perhaps to look beyond prices to financial conditions, and to note the substantial inflow of specie into the United States in 1842–43 — presumably from England — which providing a happy relief to American banking difficulties and indirectly a welcome fillip to American commodity values, may have imposed a temporarily restraining force on British commodity prices. In this manner, rather than by direct effect of price movement on price movement, British conditions exerted an influence on those of America in this year, 1843. Nevertheless, viewing the whole period, 1820–45, one is impressed with the frequency with which the course of domestic commodity values manifested response — more or less belated — to movements abroad. Obviously — as has been intimated elsewhere — no account of American business conditions, in these decades would be complete without attention to the repercussion of British difficulties upon affairs in this country, or, more generally put, without consideration of our international economic relationships.

A second means of bringing to light the international phases of the domestic situation was to be secured by constructing indices which would manifest the relative course of domestic and of foreign goods — both in the markets of the United States. Such indices were in fact elaborated, the index of domestic goods being compounded of 31 series, and that of foreign commodities being based upon 12 series. The results are exhibited in the accompanying diagram

[19] Professor Silberling's quarterly indices of prices on the base 1790 were reduced to the base 1834-42 by division by 1.033, the average of his indices for the period.

[20] See Tugan-Baranowsky, *op. cit.*, pp. 96-97; and Dewey, D. R., *Financial History of the United States* (1911 ed.), p. 230.

CHART 23. — UNWEIGHTED INDICES OF DOMESTIC AND FOREIGN WHOLESALE COMMODITY PRICES:
QUARTERLY, 1825–45

(Base: 1834–42. Vertical logarithmic scale)

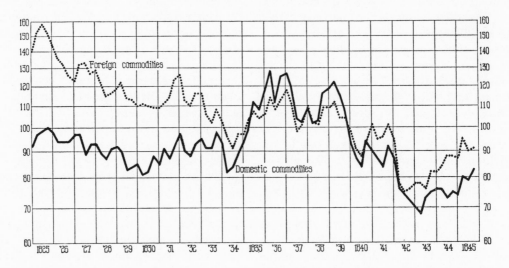

(Chart 23).[21] The features to be observed in these curves, of course, are not the synchronism or lack thereof between the two but the general tendencies of the two lines and the points of time when they cross one another. Moreover, explanation of diversity of movement is to be found, not in differences of timing here and abroad in the ebb and flow of credit, business confidence, or other force or forces which may be conceived as determinative of cyclical movements in general business conditions, but (at least proximately) in changes in the magnitude of such items, as capital inflow, which are elements in the American balance of payments.[22]

The relationship of these two curves prior to 1834 is admittedly somewhat surprising. Capital was flowing into the United States earlier than this date; and, despite the earnings of our merchant marine, we were enjoying a so-called "unfavorable" disparity of merchandise trade. The most that can be said is that seemingly the price relationship between domestic and foreign commodities was becoming generally less unfavorable

to the import of goods in the period from 1830 onward. Likewise, somewhat unanticipated is the experience of the years 1838–39; the shift in the relationship between these prices did not come immediately with the "crisis of 1837." However, we have data in Jenks' excellent study that loans and extension of credit to the United States did not cease with 1836 or 1837, but continued in sizable volume through 1839.[23]

Otherwise the story is much as one would forecast from an application of the theory of international trade to the conditions of American relationship with foreign countries in the decades under inspection. During the period of international borrowing by American States and business enterprises, the general level of domestic commodity prices rose relative to that of imported commodity values — the divergence being particularly great at the height of this bor-

[21] See Appendix B, Tables 55 and 56 for commodities employed in the two indices.

[22] For a general history of the American balance of payments, see the article by Bullock, C. J., Williams, J. H., and R. S. Tucker, "Balance of Trade of the United States" in the *Review of Economic Statistics*, Preliminary Volume I (1919), pp. 215-66.

[23] Jenks, L. H., *The Migration of British Capital to 1875* (1927), pp. 95-98. A study of Charleston prices by Dr. George R. Taylor (*op. cit.*), made along somewhat similar lines to the present one, gives general confirmation of the findings here offered, as far as the movements in the years 1825-34 are concerned. His data indicate that after 1818 prices of "domestic" goods in the Charleston market fell much more considerably than those of "imported" articles, and that this discrepancy continued until the early 'thirties. His chart (p. 861) shows a persistent though diminishing spread in the period 1825-34, much like that presented in Chart 23.

rowing movement in 1836–37. Subsequently, with the reversal of conditions and the apprehension by British investors of American securities the tide turned. As interest payments and other debit items came to exceed the inflow of new capital, net earnings in shipping and the like, the level of domestic prices fell more sharply than that of imported goods, and remained depressed through the remaining years of this period — although by 1845 domestic prices were beginning again to move closer to those of foreign commodities.

CHAPTER XII

CHANGES IN VOLUME OF TRADE

MATERIAL relating to the movement of com- modity prices, public-land sales, and com- mon stock values, though sometimes difficult to secure, is not so scarce as to render impossible a close view of the events — such a view as is af- forded by monthly or quarterly measurements of changing levels. Data of sorts are to be found with persistent search. As regards statistical material bearing upon the volume of trade, how- ever, painstaking research wins little reward. Satisfactory data simply do not exist, or at least, if they do, they have yet to be slowly pieced to-

broad interest, had not appeared even by the 'thirties and early 'forties. Individual enter- prises were small, business in large part was local, and neither the state nor the private citi- zen — with occasional exceptions — saw the utility of keeping and publishing records of the quantity or value of goods entering or circulating within the country, or for that matter any other indicia of domestic production or commerce. Especially is this true of data upon a basis other than annual — and annual figures are scarce enough.

TABLE 15. — SERIES OF INFRA-ANNUAL DATA ON THE VOLUME OF TRADE, 1824-45

Description	Period Covered	Time—Interval of Reporting	Source
Number of boats passing Lock 26 on the Erie Canal..................................	1824–45	Monthly	New York State Documents
Tolls received on all New York Canals......	1831–45	Monthly	New York State Documents
Freight carried on the Middlesex Canal.....	1830–41	Monthly	Records of the Company
Number of boats and tolls received on the Chesapeake & Delaware Canal..........	1830–45	Semi-Annually	Annual Reports of the Company
Passengers and freight carried on the Balti- more & Ohio Railroad..................	1831–36*	Monthly	Annual Reports of the Company
Receipts from passenger and from freight traffic on the Western Railroad of Massa- chusetts..............................	1840–45	Monthly	Annual Reports of the Company
Receipts from Ohio Canals................	1830–36	Monthly	Ohio State Documents
Revenue received from imports at the Port of Boston.............................	1830–45†	Quarterly	Boston *Post* and New York *Journal of Commerce*
Value of imports at the Port of New York..	1832–44††	Quarterly	*Democratic Review*
Post Office receipts.	1833–45§	Quarterly⎫	⎧29th Cong., 2d Session,
Receipts from letter postage..............	1836–45¶	Quarterly⎭	⎩Senate Doc. I.

* Data for the last quarter of 1836 missing.

† Data for the first three quarters of 1841 and the final quarter of 1845 missing.

†† Data for the last quarter of 1844 missing.

§ Data lacking from the second quarter of 1835 to the third quarter of 1836.

¶ Data lacking for the first half of 1836.

gether from such obscure sources as the surviving records of individual concerns, and cannot be expected to become available in any usable form without the lapse of many years and the expendi- ture of much labor. The day of broad interest in general economic conditions throughout the country and that of the private or public news- gathering which would be correlative to such

In nearly all of these cases, the origin of such data as are obtainable lay in the interest aroused by the exigencies of public finance, either be- cause the Government was the recipient of reve- nue derived from import duties or because it was financially concerned with the conduct of canal companies (Table 15). The very meagerness of this material upon less than annual bases would

TABLE 16. — SERIES OF ANNUAL DATA UPON THE VOLUME OF TRADE, 1815–45

Description*	Period Covered	Source
Number of boats passing Alexander's Lock on the Erie Canal ..	1824–45	New York State Documents
Number of boats arriving at and departing from tidewater.....	1828–45	New York State Documents
Freight coming to and departing from the Hudson River on Erie and Champlain Canals..........................	1834–45	New York State Documents
Tolls received on all New York Canals....................	1824–45	New York State Documents
Freight carried on the Middlesex Canal....................	1830–41	Records of the Company
Freight carried on the Lehigh Canal	1830–45	Annual Reports of the Company†
Freight carried on the Schuylkill Navigation	1830–45	Annual Reports of the Company†
Freight carried on the Union Canal......................	1830–45	Annual Reports of the Company
Number of boats passing on the Chesapeake & Delaware Canal.	1830–45	Annual Reports of the Company
Tolls received on the Chesapeake & Ohio Canal.............	1831–45	Annual Reports of the Company
Tolls received on Delaware & Hudson Canal................	1830–45	Annual Reports of the Company†
Tolls received on the Delaware Division Canal..............	1832–45	Annual Reports of the Company†
Receipts on the Ohio Canal............................	1827–45	Ohio State Documents
Receipts on the Miami & Erie Canal System...............	1828–45	Ohio State Documents
Passengers and freight carried on Baltimore & Ohio Railroad...	1831–45	Annual Reports of the Company
Passengers and freight carried on the Western Railroad of Massachusetts...	1840–45	Annual Reports of the Company
Receipts of the Boston & Worcester Railroad................	1835–45	Annual Reports of the Company
Receipts of the Boston & Lowell Railroad..................	1835–45	Annual Reports of the Company
Freight carried on the Mohawk & Hudson Railroad..........	1833–39	Annual Reports of the Company‡
Coal trade of the United States§.........................	1820–45	Pennsylvania State Documents
Trade in Onondaga salines..............................	1830–45	New York Shipping and Commercial List
Tonnage of vessels in coastwise and foreign trade............	1790–45	Merchant Marine Statistics
Number and tonnage of sailing and steam vessels built in the United States...	1815–45	Report on the Internal Commerce of the United States, 1887
Tonnage of vessels cleared for foreign trade at New Orleans...	1820–45	Report on the Internal Commerce of the United States, 1887
Number of steamboats and tons of freight arriving by river at New Orleans...	1815–45	Report on the Internal Commerce of the United States, 1887
Receipts from auction duties in New York State.............	1815–45	New York State Documents
Redemptions at the Suffolk Bank of Boston................	1834–45	Hunt's Merchants' Magazine
Woolen cloth produced at Slater Mill of Webster, Mass.......	1830–43	Records of the Company
Corporations chartered in New Jersey.....................	1830–45	New Jersey Archives‖
Corporations chartered in New York State.................	1830–45	New York Archives‖
Revenue on imports at the Port of Boston..................	1830–44 ¶	Boston Post and New York Journal of Commerce
Value of imports at the Port of Boston....................	1830–41	Boston Advertiser
Value of imports at the Port of New York..................	1832–44	Democratic Review
Value of gross merchandise imports of the United States......	1815–45	Reports on Commerce and Navigation
Value of domestic merchandise exports from the United States.	1815–45	Reports on Commerce and Navigation
Quantity of domestic exports of tobacco, wheat, and cotton...	1815–45	Reports on Commerce and Navigation
Post Office receipts...................................	1833–45ø	29th Cong., 2d Session, Senate Doc. 1.
Receipts from letter postage............................	1836–45	

* The above list represents in some measure a selection. When series are available on both a value basis (e.g., tolls received) and that of physical volume (e.g., tons of freight carried), only the latter has been enumerated here.

† Drawn from Jones, Anthracite-Tidewater Canals.

‡ Drawn from Stevens, F. W., Beginnings of the New York Central Railroad.

§ Consisting of all anthracite coal shipped on Pennsylvania coal canals.

‖ For these data, I am indebted to Prof. J. S. Davis of Stanford University.

¶ 1841 defective.

ø 1835 and 1836 defective.

suffice to render futile any hope of constructing a monthly or quarterly index of business movements; but in addition to this consideration, there may be noted the unsatisfactory character of the figures themselves — the uncertainties which alterations in import duties tend to introduce into data upon customs revenue or the value of imports, the intermittency and highly seasonal variations of canal traffic, and the like. For the most part, one must content himself with such a delineation of the course of general business as may be derived from an examination of annual figures.

Fortunately, statistical material relating to the volume of business on the latter basis is to be found in more adequate though by no means generous quantity (Table 16). Some of it has defects of serious moment, arising either from factors such as those mentioned above, or from such other disturbing elements as the varying height of canal tolls, or the changing importance of auction sales in the general system of goods-distribution. The present collection of material does have the saving grace, however, of being fairly well diversified. It relates to a variety of activities and to several sections of the country. Moreover, some defects of character may be minimized by statistical treatment and so not permitted wholly to vitiate the use of these particular series for the portrayal of "cyclical" fluctuations in the volume of general business.

With the end in view of compounding them ultimately into an index which should suggest the year-to-year changes in the volume of business transactions within the country, the following series were selected from those which are enumerated elsewhere.

The basis of this selection was the desire to secure at the same time as broad and as close a view as possible of the changing volume of business. With the first object in mind, no series was discarded without sufficient cause. With the second feature in mind, series were eliminated because their inclusion would involve duplication — as, for example, those upon the traffic of the eastern Pennsylvania coal canals if made additional to that upon the coal trade as a whole; or because they lacked accuracy as indicators of business actually transacted — as, for instance, those on State incorporations. Furthermore, when choice was possible between a series based on values and

one indicating physical volume, the latter was alone retained.[1]

TABLE 17. — SERIES USED IN THE CONSTRUCTION OF THE INDICES OF THE VOLUME OF TRADE, 1831–45

Number of boats arriving at or departing from tide-water on Erie and Champlain Canals.
Freight carried on the Middlesex Canal.
Freight carried on the Union Canal.
Number of boats passing on the Chesapeake & Delaware Canal.
Tolls received on the Chesapeake & Ohio Canal.
Receipts on the Miami & Erie Canal System.
Freight carried on the Baltimore & Ohio Railroad.
Freight received at New Orleans in the river trade.
Coal trade of the United States.
Receipts from auction duties in New York State.
Redemptions at the Suffolk Bank.
Value of gross merchandise imports of the United States.
Value of domestic merchandise exports from the United States.

Three indices were in fact constructed over as much of the period through 1845 as the material permitted. One of these included only the series pertaining to domestic commerce, and may be viewed as indicating changes in internal trade. Here, from lack of data sufficient to calculate weights, a simple arithmetic average of relatives to the lines of trend (1830–45) of the several series was employed to construct the index. The second index took only foreign trade into account, and was based merely upon the combined value of merchandise exports and imports. The third sought to unite domestic and foreign commerce into one index which should mirror the course of American business as a whole. In this case, despite the absence of information upon which to base accurate procedure, a weighting was resorted to, determined by a rough estimate of the factors involved. Since the influence of imported and exported goods would be in some measure reflected in the data upon internal commerce, and since domestic trade as a whole was undoubtedly greater than the volume of goods moving through our ports, a decision was reached to give domestic trade twice the value of foreign in the construction of this third index, which

[1] The inclusion of "Redemptions at the Suffolk Bank" might seem to some readers peculiar. Yet it is believed that the changing volume of bank notes cleared or redeemed through this Boston institution gives an unusually good indication of the movement of general business in New England.

should represent the course of aggregate American commerce.

TABLE 18. — INDICES OF VOLUME OF TRADE: ANNUALLY, 1831–45

Year	Domestic Trade	Foreign Trade	Combined Domestic and Foreign Trade
1831........	109	86	101
1832........	103	87	98
1833........	102	93	99
1834........	91	104	95
1835........	104	127	112
1836........	107	139	118
1837........	100	110	103
1838........	96	100	97
1839........	103	122	109
1840........	92	102	95
1841........	95	104	98
1842........	91	86	89
1843........	93	79	88
1844........	103	93	100
1845........	117	97	110

The results of the present inquiry into the volume of business, which are set forth in Table 18, deserve careful inspection. Particularly striking is the great amplitude in fluctuation of our foreign commerce during these years. Rising slowly but persistently in the early 'thirties, this external movement of commodities rose vigorously over the depression of 1834, which affected domestic trade severely, to reach a peak in 1836 much greater than that simultaneously attained by internal commerce. Three years later, foreign commerce was again at a high level, appreciably above the point to which domestic trade had recovered, while in 1842–43 it had fallen to a depth untouched by the latter. Even in the closing years of our period, the recovery in foreign trade was exceptionally great, although by 1845 the index was at a point very much below that registered by the rapidly reviving domestic commerce. Possibly with a clarity not conveyed by non-statistical accounts of this troubled era, the table suggests the important rôle played by foreign influences in the "crisis of 1837."

Note should likewise be taken of the truly moderate character of the fluctuations in the internal index throughout these sixteen years. The latter feature is attributable in part to the lack of synchronism in the movements of the several constituent series. For instance, the high points attained in these series individually in or around 1836 — the year when the peak in the index on foreign trade was clearly reached — were distributed from 1835 to 1839 as follows: 1835, one series; 1836, four series; 1837, two series; 1838, one series; and 1839, three series. If the relatives for these various high points be averaged, the result (121) is much closer to the value (139) attained by the index on foreign trade at its peak in 1836 than is the value (107) given for the peak of domestic trade in the index above presented. Apparently, then, there was a spottiness to domestic commerce, or a geographical variation, which prevented that trade as a whole from showing the unusual variations of our external commerce.

Noteworthy also is the attainment in 1842 of the lowest point touched by the domestic index, whereas the index for foreign commerce continued to move downward until 1843. The difference in values of the former index in 1842 and 1843 is not great, but the fact is significant that five out of the ten series carried in the index at that time moved upward appreciably, namely, from an average of 82 to one of 97. The failure of the index itself to manifest greater rise is due in large measure to marked declines in two series, receipts on the Chesapeake and Ohio Canal and auction duties in New York State — the latter being in considerable degree affected by the course of the import trade. Apparently the movement of purely domestic business must be regarded as changing direction in the earlier year.

With regard to the combined index, attention may be called both to the broken character of the course of aggregate American trade, and to the long period involved in the process of devolution after the initial break of 1836–37. Business receded unsteadily over an interval exceeding six years, and in 1843 reached a nadir — the more depressing by reason of its slow arrival — which must have seemed to the merchants of the day torpor itself when compared with the feverish activity of 1836.[2]

[2] Such infra-annual data as are available indicate that the break in the volume of trade as a whole probably came in the second quarter of 1837, and that the revival of general trade after the long decline first appeared in the third quarter of 1843. This would make the whole interval of troubled times a little more than six years — as just suggested in the text.

CHAPTER XIII

BANKING AND FINANCE

STATISTICAL evidence upon banking and finance is of varied character. Certain data are obtainable upon the condition of individual banks or groups of banks at divers intervals; and general indices of the state of money-market conditions are to be found in the interest rates prevailing in at least one financial center, and in exchange rates — both domestic and foreign. To these may be added material less directly bearing upon banking and private finance — the disparity of merchandise and gold movements, and (without going deeply into public finance) the volume of Treasury notes outstanding. In any attempt to indicate the course of events in this period all these series are deserving of notice — some, of much consideration.

Information pertaining to the first category, the condition of domestic banking institutions, is least satisfactory. To be sure, monthly data upon discounts, circulation and the like, of the Second United States Bank are available, together with annual figures of a similar sort for the same institution under Pennsylvania charter; yet except possibly for the earlier part of our period, this material cannot be looked upon as even presumably representative of general banking conditions,[1] while, of course, the data cease at a most inopportune point. Again, there exist summaries of the condition of banks in various States on an annual or in some cases on an infra-annual basis — e.g., Massachusetts, New York, Pennsylvania, and others. Unfortunately, however, these compilations, even those on the annual basis, frequently possess no regularity of date. A statement of condition for January 1835 may be followed by one for March 1836. Quarterly reports as to the first day of February, May, August, and November of 1836 may be followed by information relating to the first of January, April, June, and October of 1837. Lacking any means of computing the seasonal movement in the demands for credit, such data

are of dubious value in estimating the course of expansion or contraction, or for fixing upon the date when changes in the "cyclical" movement occurred. Moreover, the lack of similar "dates of call" for the separate States make impossible the compilation of information about individual States into aggregates which would represent the status of the country at large. Finally, there exists a rough estimate of the condition of State banks as a whole upon an annual basis.[2] These data were compiled from the returns of the several States for the dates of inquiry nearest to January 1st of each year. Since we know the irregularity with which reports were made to individual commonwealths, we are bound to have serious doubts as to the accuracy of the summary figures.

The best that appears recoverable from the whole group of State figures is a set of annual data relating to conditions in the four States, Massachusetts, Rhode Island, New York, and Pennsylvania. Fortunately this list includes three of the most important States of the country in the 'thirties and 'forties. The set of data embraces circulation, deposits, specie holdings, the ratio of loans and discounts to deposits plus circulation, and the ratio of specie to deposits and circulation combined. The period of the year to which these data refer is the fall, October to December.[3] Although admittedly far from ideal in quality, these figures are presented as the most satisfactory of an unsatisfactory collection.

Obviously there was a substantial growth in circulation and deposits (in fact, particularly in the latter) during the years up to 1836. Even if we ignore the data for the fall of 1830 — which

[1] These data upon the Second Bank are to be located in sundry Government documents, especially 23d Cong., 2d Sess., Senate Document 117, pp. 204-24.

[2] 26th Cong., 2d Sess., House Executive Document 111; and 31st Cong., 1st Sess., House Executive Document 68, pp. 1-426.

[3] Most of the figures relate specifically to October, but the Pennsylvania data with two exceptions pertain to November, and the New York reports, again with two exceptions (one, November 1st and one, December 1st), are dated January 1st. In the last case, the reports of a given January 1st are taken to represent conditions of the preceding October. Interpolations were few.

TABLE 19. — CONDITION OF THE BANKS IN FOUR STATES FOR WHICH DATA ARE
AVAILABLE AS OF OCTOBER-DECEMBER: ANNUALLY, 1830–45*

Year	Circulation (Unit: $1,000,000)	Deposits (Unit: $1,000,000)	Specie Holdings (Unit: $1,000,000)	Ratio of Loans and Discounts to Deposits plus Circulation (Unit: one per cent)	Ratio of Specie to Combined Circulation and Deposits (Unit: one per cent)
1830	19.8	16.2	5.1	185	14.2
1831	25.6	23.3	5.7	208	11.6
1832	24.7	26.8	5.5	222	10.9
1833	29.3	31.3	6.4	218	10.6
1834	25.2	36.8	10.6	222	17.1
1835	32.9	46.1	11.8	213	14.9
1836	38.5	50.0	12.0	221	13.5
1837	39.1	41.4	8.7	212	10.8
1838	42.8	39.0	13.2	205	16.1
1839	33.2	35.1	12.2	233	17.8
1840	36.5	42.3	14.0	197	17.8
1841	33.4	38.1	11.5	202	16.8
1842	27.7	35.0	15.5	202	24.7
1843	35.1	50.6	24.0	159	28.0
1844	43.8	57.8	18.3	159	18.0
1845	48.4	59.5	16.7	158	15.5

* Massachusetts, Rhode Island, New York, and Pennsylvania.

are undoubtedly defective — we find an increase in these two elements combined from approximately 49 millions in 1831 to 88.5 millions in 1836. This growth, however, was not quite regular. Especially significant is the hesitation which appeared between 1833 and 1834. On the other hand, it may be noted that the eminence reached in the autumn of 1836 was the highest peak for several years. It was not exceeded until the business revival of 1843–44. Apparently here in banking data, one may find some explanation of movements in other series such as commodity prices, although, of course, both may be viewed as reflecting yet deeper forces.

Annual data are poor guides in tracing the course of events during such a troubled period as that which succeeded 1836; but one is able to see in the combined figures of circulation and deposits some of the oscillations in business conditions that marked the years 1836–43: a slight recovery in 1838; the second revival in 1840; and finally the nadir of depression in the fall of 1842. It is clear at least that, like stock or commodity prices, these principal indices of changing bank-

ing conditions underwent divers vicissitudes in this long period of devolution.

Data on the ratio of loans and discounts to deposits plus circulation are significant for the support to speculation which the banks seem to have been giving in 1834 and 1836, and for the conservatism of their policy afterwards. On the other hand, the rise of this ratio in the fall of 1839 may perhaps be interpreted to mean that the banking institutions were pursuing an abnormally liberal policy at that time in an attempt to ease business conditions in the second major price decline then under way. The low level of this same ratio in the closing years 1843–45, is also an exception, though one of a different kind. If the extension of these data over subsequent years be taken into account (Table 32)[4] — an extension which indicates that the level reached in these years, 1843–45, was maintained over later decades — it would seem that we have to do here with a change in banking practice. As a result of the increased importance of de-

[4] See below, p. 120.

posits as a vehicle in credit operations, an average ratio of 213 for the years 1831–42 between loans and combined liabilities was replaced by one of 162.2 for 1843–60.[5]

The final column in the foregoing table (Table 19) is perhaps most interesting. It shows the precarious position of these eastern institutions in the fall of 1833, which may well have led directly or indirectly to the "high and variable" discount rates chronicled by Bigelow in the succeeding year.[6] Again, it reveals the second decline of the ratio of specie to demand liabilities in the latter months of 1837 — which also is correlated with high market rates for "money." Finally, it indicates the improvements of position which followed the receipts of specie from abroad (Table 20) in 1837–38 and again in 1842–43. By the latter years, the banks had secured an unusually ample specie reserve — in ratio, almost two and a half times that of 1837 — and undoubtedly felt themselves once more free to lend to businessmen, at that time just raising their heads from the last recession of prices and volume of trade. With the lowest money rates for many a year — 3 3/4 per cent in the latter half of 1843, according to Bigelow — business as a whole could feel that credit conditions no longer placed obstacles in the way of better times.

The various series on the state of the money market offer the most complete data available for this whole problem of the demand and supply of credit. They include monthly figures upon the discount rates in New York and Boston, and exchange rates — also with monthly frequency — of New York upon London, and upon New Orleans, Cincinnati (1838 onwards), and other domestic points. These data, of which selected series are presented in Charts 24 and 27 (see curve of discount rates), are peculiarly informative of changing business conditions.

The series relating to money rates are drawn from E. B. Bigelow's *Tariff Question* and J. G. Martin's *History of the Boston Stock Market*.[7] Bigelow defines his data as " 'street rates' on first-class paper in Boston and New York," while Martin states that his rates are those for "first-class, three to six months, bankable paper" in the Boston money market.[8] The close similarity between these two series, however, combined with our knowledge that Martin's figures appeared subsequent to Bigelow's, inclines one to believe that they are not really independent. There are, to be sure, minor differences — Martin's figures for December 1834, for example, indicating a spread of 8-10 per cent, whereas Bigelow's show a variation of 8-12 per cent — but the two have similar gaps in 1834–35, and for most months the quotations are identical. For divers reasons — this doubt as to the independence of Martin's quotations, the frequent lack of clarity in Martin's mode of expression, and the implication that Bigelow's data reflect, at least in part, conditions in the nationally important New York money market — it will be sufficient for our purposes to fasten attention wholly on the story indicated by the latter.[9]

The evidence of money rates in New York and Boston (presented graphically in Chart 27) indicates a period of tight money in 1834 when rates rose to an average of 19 per cent in January, and remained "high and variable," according to Bigelow, the greater part of the year. This episode was followed by a year of "comparatively low" rates "down to 5 per cent." The relaxation, however, was not for long. By December of this same year, an average of 9 per cent money is given, followed by rapidly rising quotations until the peak of 30 per cent money was attained in October 1836. Momentary relaxation of strain at the commencement of the succeeding

---

[5] The range for these two periods was from 197 to 233 for the earlier, and from 152 to 190 for the later.

In view of difficulties encountered in connection with New York City data (Appendix E, pp. 196–97), where such a change turned out to be due chiefly to alteration in the method of reporting "deposits," one cannot be sure of the facts above introduced. There is a possibility that the change is merely statistical, not real — or at least not so great as it seems from the above data.

[6] See pp. 83-84 and Chart 27, below.

[7] Bigelow, E. B., *The Tariff Question* (1862), Appendix 112, pp. 204-5; and Martin, *op. cit.*, p. 52.

[8] Bigelow, *op. cit.*, p. 204, footnote; Martin, *op. cit.*, p. 52.

[9] I am indebted to Dr. F. C. Macaulay for this suggestion regarding the relationship between Martin's and Bigelow's data. Martin's first book, it appears, was published in 1856, and contained no rates of discount; Bigelow's volume came out in 1862; and Martin's second edition, that of 1871, contained the figures upon interest rates — which were, in fact, preserved without change in the 1898 edition which I have used.

year was followed by money as "tight as a drum-head"[10] in April and May of 1837, when rates again approached 30 per cent. A brief return to more normal conditions was rapid; but the spring of 1838, the fall of 1839, and winter of 1841–42, all experienced convulsions of greater or less magnitude. Specially noteworthy is the height to which money rose in 1839 — 29 2/3 per cent— or approximately the highest point attained in the crisis period of 1836–37. Rates finally reached a distinctly low plane in the latter part of 1843 — 3 3/4 per cent — subsequent to which

greater part of 1842 deserve special attention. The varying fortunes of Nicholas Biddle's scheme for controlling the cotton market may have in part caused the fluctuations in these rates, but the fact that similar movements and gyrations persisted after the abandonment of his cotton-control program would seem to indicate that this element was not wholly responsible.

An examination of the exchange rates on London shows deviations from the normal that are less frequent and less persistent. On three occasions only are they worthy of special comment.

CHART 24. — QUOTATIONS OF EXCHANGE RATES AT NEW YORK ON LONDON (BANKERS' 60-DAY BILLS) AND ON NEW ORLEANS (SIGHT BILLS): MONTHLY, 1830–45

[*These curves are plotted so that par of 109.45 per cent for London coincides with par of 100 for New Orleans.*]
(*Unit: 1 per cent. Arithmetic scale*)

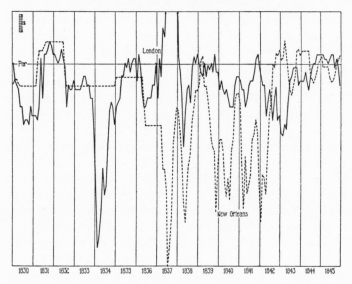

they were gradually rising to the close of the years now under discussion.

The stress of credit conditions which could provoke violent movements in money rates such as those just described, could hardly fail to have marked influence upon the course of both domestic and foreign exchanges. These data (of which the series relating to New York exchange on New Orleans and London are presented in Chart 24) in fact display gyrations of much the same order as those manifested by New York discount rates. The prolonged violent oscillations in New Orleans exchange from the beginning of troubled times in 1836 through the

[10] Martin, *op. cit.*, p. 30.

The decline in 1834 was sharp and decisive after rates had begun to fall in December 1833, and they remained low through the greater part of the succeeding year. The coincidence of this period with that of "high and variable" discount rates in the New York money market leads one to assume interaction of the two. Apparently, the convulsion in domestic credit conditions was sufficient to cause the withdrawal of funds from London, while bills on London went begging from the lack of purchasing power in New York City.

A possible, alternative explanation of the sharp fall in sterling exchange flows from a purely monetary consideration, the alteration of our

monetary system by the Act of 1834. By this Act, the mint ratio between gold and silver was changed from 15:1 to 16:1. The latter ratio overvalued gold and brought it into use within the United States. The enactment of the new law would for a time make profitable the importation of gold from England; and such importations did in fact occur after the act was passed.[11] Speculation in anticipation of the new conditions might be conceived of as depressing exchange on London.

Yet, while this alteration in our monetary system may have had some influence upon the foreign exchange market, it does not seem to have been the dominant factor. In the closing months of 1833, when the terms of the "ultimate" law could by no means be forecast — the Act being passed only in June of the succeeding year — exchange on London began to fall; and it had not only reached the nadir but recovered substantially before the "gold bill" was actually signed. On the other hand, the changes in such rates were closely synchronized with the opposite movements of New York discount rates. With the logical connection between these diverse variations suggested above, one is justified in looking chiefly to domestic credit conditions, rather than to prospective monetary change, for an explanation of the sharp decline in sterling exchange at this period.

The second extreme height reached by rates on London is merely the consequence of disturbed monetary conditions within the United States. With the suspension of specie payments by American banks in the spring of 1837, gold went to a premium — amounting at times to 10 and 13 per cent[12] — and exchange on London, which was tantamount to a command over gold, inevitably moved in a similar direction and degree. After a slump to 104 3/4 in the spring of 1838, the prospect of specie resumption at the end of that year brought exchange back within the gold points. After fluctuations in 1839–41, which sometimes carried the rates below the gold import point, appeared the third striking movement of sterling rates — the downward swing in quotations through the greater part of 1842 until bottom was reached in February 1843. This was

the time of unusually heavy importations of gold, to which reference has already been made in connection with specie holdings of domestic banks. Rates snapped back to more normal levels in the summer of 1843, and remained within the gold points through 1844–45.

Discussion of exchange rates should not be closed, however, without passing notice of the relation exhibited in these years between exchange at New York on London and that on New Orleans. Although no simple generalization is possible, inspection of the two curves seems to warrant the conclusion that the rates tended to move in sympathy. If the apparent divergence of movement in 1837 be put aside because of the part played by the suspension of specie payments in causing inflation of sterling quotations, it will be observed that the only real exceptions to the generalization proposed above occurred in 1834 and in 1843–45. In 1834 sterling was peculiarly weak, whereas exchange on New Orleans rode unaffected through the credit disturbance of that year. Possibly here, as in the case of 1837, the divergence is fictitious. Exchange on New Orleans certainly displayed a curious inelasticity for a period in which discount rates at New York and Boston were rising to an average of 19 per cent and continued "high and variable." Perhaps the quotations on the southern city were purely nominal. On the other hand, there seems no reason for doubting the accuracy of the data relative to 1843–45; and such an inverse relationship in movement may be regarded as not an abnormal condition. While cotton was being shipped to England or the Continent, American merchants and bankers were securing funds in London. Naturally they would be inclined to buy or be forced to sell exchange at relatively low figures. New York bankers at the same time would be seeking means of making payment to the original shippers of the cotton, so that exchange on New Orleans would tend to advance. It seems rather probable, then, that the close similarity of movement in 1838–42 was a phenomenon of credit conditions in the New York money market. Scarce money may well have occasioned the calling-in of funds available in the southern port, and restricted the purchasing power of northern banks over domestic exchange of any sort. For the most part, it will be observed, the course of exchange on New Or-

[11] Laughlin, J. L., *History of Bimetallism in the United States* (1901 ed.), p. 66, footnote 1.

[12] Martin, *op. cit.*, p. 31.

leans was directly inverse to the movement of money rates in New York City.

Thirdly, brief note should be made of the disparities in our merchandise and bullion trade with foreign countries. As appears at once from Table 20, the period of the 'twenties was one lacking a decisive character. In 1822 and 1828 imports exceeded exports by significant amounts — the former interestingly enough coinciding with the bulge in American commodity prices already noted[13] — but years of net import on merchandise trade were succeeded by years of net export; and corresponding conditions obtained in the movement of specie. Not until the 'thirties do tendencies become more stable. Then, from 1831 through 1837, came a persistent excess of imports on merchandise account — an excess especially great in the year 1836. For a period of seven years when, as we know, the prices of domestic commodities were generally rising more rapidly than those of foreign goods, and when, as we also know, both the investments of capital and the inflow of short-time funds favored an influx of merchandise, a net import balance of approximately $150,000,000 was built up — a notably large figure for that day and generation.

Subsequently, it will be observed, the balance varied, though the excess of imports of 1839 and of exports in 1843 are particularly significant items in the experience of these later years. The reappearance of a large import merchandise excess in 1839 after the momentary reversal of disparities in 1838 is evidence confirmatory, of course, to the position already taken in the discussion of commodity prices, that the inflow of capital and short-time credit did not cease with the initial reaction of 1837, but continued in sizable volume in 1839. Thereafter, the character of the movement is in truth altered. The continuance of troubled commercial conditions in the United States, and particularly the repudiation, or threatened repudiation, of debts by several American States, caused a temporary change in the attitude of foreign investors — with the consequence that a shift in our disparity of trade occurred in the early 'forties. For our purposes, however, it is sufficient to note here the variation in the course of these merchandise disparities as a factor contributing to an under-

[13] See above, Chart 22, p. 61.

TABLE 20. — DISPARITIES IN AMERICAN EXTERNAL TRADE IN MERCHANDISE AND BULLION: ANNUALLY, 1820–45
(*Unit: 1,000,000*)

Year Ending Sept. 30	Merchandise Trade		Coin and Bullion	
	Excess of Imports	Excess of Exports	Excess of Imports	Excess of Exports
1820........	4.76*			
1821........		.08		2.41
1822........	18.52			7.44
1823.........	4.15			1.28
1824........	3.20		1.37	
1825........		.55		2.64
1826........	5.20		2.18	
1827........		2.98	.14	
1828........	17.00			.75
1829........		.34	2.48	
1830........		8.95	5.98	
1831........	23.59			1.71
1832........	13.60		.25	
1833.........	13.52		4.46	
1834........	6.35		15.84	
1835........	21.55		6.65	
1836........	52.24		9.08	
1837........	19.03		4.54	
1838........		9.01	14.24	
1839........	44.24			3.18
1840........		25.41	.47	
1841........	11.14			5.05
1842........		3.80		.73
1843**......		40.39	20.87	
1844**......		3.14	.38	
1845**......	7.14			4.54

* Including coin and bullion. Movement of the latter is given separately only from 1821 on.

** Due to a change in the Government's fiscal year, the figure offered for 1843 includes only nine months from October 1, 1842 to June 30, 1843; and the data for 1844 and 1845 are for fiscal years ending June 30th.

standing of the volume of trade and the conditions of domestic credit during the troubled years of 1837–42.

Even more immediately significant for an appraisal of domestic credit conditions are the data (presented in Table 20) upon the excess of imports or exports of the precious metals. As also previously suggested, the decade of the 'twenties showed no clear trend. Then, in the 'thirties, appeared a period of persistent net imports — a disparity which in the years of 1832–37 added another $40,000,000 to the debit balance already large by reason of disparities in merchandise trade. The timing of the bullion movement, however, differed from that of merchandise; and year-to-year changes of the two disparities were by no means similar throughout the period. Of special moment was the heavy inflow of gold in the years 1834, 1838, and 1843. Comparison with other material already presented indicates that in each of these cases the influx of gold was followed by an easing of credit conditions and a subsequent revival of speculative and business activity.

Finally, attention may be called to the exigencies of national finance as revealed by the volume of short-term Treasury notes outstanding at the beginning of successive quarters from 1838 through 1845. Issues rose rapidly in 1838, reaching a sum of eight million dollars by October 1st of that year. A diminution followed, as the notes were turned in to the Government in payments due to it; and the outstanding volume on April 1, 1840 had shrunk to less than a million and a half. But hard times for the Government were not past. After action by Congress granting the Treasury freer hand, issues increased rapidly in the next fifteen months — again to exceed eight million dollars — and remained high for the next two years. The maxima were attained in the first three quarters of 1843, when a volume in excess of eleven million dollars was three times reported. Thereafter, however, the notes were rapidly paid off, and by October 1845, had become inconsequential. In some measure, to be sure, these issues and reissues of interest-bearing notes might be viewed as consequences of disturbed business conditions; and yet, as representing the emergency demands of an important borrower in the domestic money market, they cannot be ignored.

CHAPTER XIV

RELATIONSHIPS AMONG THE SERIES

A N exhaustive comparison of the various statistical series which have been presented in
the foregoing sections, or to which reference has
already been made, would lengthen this study to
unseemly proportions. Consideration must be
limited to those comparisons which appear to
promise the most significant results. Moreover,
by reason of the defective character of the evidence in certain respects, no elaborate statistical
devices will be employed — such as standard
deviation — to render the indices into directly
comparable terms. Rather, reliance will be had
solely upon the graphic super-imposition of
curves to suggest the relationships which the
indices bear to one another.

Two series — that representing the course of
public land sales and that indicating the movement of common stock prices — may first be
brought into consideration.[1] Here the story is
relatively simple. The first up-and-down swing
evidenced by these two items was that which culminated in 1818. In this instance, there was
striking dissimilarity in the intensity of movement, but notable similarity in the timing thereof. Receipts from land sales rose rapidly from
$700,000 for the first quarter of 1816 to an av-
erage of nearly $3,500,000 per quarter in 1818.
The peak of nearly $5,000,000 was attained in
the last quarter of that year, while by the last
half of the next year sales were again down to
$700,000 per quarter. Meanwhile, the average
of bank-stock prices had risen merely from 88
(base: 1834–42) in September 1816, to one of 105
in the middle of 1818; while the decline that set
in particularly with October of that year, simply
brought the average back by July 1819, to approximately the level from which it had depart-

ed.[2] Yet, despite this wide disparity in the degree of movement, the timing of the rise and fall
in the two cases, as already suggested, was closely similar. Both began to rise in the latter part
of 1816; both reached peak in 1818 — the maximum in land sales a bit later than that of stock
prices; and both were back to their previous
levels by the latter months of the succeeding
year. Wherefore, despite the difference in magnitude of change, it is appropriate to place these
two movements together.

Immediately after 1819, however, there appeared some real divergence of tendencies.
Stock values recovering fairly soon, reached a
point by the spring of 1822 even higher than that
touched in 1818, and suffered no considerable
recession from that level for several years thereafter. Meanwhile land sales, after a brief rise in
1820–21, slumped in the succeeding years, 1822–
23, to a level even lower than that experienced
after the break of the speculative movement in
1818. Moreover, there is dissimilarity between
the two curves, in that land sales much more
than stock prices manifested response to the
speculative movement of the middle 'twenties.
Stock prices did, in fact, lift sharply in the fore
part of 1824, but receipts from the sale of public
lands advanced from the low point of one hundred and eighteen thousand dollars in the third
quarter of 1823 to a peak of seven hundred and
twenty-six thousand dollars twelve months
later. Yet the two curves are alike in at least the
following respects. Relative to movements displayed around 1818, 1836, or even the middle
'fifties, both experienced small activity in the
middle 'twenties; both seem to have felt this
speculative force a year earlier than commodity
prices — 1824 instead of 1825; and both executed irregular and indecisive movements for several years thereafter.

[1] For the first part of the period now under review, see the
curve of quarterly receipts from public land sales on Chart 12,
p. 53, above, and that of bank-stock prices on Charts 8 and
9, both on p. 46, above. Because of the wide difference in
magnitude of movement, it appeared inadvisable to put these
two curves for land receipts and bank stocks on a single chart.

For the latter part of the period — that after 1833 — see
also Chart 25, p. 82, below, where railroad-stock values and
public land sales are brought into comparison.

[2] On the basis of average quarterly sales for the period 1834-
42 — that used in the case of bank-stock prices — the values
in sales for the periods spoken of above would be: first three
quarters of 1816, 36.6; average for 1818, 174.0; peak of last
quarter in that year, 254.0.

When the next major upward movement of values began — toward the end of the 'twenties — there was a further minor divergence of the two curves in that land sales appear to have begun this upward movement earlier than stock prices. For the former, the second quarter of 1828 yielded the smallest receipts from land sales subsequent to the first quarter of 1824; whereas the bottom of the long and slow decline of bank-stock values was reached in July 1829.

CHART 25. — PUBLIC LAND SALES, RECEIPTS BY THE UNITED STATES (QUARTERLY) AND RAILROAD-STOCK PRICE INDEX I: (MONTHLY), 1834–45

(Base: 1834–42. Different logarithmic scales have been used to make the range of fluctuation approximately the same.)

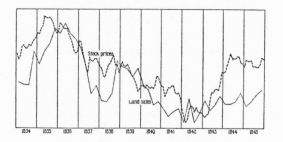

From the time when the railroad-stock index becomes available, 1834, the similarity of move-

ment is strikingly close throughout the succeeding decade (Chart 25). To be sure, the peak of land sales in 1835–36 was reached somewhat later than that of stock prices; but at least the break in stocks was not severe until after the maximum of transactions in public lands had been attained and the subsequent decline had set in. The fall in land sales in 1836–38 was more prolonged and the recovery in 1838 more pronounced; the sinking spell of such sales in 1839–42 was less broken by temporary reactions; and the revival of interest in lands at the final turn of affairs (1842–43) seems to have occurred a bit earlier. But, viewed broadly, the similarities outnumber the differences, and both series may, as already suggested, be regarded as reflecting a common element — that of the well-known speculative spirit of the country. Remembering, then, that what is said subsequently of the relationship of the stock index to other matters applies in the main also to the course of public land sales, let us turn to the second of the comparisons that seem desirable.

This second comparison lies between the course of land sales and the movement of the (weighted) index of commodity prices during the period 1816–45 (Chart 26). A brief inspection of the chart containing the curves that represent these two movements, yields the main features

CHART 26. — PUBLIC LAND SALES, RECEIPTS BY THE UNITED STATES (QUARTERLY) AND WEIGHTED INDEX OF GENERAL WHOLESALE COMMODITY PRICES (MONTHLY), 1816–45

(Base: 1834–42. In charting, different logarithmic scales have been used to make the range of fluctuations approximately the same.)

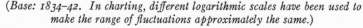
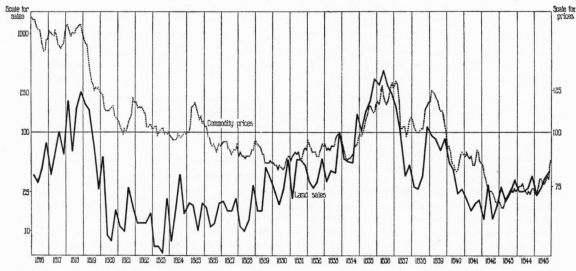

of this comparison. For our purposes, the difference in secular trend may be ignored. Also, because of the difference in scales upon which the two curves are charted, differences in magnitude need not concern us. Particularly interesting is the relative timing in the two movements. The sharp decline of values in the two cases from the end of 1818 appears to be synchronous, but, as already indicated,[3] the persistence of large receipts from land sales through 1818 was due almost wholly to special activity in the one area of Alabama. Thereafter, surely the course of land sales anticipates that of commodity prices in nearly every upward or downward change. The

tive of stock-exchange values, commodity-price movements, and New York interest rates (Chart 27) reveals many interesting divergences. Disregarding the relative amplitude of the various movements — which the chart obviously is not designed to reveal — and fixing attention upon their timings, one will observe that the course of stock-exchange values, as that of land sales just discussed, anticipates with nearly uniform persistence the movement of commodity prices. The degree of anticipation, to be sure, varies widely from time to time; but with almost infallible sequence a break in the one precedes a break in the other; resistance to further decline

CHART 27. — RAILROAD-STOCK-PRICE INDEX I; WEIGHTED INDEX
OF GENERAL WHOLESALE COMMODITY PRICES; AND
DISCOUNT RATES: MONTHLY, 1834–45

*(Base: 1834–42. Different vertical logarithmic scales have been used
to make the range of fluctuations approximately the same.)*

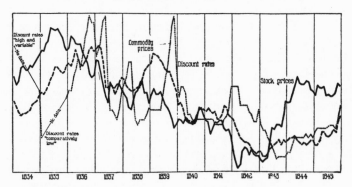

collapse of such sales in 1836 may, of course, be attributed to the chance issuance of the Specie Circular in that year; but the relationship just mentioned is much too consistent throughout these decades to be characterized as casual. As far as the events in 1836–37 are concerned, one might even assert that a sharp decline in land sales at that time would have taken place if no Specie Circular had been promulgated. Without pausing to measure the differences in the period of time by which, on one occasion or another, the course of land sales anticipated that of commodity prices — for example, 1821–22 as compared with 1828–30 — we may proceed to the third of the comparisons among the several series to which this chapter is devoted.

Super-imposition of the curves representa-

in the one case is followed by a corresponding check to further fall in the other; and recovery in the first appears before recovery in the second. Whatever the causes and whatever the significance, the essential relationship between these two curves is abundantly clear.

The position of the third movement, that of discount rates, relative to the other two, is somewhat less certain — partly by reason of a hiatus in the data for 1834 and 1835. Apparently, however, the peak and bottom of movements in interest rates were reached generally later than the corresponding points in the curves of stock and commodity prices. The characteristic relationship among these three curves may be said to be a sequence in which stock prices moved first, commodity prices second, and discount rates last. Thus in the culmination of the cycli-

[3] See above, p. 55 and Chart 16, p. 58.

cal movement surrounding 1837, railroad stocks attained their maximum in May 1835, and broke precipitately after June 1836; commodity prices continued to rise until February 1837; and interest rates did not begin to fall decisively until after May of the latter year. Again in the period of intermediate recovery in 1839–41, stock prices touched their minimum and began to advance after November 1839; commodity prices after July 1840; and interest rates after August 1841 — when stock prices had commenced again to seek lower levels. Exceptions to this general relationship are of course to be found, and perhaps would always occur in a period so confused and broken as that which embraced the devolution from the "crisis of 1837;" yet by and large, the sequence above suggested is obviously the most impressive and accurate one to be discovered among these curves.

Attention finally may be called to the broad similarity in movement between the course of commodity prices on the one hand and the volume of business on the other. Such a comparison admittedly can be only of the roughest sort, on account of the annual basis of our index on business volume. It is apparent, however, that after a few years of uncertain action preceding a decline in 1834, both movements rose to a maximum in 1836 or early 1837, fell to lower levels in 1837–38, attained a new peak in 1839, and subsequently followed a broken line of declining values until a bottom was reached in 1843. If the fragmentary infra-annual evidence upon the volume of trade can be considered acceptable as a means of determining more exactly the dates of the downturn in 1837 and the upturn in 1843, a closer similarity of the two movements is indicated. A decline in the volume of trade seems to have occurred in the second quarter of 1837, whereas commodity prices reached their highest point in February of that year and by the second quarter thereof had receded sharply. Again, a mounting volume of business appears to

be shown in the third quarter of 1843, while commodity prices had touched bottom in February of that year and by the third quarter were distinctly on a higher level. While the contrast between the course pursued by business volume and by the indices of changing stock-market and money-market values is not so great as that between the course of commodity prices and the latter, yet the conclusion seems sound that the similarity between volume of business and commodity-price movements is appreciably greater than that between volume of business and either of the other curves.

To sum up, it may be held, first, that the course of public land sales and average values of common stock prices described movements of marked general similarity — both characteristically anticipating the corresponding movements of other indices; secondly, that commodity prices and the physical volume of business moved later than these speculative indices but earlier than changes in the curve of interest rates, both in declines and upturns; and thirdly, that this last item followed all others — reaching its peaks ordinarily after stock prices, commodity prices, and the rest had been proceeding considerably on a downward path, and recovering from a temporary low point only when the other indices had made appreciable progress in an upward course. One leaves the analysis with the wonder whether this variety of relationship was maintained in subsequent cyclical movements.[4]

[4] To students of business cycles, there is no need to offer the suggestion of the similarity in this relationship among these three indices of business change to the relationship which Professor W. M. Persons discovered among series of somewhat varying sort for the period 1903-14 (cf. "An Index of General Business Conditions" in the *Review of Economic Statistics*, Preliminary Volume I (1919), pp. 111-17, and "A Non-technical Explanation of the Index of General Business Conditions," in the same *Review*, Preliminary Volume II (1920), pp. 46-47). No pretense is made that the phenomena discussed in the text conform with or substantiate the conclusions arrived at by Professor Persons. The general similarity of the two cases alone is called to the reader's attention.

SECTION III

BUSINESS FLUCTUATIONS, 1843-62
ARTHUR HARRISON COLE

CHAPTER XV

INTRODUCTION

IN conformity with the purpose already expressed of dividing the history of business fluctuations in the United States into time-periods convenient for presentation of the assembled data, we turn to the decades 1843–62. To the economic historian, however — at least to one who holds in mind a broad sweep of economic events — any subdivision of the stream of economic development into precise time-intervals seems grossly artificial. For this reason any attempt, such as this introduction purposes to make, to elaborate the background of business fluctuations in these new decades in a manner different from that employed for the period 1820–45, or by consideration of wholly novel factors, would be condemned at the outset. For the most part, the forces observed in the earlier period remained effective in the later one: the growth of population; the evolution of our transportation system; the increasing integration of American economic life, both through improved transportation facilities and through the increasing network of financial relationships; and, finally, the repercussion of foreign events upon the domestic situation. Perhaps it will suffice here to call attention to outstanding features of these continuing trends, while at the same time bringing into special prominence such new developments as the later decades provide.

The country continued to grow with rapid strides, increasing from seventeen to more than thirty-one million souls between 1840 and 1860. The line of westward settlement continued its course towards the Rockies, while in the later years came the launching of a new movement — a movement eastward from the Pacific coast, which a few decades later, by effecting junction with the westward migration, was to efface the historic American frontier. At the same time with the settlement of the West, came the beginnings of really sizable urban concentration in the East. While the total population of the country grew by less than eighty-five per cent between 1840 and 1860, New York (including all boroughs) trebled in size; Philadelphia increased

in nearly that proportion (166 per cent); while Boston and Baltimore, among other communities, exceeded the rate of growth for the country as a whole. In 1860 Philadelphia's population had reached nearly six hundred thousand and New York's had exceeded a million. The very size of these cities, especially that of New York, was beginning to count in the disposition of economic forces over the country as a whole as well as to a less degree over the course of world affairs. Past growth was an impetus to further growth, while size alone of the larger communities bred dependence of the smaller upon them.

The growth of population both in city and country was again stimulated by the inflow of immigrants. Due in large part to particular circumstances abroad — especially in Ireland and Germany — the volume of new arrivals reached unanticipated heights in the decades now under review. From a low point of seventy-two thousand in 1843, the numbers rose rapidly until a peak of four hundred and twenty-eight thousand was reached in 1854. The tide receded sharply thereafter, but it is noteworthy that in the decades 1840 to 1860, immigration brought into the country nearly one-fourth the number of souls that had constituted the total population thereof at the beginning of this period. To record the manifold effects of such an immigration movement would of course far exceed the purposes of this brief sketch. It must suffice to point out what seems a consequence, though admittedly a minor consequence, of this inflow, namely, the increase in the sale of public lands. It is notable that the peak of the last substantial speculation in the sale of public lands, i.e., 1854–55, correlates much more closely with the inflow of potential settlers from abroad than with the general movement of commodity prices and of other phenomena — of which the peaks in contemporary upward movements were not reached until 1857.

Perhaps more significant than the increase in mere numbers, or changes in the distribution of the population, were various other phenomena indicating an increase of national maturity. Conspicuous in this regard was the advance of the railroad network. A glance over maps showing the railroads in operation at successive decadal periods such as 1840, 1850, and 1860 reveals a westward extension of such transportation facilities as well as an increasing number of interconnections. In 1840 both of these tendencies were beginning to be evident, but the succeeding twenty years showed a marked advance. Here, as in other phases of American development, the decade of the 'fifties was especially productive. No such boom of railroad construction swept the United States in the middle 'forties as occurred in England, although, to be sure, the mileage completed on American railroads in the year 1847 was greater than that of any previous year excepting one — 1841. The larger expansion began in 1849 when the increase in mileage completed was double that of 1847, and reached its peak in 1856. In the latter year, the mileage added during this single twelve-month interval exceeded the total mileage in operation of 1841. From an equipment of slightly more than 4,000 miles of railroad in 1843, eight-fold that amount had been constructed and put into use by 1862. With some extension of canals and a significant improvement in the character and number of steam vessels for both coastwise and river traffic, the country found itself at the outbreak of the Civil War far more adequately equipped than it had been in any preceding decade with the facilities of transportation and communication — facilities essential to economic integration.

A further step in the integration of the country came with the development of the telegraph. At the commencement of the present period, this important agency for domestic and, later, international communication was in its very infancy. In 1844 an experimental line had been constructed by governmental subsidy from Baltimore to Washington. Successful demonstration gave encouragement to schemes of further extension and, despite difficulties of securing capital in the lean 'forties, facilities were soon broadened, until by 1850 nearly all the larger cities were interconnected by a network of wires.

Improvement in the means of transportation had its most striking, immediate effect in the opening of the old Northwest to agricultural exploitation. To be sure, cotton production in the South was increasing markedly in these decades — although aided only in a moderate degree by improvements of transportation — and even as late as 1860 cotton formed the main reliance of our export trade. Yet the production and exportation of other agricultural products — especially wheat and wheat flour — were growing at an even more rapid pace; Cincinnati was thriving on its production of pork made ready for shipment; and the Northwest, in addition to an increased export trade, was coming to supply in ever greater volume the needs of the East and South for a variety of agricultural staples. (See Chart 28 for the course of exportation, 1843–62, of cotton, tobacco, and wheat.[1]) At this time, it will be recalled, England was becoming more and more industrialized; her population was growing rapidly; and with the abolition of her "Corn Laws," England's ports were opened more widely than ever before to the inflow of agricultural foodstuffs. This spelled opportunity for American (as well as other) soils, although, as will be noted shortly, it also meant continued or even increased dependence of American business conditions upon those of our chief markets.

Although agriculture, especially in the Northwest, benefited more considerably from improvement in transportation facilities, and although the country even as late as 1860 was still predominantly agricultural, industrial activity did show important changes in the decades now under review. While the change of tariff policy after 1846 was in some measure a restraining influence, development in the means of transportation meant the opening of potential markets for eastern manufactures; and (as another favoring factor) the increase of immigration — especially Irish — provided factory owners with a working force more abundant and persisting than they had previously enjoyed. As a consequence of these and other fostering influences, real progress was being made. The cotton and wool manufactures increased in size and extend-

[1] Cotton exportation figures include both "Sea Island" and "Other" in terms of physical volume; the tobacco curve covers exportation of raw tobacco in hogsheads; while that for wheat covers the exportation of both wheat and wheat flour. The data on wheat flour have been expressed in terms of unmilled wheat by conversion on the basis that 4 1-2 bushels of wheat equals one barrel of flour.

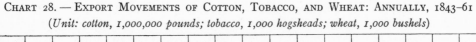

CHART 28. — EXPORT MOVEMENTS OF COTTON, TOBACCO, AND WHEAT: ANNUALLY, 1843–61
(*Unit: cotton, 1,000,000 pounds; tobacco, 1,000 hogsheads; wheat, 1,000 bushels*)

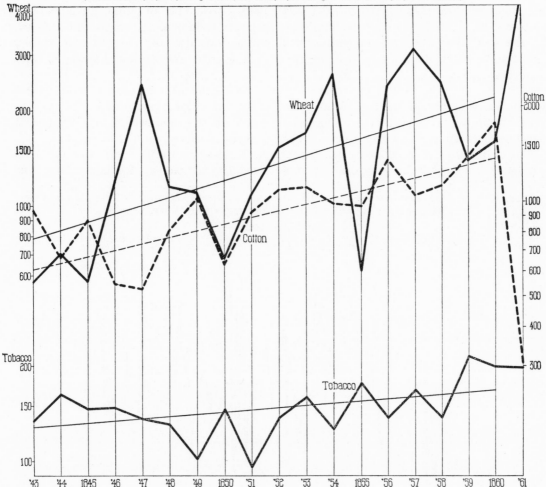

ed largely the variety of their products. The iron manufacture grew with much rapidity, and the center at Pittsburg developed. Shipbuilding enlarged exceptionally through the evolution and adoption of pre-clipper and true clipper ships. As already indicated, meat packing had reached significant scale at Cincinnati. All in all, with machine builders and flour mills, glass works and shoe factories, the face of the country was appreciably changed in the decades of the 'forties and 'fifties. Another step towards industrialization had been made.

On the financial side as well as in industrial activity, the beginnings made before 1843 were generally followed. The banking systems progressed in size and solidity, aided in appreciable measure by an increase of state supervision which the difficulties of 1837–42 did much to encourage.

The position of New York as the financial center of the nation became increasingly evident, although Philadelphia was still an active rival, and although Boston and other similar cities continued to rely mainly on their own resources. Progress was undoubtedly made in the evolution of financial — as contrasted with banking — institutions although it took the Civil War and the loans floated by the Government at that time to bring out the final steps in the evolution of a class of investment bankers comparable with that of more recent years.

In the banking and financial world as a whole, the most notable event was, of course, the discovery of gold in California with the subsequent enlargement of the basis for bank loans and for the whole pyramid of credit. While this was by no means a local phenomenon but one of world significance, it had important consequences for the United States. Data on monthly shipments of gold from San Francisco to New York (Chart 29) show a rapid rise to 1853, a moderate decline the succeeding year, but thereafter until 1862 a volume which, despite some wide month-to-month variations, averaged monthly around $3,000,000 worth. The coincidence of the first rapid rise in gold receipts in New York with the upward lift of business in 1849–52 suggests a connection between the two phenomena. The probability of such a connection is heightened when one considers that the new gold was, in a

Yet the persistence in some measure of gold shipments to the eastern States, despite this temporary breakdown of business, tended to impart a power to revival and to prevent a recurrence, in the years after 1857, of that long period of declining prices and depressed business which followed the crisis of 1837–39. All in all, the events of the period 1843–62 cannot be adequately interpreted without considerable attention to this novel phenomenon which took its rise in the placer deposits of the Pacific coast.

Domestic political events to which reference need here be made are few in number. The suc-

CHART 29. — MOVEMENTS OF GOLD FROM CALIFORNIA, MONTHLY AND ANNUALLY: SHIPMENTS TO ATLANTIC PORTS, 1849–52, AND RECEIPTS AT NEW YORK, 1850–62

(*Unit: dollars*)

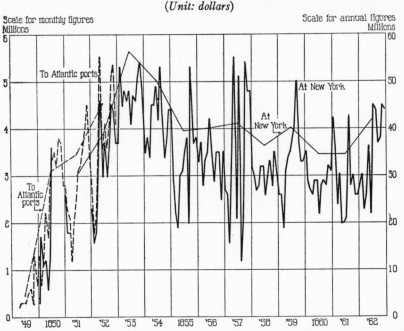

way, an added element in our export trade; that availability of increased supplies of the precious metal would inevitably impart greater confidence to loan operations of domestic banks; and that both the spectacular quality of the new development and the improving character of domestic banking and industrial conditions would serve as encouragements to European investors with loanable funds. On the other hand, the decrease in supplies of gold coming from California in the years after 1853 may have served as a brake on the tendency toward expansion of credit and general business activity, ultimately producing a strain which led to the violent reaction of 1857.

cess of the Whig party and the subsequent passage of a truly protective tariff in 1842 may have added strength to the upswing of business in 1843–47, although the evidence does not suggest a cause-effect relationship between these two events. The Democratic control of later years, with the "low-tariff" regime that came therewith, may have enhanced the intimacy of our business dependency upon Europe, but here again the case is not clearcut. Other factors, probably more potent than a somewhat reduced tariff barrier, were working in the same direction — factors such as the improvement of transportation facilities or the spread of the cotton culture. Finally, war and the threat of war must be considered. The former — conflict with Mexico — seems to have played a distinctly minor rôle in the determination of general business movements. Perhaps, like the tariff of 1842, it added somewhat to the boom of 1843–47, but its influence surely was not great. Indeed, one finds no need for reference to these hostilities to explain the more important business changes of the middle 'forties. On the other hand, the fear of possible civil conflict may have altered the course of business affairs in the years after 1857 or perhaps 1858. There is an irregularity or lack of direction in various business movements that may be interpreted as deriving from the shadow cast by the oncoming war. However, here as so often in historical inquiry, one can only surmise; one cannot prove.

The events of foreign origin which had consequence upon the American situation may also be disposed of briefly. The chief non-economic factors which ought to be noted are: first, the political revolutions of Europe in 1848 which, with the Irish famine of slightly earlier occurrence, were responsible for sending immigrants in large volume to the United States, and which may have been immediately responsible for a retardation in the business revival of that year, 1848; and, secondly, the Crimean War of the middle 'fifties which, particularly through its disturbance of the normal course of the European grain movements, had indirect influence upon the agricultural situation in this country.

The 'fifties, even more than the preceding 'thirties, formed a period of large investment by foreign, and especially British, capitalists in American enterprises. The repudiation of State debts at the close of our preceding period[2] dampened foreign enthusiasm with respect to the American investment field in the early and middle 'forties. Apparently, confidence in the United States was revived toward the end of that decade — a revival perhaps not unconnected with the misfortunes which British investors had encountered when the English railway boom exploded in the predominantly British crisis of 1847. The flow of foreign capital into the United States made special contribution once more to the rapid construction of transportation facilities (to which reference has already been made), although in some measure it aided also in the development of banking facilities and provided a certain impetus to the speculation in public lands. This influence of inflowing capital from abroad, like the California gold discoveries — with which, as already indicated, it may well have been indirectly connected — must be considered as one of the outstanding basic causes for the expansion of American business in the decade of the 'fifties. The breeze which propelled the American ship of business so rapidly forward at this time came in large measure from across the Atlantic.

Finally, it may be observed that the financial and general business affairs of the United States in the decades 1843–62, still remained sensitive to the changing fortunes of finance and business in England. Our exports were then, as in the preceding decades, financed predominantly on the London money market; our exports were largely industrial raw materials and foodstuffs — the former of which were particularly affected by alterations in general business abroad; while our carrying trade, at that time still a truly significant feature of our domestic economy, was bound to feel repercussions from the variations of prosperity and depression in the European industrial and commercial centers. Accordingly, it is of considerable value to trace the general course of business in Great Britain, the country with which our business connections were closest.

Revival of business in England after the reaction of 1839 appears to have come contemporaneously with that in the United States. The revival abroad was accompanied, as already suggested, by intense speculation in railroad construction and railroad projects. These two upward movements of trade and speculation seem to have reached peak at approximately the same time, when the so-called "railway crisis" of 1847 brought violent reaction to all business activities in the British Isles. Revival appeared in the succeeding year and in 1849 — a revival perhaps not unconnected with increasing supplies of gold from California and Australia. Expansion continued until the outbreak of the Crimean War in 1854, halted for a moment, but resumed its course until the second major crisis of this period was reached in 1857. This crisis has been described by Tugan-Baranowsky (though of course

[2] See p. 42, above.

with dubious propriety) as the first truly international crisis.[3] As far as the relation between the United States and England is concerned, it is significant that money rates in the London market had been high in 1856–57 — especially in the months immediately preceding the difficulties of both countries. The recovery from the common crisis appears to have been less rapid in England than in the United States; but the course of events in these areas after 1858 seems to have been generally similar, when allowance is made for the special non-economic difficulties and uncertainties in the United States which preceded the actual outbreak of civil war.

In summary, it appears accurate to observe that conditions of general business within the United States seemed to respond actively to the changing winds of European, and particularly of English, influence. Variation in the flow of British capital, the outbreak and close of European war, the fluctuations of prosperity and depression in British business, all these were potent factors affecting conditions in the younger, smaller, and less stable business communities of the United States. While domestic influences were undoubtedly of great immediate importance in determining the course of the country's business affairs, disregard of foreign forces would rob the picture of one of its most striking elements as well as diminish its importance from the point of view of the economic historian.

The limits of the period just discussed, 1820–45, were selected from a desire to delineate the changes in general business conditions from the close of the troubled times following the War of 1812 through the difficulties surrounding the so-called "crisis of 1837." The period 1843–62 has now been chosen to tie the closing years of the foregoing study with the outbreak of the Civil War. It seemed advantageous to start the present story with 1843, since that year marked the lowest point after the declines of the preceding six or seven years. At the other end the final year of discussion, 1862, was selected; because by then not only was the Civil War fully launched but various monetary series were already beginning to show the effects of Greenback inflation.

<hr>

[3] Tugan-Baranowsky, *op. cit.*, p. 124. The material of this volume — from 1792 on — is sufficient evidence of the "international" character of various early crises.

While this later period covers somewhat fewer years than the earlier, it manifests divers points of similarity. Each period begins at the bottom of a business decline; each manifests indecisive fluctuations over a decade or more; and each embraces an upward swing of major proportions, culminating in a crisis or crises, and followed by an irregular period which lasts until approximately the close of the decades under survey. In spite of their general likeness, however, certain differences do obtain between the two intervals — as will be narrated in detail through the subsequent pages; and possibly these differences are more significant than the similarities. Indeed, an examination of business fluctuations inclines one to draw the comforting conclusion that no two "cyclical" movements are sufficiently identical in character or even so generally similar as to make their study lacking either in interest or significance.

Material for the investigation of the period after 1843 is in several respects more satisfactory than that for the study of earlier years. Stock-exchange data are more exact and somewhat more easily obtainable; series illustrating changes in the volume of trade are more numerous and more diversified; while, toward the end of the period, information relating to banking experience becomes sufficiently homogeneous to warrant some special treatment. Inasmuch, moreover, as one can continue into this era of more abundant data the excellent series on commodity prices and public land sales, the inquirer obviously has material for a more thorough study than he had for the decades that preceded.

The many more factors involved and the wealth of data on each, increase the difficulties in choosing a point at which to begin. Perhaps as good a guide as any is the rule of working from the known to the unknown. In this case, the rule may perhaps be adapted to cover an examination first of those phases of business with which we are already somewhat familiar because of their similarity in the two periods. Later we can turn to a consideration of those other phases on which decidedly new information is obtainable. We shall start then by an analysis of commodity-price movements, and afterwards carry on with a treatment of the stock market and other aspects of business conditions.

CHAPTER XVI

COMMODITY PRICES

COMMODITY-PRICE series for the period 1843–62 are available in considerable number in the United States Treasury Report of 1863. Additional series, or data to supplement those found in the Treasury Report, were obtained for the New York market from the *New York Shipping and Commercial List*, and for the Boston district from the files of the *Boston Advertiser*. In the end eighty-four series were assembled, each one covering the whole or the major part of the decades now under consideration.[1] From this mass of material, thirty-three commodities were chosen for utilization in the construction of an unweighted index of price fluctuations. The method of selection, as well as details in the treatment of the series, are to be found elsewhere.[2]

Two indices in fact were compounded, as was done for the earlier period.[3] Originally, an unweighted arithmetic index with a broad base of average values for the eleven years 1848–58, was believed adequate; and the preliminary treatment of divergences among groups of series was carried through on the basis of comparisons with this unweighted product — of which comparisons more will appear shortly. Subsequently, with the present study in mind, and with the purpose of testing the adequacy of the unweighted index, a set of weights was devised for the construction of a new, weighted arithmetic index calculated on the same base period. The weights assigned to the several commodities had to be arrived at in rather an arbitrary fashion, since reliable data for the development of a weighting system were almost as scarce for these later decades as for the years prior to 1843. The weights assigned were, of course, not identical with those utilized in the construction of the index covering 1815–45;[4] but an attempt was made to assign weights which would reflect the importance of the several commodities in contemporary business life, especially of eastern communities.

The results of the two computations are presented herewith (Chart 30). Obviously there is little to choose between the two as far as general configuration of the curves is concerned. The degree of movement, to be sure, is somewhat more pronounced in the case of the weighted form — a result contrasting with that secured in the 1825–45 comparison, where the unweighted index for the most part moved fully as widely as the weighted. Perhaps the most interesting addition made to the narrative by this laborious treatment of the material is the indication of greater strength of commodity prices in the middle of 1857. A slight softening of prices is indicated by both indices after the peak is attained in May of that year, but on the whole the resistance to this tendency is greater in the case of the weighted than of the unweighted form; and consequently the decline after September is somewhat more precipitate. Generally, indeed, the weighted index will be seen to intensify the movements detected by use of the unweighted form, e. g., the peak in 1847, and the rise and fall in 1848–52, as well as the break in 1857 just mentioned.

However, we are getting ahead of our story. The two indices show a generally rising tendency from the spring of 1843 to June 1847. This was a rise of real significance, although it was frequently broken by recessions, especially in the spring and summer of 1846. Finally in June 1847 there came a turn of the tide — a turn tending to give support to the designation of a "crisis" in that year. The decline that followed was sharper than the rise, until, in the closing months of 1848, prices averaged no higher than they had in the spring of 1845, or even in the summer and fall of 1843. Seemingly, here we

---

[1] A list of these series together with the periods covered and the markets to which they pertain is to be found in Appendix A, Table 48, p. 161.

[2] See Appendix A, pp. 165–66.

[3] There is a slight difference in the commodities used in the two indices. For detailed description see Appendix A, Tables 50 and 51.

[4] See Appendix A, Tables 44 and 51.

CHART 30. — WEIGHTED AND UNWEIGHTED INDICES OF WHOLESALE COMMODITY PRICES: MONTHLY, 1843–62

(*Base: 1848–58. Arithmetic scale*)

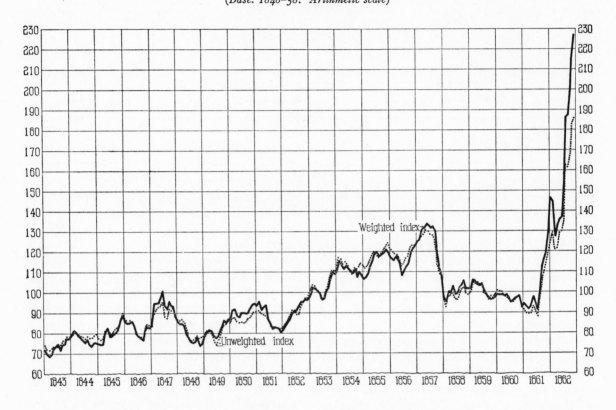

have evidence of an up-and-down movement of commodity prices possessing characteristics comparable to those which we have lately believed essential to a full-blown business "cycle."

Return of rising prices set in with the opening months of 1849; a peak was reached in February 1851; and another low point by December of that year. Possibly, if the secular trend of prices during this period is taken into account, this rise and fall over the three-year interval, November 1848 to December 1851, might also be designated a full "cyclical" swing.

A longer and more striking movement of prices ensued, lasting from December 1851 until February 1858, and concluding with a rapid and spectacular decline in the five months which followed September 1857. With this sharp fall of prices in the "crisis of 1857," moreover, and the termination thereby of a third possible business "cycle," notable changes in the general average until the onset of Greenback inflation were concluded. The indices fluctuated irregularly from February 1858 through July 1861. The very

modest rise and fall of 1858–59— especially sustained in the weighted index — is all that can be discerned.

A further broad consideration regarding these indices is the character of the secular trend revealed by Chart 30. As will be recalled, the trend for 1821–43 was found to be downward. In the later period, 1843–62, even after excluding the upward thrust of values when paper inflation began to have effect subsequent to July 1861, the movement was reversed. Moreover, the trend appears to have been initiated as early as 1843. The general upward course as here revealed runs counter to the usual conclusions regarding commodity prices in the nineteenth century. The turn from a downward to an upward trend is commonly held to have occurred after the California gold discoveries; but the data here presented seem to suggest that the influx of new gold not only gave an upward drift of prices after 1848 but perhaps prevented the "cyclical" downturn of prices after 1847 from reaching a point comparable to that from which prices had started upward in the spring of 1843. Accordingly, the latter year would appear a better point of departure for measuring the secular trend during the latter half of the nineteenth century than 1848 or subsequent years.

However, we may perhaps be excused from pursuing the implications of this last observation, and be permitted to confine attention to the period now under review. A calculation for these years, based on the weighted index, shows that a straight line fitted to the course of prices from the first half of 1843 through the first half of 1861, i.e., from low point to low point, has an annual positive increment of 2.04; whereas, it will be recalled, a similar calculation for the period 1821–43 revealed an annual negative increment of .528.[5] Possibly this reversal of trend and the considerable force of the upward tendency played a part in extending over such an unusually long interval the movement of rising prices which, as already noted, began in December 1851 and lasted until September 1857.

Let us turn next to an examination of certain special groups among the commodity series for the period 1843–62.[6] At the outset, it may be observed that perhaps the most striking general feature of the decades under review is the capacity of significant groups of commodity prices to move divergently in given time-intervals. Particularly is this true of the 'forties and early 'fifties. For example, one fairly large group, which, like nearly all the series, began to move upward in the latter part of 1843, attained its highest points in 1845 and 1846 and was coasting down again at a time when certain other series were experiencing a potent upward swing. Another set of commodities reached its highest levels in 1844 or 1848; and, if, in addition to these groups, consideration is given to certain individual series which behave erratically throughout these years, it will be seen that price movements for the middle years of the 'forties were far from uniform.

In fact, conditions in the middle 'forties were

such that Special Index I (Chart 31) should be considered as representing the course merely of the largest single group of price series with common characteristics in this period. It was possible to include but thirteen commodity series from among the considerable number of fifty active and satisfactory series collected — a num-

CHART 31. — UNWEIGHTED INDEX OF GENERAL WHOLESALE COMMODITY PRICES (IV), AND SPECIAL WHOLESALE COMMODITY-PRICE INDEX I: MONTHLY, 1843–48

(Base: 1848–58. Arithmetic scale)

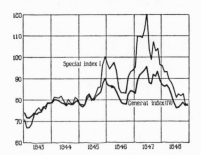

ber contrasting with the total of thirty-three items which went into one or the other of the two indices extending over the decade 1849–58. Attention should be called here, perhaps, to the eclectic character of this group of thirteen commodities as shown in the following list.

TABLE 21. — SERIES USED IN THE CONSTRUCTION OF SPECIAL WHOLESALE COMMODITY-PRICE INDEX I, 1843–48

Corn, northern	Pork, prime
Cotton, middling	Rye, northern
Cotton sheetings	Spices, nutmeg
Fish, bank cod	Spirits of turpentine
Molasses, New Orleans	Wheat, Genesee
Oats, northern	Whiskey, domestic
Olive oil	

Although certain other series also appear, the chief agricultural products, corn, oats, pork, rye, and wheat — together with industrial raw materials derived from agriculture — all find place. Apparently that rise of prices, which culminated in the middle of 1847 — in so far as any one salient or outstanding movement can be fixed upon at all — was particularly concerned with farming activities: of which more later.

In the decade subsequent to 1848, divergences among the price series gave rise to the formation

[5] The ordinates derived in the calculation for the period 1843–61 were as follows:

January to June, 1843	76.24
January to June, 1852	94.60
January to June, 1861	112.96

[6] The unweighted index is here utilized as a basis of comparison, and the special indices are also unweighted.

of two distinct groups — groups which showed rather marked dissimilarities of movement. For example, Index IIa (Chart 32) seems to indicate a complete, though brief, up-and-down swing of values between the middle of 1849 and the end of 1851; whereas Index IIb shows a retention of much of the height gained in 1849 and 1850 despite a downturn in the succeeding year. Too much weight, however, should not be

CHART 32. — SPECIAL WHOLESALE COMMODITY-PRICE INDICES IIa AND IIb: MONTHLY, 1849–58

(Base: 1848–58. Arithmetic scale)

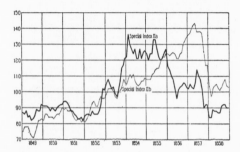

attached to the variations of these two indices in the years 1849–51. Not only, as already suggested, did a period of irregular price movements extend for nearly a decade after 1843 but also, it may be noted, the more significant nature of the price movements after 1851 was the determining factor in allocating the individual series between the two groups. However, at least this lesson is obvious: uniformity of upward trend among price series did not appear before 1852.

There is a more significant and substantial deviation in the years 1853–58 between the courses of Indices IIa and IIb. The former reaches a peak as early as February 1854 — and a peak of much higher altitude than the levels concurrently attained by Index IIb — and then describes an irregular downward course until the beginning of 1858. The latter (IIb) continues to rise until the middle of 1857 — though that rise is broken by minor, intermediate declines in 1853 and 1854 — and then undergoes a severe débâcle extending over the next nine months. Possibly the composition of these two indices, constructed from the following series, may be of interest. Obviously, the division in this case is not along lines identical with those which separated the series of Index I from the rest of the collected

TABLE 22. — SERIES USED IN THE CONSTRUCTION OF SPECIAL WHOLESALE COMMODITY-PRICE INDICES IIa AND IIb, 1849–58

INDEX IIa.

Coal, Liverpool	Sperm oil, winter
Corn, northern	Spices, nutmeg
Oats, northern	Spirits of turpentine
Pig iron, British	Wheat, Genesee
Rye, northern	Whiskey, domestic
Salt, Liverpool	

INDEX IIb.

Ashes, pearl	Olive oil
Butter, western	Pork, prime
Cognac brandy	Rosin, common
Copper, pig	Rum, New England
Cotton, middling	Spices, pepper
Fish, bank cod	Staves, white oak
Hides, Buenos Ayres	Sugar, refined, Havana
Lead, pig	Tallow, American
Leather, hemlock sole	Tobacco, Kentucky
Linseed oil, English	Whale oil
Molasses, New Orleans	Wool, merino

data in the period 1843–48; yet it is clear that for Index IIa agricultural foodstuffs and imported commodities furnished the greater number of component elements. Rye, oats, corn, and wheat are all included; and with coal, pig iron, salt, and nutmeg, these make eight out of the eleven constituent items. On the other hand, while not excluding entirely these two types of commodities — for instance, pork, butter, cognac, and pepper — the larger Index IIb is compounded with industrial raw materials and finished manufactures as its major elements. This difference in components, also, will be discussed later.

In the period after 1857 there is still another divergence in movement — one between a special group of series and the rest of the commodities — such a divergence as occurred in the case of Index I. This particular collection, compounded into Index III, was made up of the following series.

TABLE 23. — SERIES USED IN THE CONSTRUCTION OF SPECIAL WHOLESALE COMMODITY-PRICE INDEX III, 1858–61

Coal, Liverpool	Rosin, common
Corn, northern	Rye, northern
Fish, bank cod	Salt, Liverpool
Hides, Buenos Ayres	Spirits of turpentine
Leather, hemlock sole	Tallow, American
Molasses, New Orleans	Wheat, Genesee
Oats, northern	Whiskey, domestic
Olive oil	Wool, merino
Pork, prime	

The distinguishing characteristic of these commodities (Chart 33) is that on the average not only did they recover quickly from the sharp decline of 1857–58 but they executed a complete up-and-down swing between the spring of 1858 and the middle months of 1861. Nor was the movement inconsiderable. From a low point of 91.6 in February 1858, the index rises to a value of 115.7 in April 1859; dips later in that year but recovers to 112.2 by January 1860; and then slides off to 92.1 by April 1861. Furthermore, as did Indices I and IIa, this group of series includes the chief agricultural staples — although in this case they are more thoroughly intermingled with series of a different character.

CHART 33. — UNWEIGHTED INDEX OF GENERAL
WHOLESALE COMMODITY PRICES (IV) AND
SPECIAL WHOLESALE COMMODITY-PRICE
INDEX III: MONTHLY, 1858–61

(Base: 1848–58. Arithmetic scale)

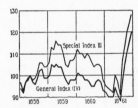

The persistency with which the prices of agricultural foodstuffs seemed to follow along the same general course and, as a group, to move substantially at variance with the prices of many other commodities, suggested the possibility of interesting results if two indices, one representative of agricultural and one of the industrial commodities, should be constructed from the data already used. This was done — except that two new series for which relatives happened to be available were added to the agricultural group.

The division of the series into these two groups is given below.

TABLE 24. — SERIES USED IN THE CONSTRUCTION OF
THE UNWEIGHTED AGRICULTURAL WHOLESALE
COMMODITY-PRICE INDEX, 1843–62[7]

Butter, western dairy	Pork, prime
Corn, northern	Rye, northern
Hams, pickled	Sugar, refined, Havana
Lard	Tobacco, Kentucky
Oats, northern	Wheat, Genesee

TABLE 25. — SERIES USED IN THE CONSTRUCTION OF
THE UNWEIGHTED INDUSTRIAL WHOLESALE
COMMODITY-PRICE INDEX, 1843–62[8]

Ashes, pearl	Molasses, New Orleans
Coal, Liverpool	Rosin, common
Copper, pig	Rum, New England
Cotton, middling	Salt, Liverpool
Cotton sheeting, brown	Spirits of turpentine
Hides, Buenos Ayres	Staves, white oak
Iron, British pig	Tallow, American
Lead, pig	Whale oil
Leather, hemlock sole	Whiskey, domestic
Linseed oil, English	Wool, merino

The industrial raw materials of agricultural origin were difficult to allocate, and a choice of purpose had to be made: i.e., should these series be placed among industrial commodities because they might be expected to reflect changing industrial conditions, or should they be placed in the agricultural group because fluctuations in their values would indicate changes in farmers' incomes? Since the former consideration seemed to come closer to the chief problem of the present study — cyclical variations in commodity prices — determination was made to put the series relating to cotton, wool, and the like into the industrial group.

The contrast between the agricultural and industrial indices (revealed in Chart 34) consists for the most part of elements which might have been forecast from the preceding analysis. This is true for the more extreme movements of the agricultural index in the middle 'forties, for the greater height attained by this same index in 1855, and for its more pronounced swing between 1858 and 1861 — all as compared with the industrial figures. On the other hand, the pro-

[7] Refined sugar was included in the agricultural group in lieu of the series for raw sugar which was defective. As the two series generally move together — except that raw sugar suffered more severely than refined in the decline after 1847 — the substitution seems permissible even though refined sugar represents a different industrial stage and in this case is of foreign origin.

It will also be admitted in passing that by inadvertence three series relating to hogs — pork itself, lard, and pickled hams — were included in the agricultural index. Although these series do not move in complete unison, unquestionably such products are thus overweighted. On the other hand, it may be noted that series of somewhat similar movement were omitted because of defects — notably, rice and beef. Both of these series showed speculative movements around 1847 and 1855.

[8] Reasons for including cotton, wool, etc., in the industrial group are presented in the text.

CHART 34. — UNWEIGHTED INDICES OF AGRICULTURAL AND INDUSTRIAL WHOLESALE
COMMODITY PRICES: MONTHLY, 1843–62

(*Base: 1848–58. Arithmetic scale*)

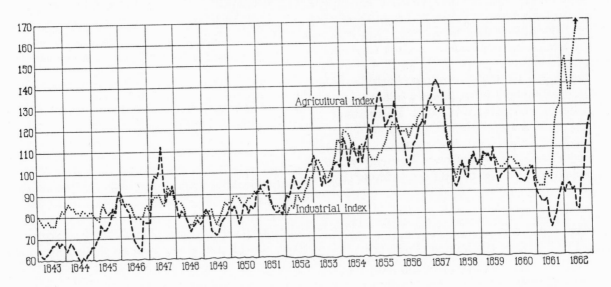

longed depression of agricultural prices in 1843–44, the height reached in 1857, and the low values of such commodities in 1861–62 are unexpected. On investigation, however, both sets of differences, expected and unanticipated, seem soluble largely on similar grounds, namely, the influence of international factors.

One such factor appears to have been of dominant force only for a brief period — during no more than the first year or two of the decades now under review — that is, while agricultural prices continued depressed through 1843 and 1844. Such a phenomenon seems attributable to the temporary reversal of our international credit position. The diminution in the flow of English capital to the United States during these years — an occurrence to which reference has already been made — had the effect of depressing domestic prices relative to foreign values, and might well have had particular incidence upon the prices of agricultural products, many of which were important items of export. Such commodities would, it seems, take the initial shock of the change, and be affected more seriously than goods which were more predominantly for domestic consumption. Such a theory is supported in some measure by the downward course in 1843-44 of certain so-called "industrial" series — notably, raw cotton, tallow, naval

stores, and pearl ashes — all of which were significant items in our export trade of the time. With returning British confidence in American securities came a revival in prices of export commodities, because of the relaxation of pressure from the side of international finance — a relaxation which is suggested by the re-establishment of an unfavorable trade balance in 1845[9] — so that such prices were free to recover a position comparable to those of other goods.

The second international factor — and one which goes far to explain the other deviations of our agricultural and industrial indices — is the influence upon American prices of the foreign markets for foodstuffs. The importance of this influence seems to be revealed by a study of British prices for the more staple cereals over this period. In consequence of the disastrous rains of the summer and fall of 1845, which helped to bring about the terrible Irish famine and which in time, as Morley put it, "rained away the Corn Laws," prices of British cereals experienced changes much like those exhibited by our agricultural index — a rise in the autumn of 1845 and again a startling upheaval in 1846–47. Possibly support was lent to this second increase in British cereal prices by a speculative

[9] See below, p. 129.

interest in England, which may well have been derived from the poor harvest for 1846 and from the immediate reduction of import duties on grains carried by the so-called Corn Law Repeal.

Data on American domestic and foreign commerce lend weight to this thesis. The tonnage of goods flowing from western states to tidewater over the Erie Canal — a movement which had been growing with some rapidity in the early 'forties — received a marked acceleration in 1846–47; and the figures of our aggregate exportations reveal similar activity. Moreover, in the field of our foreign trade, another factor is revealed. Although in 1845–46 there had been an excess of imports, and although this condition of our trade balance was to obtain for a decade following 1847, for that year itself there was a substantial though momentary excess of exports. Apparently conditions in the British market for foodstuffs — aided possibly by the export from England of short-time funds — provoked an outward movement of agricultural products from the United States sufficiently large to shift temporarily the disparity in our foreign commerce.

Similarly, the bulge in 1855 of the American agricultural index seems tied up with a corresponding movement in British cereal prices. At this time the efficient cause was the situation evoked by the Crimean War — during which Russian supplies of grain were cut off — while simultaneously some contribution was made by diminished French and British harvests. By the end of 1855, however, the close of this conflict was in sight. In March, Nicholas I had died; in September, Sebastopol had fallen; and soon the diplomats were preparing for peace. The speculative movement in cereals had come to an end; and the prices of such commodities continued to fall off rather generally throughout the next years, little affected by the conditions which soon bred the crisis of 1857. Quite similar was the course of American cereal values, although in this country they recovered somewhat in 1856–57. The combination of this partial recovery in cereals with the sharp uprush of certain other agricultural prices — notably lard, tobacco, and sugar — produced the second peak in our domestic agricultural index, the peak of 1857, which in fact exceeded the high point of 1855.

Finally, foreign market conditions may again be linked with the low level of the American agricultural index in 1861–62. The decline in agricultural prices had on the average been substantially greater than in that of industrial commodities over the turn of the years 1860 to 1861; and, though an upturn did set in almost immediately, the movement was halted in the autumn of 1861, and did not begin an ascent comparable with that already exhibited by industrial prices until the fall of 1862. To be sure, the spectacular rise of the latter toward the close of 1861 is in part attributable to the scarcity value which even at that time was beginning to attach to such southern products as cotton and turpentine. In a general way, however, prices of industrial commodities shared in a broad forward movement, while the values of agricultural commodities lagged behind — butter, sugar, and tobacco being the only exceptions. The considerable dependence of cereal values on export markets may again be looked to as a cause for the divergence of our agricultural from our industrial index. Prospects of expanding needs in certain military industries, the curtailment of supplies of particular goods from southern sources, and other forces, might send up the prices of industrial products; but, until monetary inflation had occasioned an upheaval in nominal·values, prices of surplus foodstuffs would follow the calmer course of the London cereal markets.

What, in the meanwhile, was happening to the relationship between the general level of commodity prices here and that of similar prices abroad — a relationship to which attention has already been called as far as the period 1820–45 was concerned?[10] Did domestic prices remain depressed relative to those abroad, as they were at the close of this earlier period? Let us turn to a comparison of the course of domestic and of imported commodity prices for such evidence as it can offer (Chart 35).[11]

Obviously there was no decisive alteration in

[10] See above, pp. 66, 67.

[11] As the curves reproduced on this chart are really extensions of those presented on Chart 23 (p. 68, above), the base used for the earlier period, 1834–42, has been retained. The distortion which such a procedure may impart to the later years of these indices, seems of small importance, since the chief interest in this connection is the relationship between the two curves.

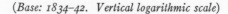

CHART 35. — UNWEIGHTED INDICES FOR DOMESTIC AND FOREIGN WHOLESALE COMMODITY PRICES:
QUARTERLY, 1843–62

(Base: 1834–42. Vertical logarithmic scale)

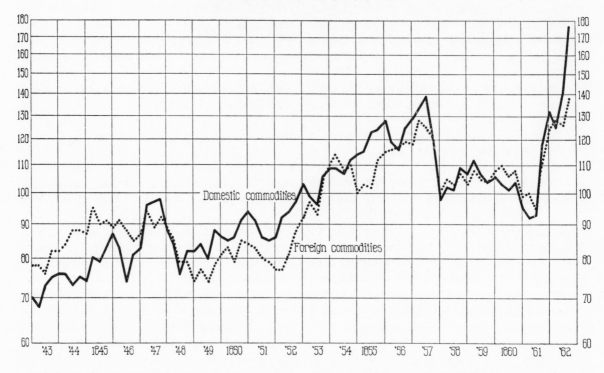

the relative position of domestic- and imported-goods prices until the close of the 'forties. The sudden bulge of domestic prices around 1847 had, to be sure, produced a temporary change; but in 1848 the earlier situation had been re-established. With the next year, however, a new era commenced. Thereafter, for nearly a decade, prices of domestic commodities ruled generally higher relative to the chosen base, than did the values of imported goods. The year of recession, 1854, forms an exception; but the next real turning point does not come until 1857. In the decline of that year, prices of domestic goods fell with greater severity than those of imported articles; and, though something of the previous relationship was renewed in 1859, the condition obviously was unstable, and the following year saw the reappearance of the situation with which this period, 1843–62, had begun.

To the student of economic history, and especially to one who has traced the vicissitudes in the external economic relationships of the United States, there is nothing surprising in these new facts — at least, if he also accepts in some

form the essentials of the classical theory of international trade adjustment. The nature of our balance of payments during these years would dictate some such alterations of relative price levels as did actually occur.[12] The temporary reversal of price levels for domestic and foreign commodities in 1847 would probably not be anticipated; nor would the brief disturbance in 1854. But such a student would expect revival of interest in the "States" by foreign investors — supported by increased net earnings of our merchant marine — to raise the prices of American goods relative to those of foreign commodities; and he would expect the greater elevation to persist as long as capital continued to flow to this country in large and expanding volume. Alteration of these dominating international influences would produce changes in the relative price levels — might even bring a reversal of relative positions. Such a result as the last surely was possible if the fears of foreign lenders regarding

[12] See the authoritative study, previously mentioned, by Bullock, Williams, and Tucker on "The Balance of Trade of the United States."

the security of their funds were pointedly aroused by the rumors of oncoming civil war.

We may stop here our consideration of domestic and foreign commodity prices with at least the following conclusions: the study of relative levels of domestic and imported commodity prices gives statistical support to the non-statistical evidence regarding the course of our international financial relationships, and the study may serve, for lack of other information, in giving indication as to the timing of the changes in these relationships.

CHAPTER XVII

VOLUME OF TRADE

HOWEVER broad may be the basis for the study of commodity-price movements, the investigator is dissatisfied if he fails to see the influence upon the changing quantum of trade, of the forces which bred these price movements, or perhaps the repercussions upon this quantum of the price movements themselves. Business is a phenomenon of both volume and price, and, if possible, inquiry should be pushed to cover consideration of changes in the physical volume of goods exchanged.

In the latter regard, it may be noted that data pertaining to the volume of business become increasingly abundant as investigation approaches the Civil-War decade. The 'fifties yield more

than the 'forties, and the latter more than the 'thirties; yet difficulties are numerous. In particular, series of long duration are rarely encountered — series which would enable one, for example, to contrast the events around 1857 with those of the "crisis" period a decade earlier. Again, series of greater than annual frequency are especially scarce until railroads began, in the 'fifties, to make their earnings available on a monthly basis. For the most part, then, the investigator is forced to make use of what he can gather together from divers sources rather than permitted to select the best of an abundant store.

Enumeration of the statistical evidence which

TABLE 26. — SERIES OF ANNUAL DATA UPON THE VOLUME OF TRADE, 1843–62*

Description	Period	Source
Tonnage received at New Orleans from the interior..........	1843–62	Congressional Documents
Tonnage carried on the Western Railroad of Massachusetts...	1843–62	Annual reports of company
Tonnage carried on all New York State canals..............	1843–62	New York State Documents
Total revenue from the main stem of the Baltimore & Ohio Railroad...	1843–62	Annual reports of company
Receipts on the Boston & Lowell Railroad..................	1843–62	Annual reports of company
Anthracite coal shipped from the Schuylkill, Lehigh, and Wyoming regions..	1843–62	*Mineral Resources of the United States*
Tonnage carried on the Chesapeake & Delaware Canal.......	1843–62	Annual reports of company
Tolls received on the Ohio State canals....................	1843–62	*History of the Ohio Canals†*
Tonnage of vessels built in the United States...............	1843–62	Congressional Documents
Auction duties paid in New York State....................	1843–62	New York State Documents
Bushels of salt made at the Onondaga salt springs...........	1843–62	New York State Documents
Redemptions at the Suffolk Bank.........................	1843–56	*Bankers' Magazine*
Tonnage carried on the Lehigh Canal......................	1843–62	Annual reports of company
Tonnage carried on the Morris Canal......................	1843–62	Annual reports of company
Tonnage carried on the Schuylkill Canal...................	1843–62	Annual reports of company
Tolls received on the Delaware & Hudson Canal.............	1843–62	Annual reports of company
Tonnage carried on the Union Canal......................	1843–62	Annual reports of company
Receipts on the Boston & Worcester Railroad...............	1843–62	Annual reports of company
Tonnage carried on the Philadelphia & Reading Railroad.....	1843–62	Annual reports of company
Value of gross merchandise imports of the United States......	1843–62	*Reports on Commerce and Navigation*
Value of gross merchandise exports from the United States....	1843–62	*Reports on Commerce and Navigation*
Stocks of leaf tobacco at the New York warehouse (monthly series)..	1843–60	*New Orleans Price Current*
Gross earnings of individual railroads (monthly series)‡.......	1853–62	Annual reports of the several companies

* Annual series, except for the last two items.
† Ohio Archeological and Historical Society.
‡ See Table 29 for a list of the individual railroads.

has been brought together for the present study is made in the accompanying table (Table 26) with information as to source, duration, and frequency of report. It may not be properly pretended that these data exhaust the available supply. Certain other series are to be secured by scrutiny of *Hunt's Merchants' Magazine* and the documents of the several States. For instance, various series relating to the whole or parts of the New York State canal system are to be found in the annual reports of the New York Canal Commissioners; and information upon the import trade through particular ports is available in the magazine just mentioned, or in other journals such as the *New York Shipping List*.[1] Nevertheless, it is believed that the more significant series have been secured — those which best reflect alterations in the volume of American business activity.

Inspection of the accumulated data reveals at once the futility of attempting to devise for the latter 'forties or early 'fifties an index of greater than annual frequency. A sufficiently large number of series on a monthly basis or even on a quarterly basis simply does not exist. Yet annual data are not without value. Despite the inconsiderateness of business fluctuations in failing to conform to a periodicity of calendar years — or, for that matter, to a periodicity derived from any other twelve-month interval — the crude measurement of change provided by an annual index seems decidedly preferable to no index at all. Moreover, it may be remarked that an annual index on the calendar-year basis has greater validity in the 'forties and 'fifties than it would have today. Canal transportation was still important, leading to a midwinter slump in trade; and the marketing of agricultural output was still slow, so that the effects of one year's crops were felt mainly in the succeeding calendar year.

At all events, an annual index of the volume of trade was compounded from eleven of the significant series above mentioned, extending from the close of the preceding business downturn (1843) to the beginnings of Civil-War inflation

[1] Some series known to exist relating to the trade of New Orleans and other southern ports are purposely omitted from this list, inasmuch as the tabulation would be much lengthened by the addition of the various items available in the *New Orleans Price Current*.

(1862). The eleven components of this index follow.

TABLE 27. — SERIES USED IN THE CONSTRUCTION OF THE INDICES ON THE VOLUME OF TRADE, 1843–62

Tonnage carried on all New York State canals
Tonnage carried on the Chesapeake & Delaware Canal
Tolls received on the Ohio State canals
Total revenue from the main stem of the Baltimore & Ohio Railroad
Receipts on the Boston & Lowell Railroad
Tonnage carried on the Western Railroad of Massachusetts
Tonnage received at New Orleans from the interior
Auction duties paid in New York State
Total tonnage of coal trade in the United States
Tonnage of vessels built in the United States
Total value of foreign merchandise trade (imports plus exports)

In the treatment of these series, no intricate statistical procedure seemed desirable or warranted. To be sure, a growth element of varying proportions in the several series had to be removed in order that cyclical changes might be more readily observed. To that end, the secular trend was computed for each.[2] Subsequently, the annual values for the several series were expressed as relatives to the respective lines of trend.

Three separate indices were in fact constructed. One included only the series pertaining to domestic commerce, and may be viewed as indicating changes in internal trade. Here, from lack of data sufficient to calculate weights, a simple arithmetic average of relatives was employed. The second index took only foreign trade into account, and was based merely upon the combined value of merchandise exports and imports. The third sought to unite domestic and foreign commerce into one index which should mirror the course of American business as

[2] The terminal years employed for these trends were 1843 and 1860; 1860 was preferred to 1862 because of the Greenback inflation of values in the latter year. Those of our series which were expressed in money terms were likely to be affected by this inflation.

A single straight-line trend was employed, except in the case of receipts on the Ohio State canals and of shipping construction in the United States. An abrupt and marked change of trend in these latter cases, manifesting itself near the middle of the period 1843–62, suggested the desirability of breaking the trends for the two series at 1850 and at 1854, respectively.

a whole. In this case, despite the absence of information upon which to base accurate procedure, a weighting was resorted to, determined by a rough estimate of the factors involved. Since the influence of imported and exported goods would be reflected in some measure in the data upon internal commerce, and since domestic trade as a whole was undoubtedly greater than the volume of goods moving through our ports, a decision was reached to give domestic trade twice the weight of foreign in the construction of this third index which should represent the course of aggregate American commerce.[3]

TABLE 28. — INDICES OF VOLUME OF TRADE, 1843–62

Year	Domestic Trade	Foreign Trade	Combined Domestic and Foreign Trade
1843.........	98	111	102
1844........	104	108	105
1845........	102	98	101
1846........	104	99	102
1847........	108	100	105
1848.........	102	90	98
1849........	94	88	92
1850........	88	97	91
1851........	93	97	94
1852........	94	98	95
1853.........	101	108	103
1854........	106	102	105
1855........	108	102	106
1856........	104	114	107
1857........	97	102	99
1858.........	91	96	93
1859........	98	104	100
1860.........	114	91	106
1861........	86	64	79
1862........	96	57	83

Of the various changes suggested by the indices (Table 28), the following are important for our purposes. First, it will be noted that the

[3] The results presented in the accompanying table include minor adjustments in the first year and the last two years. For 1843, the item of earnings on the Baltimore and Ohio Railroad was far out of line with the other evidence and has been excluded from the average for that year. The items of receipts on the Ohio State canals (1862), tonnage received at New Orleans from the interior (1861 and 1862), and tonnage of vessels built in the United States (1861 and 1862) were excluded in computing the averages for 1861 and 1862. These items showed such large deviations from the general tendencies exhibited by the other series that their inclusion would have appreciably distorted the index.

rise and the decline of domestic trade in the middle 'fifties were of substantially greater proportions than the somewhat similar movements around 1847. To be sure, the advance from 1843 to 1847 was considerable — much more than would be anticipated from an examination of the course of commodity prices or of other series in this period. Yet the movements in 1850–58 were more general, in that both domestic and foreign trade swelled and fell off; and the combined index for foreign and domestic trade stood at a higher level, as compared with the trend, in 1856 than it had in 1847. Secondly, it becomes apparent that the movement of 1850–58 was of substantial duration. This swing, although not quite equaling the rise and decline which terminated in 1843, was certainly longer than the average of post-Civil-War cycles. It is obvious that improvement in trade began as early as 1850, and that the next definite low point is not found until 1858. An advance and a decline that rule an eight- or nine-year interval are entitled to real respect. Finally, it will be observed that the volume of trade as indicated by the combined index reached peak in 1856 and was quite reduced by the crisis year, 1857. The location of the exact turning point is in fact somewhat dubious, especially in view of the small increase in the combined index between 1855 and 1856, and of the peak of domestic trade which clearly came in 1855. Annual data on railroad activity, however, may be adduced as additional evidence. These data — information on gross earnings of twenty-one roads during these years — suggest clearly that 1856, not 1855, was really the maximum year.[4] An annual index, nevertheless, is at best a crude instrument by which to select the precise point at which trade ceases to expand and retrogression sets in. For this purpose monthly data are most desirable; although, of course, even when such data are employed, precision is far from absolute.

Fortunately, it is possible to supplement this general accumulation of annual data with

[4] Such earnings (to which further reference will shortly be made) give relatives to their line of trend as follows:

1853	79	1858	94
1854	100	1859	89
1855	110	1860	98
1856	121	1861	102
1857	109	1862	128

monthly material for the important series of gross earnings for domestic railroads — to which reference has just been made. Beginning with 1853, information as to such earnings is available upon a monthly basis for a group of railroads sufficiently large in number to make month-to-month variations of some significance (Table 29).[5] The group indeed is large enough to permit division by geographical areas and the compilation of aggregates for the various sections, so that changes in conditions within these several regions are in some measure represented. The roads were, in fact, divided into three subgroups: New England, central-Atlantic, and western. The monthly aggregates for these sub-groups, together with corresponding data for the three groups combined, are presented herewith (Chart 36).

TABLE 29. — SERIES OF RAILROADS FOR WHICH MONTHLY DATA ON GROSS EARNINGS ARE AVAILABLE, 1853–62

New England sub-group
  Boston & Maine
  Cheshire
  Connecticut River
  Worcester & Nashua
  Vermont & Massachusetts (no data, December 1859–November 1860)
  New York & New Haven
Central-Atlantic sub-group
  New York Central
  Pennsylvania
  Philadelphia & Reading
  New York & Erie
  Baltimore & Ohio
Western sub-group
  Cleveland, Columbus & Cincinnati
  Sandusky, Dayton & Cincinnati
  Little Miami (no data, December 1857–November 1858)
  Michigan Central
  Michigan Southern & Northern Indiana
  Illinois Central (beginning January 1855)
  Galena & Chicago Union
  Chicago & Rock Island (beginning August 1853)
  Milwaukee & Mississippi
  St. Louis, Alton & Chicago (beginning January 1855)

---

[5] Data were not available for the Chicago and Rock Island, January–July 1853; for the Vermont and Massachusetts, December 1859–November 1860; for the St. Louis, Alton and Chicago, and the Illinois Central, 1853–54; and for the Little Miama, December 1857–November 1858. In each case, extrapolated or interpolated figures were secured by assuming that

Obviously, each combination of original data contains a marked seasonal movement. The seasonal variation is, indeed, so notable that it seems worth while to compare it with that of more modern times. The results, as far as the all-inclusive aggregates are concerned (exhibited in Chart 37), are most interesting.[6] A certain similarity between the two curves, to be sure, does appear: for example, both are lowest in February and reach peak in October; but the violence of movement is strikingly greater for the earlier decade. Not only is the maximum spread twice as great (46 points as compared with 23), but the rates of change are greater, month to month. Note, for instance, the decided slump in volume from April to July in the 'fifties, and then the tremendous upward thrust between July and September. This seasonal variation, it may be remarked parenthetically, should be taken into account in judging the effectiveness of our transportation facilities in the earlier days. Explanation of its peculiar features would involve the elements of greater predominance of agricultural production in the pre-Civil-War decades, the technical difficulties of maintaining service during the winter months,

the items for the missing series showed the same relative month-to-month movements (differences in form of seasonal variation being allowed for, except in the first two cases) as were exhibited by the average for the remaining series of the group to which the railroad in question had been assigned. For the first two roads, the differences in seasonal movement were of slight importance, and hence were neglected in making the extrapolation.

Again, it must be admitted that little endeavor has been made to eliminate the effect of such irregularity of company earnings as would derive from consolidations of previously independent railway lines or from the more gradual extension of each company's network of road. Where choice was readily possible, a uniform basis was sought, e.g., "the main stem" of the Baltimore and Ohio. Otherwise, reliance was placed upon discriminating interpretation of the data — as, for example, allowance for the element of growth — to supply the place of more accurate original material. When consideration is given the essential character of these series and the purpose to which the data were to be put, this procedure appears wholly appropriate.

[6] The index of seasonal variation for the gross earnings of railroads in the period 1853–62, computed by the link-relative method, is brought into comparison on the accompanying chart with an index similarly derived for gross earnings of ten leading railroads in the years 1903–16. The latter index was computed by Professor W. M. Persons and published by him in the first number of the *Review of Economic Statistics, op. cit.*, pp. 76–77.

CHART 36. — GROSS EARNINGS OF AMERICAN RAILROADS, MONTHLY, 1853–62: ORIGINAL DATA, AND DATA ADJUSTED FOR SEASONAL VARIATION

CHART 37. — SEASONAL VARIATION IN GROSS EARNINGS OF AMERICAN RAILROADS, 1853–62 AND 1903–16

(*Average for year = 100*)

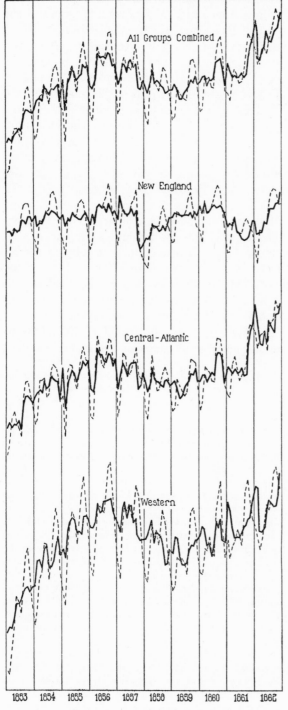

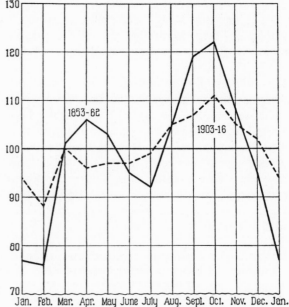

Adjustment of the original series for seasonal variation is helpful in bringing to light changes in the general course of railroad earnings (Chart 37).[7] It now appears that the conclusion suggested by the annual data is really correct: the peak in the volume of trade came in 1856, not 1857. Some months before the failure of the Ohio Life Insurance and Trust Company (August 1857), the quantity of goods exchanged — at least, as indicated by this additional, important index of that movement — was appreciably declining. It is true that a partial recovery occurred in the spring and summer of 1857 — which, indeed, terminated abruptly a month after this notable failure — but this recovery did not carry quantities to the levels reached in April to October of the preceding year.

The degree of enhancement in business activity in the years around 1856–57 obviously differed in the several sections of the country, if variation in railroad earnings be taken as in-

and the greater competition of canals and other waterways for traffic in the spring and summer.

[7] It seemed hardly worth while to attempt the removal of secular trend in these series. Only in the case of earnings for western roads is the trend sufficiently great to interfere with an immediate appraisal of the situation as revealed by the original figures or the figures adjusted for seasonal variation.

dicative of this fact. The earnings of the New England roads manifested little rise, at least in the period for which we have monthly data; and they recovered quickly from the slump after the crisis. The railroads of the central-Atlantic group showed somewhat greater advance and recession. Most striking of all, however, even if allowance be made for secular trend, was the increase of earnings by the western carriers from 1853 through 1856, and the subsequent prolonged and considerable decline until the spring of 1859. Evidently, here as in the case of other phenomena of the pre-Civil-War period, it is fruitful to differentiate the various regions of the country.

Note may also be taken of the fact that after the conclusion of the recession in 1857, no series except that pertaining to the New England railroads manifested up-and-down swings in the next few years. The course of business activity as indicated by these various data on railway receipts is indeed quite different from that which might be inferred from a study of stock values, or the prices of commodities. There is less indication here than in either of the series just mentioned, of a "short and sharp" crisis — the type of revulsion which the crisis of 1857 is sometimes assumed to have been. The series of earnings for all groups combined moved irregularly downwards until the latter half of 1859. Recovery, it seems, was well on its way when Lincoln was elected and when, soon thereafter, the country drifted into civil war.

Finally, brief consideration should be given variations in the volume of business as indicated by changes in bank clearings of New York City institutions — a matter which will be examined in greater detail later.[8] Data on such clearings, treated to eliminate secular trend and seasonal variation, show two fairly clear-cut cycles between 1855 and 1861 (Chart 42). Inasmuch as we lack data for any considerable period prior to 1855, we may perhaps assume the first cycle to have begun in the spring of this latter year. It reached a peak of considerable altitude in 1857.

[8] See below, p. 123.

The decline registered for August was moderate, but thereafter the drop was most precipitate. By October, the volume of clearings was as much below its line of trend as in July it had been above.

The recovery from this first movement was prompt; and the tendency was upward, with few signs of hesitation, until another peak was attained in October of the eventful year of 1860. The slump was again precipitate although less pronounced than in the preceding case; and bottom was reached by May 1861.

The points of chief interest in these data are: the existence of two fairly definite swings in this period of a little more than six years; the persistence of the upward trend in the first cycle past the middle of the "crisis" year; and the prompt rehabilitation that followed in 1857–58. In these particulars, there is considerable contrast between the movement of New York City clearings and that of the other indices of changing volume of trade, on the one hand, or the prices of stocks or commodities, on the other. Apparently, even as early as the latter 'fifties, the volume of combined business and financial transactions in New York City differed in performance from that of the country at large.

In sum, such evidence of all types as we have on the volume of trade in the period 1843–62 suggests (a) that after a rise and decline of moderate proportions around 1847, another advance of appreciably greater magnitude was launched with the turn of the decade; (b) that the latter movement came to a peak in 1856, probably in early autumn of that year, after which followed a broken decline lasting until the fore part of 1859; (c) that, as among regions, this principal swing in the volume of trade was least pronounced in New England and most striking in the West; (d) that after the secondary recession of September–November 1857, the course was without clearly defined movement until the autumn of 1859 when the Civil War was not far distant; and (e) that as far as New York City is concerned the movements were quite variant from those outside this growing metropolis, both in character and timing.

CHAPTER XVIII

STOCK PRICES AND PUBLIC LAND SALES

HAVING acquired a standard of comparison by examination of the course of commodity prices and fluctuations in the volume of trade, let us turn to those features of the business situation in the years 1843–62, which are commonly characterized as "speculative" — the movement of stock prices and changes in the volume of public land sales.

Reliance in the task of tracing the course of stock values may, in this period, be placed wholly upon the indices of railroad-stock prices to which reference has already been given;[1] and we

specie payments, and possibly other factors — such as the growing realization of the splendid future in store for railroads as a whole — had a marked influence upon the value of railroad stocks. From February 1843 to May 1844, there was a sharp and almost continuous rise in stock prices, which took the average of Index I from a level of 32 to one of nearly 75 — a rise more spectacular than that which had preceded the break in 1835, or, in fact, any that occurred after 1844 and prior to the advent of Greenback inflation in 1862.[3] This Index I, it will be re-

CHART 38. — INDICES OF RAILROAD-STOCK PRICES, MONTHLY, 1843–62: INDEX I (8 SELECTED STOCKS), 1843–52; INDEX IIc (18 SELECTED STOCKS), 1853–62; AND ALL-INCLUSIVE INDEX, 1843–62

(Base: 1853. Logarithmic vertical scale)

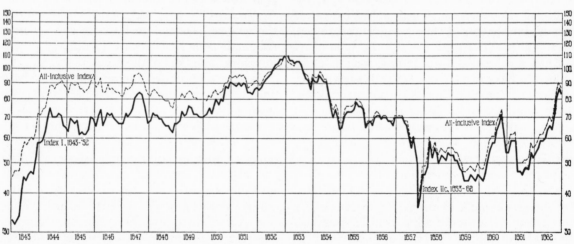

may turn at once to an inspection of the general course of such values as indicated by the all-inclusive and the special indices presented herewith (Chart 38).[2] The story may be recounted briefly.

The reappearance of cheap money in 1843, the return of confidence after the banks had resumed

called, represents the average movement of eight stocks — a group which survived after insensitive and erratic series had been discarded from the whole number collected. However, lest it seem to appear that this "sensitive" index alone experienced the sharp advance just mentioned, it may be noted that even the all-inclusive index — the one which embraced all the series available for this period — manifested a rise from a level of 45 in January 1843 to one of 88 in May 1844.

---

[1] See above, pp. 48 *seq.*

[2] The all-inclusive index, as its name suggests, embraces the whole group of available series, whereas the special indices are based upon the movement of series selected because of their representative character (see below Appendix C, pp. 177–83).

[3] The base here employed is 1853 = 100.

Thereupon values steadied. Index I reveals a flat trend for the succeeding four years, and the all-inclusive index a slightly receding one. After a small decline in 1848, these indices started upward again in December of that year, and rose quite steadily to a high point four years later (December 1852) which, indeed, was the peak for railroad-stock prices until paper money had wrought havoc with values.

In the perspective supplied by our indices, even the episode of 1847 — sometimes spoken of as a "crisis" and referred to more accurately in *Business Annals* as a "panic"[4] — appears quite different in magnitude from the movements culminating in 1835 and 1852. Although shown by our sensitive Index I as a "bulge" — or brief upheaval in the stock market — the flurry was closely encompassed within the year 1847, and occasioned no prolonged deviation of these prices from their general trend. When observed from the broader plane of our all-inclusive index, this particular rise and fall appears to be of still less moment; should not be accepted as representing a true major speculative movement; nor, of course, considered at all comparable with the British crisis of 1847 — with which, to be sure, it probably was not unconnected.

The movement of railroad-stock prices after 1852, as after the break in 1835, offers many a surprise when compared with the picture of the 'fifties as seen through the usual non-statistical accounts. From them alone, one would gain the impression of an ever-welling flood of speculation, stimulated by the rapid growth of the country, the increase of gold supplies, the rise of prices, and the renewed inflow of foreign capital — a flood of speculation which, after the sudden collapse of the Ohio Life Insurance and Trust Company, finally broke its levees; and, as Sumner says, "stocks fell 40 or 50 per cent."[5]

In fact, the movement of stock prices over these years contrasts broadly with the descriptive accounts available: it is both less spectacular and less simple. Generally speaking, it exhibits a downward course, which may be taken as representing the average change in values up to 1857. This is the picture given by Index IIc,[6]

and it is also presented by the all-inclusive index over the years 1853–62. But the downturn after 1852, as indicated by either measure, was not regular. While the declination was fairly persistent for five years, it was accelerated by rather sharp and sizable sinking spells in 1854 and 1857. With the latter, the long speculative movement which began in 1843 may be considered to have come to a close. Thereafter followed a more mixed period. Three shorter swings — 1857–59, 1859–61, and, despite the influence of paper money, 1861–65 — are revealed; and our indices end on a gentle rise of stock prices — a rise which, in fact, was not to be concluded until after the notable crisis of 1873.

In the investigation of this subject, evidence accumulated indicating that the movement of stock prices in the period 1853–62 could not be regarded as simple and uniform; nor could this movement be studied profitably as a single entity. Separation of the series into two groups appeared desirable. This was done, and the indices derived from these groups, Indices IIa (8 stocks) and IIb (10 stocks), were found to present quite diverse movements (Table 30 and Chart 39). The course described by Index IIa is

TABLE 30. — SERIES USED IN THE CONSTRUCTION OF RAILROAD-STOCK-PRICE INDICES IIa AND IIb, 1853–62

Index IIa
  Boston & Providence
  Boston & Lowell
  Eastern of Massachusetts
  Philadelphia, Wilmington & Baltimore
  Hudson River
  Panama
  Camden & Amboy
  New York & Harlem
Index IIb
  Baltimore & Ohio
  Philadelphia & Reading
  Michigan Central
  New York Central
  Illinois Central
  Cleveland & Toledo
  Chicago & Rock Island
  Chicago, Burlington & Quincy
  New York & Erie
  Michigan Southern
Index IIc is a combination of the stocks included in Index IIa and Index IIb.

typical series. As indicated by Table 30, Index IIc is a combination of Indices IIa and IIb which for part of the period now under discussion showed divergent movements.

[4] Thorp, *op. cit.*, p. 124.

[5] Sumner, *History of American Currency*, p. 183.

[6] Index IIc (1853–62) may be looked upon as a continuation of Index I (1834–52). Each represents the course of

rather surprising. Beginning in January 1853, the curve shows a pretty steady decline through the next five years, broken in notable fashion only by a particularly sharp downturn in the summer and fall of 1854 and by a minor recovery in the succeeding year. Indeed, with the advent of the "crisis" year, 1857, these stocks already had been so "deflated" that the storm of that spring and summer could force them but little lower. The speculative element had been squeezed out of them in the preceding interval.

— the "demand notes" — caught these stocks in its flow, and started them on a mad upward career — a wild ride which did not terminate until expectation of the War's sure close served to moderate the speculative tendencies of the stock market.

In the meantime — from 1853 to the period of abundant paper money — the stocks included in Index IIb had been experiencing, on the average, quite a different fate. For a while they followed the same general course as those of Index IIa,

CHART 39. — INDICES OF RAILROAD-STOCK PRICES, MONTHLY, 1853–66: INDEX IIa (8 SELECTED STOCKS) AND INDEX IIb (10 SELECTED STOCKS)

(Base: 1853.   Logarithmic vertical scale)

Moreover, the rebound of these particular stocks was quick and persistent. Progress upwards began immediately after the low point of October 1857 had been touched, and continued with scarcely an intermission until October 1860. This rise, too, was of sizable dimensions — from a nadir of 40 to a peak of 90. The decline thereafter, which lasted for a year, was undoubtedly caused by uncertainties that the election of Lincoln inspired. It did not carry Index IIa to a level anything like that from which it had departed in 1857, but a fall from 90 to 64 in a year's time is quite substantial evidence of public apprehension. During the summer of 1861, the downturn was checked; and, in the closing months of the year, renewed confidence, or the first issue of government currency

and moved downward through 1853 and 1854; but with the turn of the year 1855 they received a new impetus, and continued broadly upwards till the opening of 1857. For these stocks, 1857 was undoubtedly a "crisis" year. Their values fell precipitately from an average level of 86 in January to one of 33 in October. No débâcle corresponding to this is evident in any other of our general indices during the decades which we have had under review.

As occurred also in the case of Index IIa, the recovery of these stocks appeared promptly. In fact, their rebound was more rapid than in the other case; and by March 1858, Index IIb had regained an average level almost equal to that which it had held in July 1857. But the recovery was not sustained; and after March 1858, another decline had set in, which by the close of the succeeding year had brought prices to a point approximately equal to that of October 1857. Once more, however, an advance followed — an advance of considerable proportions — only again to suffer a substantial collapse in 1860–61. With the war years came a third upswing and after April 1864, another downturn — both of which were proportionately greater than the similar movements in Index IIa.[7]

An analysis of stock prices, then, of the period 1853–66 brings to light two quite different movements. The course of Index IIa is more orderly and shows a smaller amplitude of variation than that of Index IIb. The latter is more vigorous; more given to false starts; and, in short, more distinctly dominated by the speculative element.

Before going further into a discussion of what occurred after 1857, let us look once more at the general picture presented by the all-inclusive or special indices (Chart 38) for the period 1847–57. Whatever the differences between Indices IIa and IIb in the 5-year interval, 1853–57, unquestionably a broad movement of rising and falling values ruled stock-market prices from the spring of 1843 to the latter months of 1857 — a period of nearly a decade and a half. This general course of change embraced a rapid rise of values in 1843–44; a long interval of more gradually increasing and decreasing values, with a peak at the turn of the years 1852–53 — a peak, by the way, which had failed of notice in non-statistical material — and a precipitate decline in 1857.

Such a curiously sustained movement demands explanation. None is immediately evident. One's first thought might well be that this was another manifestation of the power exerted by the newly found California gold; but the facts appear not to bear out this view. Short-time credit for speculative purposes was not superabundant in these decades. The "plethora in the money market," which Martin notes for 1843, seems to have been rapidly absorbed; and after that date, says this same author, "the demand for money, up to 1857, was

constantly active, the Spring and Summer of 1852 being the only exception" (the latter period, it may be observed, being one of rather rapid rise in our railroad-stock index).[8] This situation of generally tight money was accounted for by Martin as due to "the immense absorption of capital by railroads, and they being constant borrowers in the market at high rates of interest. For a period of thirteen years, there was hardly a time when money could be had outside of banks at six per cent, except in 1852." As a matter of fact, money rates in the New York market ranged around eight to ten per cent through most of these years. What must they have been in other, less well developed parts of the country? No, cheap and plentiful credit for speculation does not seem to have been the sufficient cause.

Explanation of this long-continued swing of values is perhaps best found in the contributions of several factors. Cheap money may in truth have caused the sharp rise of 1843–44; but the sustained strength thereafter seems due to the rapid development of the country; the inflow (with the later 'forties) of much capital from abroad; and perhaps even the high short-time and, presumably high, long-time rates themselves since these high rates possibly served to check such violent speculation as would have led soon to overextension of credit and the collapse of the "house of cards." Possibly the concomitance of a prosperous country, inflowing capital, and high interest rates, all acting together, was adequate to create stability.

Of the period 1858–66, little need be said. It comprises the least interesting years of the decades now under review. The first three or four years were characterized by false starts, alternate fevers and chills, which probably were not unconnected with the uncertain political situation; while the final downturn, that of the autumn of 1860, was undoubtedly a premonition of approaching conflict. Thereupon followed a somewhat longer swing of prices, lasting until 1865, which, as already intimated, was chiefly a creature of cheap money, war-time prosperity, and (as to its culmination) the subsequent prospect of peace. Little distinguishes this movement from many later ones, beyond the great enhancement of values which flowed from the

[7] A comparison of the two indices on this latter point is interesting. The low and high points are, respectively:

	Low point in 1861	High point in 1864	Low point in 1865
Index IIa	64	164	130
Index IIb	36	134	87

[8] Martin, *op. cit.*, p. 34.

CHART 40. — GEOGRAPHICAL INDICES OF RAILROAD-STOCK PRICES, QUARTERLY, 1843–62;
NEW ENGLAND, 1843–62; CENTRAL-ATLANTIC, 1843–62; AND WESTERN, 1853–62

(Base: 1853. Logarithmic vertical scale)

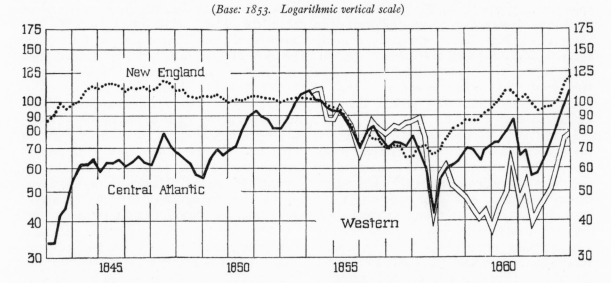

Greenback inflation. The curtain may be quickly drawn, while we turn to another aspect of the present study.

GEOGRAPHICAL DIFFERENCES

Ascertainment of significant differences in the movements of Indices IIa and IIb naturally provoked interrogation as to cause. Was there anything in the constitution of these indices which would account, at least in part, for the variant actions of the two curves? And at once attention was drawn to the fact that each index was constructed largely from series which pertained to railroads in a particular section of the country. Index IIa was predominantly an eastern index; while in Index IIb the western stocks outnumbered the eastern. Moreover, it was found that many of the series previously discarded in the make-up of Index I (for 1834–53) represented stocks of railroads located in still another part of the nation.

Although it was realized that the story could be fairly well deduced from the evidence already at hand, it was decided for purposes of clear determination to bring together into a trio of supplementary indices the stock-price series related, respectively, to the New England, central-Atlantic, and western states.[9] In each group none were to be eliminated, excepting those which showed peculiarly erratic movements. The re-

sults (presented in Chart 40) were worth the additional effort.

The contrasts among these three indices are striking. Note, for example, the moderate and restrained character in the movement of the New England railroad stocks. Regarding these securities, it will be recalled that the course of values in the period 1834–43 had been phlegmatic: the rise and fall in 1834–37 had been distinctly moderate; the recovery after 1837 came

[9] Series used in the construction of these geographical indices were:

New England group
    Boston & Lowell
    Boston & Providence
    Boston & Worcester
    Eastern of Massachusetts
    Western of Massachusetts

Central-Atlantic group
    Baltimore & Ohio
    Camden & Amboy
    Philadelphia & Reading
* { Mohawk & Hudson
    Philadelphia, Wilmington & Baltimore
* { Paterson
    Hudson River
    New York Central (beginning with July 1853)

Western group
    Chicago & Rock Island
    Chicago, Burlington & Quincy
    Cleveland & Toledo
    Illinois Central
    Michigan Central

* Adjusted to form a continuous series.

with promptness; and the high level when once attained had been well maintained.[10] Accordingly, the index of these stocks starts in 1843 at quite a different level from that of the central-Atlantic railroad group. Now, in the years through 1862, these New England securities manifested a peculiar quality. Their rise in 1843–44 was small; after 1847, a downward trend became evident, even while the values of the central-Atlantic group were still rising; these stocks appear to have been "deflated" before the crisis of 1857 supervened; and they advanced fairly steadily throughout the remainder of our period.

As might well be suspected, the index for the central-Atlantic group follows largely the course of Indices I and IIa (Charts 38 and 39) — in the construction of which its series played a dominant rôle. Some differences, however, are to be observed. For instance, in this new geographical index, the upward rush after the spring of 1843 is somewhat less considerable than that in the special Index I, and the decline after 1852 is of somewhat smaller magnitude prior to the sidewise movement in 1855–56. However, the general contour remains the same.

Similarly, the index for the western group is closely akin to Index IIb. In fact, it is not easy to discover differences between these two. The only notable one is the varying persistence of speculation before the break in 1857. Whereas the turn in Index IIb came with January of that year, the decline in the index for the western roads did not appear until July — in fact, a month later even than when the other general index, IIa, already much deflated, began appreciably to feel the force of the disturbed conditions.

These varying contours of the indices for the central-Atlantic and western groups, in so far as they cover similar time-periods, call for explanation. Obviously, while both groups of stocks were affected by the high interest rates which ruled in 1853 and 1854, the central-Atlantic railroads suffered less than the western roads. On the other hand, values of the former did not respond so actively to the subsequent, very moderate easing of the money market: the index for the western roads rose in March 1857 to a point nearly as high as that held in June 1854, while that for the central-Atlantic moved sidewise until it began to fall precipitately in the early part of 1857. The decline for the central-Atlantic group, at this time, while more rapid, was not appreciably greater than had occurred in 1853–54; whereas in the case of the western roads, the fall of values, compressed chiefly between June and October 1857, was particularly abrupt. Such peculiarities of the latter index, together with the sudden rebound of prices up to March 1858, the renewed deflation in 1858–60 (when the eastern part of the country on the whole was enjoying prosperity), and the sharp rise and fall of 1860–61 — all seem to suggest a predominant speculative element in the western securities.

These western stocks were, to be sure, much more tarred with speculation than those embraced in the central-Atlantic group. While, of course, the possibilities of development were hardly touched in such cases as the growing trunk lines, the future of the Paterson or the Hudson River railroads could be more accurately appraised than that of such lines as the Illinois Central or Michigan Southern. Moreover, land grants by the national government and the various States attracted attention to the western roads at this time, making them seem more desirable objects of investment. Foreign capital, as well as domestic, flowed into these railroad shares, a particularly well-known incident being the interest taken by Richard Cobden in the Illinois Central.[11] Supported in such ways, speculation persisted longer in the face of worsening conditions than in the case of eastern roads; and the deflation after 1857, lasting till the spring of 1860, was in part the cost to speculators of the early enthusiasm which, as it turned out, had had insufficient foundations.

In short, there appears here a westward movement. In the period before 1845, a contrast existed between the New England and the central-Atlantic railroads, when the latter provided greater possibilities of future gain than roads hampered by the conservative attitude of the Massachusetts legislature.[12] Subsequent to

[10] See pp. 49–51 above.

[11] Morley, John, *Life of Richard Cobden* (1908), vol. 2, pp. 202–3. See also Jenks, *op. cit.*, pp. 169–70.
[12] See above, p. 50.

that date, speculative interest shifted to the newer areas, leaving the railroads of the central-Atlantic states in an intermediate position, not so well established as the lines around Boston, but also not so subject to the play of speculative forces as those located in the untried West.

Public Land Sales

The chief medium of speculation, during the decades 1843–62, other than common stocks was public lands. Two major rises of speculative dealings in the sale of lands — those which reached peak in 1818 and 1836 — had not sufficed to cure the country of recurrent excess of enthusiasm for investment in the public domain. The years under survey include two periods of speculation in public lands, one culminating in 1847 and the other in 1854–55 (see heavy line in Charts 13–16).[13]

The first of these upswings in the sale of public lands was minor in comparison with the heights attained in 1818, 1836, or 1854–55. Receipts in the maximum (third) quarter of 1847 did not quite total $1,000,000, whereas the corresponding peaks in the other speculative periods fell little short of $5,000,000, $8,500,000, and $4,000,000, respectively. In the middle 'forties, to be sure, there was less uniformity of movement in the curves for the individual States than is true of these other occasions (see charts just mentioned). Yet the contour of the curve for total land sales does follow a rising and falling course between the third quarter of 1842 and the second quarter of 1850, and there is sufficient similarity of movement in sales by the several States so that the upward and downward course of the national data cannot be looked upon as chaotic or due to the operation of local factors. The rise after 1842 is particularly marked in the case of Indiana, Wisconsin, Iowa, and Florida, but other States, such as Mississippi or even Ohio, shared in the movement to greater or less degree.

The culmination of the upward movement, as just indicated, came in the third quarter of 1847, although, of course, the variations in movement among the several States gives less significance to this peak than might otherwise be the case. The fact that the turn occurs in 1847, however,

becomes of greater significance when the course of land sales is brought into comparison with that of commodity prices. It will be recalled that the index of commodity values, and especially that of agricultural goods, moved upward from 1843 to 1847, and then downward. The coincidence of movement of land sales with that of agricultural prices gives additional support to the notion that this "crisis" of 1847 was particularly western and non-industrial in character.

A more striking movement appeared in the middle 'fifties, as already suggested. Powerful forces of wide incidence appear to have been operating, as was the case in the movement which reached its peak in 1836. Here again nearly all the States were more or less affected. In some, e.g., Ohio and Indiana, there was, admittedly, no appreciable upswing, but a halt did occur for a few years in a movement of decline that was well begun; and this halt was followed by a decrease too precipitate to be attributed to particular or local causes. In other cases, notably Wisconsin, Minnesota, and Iowa, the boom was exceptionally pronounced. At this time, as in earlier occasions, the newer areas were those specially affected. Indeed, here is again evidence of that western movement in the speculative purchases of public lands to which attention has already been called.[14]

This extraordinary increase in public land purchase, which in 1854 and 1855 reached levels not far below those attained in 1818, is of further interest by reason of its peculiar timing. It was not a movement which, like that of 1818 and 1836, was closely tied up with a major business crisis. Apparently, it rose and fell without appreciable effect upon the business conditions of the period. Moreover, this movement does not march in step with the major changes in stock prices or with the course of commodity values. The most that appears possible in the way of explanation is that an expansion in public land transactions which had its genesis in the rising tide of immigration (after the Revolution of 1848 in Europe), the prospective enactment of the graduation scheme, and possibly the enlivened interest in the West which was derived from the California gold discoveries, attracted the attention and resources of speculators after the downturn of stock values at the beginning

[13] See pp. 55-58, above.

[14] See above, p. 56.

of 1853. But the dénouement is still something of a mystery. Surely not all these huge areas transferred to private possessors in 1854–55 went at once to *bona fide* settlers. If not, how did the falling off of interest in public lands after 1855 occur — a falling off evidenced by sharply reduced new sales — without upsetting general business conditions? Was the capital brought over by immigrants, together with that being sent over at this time by their compatriots for investment in the rising young country, sufficient to keep the land speculators from serious, immediate financial loss? Surely with New York money rates what they were at this period — ranging around ten per cent and in December 1854 shooting up to fifteen per cent — an explanation which relied wholly on the influence of domestic factors must be unsatisfying. Yet the hypothesis implied in these latter comments is offered with great hesitation and only in the hope of stimulating research looking toward the right solution.[15]

[15] For a complete picture of the public land activity in the period of the 'fifties, note should be made of the influence of the graduation scheme. Little attention was given to this feature since its effect was social rather than financial. In consequence of its provisions, more land passed from the Government into private hands, but this did not have appreciable effect upon the business situation.

In 1854 Congress passed the graduation scheme, as it was called, under the terms of which land that had been in the market for a given period was to be lowered in price according to a specified gradation. Substantial areas of land were taken up under this Act, and accordingly a disparity appeared between the data on receipts by the Treasury and on acreage sold. Prior to 1854, as already stated, these two series moved with almost exact similarity. Under "graduation," however, the two series diverged. Utilizing the low point in sales of 1852 as a base (100) the movement of the two elements in subsequent fiscal years through 1860 may be indicated by the following series of relatives:

	1853	1854	1855	1856	1857	1858	1859	1860
Receipts.......	372	846	769	342	220	119	134	108
Acreage	423	1433	1337	586	471	409	448	284

Although the data on acreage transferred to private ownership are valuable chiefly for purposes other than the present

At least the following conclusions may be drawn from this brief survey of the sale of public lands in 1843–62: (a) two up-and-down swings occurred during this period, one of minor character culminating in 1847 and the other of extraordinary proportions possessing a double peak in the years 1854–55; (b) there was a westward trend in the areas most affected in these movements, especially as compared with similar episodes in the earlier decades; and (c) the timing of the peaks in the movements of these decades, relative to the course of commodity prices, tended to agree with that observed so clearly in the years 1818–45, i.e., anticipation by land sales of commodity-price declines. To be sure, the case is not clear in 1847. There are two peaks in land sales at about that turning point, one in the second quarter of 1846 and another — slightly lower — in the third quarter of 1847; while the lack of uniformity of movement in land sales among the several States at this time makes the possible argument in favor of the earlier date of dubious value. Surely, however, the break in land sales during the 'fifties anticipated by almost two years the collapse of commodity prices. While, then, the evidence favors the relationship observed in the earlier decades, perhaps we had best postpone further discussion of this matter until other series — banking and financial data — may conveniently be brought into consideration.

study, it is of interest to note that as far as volume of land sales on the acreage basis is concerned, the heights reached in 1854–55 compare much more favorably with that of 1818 or 1836 than do the Treasury receipts from these sales. Again, using 1852 as a turning point (100) the quantity of land transferred in 1818 was about fourfold (a relative of 391 on this base), and that in 1836 was approximately twenty-two times (a relative of 2242); whereas, as just indicated, sales in 1854 and 1855 were respectively over fourteen and thirteen times those of 1852.

Data used in the above computation are drawn from the Annual Reports of the General Land Office. They differ from those presented by Hibbard (*op. cit.*, p. 106). His figures through 1850 appear to be for calendar years, whereas thereafter they relate to fiscal years ending June 30th.

CHAPTER XIX

BANKING AND FINANCE

OF all types of business data, those relating to banking and to certain phases of finance are among the most difficult to secure for the decades before regular and trustworthy state or federal reporting systems had been devised. Even though no index of commodity prices is immediately available in the news-sheets of the 'forties and 'fifties, the raw material for such an index is procurable with relative ease; and the same is true in greater or less degree of stock values and of the volume of trade. On the other hand, not only are there no indices available in the fields of banking and finance, but the few good series pertaining to these fields that are obtainable cannot be increased in number without exceptional research. In fact, it is very doubtful if we shall ever have much more evidence of a statistical character upon these aspects of the pre-Civil-War decades than we possess now — and that is all too little of a desirable sort.

Let us examine the banking field. Here the best figures exist — quite a handful. Of course, no series of such figures derive from contemporary direct inspection or investigation by federal authorities. Of State figures, many must be discarded as too irregular or too broken to give an adequate or accurate picture of banking experience in these years. The data with respect to a number of States have gaps especially around 1852–53. Moreover, reports dated March and August in one year may be followed by summaries for January and October in the succeeding year. Without data for the removal of seasonal variation (an element which from various sources we have come to believe must have been of considerable importance in all parts of the country), such statistics are of dubious value in tracing year-to-year or infra-annual changes in the volume of credit outstanding, in the ratio of deposits to specie, and the like. Something of the condition of these State figures is secured from the accompanying tabulation.

Inspection of such a tabulation necessarily throws considerable doubt upon the figures published by the Secretary of the Treasury for aggregates representing banking conditions for the United States as a whole — figures which for lack of better data have been sometimes employed in the study of conditions before the Civil War.[1] Especially misleading are the aggregates for loans and discounts in the first half of the 'fifties. Investigation of the constituent series indicates that undoubtedly there was no such rapid rise in the volume of loans and discounts between 1853 and 1855 as the Treasury figures suggest (from 208 millions to 576 millions). The aggregates with respect to circulation are also untrustworthy for these same years; while in all probability the series with respect to specie and deposits contain some errors, as, for example, the increase in deposits from January 1857 to January 1858. Finally, it may be remarked that the series for the important State of New York were found defective as presented in the reports of the Secretary of the Treasury — as, for example, through the confusion of individual and total deposits; and the data could be purified only after a thorough recasting of the State quarterly returns, sometimes even by recourse to the returns of individual banks.[2]

The possibility of securing results of some value, however, exists in the fact that for the States most important from the banking point of view — namely, Massachusetts, Rhode Island, New York, and Pennsylvania — annual data may be obtained relating to the fall months; while for another group of States located chiefly in the South and West — namely, Maryland, Virginia, Ohio, Kentucky, Alabama, Louisiana, and Missouri — annual data are obtainable rel-

[1] See the Annual Reports of the Secretary of the Treasury on the "Condition of State Banks," op. cit. See p. 74, footnote 2. The aggregates are said to represent conditions "according to returns nearest to January first."

[2] To some extent, resort was necessary to interpolation in the acquisition of these composite figures. For example, data were missing for the years 1843 and 1844 in the case of Rhode Island. In such cases it was assumed that the figures in the defective series moved with those in the series for which full data were available.

TABLE 31. — SERIES OF ANNUAL BANKING DATA AVAILABLE, 1843–62

	Period	No. of Years	Months in which Banking Data were Reported	No. of Times
State Banks				
Alabama.....................	1843–51	18	January	14
	1853–61		November	2
			December	2
Connecticut...................	1843–60	19	January	1
	1862		March	3
			April	13
			May	2
Delaware....................	1843–51	18	January	17
	1853–61		December	1
Indiana......................	1843–60	18	October	4
			November	13
			December	1
Kentucky....................	1843–62	20	January	20
Louisiana....................	1843–61	19	January	8
			April	1
			October	2
			December	8
Maine.......................	1843–62	20	January	11
			October	7
			December	2
Maryland....................	1843–45	18	January	17
	1847–51		December	1
	1853–62			
Massachusetts................	1843–62	20	May	1
			July	1
			August	3
			September	4
			October	11
Michigan....................	1843–60	18	January	9
			December	9
Mississippi...................	1854–58	5	January	5
Missouri.....................	1843–50	18	January	13
	1853–62		November	1
			December	4
New Hampshire...............	1843–61	19	Semi-annually from 1847 on	
			June	19
			September	1
			December	15
New Jersey...................	1843–51	19	January	18
	1853–62		"Near close of year"	1
New York....................	1843–62*	20	Quarterly	20
Ohio........................	1843–62†	20	Quarterly	20
Pennsylvania.................	1843–62	20	October	1
			November	19
Rhode Island.	1845–62	18	January	2
			September	8
			October	3
			November	2
			December	3

* Second quarter 1843 missing.

† Many entries missing.

TABLE 31. — (*Continued*)

	Period	No. of Years	Months in which Banking Data were Reported	No. of Times
Tennessee......................	1854–61	8	January	7
			October	1
Vermont.......................	1843–62	20	July	1
			August	17
			October	2
Virginia.......................	1843–51	19	January	18
	1853–62		November	1
Wisconsin.....................	1854–62	9	January	9
City Banks				
Baltimore.....................	1843–62	20	January	20
Boston........................	1843–62*	20	May	1
			July	1
			August	3
			September	3
			October	11
			November	1
New York.....................	1843–62†	20	Quarterly	20
Richmond.....................	1843–48	16	January	16
	1850–52			
	1854–60			

* Weekly from June 1854.

† Weekly from Aug. 1853, 1843–48 defective, especially as regards deposits.

ative to the winter months — that is, around January first. For those two groups — which for convenience we will designate as Groups A and B — the movements of the more important series are indicated in the following tabulation (Table 32) — namely, loans, deposits, circulation, the ratio of loans and discounts to deposits plus circulation, and the ratio of specie to combined circulation and deposits.[3]

As one scans these data, he is impressed by a number of rather significant phenomena. For example, he is struck with the rather slow development of banking resources in the decade of the 'forties. It will be recalled that the year 1843 marks a low point in a downward movement of business conditions which had been long continued and severe. Recovery in 1844 and 1845 was to be anticipated, but after the latter date expansion was small for several years — especially as compared with the movement which set in with 1850. Possibly the sluggishness of the banking growth in the later 'forties is trace-

[3] Cf. explanatory note for Group B, Table 32.

able ultimately to the failure of foreign loans to flow into the country in the volume which obtained prior to 1840 and again, after the restoration of British confidence, in the 'fifties; while the more rapid rise of the banking series after 1849 is traceable not only to the latter factor but to the expansion of specie holdings which derived, of course, from the increased gold production of this period.

Another feature of these figures is the lack of any general cyclical movement around the so-called "crisis of 1847." In the eastern States (Group A), to be sure, there is a distinct advance between 1846 and 1847 in the volume of loans and discounts, deposits, and circulation (although a part of this increase is merely recovery from a decrease registered for the preceding year); and this advance was followed by a considerable decline before the autumn of 1848. Moreover, there appeared a marked increase in the ratio of loans and discounts to deposits plus circulation between 1847 and 1848 — as if the banks had at that time found themselves under the necessity of coming to the support of business; while the specie ratio in the same period fell to a new low point. On the other hand, the banks in the West and South (Group B) appear to have ridden through this "crisis" without significant difficulty. A rise and fall in the volume of circulation does appear in a minor degree around 1847, but otherwise the most that may be observed in these banking data is a hesitation in rapidity of growth — not a real cyclical movement. Though agricultural prices were affected more than industrial,[4] and though public land sales rose and fell around this year,[5] the evidence on banking matters points to a geographically restricted incidence of the disturbances that reached peak in 1847. Possibly western banks did call for aid from their correspondent and reserve-holding institutions in the East — and maybe the changes in eastern bank data are evidence of such "calls;" but perhaps the New York and other eastern institutions were able fully to meet these requests for help, and the difficulties subsided before the banks in the West began to show signs of strain. The fact that the "crisis" broke in the summer instead of the fall is significant in this regard.

On the other hand, the existence of strained and, on the whole, worsening banking conditions in the years preceding 1857 is abundantly evident. Especially noteworthy is the persistently low ratio of specie to deposits plus circulation. Deposits expanded with particular rapidity; while the volume of specie holdings of the banks — despite the California gold output — did not increase so fast. Here, however, it is worth noting that the expansion of deposits plus circulation was distinctly greater in the case of the States of Group A than in those of Group B — particularly in the years immediately preceding the crisis of 1857. Circulation in the Group B areas showed no significant increase after the high point of 1853, and deposits expanded only 10 per cent. To be sure, the peaks in 1853 represented the culmination of a considerable rise, but this advance (after 1848) was no greater than that contemporaneously experienced in the Group A region. If the States of the latter group be taken as representative of the more

populous and more industrial East, and the States in the former as typical of the western and southern areas, the crisis of 1857 would seem to have had at least its germination in the eastern area. When the crisis descended, on the other hand, the two sections appear to have shared almost equally in the later collapse. Indeed the decline in deposits plus circulation in 1856–57 was in fact somewhat larger proportionately for the Group B than for the Group A banks (26 per cent as compared with 22 per cent). As to whether, as sometimes asserted, this "crisis" was particularly, if not predominantly, an eastern phenomenon, the data are by no means clear.[6]

Additional features of these data are the severity of the reaction in 1853–54 experienced by the southern and western regions (Group B) — a reaction which the communities of the East as a group appear to have almost wholly escaped;[7] the persistent low ratio of specie to demand liabilities in the case of Group A banks from 1853 through 1856 — a situation suggesting continued strain on these eastern institutions and a failure on their part to make ready for even worse business conditions; and the advance with respect to both groups of banks in the ratio of loans and discounts to demand liabilities between 1856 and 1857, as if banking institutions the country over came to the rescue of business after the outbreak of crisis conditions in August 1857.

Finally, it may be noted that the crisis of 1857 produced no long-extended or severe re-adjustment of banking conditions. In nearly all cases, the year 1858 gives evidence of a considerable upward reaction; while in the succeeding year, tendencies apparent in the foregoing period reappear. For example, in the States of both Group A and Group B, deposits again reached record volume, and the ratio of specie to deposits plus circulation was again normal (or better). Possibly, the greater volume of gold resulting from the new mining had the effect of permitting

[4] See above, p. 98.
[5] See above, p. 114 and Charts 13–16.

[6] See below, pp. 131 et seq.
[7] New York City banks did not escape (cf., pp. 122–25, but these have a special relation to western institutions as caretakers of reserves for the latter banks. Seemingly, here, the difficulties of the East were confined to the banking center, although in 1847 troubles had been severe enough to affect the eastern banks generally — probably in repercussion from New York City.

TABLE 32. — CONDITION OF BANKS FOR FOUR STATES (GROUP A) FOR WHICH ANNUAL DATA ARE AVAILABLE AS OF THE LATE FALL; AND OF SEVEN STATES (GROUP B) FOR WHICH ANNUAL DATA ARE AVAILABLE AS OF THE FIRST OF THE YEAR, 1842–62

Group A*

Year (c. Nov. of year)	Loans and Discounts Unit: $1,000,000	Deposits Unit: $1,000,000	Circulation Unit: $1,000,000	Ratio of Loans and Discounts to Deposits plus Circulation (Unit: one per cent)	Ratio of Specie to Deposits plus Circulation (Unit: one per cent)
1842	127	35	28	202	25
1843	136	51	35	159	28
1844	161	58	44	159	18
1845	170	60	48	158	16
1846	165	55	51	157	14
1847	187	62	61	152	15
1848	172	51	48	173	13
1849	194	65	53	164	13
1850	222	80	58	161	13
1851	229	81	62	160	12
1852	276	107	69	157	12
1853	308	121	81	153	11
1854	322	124	78	159	11
1855	344	136	77	162	11
1856	382	152	83	162	10
1857	350	124	60	190	12
1858	371	163	63	165	24
1859	376	162	67	164	17
1860	411	177	76	164	14
1861	372	179	67	152	24
1862	386	280	101	101	15

* Group A. — Massachusetts, Rhode Island, New York, and Pennsylvania.

a more rapid and substantial rehabilitation of financial conditions.

Additional evidence concerning banking conditions in the decades after 1843 is supplied by the data relating to New York City banks.[8] As the result of the supervision of banking in New York State, which began as early as 1829 and which was extended and improved in 1843 and again in 1853, information regarding New York City banks is available in quite regular quarterly figures from 1843 on.[9] In fact, weekly

figures may be secured subsequent to the middle of 1853. While the data for the years 1843 onward are not without defects in quality, they are (when purified) of sufficient abundance and accuracy to give us a fairly satisfactory picture of changing circumstances in the New York money market.[10]

While these data in their crude form are dominated by the element of growth, variations due apparently to changes in general business conditions are not wholly obliterated. Following the sharp recovery of 1843–44, such series as deposits and circulation show steady, though less rapid, advances into the early fall of 1847. The increase was particularly pronounced in the last twelve months of the rise, and the reaction

[8] As already indicated in Table 31, material is available regarding both Boston and Baltimore banks as well as those in New York City. Although these data were transcribed and examined, they did not seem to warrant the discussion here of their peculiar features.

For further discussion of the New York City material itself, than appears in the subsequent paragraphs, see below, p. 126 ff.

[9] Infra-annual data for the years 1829–42, are rather fragmentary.

[10] The data regarding New York City banks and their operations are unsatisfactory in many regards. For a detailed description of sources, see pages 196–97 of Appendix E.

TABLE 32. — *(continued)*

Group B*

(Although these data relate to January first or close to that date, it was thought that they more accurately portrayed the condition of the banks for the end of the preceding year rather than of the year following January first. They have therefore been labeled as of the year preceding January first in each case, and are therefore comparable with data of Group A which relate to the fall months.)

Year (c. Jan. 1st of year following)	Loans and Discounts *Unit: $1,000,000*	Deposits *Unit: $1,000,000*	Circulation *Unit: $1,000,000*	Ratio of Loans and Discounts to Deposits plus Circulation	Ratio of Specie to Deposits plus Circulation	
					Louisiana included *(Unit: one per cent)*	Louisiana excluded *(Unit: one per cent)*
1842	60	13	12	232	46	38
1843	55	18	17	159	55	42
1844	62	20	20	151	47	35
1845	72	24	27	141	36	29
1846	74	25	31	133	34	29
1847	80	25	36	132	36	29
1848	82	26	35	135	36	28
1849	84	27	40	125	32	27
1850	93	30	45	124	28	25
1851	100	29	44	137	27	24
1852	97	38	47	114	25	22
1853	121	41	55	126	25	21
1854	107	35	43	137	26	23
1855	119	44	54	122	28	25
1856	126	44	56	126	22	20
1857	106	36	38	142	32	24
1858	128	54	59	113	32	25
1859	147	54	62	126	27	22
1860	136	48	62	124	30	22
1861	108	40	58	110	34	28

* Group B.—Maryland, Virginia, Ohio, Kentucky, Alabama, Louisiana, and Missouri.

of the later months brought the values by May 1848 down to approximately the same level as those for August 1846. This sudden rise and fall is quite similar to that displayed by commodity prices in the same interval.[11] Later reactions, particularly obvious in the figures for deposits but evident also in those for circulation and discounts, put in an appearance in the middle of 1851, in 1853–54, in 1857, and in 1859. The events of 1854 seem fully as striking as those of 1857, while the reactions of 1851 and 1859 appear less considerable in degree.

So important are these New York City data for a study of business conditions in the country that it has seemed worth while to submit them to minor statistical treatment. In the case of loans and discounts and of "net" deposits (i.e.,

[11] See Chart 30, p. 94, above.

"due depositors") — cases in which the data are most complete — the quarterly values have been expressed as relatives to the line of trend for the whole period 1843–60. The results thereby attained (Chart 41) confirm in some measure the observations drawn from a view of the original material. For the first years, to be sure, there is an unexpected phenomenon. In loans and discounts and in deposits appeared a rise and fall extending from 1843 to 1848. In large measure, however, the decline after 1844 is due to the statistical procedure employed in the attempt to correct for growth. Even though a compound interest curve was used, the sluggishness of the advance of the absolute quantities in 1844–46 yielded declining values when these actual data were expressed as relatives to the line of trend. While the retardation of bank expansion at this

CHART 41. — TOTAL LOANS AND DISCOUNTS, AND NET DEPOSITS (DUE DEPOSITORS) OF
NEW YORK CITY BANKS: QUARTERLY, 1843–62

(Actual data expressed as relatives to their respective lines of trend for the period 1843–60)

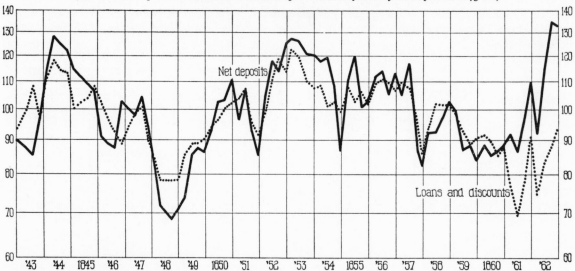

period is not without significance, of greater importance for our immediate purposes are the advance in 1843–44 and the brief rise and fall especially noticeable in deposits in the years of 1846–47 — a rise and fall which elimination of trend does not obscure.

Toward the close of the succeeding year another advance set in which, broken by a substantial recession in 1851, reached its peak in the spring of 1853. After a gradual decline of nearly two years' duration — especially precipitous in the fall of 1854 — came a recovery which kept values high until the middle of the crisis year, 1857. In this connection special note may be made of three features, namely: (a) that the high point with respect to both net deposits, and loans and discounts was reached in 1853, more than four years prior to the outbreak of major crisis conditions; (b) that the volume of net deposits exhibited a sharp decline followed by an equally rapid recovery between the middle of 1854 and the summer of 1855; and finally, (c) that for both deposits, and loans and discounts, there is evidence of a long-continued movement lasting from the middle of 1848 until the end of 1857, in which the reverses of 1851 and 1854

may be looked upon as recessions instead of terminal points in true "cyclical" swings.[12]

Subsequent to the crisis of 1857, recovery in the succeeding year soon spent itself, and a decline early in 1859 ushered in a year or two of uncertain movements until the banking system began to feel the effects of the War and of wartime inflation.

For the period after the middle of 1853, it is possible to secure still more detailed records of events in the New York money market. From the weekly figures of loans and "net" deposits which, with other banking data, were required to be published each week by the New York institutions and which were assembled for publication by the newly organized Clearing House, it is possible to derive monthly averages for both these important series. Moreover, after September 1853, it is possible to utilize the data on total clearings of New York City banks, now for the first time gathered and published by the new Clearing House organization. After the elimination of trend and correction for seasonal variation, these data of both varieties show, even more clearly than the quarterly figures above described, the ups and downs of banking

[12] The curve for loans and discounts might be regarded as having reached bottom in 1861 rather than in 1857. Inasmuch, however, as the sharp decline in the spring of 1861 is undoubtedly associated with apprehension of bankers over political conditions, this last phenomenon may legitimately be

disregarded. If so, the movement of this series, like that of deposits, becomes one of substantially even trend in the years after the crisis; and, accordingly, the earlier date (1857) may be considered the close of any such prolonged movement as that spoken of above.

conditions in the years which these figures cover (Charts 42 and 43).[13]

Unfortunately the data on loans and on deposits are defective for the first year or so (through June 1854). One cannot be certain of the exact character of the figures presented as "loans and discounts" or as "deposits" for these months. Accordingly, Chart 43 has been abbreviated to cover only the period subsequent to June 1854. For somewhat similar reasons, this chart is also made to end with the year 1860.

Our consideration of the quarterly figures suggested that the movements evidenced in 1853 and 1854 by these adjusted data are to be interpreted as features of an up-and-down swing which probably began in 1848. Subsequent to the close of 1854, however, the variations described by these several monthly series may be considered quite apart from the quarterly data already presented.

cipitate decline, with the result that by October of that same year, the curve was as much below the line of trend as in July it had been above. Recovery was fairly prompt, and again values moved upwards, reaching peak towards the close of 1860 — specifically, in October. The subsequent decline lasted until May of the next year, after which time values became so confused by paper-money issues that (unadjusted) they ceased to mirror true "cyclical" changes.

Both of the other series manifest something of the same general movement described by clearings, although loans show greater similarity than deposits. Two up-and-down swings appear in the cycle figures for loans: the one, December 1854 through to November 1857; the other, commencing two months later and ending in the middle of 1861.[14] Although this second swing is broken by a subsidence and recovery in 1859, the general contour over the eight-year period

CHART 42. — CYCLES OF TOTAL CLEARINGS FOR NEW YORK CITY BANKS: MONTHLY, 1853–62

CHART 43. — CYCLES OF LOANS AND NET DEPOSITS FOR NEW YORK CITY BANKS: MONTHLY, 1854–60

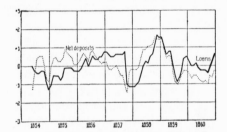

In all these cases, it will be noted that clear-cut swings are in evidence for the greater part of the remaining period. Of the series studied, the course displayed by that of clearings is the most simple as well as the most extreme. From a low point in March 1855, an advance began which proceeded with little hesitation until July 1857. The crisis brought an exceedingly pre-

is on the whole similar to that of clearings. The divergences are, briefly: a more decided downward tendency in 1854 (probably due to changing character of the original data); a later break in the crisis year of 1857 (October instead of July); and the second break and recovery of 1859 just mentioned. The last phenomenon, like the corresponding one in deposits, is, of course, of limited general significance, being connected undoubtedly with the pre-war uncertainties.

Although the movement of deposits shares in some measure that of the other two, the divergences of this movement alone need comment here. The downward swing which culminated in 1857 had its beginning at least as early as July 1855. The second rise and fall occupied

[13] In an earlier study (*Review of Economic Statistics*, 1929 and 1930, vols. 11 and 12, pp. 164–70 and 30–38) where these data were first presented, the line of trend for all these banking data was based on the years 1854–61. Despite the subsequent discovery of certain defects in the data on loans and deposits for early 1854 and for 1861, no recalculation was carried through. Inspection of the data themselves suggested that no appreciable alteration in nature or timing of the "cyclical" movements would have resulted therefrom.

For a brief discussion of seasonal variation, see Notes, Section III, p. 139.

[14] Statement based on weekly data (as accurate as obtainable) not exhibited in Chart 43.

only the twenty-two months between October 1857 and August 1859. Thereafter no definite movement is evident through 1860.

Without pausing longer to note further variations among all three series, let us proceed to a somewhat more detailed examination of the relative movements of loans and deposits — two elements the interaction of which reflects positive banking policy. A comparison of curves representing cyclical changes in these two series reveals several interesting features (Chart 43). One notes immediately that throughout the earlier years, or more specifically from 1854 through 1858, the larger movements of the curve based on deposits regularly anticipated corresponding movements of the curve derived from loans. In the upswing from 1854, in the downturn culminating in 1857, and again in the recovery throughout the whole of 1858, the curve for loans always lagged behind that for deposits. On the other hand, smaller oscillations in the two curves appeared generally simultaneously; and, more important still, after 1858 the two series moved together even in their major changes.[15]

Explanation of the rather persistent lag of loans behind deposits up to 1859 appears to be connected with changing banking practice. By reason of the rapid increase in the use of deposits instead of notes — a phenomenon particularly noteworthy with respect to New York City banks after 1853[16]— loans at this time may well have been the result of deposits. Deposits bred loans and not loans deposits.[17] The synchronism of changes after 1858, on the other hand,

may well have been the result of an increased sensitivity of the money market which was still remembering the difficulties of the recent crisis period, and already perhaps becoming apprehensive over a threatening civil conflict. It is evident that in these years, however, the increase in volume of loans in 1859–60, as well as a striking decline of loans in the first half of 1861 (not pictured in Chart 43), had much less than commensurate effects upon the course of deposits.

The movements displayed by specie holdings of the banks, and by the ratio of such holdings to the sum of "total deposits" plus circulation (as shown by the weekly data), are also interesting and significant. Since the course of the former in this case so largely determined the movements of the latter, it will suffice to confine attention to one series; and inasmuch as the ratio to total demand liabilities is on the whole the more important, we will restrict our story to its movements.

The specie ratio in New York City banks had fallen to a strikingly low level (around 12–14 per cent) in the spring and early summer of 1854 — a level not materially above that touched in the later, crisis year when the low points reached 10–13 per cent. Thereafter it rose smartly until by February 1855 a really high figure of 22 per cent had been attained. Then, however, with the expansion of deposits and circulation, and with an actual diminution of specie holdings, the curve shows a substantially steady decline (broken in 1856 when high points of about 17 per cent occurred in February and June) until in February 1857, and again in August of the same year, extreme figures were touched of 10.9 and 9.9 per cent, respectively. In short, between 1854 and 1857, something like a cyclical movement was displayed.

As will be narrated in greater detail below,[18] gold flowed to New York in astonishing volume in the months immediately following the outbreak of crisis conditions in that center. In the three months from October 1857 to January 1858, the specie holdings of New York City institutions jumped from 7.8 millions to the impressive sum of 31.3 millions — a movement as extraordinary as the precipitous slump of clearings in the early fall of 1857. The ratio of specie

[15] Something of the feature first mentioned — the lag of loans behind deposits — is to be observed in the curves for earlier years (see Chart 41, above).

[16] See Cole, Arthur H., "The New York Money Market, 1843–62," in the *Review of Economic Statistics*, vol. 11 (1929), pp. 164–70.

Incidentally, note may be made that the data on deposits employed in the article just mentioned have since its publication been found to be inaccurate. Chart 41 is based on the corrected data.

[17] It is interesting to speculate whether or not this condition set the tradition as a result of which bankers even as modern as W. L. Leaf, (*Banking*, 1927, pp. 101–102) insist that "the banker's business is founded on deposits, and limited by them." In a similar manner economists continued to describe transactions in foreign exchange as transfers of real bills between merchants, long after the facts had ceased to hold on which presumably they based their early descriptions.

[18] See Chart 45, p. 130, and p. 133.

to liabilities shot up with corresponding rapidity, thanks in part also to a diminution of deposits as well as to the accretion of gold. A ratio of 9.9 per cent for August 29, 1857 became one of 34.7 per cent in January 1858. But the banks were able neither to retain the gold nor to maintain this notably high ratio, chiefly, it seems, by reason of the drainage of specie to other sections of the country. Now came a practically steady decline of the gold holdings and of the ratio, until by January 1860 the latter reached a new low value of 16.8 per cent; and a second up-and-down swing — one notably similar to that described by clearings in approximately the same time-period — came to its close.

To complete the narration up to the War, it will suffice to say that after moving throughout the year irregularly around the low figure reached at the opening of 1860, the specie ratio again shot up with surprising force in the first part of 1861. Large receipts of specie coincided with a rather stagnant level of deposits and circulation. In consequence, the middle of 1861 found the New York City banks with the abundantly safe specie ratio of 43.4 per cent — at which point we may turn our attention elsewhere.

DISCOUNT RATES

Another important financial series for the period now under review is that of monthly "American" discount rates, procurable from Erastus B. Bigelow's *Tariff Question in the United States*.[19] As already indicated, research has as yet failed to unearth the source or the exact character of Bigelow's data, or to secure similar material by which to check this single series.[20] Probably Bigelow's data are representative of short-time interest rates in New York City; but, lacking other material, we must accept his evidence as indicative of the general movement in short-term money rates for the country as a whole. Although these data will come up shortly for consideration in another connection,[21] certain features of their story deserve comment here.

Extraordinary was the course of these discount rates between 1843 and 1848 (Chart 44).[22] According to Bigelow, the closing months of the earlier year had witnessed particularly great money ease, when credit brought only an average of 3¾ per cent. With the succeeding spring, the price of accommodation began to rise, fluctuated widely in 1846 and 1847, and finally attained in 1848 a plateau of high values that has rarely, if ever, been duplicated in the decades for which we have any sort of data. Rates did not fall below 13½ per cent for any month throughout the whole calendar year 1848, and they averaged nearly 15½ per cent in those twelve months. What the explanation of this strange phenomenon is we have yet fully to discover. To be sure, stock prices had risen considerably from their nadir of 1843, and they had exhibited a sharp bulge in the middle of 1847. Commodity prices also had advanced in somewhat the same manner, though not in the same degree; and trade — especially domestic trade — had swelled to a peak in 1847. But none of these phases of the business situation showed the extravagant character which had marked the speculation of the middle 'thirties, and none of them that especial intensity which might reasonably breed extraordinary and prolonged credit stringency. Nothing can be found in the political events of the period or in the international economic or political conditions to explain the unusual occurrence. For example, the rates of discount at the Bank of England display no movement corresponding to that of the Bigelow figures for New York and Boston. The only suggestion of possible cause is that contained in a survey of the New York money market published in the *Democratic Review* of February 1848.[23] From this account it would appear that the New York banks had in 1845–47 participated in an over-issue of banknotes based upon the rising values of the securities which under the relatively recent "free banking" law of the State might be deposited as collateral for issued notes.

[19] Bigelow, *op. cit.*, pp. 204–205. This series must be supplemented for 1861–62 by data from Martin, *op. cit.*, p. 53.

[20] Strictly speaking, another series does exist in Martin's volume just cited; but, as above suggested, this is believed not to constitute an independent set of data (see p. 76, above).

[21] See below, pp. 136–38.

[22] Chart 44 is based on the average for the month of Bigelow's figures for 1831–60 and Martin's for 1861–62. The actual data as given by Bigelow and Martin appear in Appendix E, Table 74.

[23] *Democratic Review*, vol. 22 (1848), pp. 182–83. My attention was called to this reference by Dr. George R. Taylor of Amherst College.

CHART 44. — RATES OF DISCOUNT IN NEW YORK CITY: MONTHLY, 1843–62

(Unit: 1 per cent. Average for the month. Vertical logarithmic scale)

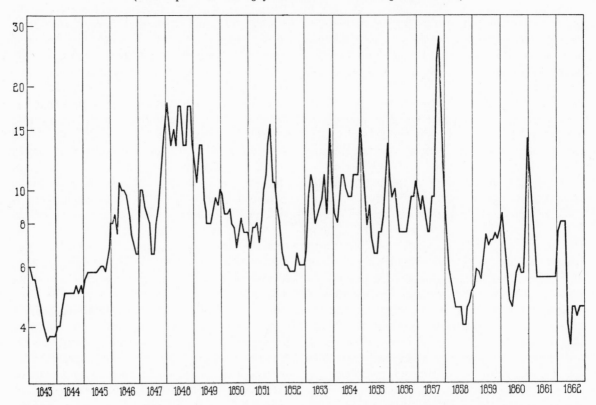

Twenty-two New York institutions, runs this story, "supposing that specie would not be demanded of them, or if it was that there was plenty to be got, engaged to pay on demand $1,879,151 of specie. They had but $29,848, but they supposed that they could get it if called for, by selling their stock. In the meantime specie left the city for the South and West, $6,000,000 was sent abroad, and the demand for it continued. These banks are called upon to meet their promises, and they are 'cornered.'" The banks were forced to dump their collateral in order to secure specie; values of the securities fell and as a result of this "bank mania" the institutions found themselves in a difficult position. The observer for the *Democratic Review* noted in February 1848, "Money is now, and will continue to be, tight." If such were the true explanation of the extraordinary rates which ruled in the month just mentioned and which "continued" to rule throughout the year 1848, obviously the figures chronicled by Bigelow and employed in Chart 44, above, surely could not be

taken as probably representative of the country as a whole. The figures might represent a local New York City situation and not necessarily reflect the rates for short-time money in the other money centers of the United States.

With the summer of 1849, interest rates ultimately softened, and, except for a brief (though vigorous) stringency in the fall of 1851, the tendency was persistently downward until the summer of 1852. Once more, however, the tide turned. Rates ranged higher during 1853 and 1854, subsided in the next two years, and then shot up to panic values in the closing months of 1857. Normal ease in the succeeding, post-crisis year was followed by generally rising figures for these money rates — and soon by the interjection of political events that altered the whole aspect of the business scene.

Inspection of these data (Chart 44), however, leads to other inferences. One notes, for example, the long-range up-and-down swing of values between the close of 1843 and the latter part of 1858; and, on contemplation, he recalls a similar, long-range movement in the case of stock prices.[24] There are, of course, many differences, including the important one of relative timing; and yet the general similarity is arresting. Here, as in the case of the longish up-and-down swings of commodity prices and of banking data (deposits, and loans and discounts), there evidently were forces which, acting slowly, gave decade-long sustaining power to values.

Again, one sees portrayed the generally high level of money rates throughout most of these two decades — especially during the years 1846–57, a period in which there was a constantly increasing gold supply! If such levels — and possibly higher — be taken as the experience for the country as a whole, one can conclude only that, though gold supplies may have increased and though they may have had effect on commodity prices and the like through the expansion which they made possible in total purchasing power, the pressure of the demand for accommodation at the banks was steadily too large and too insistent to permit softening of money rates for any considerable periods. Even the concomitance of enlarging gold supplies, of increasing bank capitals, and of swelling imports of foreign capital could not satisfy the credit needs of a young country whose mixture of productive factors was so specially compounded as that of the United States in the 'forties and 'fifties of the last century.

Finally — if one may disregard other tempting excursions — he will observe the frequency with which money rates tended to advance sharply in the fall of the year: not only in 1847 and 1857 — the "crisis" years — but also in 1851, 1853–55, and 1860 (after Lincoln's election), with minor thrusts in other years. Indeed, an index of seasonal variation based on the decade 1850–60 shows heights attained in November and December appreciably above an index based on more modern data (see Chart 48). For example, the value for December in the former reaches 122 per cent, whereas the index of seasonal variation for the years 1900–13 shows a high point in December of only 113.4 per cent.[25] In some ways the extremes of these late autumnal movements are more interesting than the normal or

average heights — particularly when one reflects that such strong upward thrusts must indicate severe strains on the whole banking system. The tendency for "panics" and "crises" in this country to appear in the fall of the year has its roots in such banking strains as these data reveal.

EXCHANGE RATES AND AMERICAN EXTERNAL TRADE IN MERCHANDISE AND BULLION

In addition to strictly banking figures (including money rates in New York City), other financial data may be marshalled to give evidence regarding changing business conditions of the country in the decades 1843–62, notably, (a) the variations of exchange on London and on such domestic centers as New Orleans and Cincinnati; and (b) alterations in the American disparity in international trade, both of merchandise and of bullion. Let us turn to a brief consideration of these items.

Of exchange rates, it is necessary to make two observations. First, an investigation into the course of exchange on London over decades for which we have definite quotations indicates that a distinct change of tone appeared in the sterling exchange market in 1848 and sets off the period thereto from the years (up to the Civil War) that come thereafter. This change of tone is evidenced in a marked steadying of exchange rates — a steadying which replaces widely ranging quotations of previous decades and which, coming suddenly in 1848, persists for at least the subsequent thirteen years.[26] It is interesting to note that this change came at the time of the gold discoveries, of reviving confidence of British investors in American securities, and of the advent of high discount rates at least in the leading financial center of this country. Perhaps all these factors were in some measure contributory to this development; and perhaps their continued operation — including the net exportation of gold, to which reference will soon be made — had the effect of maintaining the steadied rates in the years that followed.

The second observation with respect to exchange rates relates to their action during periods of financial stress. Their activity at such

[24] See Chart 38 and p. 109 above.
[25] The index for the period 1900–13 was constructed by the Harvard Economic Society for Professor W. L. Crum.

[26] See the article by Arthur H. Cole, "Seasonal Variation in Sterling Exchange Rates" in the *Journal of Economic and Business History*, vol. 2 (1929), pp. 203–18.

times, like that of money rates, is symptomatic of the true financial situation in the center to which they pertain; but they have the advantage over money rates in that they enable us sometimes to make deductions as to what was happening in the area on which they were quoted, i.e., London, New Orleans, Cincinnati, etc. For example, the probability that the "crisis" of 1847 was chiefly an eastern affair and one influenced largely by events abroad is strengthened by an inspection of exchange rates at this period. Exchange on New Orleans and Cincinnati rode through this year without deviation from normal quotations.[27] On the other hand, exchange on London was affected. Moreover, it was affected as early as November 1846, when it fell to 1.06 (parity then being approximately 1.094/5). It touched as low as 1.045 in April of 1847, and was not back to normal levels until October.[28] Yet commodity prices in this country, it will be recalled, continued to rise until June 1847! And discount rates in New York, though oscillating between 7 and 10 per cent in 1846 and early 1847, did not shoot up toward spectacular heights until November of the latter year. Apparently the speculative advance of prices abroad had given rise to abnormally large exports;[29] these had created unusual American balances in London; and the drawing of bills to recover these funds sent sterling below the gold import point.[30] Gold imports kept money rates in New York City at reasonable levels throughout the winter and spring of 1846-47, and gave support to the rising price of commodities. The end came with the advent of difficulties in London.[31]

Exchange rates—both domestic and foreign—for the subsequent period may be dealt with summarily here, since they are examined with considerable detail in the succeeding section.[32] Suffice it to say that domestic exchange rates manifested significant movements only in 1854 and 1857. At the first occasion, the alteration from a placid normal was almost as important by reason of the negative as of the positive phenomena. Exchange rates in New York on Baltimore, St. Louis, and San Francisco pursued the even tenor of their ways. New Orleans rates were moderately affected through the summer and fall, declining to as much as $1\frac{3}{8}$-$1\frac{1}{2}$ per cent discount. That of New York on Cincinnati showed the most striking decline. From a customary 1-$1\frac{1}{2}$ per cent discount, it fell to $2\frac{1}{4}$-$2\frac{1}{2}$ per cent below parity in the autumn months, and to an extreme of $3\frac{1}{2}$-$3\frac{3}{4}$ per cent discount in December. Apparently, however, even this somewhat localized disturbance was short-lived. By March of the next year, the New York rates on these western cities were back to their usual positions.

On the next occasion, 1857, all exchanges were affected, and affected for a longer period. In September of that year, exchange rates generally began to fall way; in October, all were low—very low. Following this, first the exchange on London, later that on Baltimore, and finally the others recovered; but it was not until March 1858 that all traces of the recently past "unpleasantness" were removed from every portion of the exchange market. The evidence from the exchanges, then, indicates that the crisis of 1857 was of widespread incidence. Data of other sorts, such as those on banking conditions proper, or on the volume of trade, suggest that the reaction in the South and West was by no means so severe as in the eastern communities; but these exchange figures lend presumption to the

[27] Exchange on Cincinnati, however, was below normal from May through December in 1846 — 2 to 3 per cent discount — although by January 1847 and throughout that year it ran steadily at 1 to 1 3-4 per cent discount.

[28] The above quotations relate to bankers' sterling 60-day bills at New York as of the first day of the month, and are taken from Martin (*op. cit.*, p. 28). For explanation of the manner of quoting sterling exchange at this period, see the article by Arthur H. Cole, "Evolution of the Foreign Exchange Market of the United States" in the *Journal of Economic and Business History*, vol. 1 (1929), pp. 406–7.

[29] Note the appearance of a large excess of exports in our merchandise balance for the fiscal year ending June 30, 1847 (Table 33, below).

[30] An extraordinary excess in the importation of coin and bullion took place in the fiscal year ending June 30, 1847. See Table 33, below. *Cf.* also the *Democratic Review*, vol. 22 (1848), p. 83.

[31] Discount rates in the London money market remained normal until May 1847. They ranged from $5\frac{1}{2}$ to 7 per cent in the six months of May–October; jumped to 10 per cent in November; returned to 6 per cent in December; and were again at ordinary figures by January of the following year (Bigelow, *op. cit.*, p. 205).

[32] See p. 132 below.

view that the former areas did not escape all repercussion from the primarily eastern upheaval.

For subsequent years, it remains merely to note that exchange on London fell rapidly after Lincoln's election and the forecast of civil war which that event appeared to carry; and it continued low for a year thereafter. With such occurrences, so closely connected with the oncoming war, it is not necessary here to concern ourselves. We may merely notice that this movement of exchange rates, deriving chiefly from the apprehension of American bankers, north and south, is adequate to explain the large net importation of gold (into this important gold-producing country!) which featured the fiscal year of 1861.

TABLE 33. — DISPARITIES IN AMERICAN EXTERNAL TRADE IN MERCHANDISE AND BULLION: ANNUALLY, 1843–62

(*Unit: $1,000,000*)

Fiscal Year Ending June 30	Merchandise Trade		Coin and Bullion	
	Excess of Imports	Excess of Exports	Excess of Imports	Excess of Exports
1843*.......		40.4	20.9	
1844........		3.1	.4	
1845........	7.1			4.5
1846........	8.3			.1
1847........		34.3	22.2	
1848........	10.4			9.5
1849........	.9		1.2	
1850........	29.1			2.9
1851........	21.9			25.0
1852........	40.5			37.2
1853........	60.3			25.3
1854........	60.8			34.5
1855........	38.9			52.6
1856........	29.2			41.5
1857........	54.6			56.7
1858........		8.7		33.4
1859........	38.4			57.5
1860........	20.0			58.0
1861........	69.8		16.5	
1862........		1.3		20.5

* Nine months from October 1, 1842 to June 30, 1843.

Turning briefly to the last items on our docket, we may observe that the data upon the country's

disparities in international trade—both of merchandise and of bullion—suggest the influence of foreign conditions upon the American business situation (Table 33). The net export of merchandise in 1843 probably represents the tag-end of readjustment following the downturn of business which began in 1837. The sharp fall of commodity prices, greater proportionately than the corresponding fall in England, together with the alteration in capital flow (already often mentioned), gave a stimulus to exportation of goods—so great a stimulus, indeed, that the country was able to draw a large supply of gold from abroad. Again the heavy excess for the fiscal year 1847 is tied up with the speculative movement in England, just referred to above.[33] On the other hand, the meagreness of the import disparity in the years 1845-46 and 1848-49 reflect the changed position of the United States on capital account; while the heavy excess of commodity imports in 1853-54 and again in 1857-61 indicates years of marked inflow of foreign funds. The reversal of disparity in the commodity balance for the fiscal year 1858 obviously manifests merely a temporary halt in that inflow which came as an aftermath of the crisis of 1857.

Something of the same picture is evident in the equivalent data upon the trade in coin and bullion. Note the heavy net importation of gold in 1843 and 1847, and the meagre disparities in other years even as late as that ending June 30, 1850. From that time forth, however, gold in American trade was more a commodity than a means for the short-term adjustment of price disequilibria. But it had not altogether lost the latter function. While exports of gold went on in fairly steady volume, importation of coin and bullion increased notably in the fiscal year ending June 30, 1857, and even more markedly in that ending June 30, 1858: note the decline of net exportation. Before the crisis actually broke, premonitions had sent sterling exchange to unusually low levels, until (as monthly data indicate) the net export of bullion became a mere trickle. Again, immediately after the crisis came, New York bankers threw pressure upon the London money market, and the precious

[33] See also the relative movements in the prices of domestic and imported goods in this period, Chart 35, p. 100, above.

metals were hurried to this shore in aid of our banking structure.[34]

THE CRISIS OF 1857 IN THE NEW YORK MONEY MARKET

The increased volume of information regarding financial conditions in New York City during the years surrounding the crisis of 1857 suggests the appropriateness of a section of the present study devoted specifically to a survey of events in that center during this important period. Moreover, the continued advance of New York as the financial center of the country gives reason for such special consideration. In this crisis more than in any of its predecessors, banking conditions in New York City played an important rôle. In 1837–42, events transpiring in New Orleans or Philadelphia or London were of something like equal importance with those of New York City; but by 1857 New York had become so significant in the financial affairs of the country — especially as a custodian of the reserves of out-of-the-city banking institutions — that the events of the metropolitan area were bound to have reactive effect upon the nation as a whole.

Even when dealing merely with the experiences of the New York money market itself in the period surrounding the crisis of 1857, one may still be electic. The data which form the basis of this study make no new contribution concerning the growth of inter-bank deposits in the New York institutions; concerning the conditions which impelled outside banks to withdraw their funds after the startling failure of the Ohio Life Insurance and Trust Company in August 1857; or concerning the existence of the possibility that, between August and October, the New York banks might have arranged to avoid the suspension of specie payments. In short, the data used are merely descriptive of what happened, and are of themselves inadequate to provide material for a general treatment of the crisis.

Attention may be focused particularly on three points; first, the actions of the New York banks prior to the precipitation of disturbed conditions by the failure of the Ohio Life Insurance and Trust Company; secondly, the gen-

eral course of affairs in the New York money market between August and October 1857; and thirdly, the events which occurred in the period following the suspension of specie payments and terminating in their resumption on December 12, 1857.

To aid in such analyses, the weekly data respecting New York City banks from 1853 through 1860 are presented (on a logarithmic scale) in their original form (Chart 45): data on loans (really "total loans" minus "loans to brokers and directors"), total deposits (closely approximating "due depositors" plus "due banks"), "net deposits" (roughly "due depositors"), and specie holdings.[35] Except for the increase in complexity of the chart, another curve might have been included, based on the movement of circulation. But the story in this

CHART 45. — NEW YORK CITY BANK DATA, WEEKLY 1853–60: LOANS AND DISCOUNTS; TOTAL DEPOSITS; NET DEPOSITS; AND SPECIE

(Unit: $1,000,000. Logarithmic vertical scale)

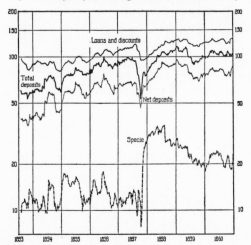

regard is simple. The volume of notes outstanding varied little from week to week or year to year. It did not exceed $9,800,000 (May 1854) nor fall below $6,700,000 (January 1855), with the exception of a few months around the turn of the years 1857–58 (November 1857 through February 1858) when it fell slightly below the latter figure. And the trend throughout this period, 1853–62, was flat at an average value of approximately $8,000,000. With these addi-

[34] See below, pp. 133–34.

[35] Weekly data on loans and discounts inclusive of "loans to brokers and directors" are not available.

tional facts in mind, we may turn to the chart itself and to the story in the clarification of which it gives aid.

An analysis of activities within the New York money market antecedent to the outbreak of the crisis calls special attention to the ratio of loans to "net" deposits (approximately "due depositors") plus circulation, and the ratio of specie to current liabilities. The former ratio in terms of monthly averages of weekly figures had risen to a peak of 160 per cent in November 1854, but soon subsided to its normal level of 135–155 per cent. In the succeeding two and a half years, the range was from 133 to 154 per cent. With the summer of that year loans expanded rapidly, though this increase was not accompanied by a sustained proportionate advance in deposits which began to fall off in July. The ratio between the two items rose from 135 to 154 per cent, or, as Gibbons put it, in terms of the curves of the original items themselves, "a new gap was opened between the loans and their basis."[36] The level reached by October 1856 was maintained with only a minor diminution through June 1857, whereupon a further lift occurred which by August had brought the ratio to 163 per cent.

The ratio of specie to demand liabilities — "total" deposits plus circulation — described for the most part a downward course in the year or two immediately preceding the crisis of 1857, as has already been suggested. The spring of 1854 had been a period of strain due in large measure to internal disturbances, when the ratio dropped to levels nearly as low as those reached three years later; but recovery had been reasonably prompt, so that by the first months of 1855 this ratio registered a peak of approximately 22 per cent. Thereafter, this percentage moved generally lower until by August 1857 it had attained a minimum figure of 9.9 per cent. The year 1857, it may be noted, had not itself been a year of continuing decline in this ratio. A point (10.4) almost as low as this of August 1857 had already been reached in the preceding February, from which, however, a recovery had been started, until in July the ratio stood at 13 per cent.

The course of affairs in the New York money

market between August and October 1857 may be considered from two viewpoints — the condition of the banks themselves, and the course of interest and exchange rates. The analysis of banking data for these months reveals one particularly significant result. In previous accounts of the crisis, it has been generally held that, following the failure of the Ohio Life Insurance and Trust Company in August, New York banks contracted their loans in so rapid a manner as to cause difficulties throughout the country. Thus Gibbons asserted that "the banks took the initiative in forcing down their loans" and that "this unmistakable indication of the course of bank policy was everywhere accepted as evidence of existing panic."[37] There was the further allegation that this contraction of loans was the result of a conspiracy among a few institutions. B. Douglass and Company, a mercantile agency of the time, corresponding somewhat to Dun's and Bradstreet's of the present day, asserted after the crisis, that they entertained "the common opinion that action of the officers of four or five of our strongest banks was the chief cause of the great disasters of the season. They concerted together and forced a rapid and merciless contraction upon all our city banks, carrying along with them those of the country."[38]

Data upon the ratio of loans to net deposits plus circulation, however, show an increase in these months from 163 to 176 per cent. (See also the lag of loans behind deposits in the "cyclical" movements above described.) Undoubtedly, loans were contracted — as the figures on loans themselves indicate — but deposits declined even more rapidly. This decline in deposits was alleged to have been due largely to the action of the country banks. Gibbons says that "a full three-quarters" of the decrease between August 22 and September 26 was due

---

[36] Gibbons, J. S., *op. cit.*, p. 367.

[37] Gibbons, *op. cit.*, pp. 350, 361. See also C. F. Dunbar, *Economic Essays* (1904), pp. 278–80; Evans, D. M., *History of the Commercial Crisis of 1857–58 and of the Stock Exchange Panic of 1859* (1859), p. 34.

[38] Letter of B. Douglass & Co., quoted in Evans, *op. cit.*, p. 123. Dunbar does not seem to accept the assertion of conspiracy although he does say that "it proved to be impossible to convince a large part of the banks, and among these some of the largest and strongest, that they were required to consult anything except their own safety, or that this could be found in any other course than that of contraction" (*op. cit.*, p. 280).

to this element.[39] In addition, hoarding appears to have been going on at the same time.[40] At any rate, the rise of the ratio of loans to deposits in the New York City banks runs directly counter to the general story of events. While these banks may not have served the community and the country in the measure of which they were capable — especially through joint action — they can hardly be charged with complete disregard of the business situation. The changing spread between total deposits (which included "due banks") and net deposits (Chart 45) is confirmatory of this whole analysis.

The data on interest and exchange rates likewise modify the story which is customarily told of this crisis period — that of panic following the failure of the Ohio institution. In September 1857, to be sure, money rates in New York City did rise, according to the monthly figures chronicled by Mr. Bigelow. From an average level of 9½ per cent in August, the rate rose to 24 per cent in September, and reached peak of 28 per cent in October.[41] On the basis of this Boston and New York series, one could not fail to conclude that business conditions were disturbed throughout the greater part of the period between August and October.

The material on exchange rates reveals a somewhat different picture. The data on sterling exchange suggest that values held up fairly well through the twentieth of September, while the weekly quotations of domestic-exchange rates indicate no appreciable break until the very end of September (Chart 46). New Orleans exchange had been somewhat soft during the whole summer — in fact, ever since March — but registered no precipitous decline until the week ending September 30. In the case of other exchanges, the weekly data manifested reaction, it is true, almost immediately after the news of the failure of the Ohio Life Insurance and Trust Company — as, for example, when exchange on Baltimore fell from ¼–½ per cent discount on August 26

to 1–1½ per cent on September 9; or that on St. Louis from 1–1¼ per cent discount to 2–4 per cent at corresponding dates. For the succeeding two weeks, however, no further declines in such domestic-exchange rates were registered. Not until the week of September 30 did a change occur, when simultaneously all domestic-exchange rates slumped precipitously — for example, Baltimore to 10–15 per cent discount; St. Louis to 5–10 per cent; and New Orleans to 4–7. In short, only minor pressure is indicated by these weekly figures for nearly a month after the above-mentioned failure, and no decided collapse is shown until the end of September. Meanwhile, it seems, difficulties had been increasing more rapidly outside of New York than within the city itself; and "between the twenty-fifth and twenty-ninth of September, no less than 150 banks in Pennsylvania, Maryland, Virginia, and Rhode Island, suspended specie payments."[42]

CHART 46. — QUOTATIONS OF DOMESTIC EXCHANGE AT NEW YORK ON NEW ORLEANS, BALTIMORE, AND CINCINNATI, AND OF 60-DAY BILLS ON LONDON: WEEKLY, JULY 1857–FEBRUARY 1858

(*Unit: 1 per cent. For domestic exchange the mean of range was used; for 60-day bills, the low of range relative to par 109.5*)

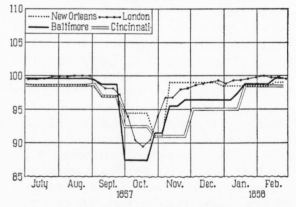

The aggregate evidence suggests that the concept of a sharp panic after the failure of the Ohio Life Insurance and Trust Company had been announced might well be amended along the following lines. As the news of this failure was bruited about the country, banking institutions began to look to their own safety, and started to draw money out of New York City

[39] Gibbons, *op. cit.*, p. 355.

In 1857, the deposits of outside institutions with New York City banks were estimated to amount to fifteen million dollars — or something better than one-fifth of the aggregate "net" deposits of the New York banks (Gibbons, *op. cit.*, p. 359).

[40] Dunbar, *op. cit.*, p. 281.

[41] See Chart 44, above.

[42] Evans, *op. cit.*, p. 34.

banks. Pressure increased gradually, in spite of some effort on the part of New York institutions to ameliorate conditions by maintaining a fair ratio of loans to deposits. By the end of September, however, the situation had become acute in the City itself; New York banks could no longer withstand the strain, and shortly were forced to suspend specie payments. The major difficulty here, as in the case of crises under the national banking system, was the arrangement by which outside banking institutions kept their surplus funds in New York where they were loaned on the call-money market. As Gibbons asserts, these country deposits "allured by competing rates of interest made sufficient ground for an extraordinary pressure when a reduction [of credits] was to be effected."[43]

The events subsequent to the outbreak of real difficulty, which came at the turn of the months, September-October, may be disposed of briefly. For the most part, they have to do with the extraordinarily rapid recovery by the banks of adequate gold reserves. As the fundamental weakness of the position of the New York City banks prior to the crisis had been the inadequacy of their gold holdings, so renewal of this vital element made possible the reëstablishment of confidence, and enabled New York banks even without joint action to come to the support of business.

The course of specie holdings by these New York institutions after October 1857 is indeed spectacular. As already indicated, the amount of specie held increased precipitously from a low point of less than 8 million dollars in October to more than 24 million in November and to over 31 in January 1858; while the ratio of specie to the sum of total deposits plus circulation rose to a level of 28.3 per cent in November and reached almost 35 per cent two months later. Gibbons' remarks on this course of events are particularly sound: that the phenomena could not fail to "excite astonishment . . . that suspension [of specie payments] could have occurred while they [the means of relief] were within such speedy grasp."[44]

The factors which went to provide this renewal of gold reserves were numerous. The underlying factor appears closely related to the flow of new gold from California. At that time it chanced that the accessions from California were unusually favorable. Receipts of gold at New York had been highly variable in the summer of 1857, but in the late fall, October-December, arrivals ran unusually large — in fact an increase of approximately 50 per cent over the corresponding months either of 1856 or 1858 (Chart 29).[45] With such receipts of new gold from the West, reconstitution of the banking reserves was possible if only the banks could retain this new bullion. In part, the banks were enabled to do so by reason of the smaller payments of duties on imports, which came about through the diminution of inflow of goods. Smaller payments for such taxes meant smaller loss of gold into the coffers of the Government's Independent Treasury.[46] Secondly, the retention of gold was possible if exports thereof were to diminish. Net exports, which from June to August had been proceeding at the rate of nearly 6 million dollars per month, fell in September to scarcely 100 thousand dollars, and again in November were down to 200 thousand dollars.

Meanwhile, another source of specie supplementary to that from domestic gold mining had begun to be tapped. The fall of sterling rates in September and October had occasioned an import of gold from London; and possibly imports from other European monetary centers were induced by similar conditions. The result was a net importation of specie into the port of New York amounting to $2,200,000; and this is the more striking since on no other occasion from 1853 through 1862 did a net importation

[43] Gibbons, op. cit., p. 362.
[44] Gibbons, op. cit., p. 361.

[45] See Table 75, p. 195. Perhaps these heavy receipts were not due to mere chance. The high variability of receipts in the late spring and summer of the year may indicate repeated efforts of New York banks — realizing their precarious position — to acquire California gold. However, on account of the fact that the telegraph had not reached the Pacific Coast previous to 1861, and accordingly it would have taken two or three months for orders from New York to result in arrivals of gold in that city; that the failure of the Ohio Life Insurance & Trust Company occurred only in August; and that shipments would be limited by the current production, it seems probable that some element of luck entered in.

[46] Importation of goods into the port of New York, which had been running at the rate of 12.4 million dollars per month during the first half of 1857, and had reached a peak of 28 millions in July, fell rapidly away until, in the final quarter of the year, they averaged less than 5 million dollars per month.

occur until the threatened outbreak of the Civil War.

The retention of new gold and the attraction of bullion from abroad were possible, of course, only by alteration of our relation to foreign money markets. In large measure, this alteration came through what we now would consider normal developments. Our debit account with Great Britain, for instance, was lightened by a decrease in commodity importations. Our credit balance with foreign nations, also, was increased by sales of securities to their citizens. Stock prices in the New York market had begun to sag after March and broke sharply in September and October. This movement was perhaps intensified by the return of stocks from abroad; but soon, it seems, the tide turned, and even at the height of the crisis, "it was stated in New York that orders for the purchase of stocks to a considerable amount had been received from abroad."[47] It was as a consequence of these forces that the net export of gold from the port of New York was cut down sharply in September, and a net import secured in the succeeding month. The shift in our balance of gold movements appeared at a time too early to have been provoked by the extreme difficulties of the New York money market, although the crisis did occur in that same month of October.[48] It will be recalled that the banks of New York did not suspend specie payments until October 13, and that there existed in those days no transatlantic cable by means of which information could be quickly transmitted to London.

Despite the dominance of the elements above mentioned, however, some protection was given the American supply of gold, especially subsequent to the definite outbreak of crisis conditions in October, by forces of a less normal sort. The domestic banking mechanism had actually broken down, and with it had fallen the machinery for dealing in bills of exchange. In this situation the international bankers of the period — acting independently or in coöperation with commercial banks — sent bills to London for collection, and demanded gold for the purpose

of aiding New York banking institutions.[49] At this time the Bank of England was steadily advancing its rate until by December it was charging an extraordinary discount of nine per cent on bills of exchange. The sterling exchange rates in New York fell to a level of at least five or six per cent below the normal specie import point; and bills of exchange, when accompanied by bills of lading, were said to be negotiable only with "great difficulty."[50] Meanwhile, gold was in fact becoming redundant in the New York money market — the foreign trade figures showing a net export of gold both in November and December 1857 — and the financial editor of *Hunt's Merchants' Magazine* noted the "strange anomaly" of a double current of gold between the same points, since "at the same moment that gold arrived here from Liverpool an almost equal amount was exported in return shipments."[51]

In summary, the investigation of banking data may be said to reveal: (a) that disturbances around 1847 had effect, as far as banking was concerned, almost wholly on conditions in the East, and produced scarcely a ripple in such affairs of the West and South; (b) that banking series thereafter seem to have gone through a succession of advances and recessions not unlike those revealed by non-banking data; (c) that the timing of such movements, however, did not always correspond with the timing of advance and decline in such non-banking series as commodity prices — although, it must be admitted, comparison is here being made between (chiefly) New York City banking data and other series not so localized; (d) that, broadly speaking, the period 1848–57 may be conceived as one prolonged movement with intermediate recessions

[47] Dunbar, *op. cit.*, p. 285.

[48] Exchange on London fell away somewhat in the earlier part of September, and was particularly weak after the twentieth of that month (see Chart 46 based on data from *Hunt's Merchants' Magazine*).

[49] Even as early as October 17, 1857, *The* [London] *Economist* remarked that there was "some considerable pressure upon this [London] market for relief of the money market of New York," and was of the opinion that the gold was "sent chiefly to strengthen the reserve of different banks rather than with a view to any profit that can be derived from it as an exchange speculation" (*The* [London] *Economist*, vol. 15 (1857), p. 1146). *Hunt's Merchants' Magazine* commented in December that despite increases in the discount rate of the Bank of England, the flow of gold from that quarter could not at once be checked, "orders having been positive to remit for bills sent out for collection" (*Hunt's Merchants' Magazine*, vol. 37 (1857), pp. 711–12).

[50] *Bankers' Magazine*, n.s., vol. 7 (January 25, 1858), p. 684.

[51] *Hunt's, op. cit.*, vol. 37 (1857), p. 711.

in 1851 and 1854; (e) that the disturbance in 1854 was largely a western affair, particularly severe in the Cincinnati area; (f) that the crisis of 1857 was characterized particularly by an internal drain of specie out of New York City, a fair response of the New York City institutions to the demands of the situation, and a rapid restoration of normal banking conditions with the acquisition of an adequate, even abnormally large stock of gold; and (g) that the period after 1857 presents a confused picture, in which recovery from the preceding crisis was soon met by apprehension over the approaching political difficulties.

CHAPTER XX

RELATIONSHIPS AMONG THE SERIES

IN preceding chapters attempt has been made to portray the course of various statistical series which, in one way or another, are connected with the ups and downs of business conditions during the decades subsequent to 1843: stock prices and the volume of land sales; commodity prices; the volume of trade; and diverse banking and financial factors. A synthesis of the various elements which would be wholly satisfying to the economic historian would, as elsewhere indicated, require the addition and inclusion of various elements not statistically measurable — as, for example, changing business organization, shifting of the psychological background, and variations in the inflow of foreign capital — in short, the subordination of these statistical measurements in an elaboration of a broadly conceived economic history of the United States. Inasmuch, however, as the development of such a history lies beyond the purposes with which this present investigation was initiated, a synthesis appropriate to the narrower scope of the present volume may be found in a comparison of movements of the more important series described above; stock-market values, land sales, commodity prices, volume of trade, and interest rates. Three of these series are made directly comparable by their superimposition in the accompanying chart (Chart 47).[1]

Among the various phenomena therein portrayed, to which attention might be called, we may select the following:

(1) It will be noted that stock prices and commodity prices began an upward movement in the late spring of 1843 — a movement which perhaps had its generating power from the declining money rates. The rise of stock prices began slightly earlier than that of commodity prices, and was much more striking. At this time the volume of trade was also expanding — especially as far as the domestic movement of goods was concerned.

(2) Subsequent to this expansion of business and the accompanying rise of both stock and commodity prices in 1843–44, came a period of three or four years of broken and irregular movements difficult to interpret. The only reasonably clear episode is that which affects particularly the years 1846–48. The volume of domestic trade surely swells significantly in the so-called "crisis" year of 1847. Stock prices bulged impressively at that time, although they might be observed to have experienced a rise and fall of considerably greater length extending from September 1845 to November 1848. Commodity prices also advanced and fell decisively, although here again the exact points of commencement and conclusion are not clearly discernible. Possibly the latter are best conceived as September 1846 and November 1848, respectively. In the meanwhile, discount rates had advanced from an unusually low point — at least, unusual for those times — of $3\frac{3}{4}$ per cent in the fall of 1843 to relatively normal though fluctuating levels in 1846 and 1847. A sharply declining movement in such rates, which set in with the spring of 1847 and which in part reflects the normal seasonal variation of discount rates in this period, was soon reversed when between July of that year and January 1848, money rates rose from $6\frac{1}{2}$ to 18 per cent.

The year 1848 reveals in fact an extraordinary condition of discount rates, inasmuch as they averaged 15 per cent during that twelve-month interval, and never fell below $13\frac{1}{2}$ per cent for any one month. The preceding expansion of business and rise of prices seem insufficient to explain this curious phenomenon. It is noteworthy, for instance, that much more extreme movements in business around 1854 and 1857 produced no such long-continued rise of money rates. Nor is there any adequate explanation to be found in speculation in public lands within the country. Possibly the reëstablishment of

---

[1] On Chart 47, the stock-price index is a combination of Index I and Index IIc, above described (p. 109); the commodity-price index is the weighted form spoken of above (p. 93); and the discount rates are the monthly averages of Bigelow's (and Martin's) figures previously referred to (p. 76).

CHART 47. — INDEX OF RAILROAD-STOCK PRICES; WEIGHTED INDEX OF GENERAL WHOLESALE
COMMODITY PRICES; AND DISCOUNT RATES: MONTHLY, 1843–62*

*(Different logarithmic vertical scales have been used to make the range of
fluctuation approximately the same for the three series)*

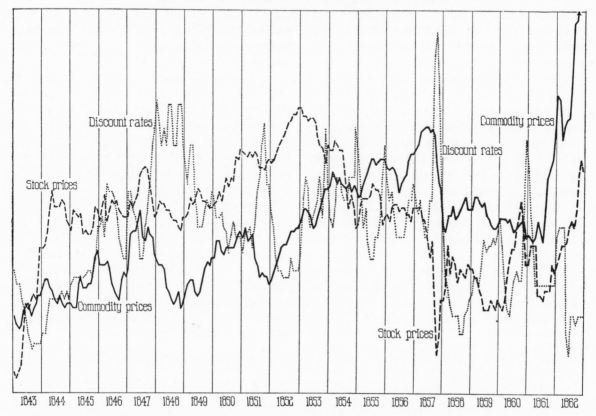

* The curve for the index of railroad stock prices is made up of Index I, 1843–52, and Index IIc for 1853–62.

the Independent Treasury in 1846 may have had such a considerable, though delayed, influence upon conditions in the money market. More likely, it seems, that those high American rates reflected the crisis conditions of the English money market of the preceding half-year and an especially thin inflow of British capital in 1848 — a diminution which was the immediate consequence of the British "railway crisis."

(3) The years 1851 and 1854 were periods of recession. In the former case, stock prices had ceased to go higher with the very opening of the year; commodity prices soon turned downward, and fell with startling rapidity in the summer months; while discount rates pushed upward to a peak of 15½ per cent in October. But confidence soon revived, and with the close of the year the improvement was becoming manifest. The decline three years later found the rôles

of stock and commodity prices somewhat reversed. Stocks took a precipitous tumble, while commodity values decreased but moderately. Discount rates again rose, though sharply only in the month of December; while, as in the early case, the close of the year found conditions once more improved.

(4) Turning now to the events of later years, we may note that the general advance which foreran the "crisis of 1857" began, for common stock values, with December 1848 (if not indeed with the early months of 1843); for commodity prices, with August 1849; for the volume of trade, with the year 1851; and, lastly, in the case of the highly irregular New York discount rates, with the middle of 1852.

The peak of stock-market prices, it will be observed, was reached at the turn of the years 1852–53. Thereupon a broken decline supervened, with a particularly sharp and final plunge of values between March and October 1857. Meanwhile, a speculative movement in the sale of public lands had come and passed. Receipts of the Government from the disposal of its western territory shot up from $1,400,000 in 1852 to more than $11,000,000 in both 1854 and 1855, and had receded to a bare $3,000,000 by 1857.[2]

The volume of trade rose steadily from 1850 through 1856, with a special expansion apparent in the western area; and commodity prices advanced, despite important recessions in 1851 and 1856, until they reached a peak in May-June 1857. In New York City, already the financial center of the country, the volume of transactions continued to expand for a short time longer — at least as indicated by the volume of clearings. The maximum for clearings of New York City banks, adjusted for seasonal variation and trend, came in July 1857.[3]

The course of discount rates is less easily summarized. A casual inspection of the curve for

[2] See above, pp. 57, 58.
[3] See above, p. 123.

such values would show a peak of 28 per cent for the month of October 1857 — the rate having in fact touched 36 per cent for the last week of September and the first week of October. Unlike the peak attained in 1854 the crisis levels reached in September and October 1857 were followed by real ease of money rates in the succeeding year.

(5) Low points after the outbreak of crisis conditions upon the announcement of failure by the Ohio Life Insurance and Trust Company in August 1857 were for the available series, respectively: stock prices, October 1857; commodity prices, February 1858; volume of trade, probably the spring of 1858; and interest rates, the summer of that year.

Here one may stop. The period intervening between the post-crisis troughs and the outbreak of the Civil War is too confused to permit effective summary. On the whole, however, there appears here, as elsewhere, a persistence of the general relationship evident in the analysis for the earlier period of 1820–45 — namely, a sequence in movement of stock values, commodity prices, and interest rates.

NOTES

SEASONAL VARIATION

As already indicated, relatively little attempt was made in the foregoing study to apply refined statistical procedure to the data assembled. Accordingly, only occasionally were indices of seasonal variation secured. A few, however, were computed relating to certain phenomena of the 1850's. For the benefit of those who may find such indices useful in their studies, two of them are reproduced herewith (Chart 48).

First is that based on Bigelow's rates of discount in New York and Boston, with which a more modern measure is brought into comparison, an index based on 60- and 90-day commercial paper rates for the years 1900–13, prepared by the Harvard Economic Society for Professor W. L. Crum.[1]

The second is that based on the clearings data compiled by the New York Clearing House; and again a modern measure is brought into contrast, that evolved by Professor W. M. Persons, and published by him in the *Review of Economic Statistics*, Preliminary Volume I (January, 1919), p. 50.[2]

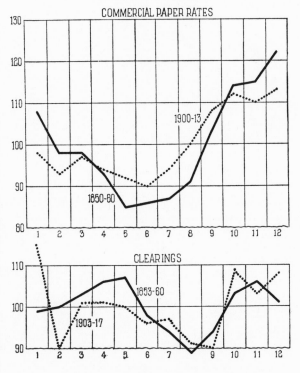

CHART 48. — MONTHLY INDICES OF SEASONAL VARIATION: COMMERCIAL PAPER RATES, 1850–60, AND NEW YORK CITY BANK CLEARINGS, 1853–60, WITH LATER PERIODS

[1] The index of seasonal variation based upon Bigelow's rates of discount through the period 1850–60 shows a decline from a value of 108 in January to one of 85 in May, and a subsequent continued rise — especially marked after August — until in December an altitude of 122 is reached. On the other hand, the index relative to the modern period shows a decline from 97.6 per cent in January to 90.3 per cent in June, and then a sharp rise until a peak of 111.5 per cent is reached in October. While other changes in the configuration of these two indices are not without interest, particularly worthy of

note is the degree to which the increase of rates in the fall had cut down in the intervening fifty or sixty years.

[2] For the interval 1903–17 the indexes apply to monthly aggregates, whereas those for the earlier interval apply to daily averages. Corresponding allowances should be made in comparing the two curves.

APPENDICES

INTRODUCTION

The methods employed in the less complicated cases of index construction, such as those relating to the volume of trade, bank stocks, or the data on banking operations have been previously described in the text. They will be omitted, therefore, from the discussion here. The major part of the descriptive matter will be devoted to the various commodity-price indices and to the several railroad stock indices.

APPENDIX A

Sources of Data and Statistical Methods used in the Construction of Monthly Indices of Wholesale Commodity Prices, 1792–1862

Commodity Price Indices, 1792–1820

Data and their sources: (See Table 34.) Data on wholesale commodity prices for the period 1792–1820 were transcribed from the *American Apollo* for the months of October 1792 to December 1794 inclusive; from the *Boston Price Current and Marine Intelligencer* from September 1795 to May 1798; from *Russell's Gazette* from June 1798 to September 1800; and from the *Boston Gazette* from October 1800 to December 1820. Files of these newspapers are to be found in the Boston Public Library, the Library of the Massachusetts Historical Society, and the Boston Athenaeum.

TABLE 34. — SERIES OF WHOLESALE COMMODITY PRICES TRANSCRIBED, 1792–1820

Commodity	Unit	Total Period Covered	Commodity	Unit	Total Period Covered
Alum[1]	cwt.	1795–1820	Lead, white, dry	cwt.	1795–1820
Ashes, pearl	ton	1792–1820	Leather, sole	lb.	1795–1820
Barley	bu.	1800–1820	Linseed oil, American	gal.	1800–1820
Beef, mess[1]	bbl. (200 lbs.)	1792–1820	Lumber	M ft.	1795–1820
Brandy, French[1]	gal.	1792–1820	Boards, clear (1795–1802)		
Brimstone, roll[1, 2, 3]	cwt.	1801–1820	Ken and Mach (1803–1809)		
Butter, shipping	lb.	1800–1820	Quad and Mach (1809–1820)		
Candles, American tallow[1]	lb.	1792–1820	Molasses	gal.	1800–1820
Cheese, American	lb.	1792–1820	Nails, 10 d.	M	1794–1820
Coal, American	chaldron	1795–1820	Oats	bu.	1800–1820
Coal, foreign[1]	chaldron	1795–1820	Pepper	lb.	1800–1820
Cocoa, Caracas[2]	cwt.	1800–1820	Pork, cargo[1]	bbl.	1792–1820
Coffee, West Indian[1]	lb.	1792–1820	Raisins, Malaga	cask	1800–1820
Copper, sheets[2]	lb.	1794–1820	Rice[1]	cwt.	1792–1820
Corn, southern Indian	bu.	1792–1820	Rum, New England	gal.	1795–1820
Cotton, Georgia upland	lb.	1792–1820	Rye	bu.	1800–1820
Duck, Russia[1, 2]	bolt	1792–1820	Salt, Liverpool	8 bu.	1792–1820
Fish, alewives	bbl.	1795–1820	Saltpeter, refined[1]	lb.	1802–1820
Flour, rye	bbl.	1801–1820	Soap, white American	lb.	1800–1820
Flour, superfine[2]	bbl.	1792–1820	Steel, English blistered[2]	lb.	1795–1820
Fur, beaver	lb.	1800–1820	Sugar, Havana brown	cwt.	1792–1820
Glass, Bristol (8x10)[1]	100 ft.	1794–1820	Staves, white oak hhd.[2]	M	1792–1820
Glue, American	lb.	1801–1820	Tar, Wilmington[1]	bbl.	1792–1820
Gunpowder, foreign	lb.	1800–1820	Tea, Young Hyson	lb.	1801–1820
Gunpowder, American	lb.	1795–1820	Tea, Hyson	lb.	1792–1820
Hemp	ton	1792–1820	Tin, Plates, No. 1. 3dX	box	1795–1820
Iron, Swedish	ton	1792–1820	Tobacco[1]	cwt.	1792–1820
Lard	lb.	1800–1820	Turpentine[1]	bbl.	1800–1820
Lead, pig[2]	cwt.	1795–1820	Whale oil, common	gal.	1792–1820

[1] Minor changes in specifications.
[2] This series has a gap of a year or more about the year 1808.
[3] This series has a gap of several months or a year sometime between 1812 and 1815.

Series discarded: Generally speaking, series were discarded for four reasons: they were lacking in homogeneity and continuity, or they were not responsive to changes in the business situation, or they duplicated the movement of other price series, or lastly they were economically unimportant. A list of series discarded is given in Table 35.

TABLE 35. — SERIES DISCARDED FOR USE IN WHOLE-SALE COMMODITY-PRICE INDICES, 1792–1820

Series	Reason
Barley	Unimportant
Butter	Dairy products better represented by cheese
Coal, American	Unimportant
Cocoa, Caracas	Unimportant
Flour, rye	Unimportant
Fur, beaver	Insensitive
Glue, American	Insensitive
Gunpowder, American	Relatively unimportant
Lard	Unimportant
Lead, pig	Essentially a duplicate of white lead
Linseed oil	Unimportant
Molasses	Essentially a duplicate of sugar
Oats	Unimportant
Pepper	Unimportant
Raisins, Malaga	Unimportant
Rum, New England	Showed both foreign and domestic influences
Rye	Unimportant
Saltpeter	Incomplete
Soap, white American	Inflexible
Tea, Young Hyson	Less important than Hyson
Turpentine	Less important than tar

Index numbers: The following index numbers are herewith given for the period from 1792 to 1820.
(1) An all-commodity index number of wholesale commodity prices as quoted in Boston, 1792–1820. (See Table 36.)
(2) An index number of wholesale commodity prices of domestically produced goods as quoted in Boston, 1792–1820. (See Table 37.)
(3) An index number of wholesale commodity prices of imported goods as quoted in Boston, 1792–1820. (See Table 38.)
These index numbers are weighted aggregative indices with the year 1802 as the base. The weights used in the construction of these index numbers are indicated in Tables 1, 2, 3, and 4 in the text.

The index numbers are perfectly homogeneous from 1795 to 1820. Between 1792 and 1794 all of the series used in the 1795–1820 index numbers were not available. In the construction of this earlier index number only the following domestic prices were used: pearl ashes, beef, tallow candles, American cheese, Indian corn, cotton, superfine flour, whale oil, mess pork, rice, staves, tar, and tobacco. The index of prices of imports between 1792 and 1794 was made from the following series: brandy, coffee, Russia duck, hemp, Swedish iron, Liverpool salt, brown sugar, and Hyson tea. The weights on the reduced list of commodities used in the indices for this early period were adjusted. These short index numbers are also on an 1802 base.[1]

(4) Regional index numbers of domestic wholesale commodity prices in Boston, New York, Philadelphia, and Baltimore, 1810–1817. (See Table 39.)

Data and their sources: The Boston index has already been described in connection with the index numbers from 1792 to 1820.[2] The New York data came from the *New York Price Current* (1810–1815) and from the *New York Shipping and Commercial List* (1815–1817). Statistics of commodity prices in Philadelphia were obtained from *Hope's Philadelphia Price-Current* (1810-1813), *Scott's Philadelphia Price-Current* (1813), and *Grotjan's Public-Sale Report* (1813–1819). All of the commodity price quotations for Baltimore were taken from the *Baltimore Price-Current*. The New York journals are to be found in the New York Public Library and the library of the New York Historical Society; the Philadelphia materials are on file with the Library Company of Philadelphia (Ridgeway Branch) and the library of the Pennsylvania Historical Society. The *Baltimore Price-Current* is in the library of the Maryland Historical Society.

Construction of the regional indices: For the construction of these indices, see the *Review of Economic Statistics,* vol. 9, pp. 171–180. The series used are identical with those used for the aggregative index numbers (see Table 1) of domestic commodities with the following differences: American coal and New England rum were included in the regional index numbers, and rice and tobacco were omitted.

The index numbers of domestic commodity prices for the cities mentioned above have as a base the average of prices in 1810. The formula for averaging is the unweighted geometric mean.

---

[1] It should be noted that for the years 1792–1794 prices were quoted in shillings and pence. From a contemporary account in the *Boston Price-Current* the rate in New England was six shillings to the dollar. This rate was used therefore in converting prices to a dollar basis.

[2] See p. 143, above.

TABLE 36. — WEIGHTED ALL-COMMODITY INDEX (A PLUS B) OF WHOLESALE PRICES IN BOSTON: MONTHLY, 1792–1820[1]

(*Base: 1802*)

	Jan.	Feb.	March	April	May	June	July	Aug.	Sept.	Oct.	Nov.	Dec.
1792	...	...	...	...	...	...	...	...	...	85	89	89
1793	91	89	86	93	95	93	95	91	89	87	88	88
1794	93	93	92	94	91	94	95	97	98	101	102	103
1795	...	...	...	...	...	...	...	...	119	119	125	121
1796	122	125	128	127	125	123	118	118	123	127	126	125
1797	123	122	118	116	116	115	112	114	120	116	119	117
1798	117	115	110	109	108	110	111	111	110	112	112	114
1799	115	116	115	114	116	115	117	117	117	121	127	122
1800	115	114	109	108	113	112	115	118	117	121	127	122
1801	123	128	132	130	132	127	127	123	119	119	120	107
1802	103	99	100	101	101	99	98	98	98	99	102	102
1803	101	101	101	102	105	104	110	113	112	113	115	114
1804	112	111	112	111	109	107	108	107	111	113	118	118
1805	119	122	126	125	125	123	120	118	117	118	120	119
1806	119	119	118	112	114	114	114	117	117	115	116	118
1807	120	119	119	116	114	113	111	109	107	107	108	107
1808	101	100	98	96	95	93	93	95	96	101	102	106
1809	103	107	115	111	112	110	104	104	103	102	104	108
1810	108	109	110	108	108	107	109	110	108	110	113	110
1811	111	108	104	103	103	103	102	103	100	101	104	100
1812	105	107	107	102	100	104	105	107	110	113	113	114
1813	118	122	121	127	136	132	134	137	139	150	155	161
1814	...	161	155	155	152	154	156	157	162	169	...	155
1815	...	150	134	129	129	131	131	131	131	133	136	134
1816	135	137	137	133	130	126	123	121	123	125	132	134
1817	135	136	134	138	137	127	124	128	125	125	128	134
1818	136	137	135	130	128	132	130	133	134	136	139	134
1819	128	124	121	112	106	101	101	99	101	101	101	99
1820	95	93	89	88	89	87	90	90	90	88	88	88

[1] For a discussion of this index, see p. 8.

TABLE 37. — WEIGHTED INDEX (A) OF WHOLESALE DOMESTIC COMMODITY PRICES IN BOSTON: MONTHLY, 1792–1820[1]

(Base: 1802)

	Jan.	Feb.	March	April	May	June	July	Aug.	Sept.	Oct.	Nov.	Dec.
1792	...	...	...	...	...	...	...	...	...	82	87	87
1793	89	89	87	96	99	96	97	92	88	87	86	86
1794	93	90	90	92	88	92	95	97	98	101	102	102
1795	...	...	...	...	...	...	...	...	127	127	135	130
1796	130	134	138	137	135	131	124	123	130	135	132	131
1797	127	127	122	119	118	116	114	116	125	120	123	122
1798	120	117	110	108	106	106	107	107	107	110	110	112
1799	113	113	113	113	116	115	118	117	118	123	120	120
1800	115	115	108	108	116	115	119	123	121	127	135	125
1801	128	134	141	138	140	133	131	129	126	124	123	109
1802	103	99	100	101	101	98	97	98	98	99	103	101
1803	99	100	101	102	103	102	111	112	112	112	113	112
1804	109	107	107	107	106	104	105	107	111	112	120	119
1805	121	124	130	129	131	127	124	121	119	121	122	120
1806	120	121	117	110	113	114	114	118	118	117	118	119
1807	121	120	119	117	116	114	117	108	108	108	110	108
1808	100	96	93	91	88	84	84	86	85	89	91	87
1809	85	91	101	98	104	104	99	98	96	95	98	100
1810	103	104	105	103	104	103	105	108	106	109	113	111
1811	112	108	103	103	102	101	101	101	96	95	98	93
1812	100	103	102	94	90	94	90	93	97	102	104	104
1813	101	106	112	120	131	125	126	124	130	142	147	151
1814	...	147	144	146	146	149	151	148	150	155	...	140
1815	...	132	128	123	123	125	127	130	129	134	139	139
1816	141	143	143	138	135	135	137	129	131	135	145	148
1817	149	150	149	154	154	140	137	142	136	135	138	144
1818	147	147	143	138	135	141	139	142	144	146	150	145
1819	138	132	127	114	107	100	102	98	100	101	101	98
1820	94	91	86	84	85	83	86	87	88	85	84	83

[1] For the commodities and weights used in the construction of this index, see Table 1, p. 9, and Table 3, p. 11.

TABLE 38. — WEIGHTED INDEX (B) OF WHOLESALE IMPORTED COMMODITY PRICES IN BOSTON: MONTHLY, 1792–1820[1]

(*Base: 1802*)

	Jan.	Feb.	March	April	May	June	July	Aug.	Sept.	Oct.	Nov.	Dec.
1792	...	...	...	...	...	...	...	...	...	94	94	94
1793	97	88	84	83	85	85	90	88	90	90	91	92
1794	93	103	98	100	101	100	95	97	96	101	102	105
1795	...	...	...	...	...	...	...	...	102	103	104	103
1796	105	106	106	107	106	107	107	108	109	109	112	113
1797	113	111	111	111	111	112	108	109	110	109	109	107
1798	110	110	112	111	112	117	118	119	117	117	116	118
1799	121	121	119	117	117	115	117	117	116	114	117	115
1800	115	112	110	108	108	106	108	107	108	110	112	114
1801	114	115	116	113	115	114	118	109	105	109	110	104
1802	101	99	101	101	101	100	99	98	98	99	100	102
1803	103	103	103	104	109	109	110	114	113	114	119	119
1804	117	121	120	119	114	114	113	109	110	113	115	115
1805	116	117	117	115	114	114	112	112	113	113	116	116
1806	117	116	118	116	118	115	114	115	114	113	113	116
1807	116	116	119	112	111	110	110	109	106	105	105	106
1808	107	109	109	107	108	111	112	115	119	124	125	145
1809	140	142	142	137	130	123	115	118	117	117	116	119
1810	117	120	120	119	116	115	115	115	113	112	111	109
1811	109	107	106	104	103	105	106	107	107	112	117	115
1812	116	117	118	118	119	122	135	137	136	135	133	135
1813	140	141	140	142	147	146	149	154	156	166	173	183
1814	...	190	180	174	166	165	167	176	188	197	...	186
1815	...	185	146	143	141	145	138	134	134	131	128	124
1816	125	124	124	123	119	114	106	104	106	105	105	106
1817	106	107	104	105	102	100	99	101	103	104	108	113
1818	115	117	117	115	113	113	112	113	115	116	117	111
1819	108	108	109	107	105	105	100	100	101	101	103	101
1820	99	97	95	95	97	94	96	96	95	94	96	98

[1] For the commodities and weights used in the construction of this index, see Table 2, p. 10, and Table 4, p. 11.

TABLE 39. — UNWEIGHTED REGIONAL INDICES OF WHOLESALE DOMESTIC COMMODITY PRICES IN BOSTON, NEW YORK, PHILADELPHIA, AND BALTIMORE: MONTHLY, 1810–1817[1]

(*Base: 1810*)[2]

		Jan.	Feb.	Mar.	April	May	June	July	Aug.	Sept.	Oct.	Nov.	Dec.
1810	Boston.................	99	99	99	98	99	99	100	99	99	100	104	103
	New York..............	101	100	98	99	97	97	100	99	99	101	103	103
	Philadelphia............	98	100	98	98	99	98	99	100	98	99	103	104
	Baltimore..............	96	97	96	96	100	100	100	102	100	103	102	106
1811	Boston.................	103	102	100	99	99	97	96	97	92	94	95	96
	New York..............	103	100	98	96	95	93	92	95	95	96	92	95
	Philadelphia............	110	108	107	103	101	101	99	100	99	95	96	100
	Baltimore..............	106	101	99	98	99	97	96	95	95	95	96	96
1812	Boston.................	98	99	98	94	92	93	93	92	94	97	97	97
	New York..............	95	97	98	94	92	93	93	95	96	100	103	103
	Philadelphia............	100	100	98	94	93	93	95	95	102	101	101	99
	Baltimore..............	98	99	98	93	91	92	98	96	97	104	103	102
1813	Boston.................	102	103	104	108	116	114	115	118	118	123	128	134
	New York..............	108	108	109	117	116	119	119	122	125	130	134	142
	Philadelphia............	100	103	103	108	109	...	...	112	114	117	119	130
	Baltimore..............	106	104	103	106	107	108	109	116	118	122	134	147
1814	Boston.................	...	135	136	140	136	140	142	140	140	144	...	136
	New York..............	155	152	153	154	150	147	148	143	144	147	152	151
	Philadelphia............	135	137	134	138	132	131	127	127	128	136	140	142
	Baltimore..............	149	143	142	143	137	141	142	142	...	155	161	157
1815	Boston.................	...	133	128	125	124	122	124	122	123	125	127	121
	New York..............	152	155	143	136	138	140	144	144	146	151	153	146
	Philadelphia............	144	143	130	124	123	127	132	132	134	140	142	141
	Baltimore..............	157	160	134	127	133	134	141	141	146	154	154	153
1816	Boston.................	124	124	122	116	113	111	107	106	104	109	112	113
	New York..............	146	146	138	129	128	126	125	119	113	112	113	112
	Philadelphia	139	137	132	129	128	134	135	133	130	124	126	124
	Baltimore..............	149	147	141	136	137	136	136	132	128	128	131	134
1817	Boston.................	117	117	116	120	119	114	109	111	109	108	110	114
	New York..............	116	120	122	121	122	118	115	114	114	113	113	117
	Philadelphia............	123	124	125	122	117	113	110	109	107	105	105	107
	Baltimore..............	132	133	129	126	122	117	116	112	115	114	117	116

[1] For the commodities and methods used in the construction of these regional indices, see p. 9 and the paragraphs under (4) above, p. 144.

[2] To shift the Boston index to the base July-December 1802, multiply by 1.0744.

COMMODITY PRICE INDICES, 1815-45

Sources of data: For the decade 1815-24, data were drawn from various contemporary newspapers, principally the *New York Shipping and Commercial List;* the *Boston Commercial Gazette;* the *Boston Daily Advertiser;* the *Philadelphia Gazette;* and, in a few cases, *Grotjan's Philadelphia Public-Sale Report.* For the period 1825-45, recourse was first had to the Report of the Secretary of the Treasury for 1863 (38th Congress, 1st Session, Executive Document, No. 3), hereinafter spoken of as the *Finance Report.* All the series which were there presented complete or substantially complete for the two decades, 1815-45, were transcribed. In the cases of important commodities for which quotations in the *Finance Report* were defective, and in those of commodities for which the market or point of sale might be a factor of considerable influence, additional data were transcribed from contemporary newspapers. Substantially a full series of monthly quotations was made a prime requisite for acceptance, interpolation being resorted to only in a few cases, for not more than brief intervals, and only after cognate series had been transcribed from all available sources.

In the end, price series for about ninety different commodities were obtained, nearly all of them covering the whole of the period under investigation. The list of commodities for which price series were secured, together with information as to the description, unit, dates, and sources for the period covered is given in Table 40. Of these series, about seventy are based on quotations from the New York market, twelve from the Boston, seven from New York and Boston combined, and five from Philadelphia.

It will be noted that practically all commodities which were economically important during the years 1815-45 are represented on this list, while leading commodities such as upland cotton, molasses, wool, *et cetera*, usually appear in two or more varieties or grades. There are many cases in which similar series from more than one source were transcribed. Most of these were sought by reason of a desire either to secure a second set of data from an additional market, or to corroborate doubtful, insensitive or defective series. For example, a complete or even substantially complete series for the important article, wheat, was peculiarly difficult to secure. Many series of wheat prices — for instance those appearing in the *Finance Report* — failed to give homogeneous monthly quotations for considerable intervals during the critical years, 1835-39. Only by recourse to the Philadelphia market and by use of data from the New York market — since no one series was complete in itself — was a set of quotations covering the two decades from 1825 to 1845 finally obtained. However, the acquisition of several series for certain commodities such as wheat, fish, cotton, and cotton goods did not mean their inclusion in the indices of prices finally constructed. As will appear, by an inspection of the list in Table 42 several series were discarded to avoid overweighting specific commodities.

The list of price series given in Table 40 includes representatives of practically all phases of the economic life of the period — agriculture, fishing, lumbering, mining, and manufacturing. Likewise the list embraces, as far as data are available, commodities in various stages of fabrication — raw materials, such as whale oil or indigo, semi-manufactured goods, such as cotton yarn and British bar iron, and articles ready for the consumer, such as sheetings, gunpowder, and rum. Additional series could undoubtedly have been secured by further thumbing of newspapers or "commercial lists," but it is unlikely that they would have contributed sufficiently to the general index to have made the research worth while. The list as given is broad and diverse enough to mirror the important movements of general prices.

TABLE 40. — SERIES OF WHOLESALE COMMODITY PRICES TRANSCRIBED, 1815–45*

In some cases, series were not transcribed in the full period for which they were available, as, for instance, when observation of quotations for a number of years indicated that the series were insensitive to changes in business conditions.

(Series used in the construction of the weighted commodity-price index are marked by an asterisk)

Commodity	Years	Unit	Total Period Covered	Source of Data
*Ashes, pearl	....		1815–45	
	1815–30	ton		New York Shipping List
	1830–45	100 lbs.		New York Shipping List
*Beef	....	bbl.	1815–45	
mess	1825–39			U. S. Finance Report
mess, country	1840–44			U. S. Finance Report
mess	1845			U. S. Finance Report
mess	1843–45			New York Shipping List
*prime	1815–24			New York Shipping List
*prime	1825–45			U. S. Finance Report
Boards, North River	....	M ft.	1826–31	U. S. Finance Report
*Butter	....		1815–45	
*first sort	1815–24	firkin		Boston Commercial Gazette
first quality	1821–24	lb.		New York Shipping List
*western dairy	1825–39	lb.		U. S. Finance Report
*state	1840–45	lb.		U. S. Finance Report
*Candles, sperm	....	lb.	1815–45	
	1815–24			Boston Commercial Gazette
	1825–45			U. S. Finance Report
*Coal	....		1815–45	
*Liverpool	1815–24	chaldron		New York Shipping List
*Liverpool	1825–45	chaldron		U. S. Finance Report
Virginia	1815–24	ton		New York Shipping List
Schuylkill	1825–30	ton		U. S. Finance Report
anthracite	1830–45	ton		U. S. Finance Report
*Coffee	....	lb.	1815–45	
West Indies, best green	1815–24			Boston Commercial Gazette
*West Indies, 2nd grade	1815–24			Boston Commercial Gazette
*Brazil	1825–45			New York Shipping List
Brazil	1825–45			U. S. Finance Report
Cognac brandy	....	gal.	1825–45	U. S. Finance Report
Copper, pig	....	lb.	1825–45	
	1825–45			U. S. Finance Report
	1825–45			New York Shipping List
*Corn, northern	....	bu.	1815–45	
*northern, yellow	1815–24			New York Shipping List
*northern, (not qualified)	1825–45			U. S. Finance Report
Corn meal, northern	....	bbl.	1825–45	
northern, (not qualified)	1825–36			U. S. Finance Report
northern, Jersey	1837–44			U. S. Finance Report
northern, (not qualified)	1845			U. S. Finance Report
*Cotton, upland	....	lb.	1815–45	
*Georgia and North Carolina	1815–24			Boston Commercial Gazette
*(not qualified)	1825–31			Boston Daily Advertiser
*good to prime	1832–33			Boston Daily Advertiser
*fair to good	1834–43			Boston Daily Advertiser
*fair to prime	1844–45			Boston Daily Advertiser
(not qualified)	1825–37			U. S. Finance Report
middling	1838–44			U. S. Finance Report
(not qualified)	1845			U. S. Finance Report

TABLE 40. — *Continued*

Commodity	Years	Unit	Total Period Covered	Source of Data
Cotton sheeting, brown, 4–4.............	....	yd.	1825–45	New York Shipping List
*Cotton yarn, 5–10–14...................	....	lb.	1823–45	New York Shipping List
*Fish.........................	....	qtl.	1815–45	
*table, Isle of Shoals..................	1815–24			Boston Commercial Gazette
*bank cod....................	1823–35			Boston Daily Advertiser
*bank and bay cod...................	1836–38			Boston Daily Advertiser
*bank cod....................	1839–45			Boston Daily Advertiser
dry cod.....................	....	cwt.	1825–45	U. S. Finance Report
mackerel....................	....	bbl.	1815–45	
No. 1.....................	1815–24			Boston Commercial Gazette
No. 1.....................	1825–43			U. S. Finance Report
No. 1, Massachusetts...............	1844–45			U. S. Finance Report
Flax........................	....	lb.	1825–45	
American.....................	1827–45			New York Shipping List
American.....................	1825–45			U. S. Finance Report
Russian......................	1826–45			U. S. Finance Report
Furs, beaver, northern...............	....	lb.	1825–45	
	1825–45			U. S. Finance Report
	1825–45			New York Shipping List
Gin........................	....	gal.	1825–45	
Scheidan.....................	1825–29			U. S. Finance Report
Holland.....................	1830–45			U. S. Finance Report
Glass, American....................	....		1825–44	
	1825–30	100 ft.		U. S. Finance Report
	1831–41	50 ft.		U. S. Finance Report
	1842	box		U. S. Finance Report
	1843–44	50 ft.		U. S. Finance Report
Gunpowder, American................	....	25 lbs.	1825–45	U. S. Finance Report
Hams, smoked....................	....	lb.	1825–45	U. S. Finance Report
Hides.......................	....	lb.	1825–45	
La Plata.....................	1825–28			U. S. Finance Report
Buenos Ayres...................	1829–43			U. S. Finance Report
La Plata.....................	1844			U. S. Finance Report
Buenos Ayres...................	1845			U. S. Finance Report
Hops, first sort....................	....	lb.	1825–45	U. S. Finance Report
Indigo.......................	....	lb.	1825–45	
Bengal.....................	1825–45			New York Shipping List
Manilla.....................	1825–45			U. S. Finance Report
*Iron, English bar...................	....	ton	1818–45	
*assorted.....................	1818–24			New York Shipping List
*assorted.....................	1825–30			U. S. Finance Report
*common.....................	1831–45			U. S. Finance Report
Iron, pig.....................	....	ton	1815–45	
English.....................	1815–24			Boston Commercial Gazette
English.....................	1820–24			New York Shipping List
English.....................	1825–26			U. S. Finance Report
Scotch.....................	1827–45			U. S. Finance Report
*Lard.......................	....	lb.	1821–45	
	1815–20			Boston Commercial Gazette
	1821–24			New York Shipping List
	1825–45			U. S. Finance Report
*Lead.......................	....	cwt.	1815–45	
*pig.......................	1815–24			Boston Commercial Gazette
*pig.......................	1824–31			Boston Daily Advertiser

TABLE 40. — *Continued*

Commodity	Years	Unit	Total Period Covered	Source of Data
*Lead (*continued*)				
*pig and bar, Missouri.................	1832–35			Boston Daily Advertiser
*pig............................	1836–45			Boston Daily Advertiser
pig............................	1825–37			U. S. Finance Report
*Leather, hemlock sole...................	....	lb.	1815–45	
	1815–20			Boston Commercial Gazette
	1821–24			New York Shipping List
	1825–45			U. S. Finance Report
*Linseed oil.........................	....	gal.	1816–45	
*American.........................	1816–24			New York Shipping List
*(not qualified).....................	1825–45			U. S. Finance Report
*Molasses............................	....	gal.	1815–45	
*Havana..........................	1815–24			New York Shipping List
*Havana..........................	1825–44			U. S. Finance Report
*Havana and Matanzas..............	1845			U. S. Finance Report
*New Orleans.....................	1817–24			Boston Commercial Gazette
*New Orleans.....................	1825–45			U. S. Finance Report
*Nails............................	....	lb.	1820–45	
*assorted sizes......................	1820–26			Boston Commercial Gazette
*assorted sizes......................	1827–45			Boston Daily Advertiser
cut............................	1830–45			U. S. Finance Report
*Oats............................	....	bu.	1815–45	
*(not qualified).....................	1815–20			Boston Commercial Gazette
*northern.........................	1821–24			New York Shipping List
*northern.........................	1825–40			U. S. Finance Report
*state, northern....................	1841–45			U. S. Finance Report
*Olive oil............................	....	gal.	1815–45	
*Sicily............................	1815			Boston Commercial Gazette
*Sicily............................	1816–17			New York Shipping List
*(not qualified).....................	1818–45			U. S. Finance Report
Paint, red lead........................	....	lb.	1830–45	U. S. Finance Report
Pepper............................	....	lb.	1825–45	U. S. Finance Report
*Pork............................	....	bbl.	1815–45	
cargo............................	1815–24			Boston Commercial Gazette
*navy mess.........................	1816–24			Boston Commercial Gazette
*mess............................	1825–45			U. S. Finance Report
prime............................	1825–45			U. S. Finance Report
*Rice............................	....	cwt.	1815–45	
*(not qualified).....................	1815–24			Boston Commercial Gazette
*ordinary...........................	1821–24			New York Shipping List
*ordinary...........................	1825–45			U. S. Finance Report
*Rosin, common.......................	....	bbl.	1815–45	
	1815–24			New York Shipping List
	1825–45			U. S. Finance Report
*Rum............................	....	gal.	1815–45	
Jamaica............................	1825–45			U. S. Finance Report
*New England......................	1815–24			Boston Commercial Gazette
*New England......................	1825–31			Boston Daily Advertiser
*New England, pure..................	1832–45			Boston Daily Advertiser
*Rye, northern.......................	....	bu.	1815–45	
	1815–24			New York Shipping List
	1825–45			U. S. Finance Report
Rye flour, fine........................	....	bbl.	1815–45	
	1815–20			Boston Commercial Gazette
	1821–24			New York Shipping List
	1825–45			U. S. Finance Report

TABLE 40. — *Continued*

Commodity	Years	Unit	Total Period Covered	Source of Data
*Salt, Liverpool......................	....		1815–45	
blown.............................	1815–24	bu. sack		Boston Commercial Gazette
blown, fine.......................	1815–18	bu. sack		New York Shipping List
ground, (fine)....................	1819–24	bu. sack		New York Shipping List
*coarse†..........................	1815–24	8 bu.		Boston Commercial Gazette
fine..............................	1820–23	4 bu.		Boston Commercial Gazette
*fine.............................	1825–45	4 bu.		U. S. Finance Report
Sheetings...........................	....	piece	1825–45	
Russia, brown.....................	1826–45			U. S. Finance Report
Russia, white.....................	1826–45			U. S. Finance Report
Soap......	....	lb.	1825–45	
American, No. 1...................	1830–43			Boston Daily Advertiser
New York.........................	1825–45			U. S. Finance Report
Sperm oil...........................	....	gal.	1825–45	
winter............................	1825–41			U. S. Finance Report
winter, manufactured..............	1842–44			U. S. Finance Report
winter............................	1845			U. S. Finance Report
*Staves, white oak, hhd..............	....	M	1815–45	
	*1815–45			New York Shipping List
	1815–24			Boston Commercial Gazette
Steel, American......................	....	lb.	1825–28	New York Shipping List
*Sugar..............................	....		1815–45	
*New Orleans, prime...............	1815	cwt.		Boston Commercial Gazette
*New Orleans, prime...............	1816–24	cwt.		New York Shipping List
*New Orleans, (not qualified)......	1825–45	lb.		U. S. Finance Report
*Tallow.............................	....	lb.	1815–45	
*American..........................	1815			Boston Commercial Gazette
*American..........................	1816–24			New York Shipping List
*American..........................	1825–35			U. S. Finance Report
*(not qualified).....................	1836–37			U. S. Finance Report
*American..........................	1838–41			U. S. Finance Report
*(not qualified).....................	1842			U. S. Finance Report
*American..........................	1843–45			U. S. Finance Report
Tea, Young Hyson....................	....	lb.	1815–45	
	1815–24			Boston Commercial Gazette
	1825–45			U. S. Finance Report
*Tobacco............................	....	lb.	1815–45	
Bull's Eye.........................	1828–45			Boston Daily Advertiser
*Kentucky.........................	1815–24			New York Shipping List
*Kentucky.........................	1825–45			U. S. Finance Report
manufactured, No. 1...............	1826–45			U. S. Finance Report
*Turpentine, spirits of..............	....	gal.	1816–45	
	1816–24			New York Shipping List
	1825–45			U. S. Finance Report
*Whale Oil..........................	....	gal.	1816–45	
*(not qualified).....................	1815–24			Boston Commercial Gazette
(not qualified).....................	1816–24			New York Shipping List
*(not qualified).....................	1825–39			U. S. Finance Report
*southern..........................	1840–42			U. S. Finance Report
*(not qualified).....................	1843			U. S. Finance Report
*southern..........................	1844			U. S. Finance Report
*(not qualified).....................	1845			U. S. Finance Report

† Adjusted and used with "fine."

TABLE 40. — *Continued*

Commodity	Years	Unit	Total Period Covered	Source of Data
Wheat..................................	....	bu.	1825–45	
Genesee, (not qualified)...............	1825–29			New York Shipping List
Genesee, (not qualified)...............	1832–39			New York Shipping List
Genesee, (not qualified)...............	1826–38			U. S. Finance Report
Genesee, prime white..................	1839–44			U. S. Finance Report
Genesee, (not qualified)...............	1845			U. S. Finance Report
Delaware.............................	1827–29			Philadelphia Price Current
Delaware and Maryland...............	1830–31			Philadelphia Price Current
southern.............................	1832–45			Philadelphia Price Current
North River, red......................	1825–40			New York Shipping List
Pennsylvania, white...................	1825–27			Philadelphia Price Current
Pennsylvania, red.....................	1825–27			Philadelphia Price Current
Pennsylvania, (not qualified)..........	1827–38			Philadelphia Price Current
Pennsylvania and Ohio................	1838–41			Philadelphia Price Current
Pennsylvania and western.............	1842			Philadelphia Price Current
Pennsylvania, red.....................	1843–45			Philadelphia Price Current
Virginia, white.......................	1825–40			New York Shipping List
*Wheat flour, superior.................	....	bbl.	1815–45	
Baltimore, superfine..................	1819–24			Boston Commercial Gazette
Philadelphia, superfine...............	1815–18			Boston Commercial Gazette
New York, superfine..................	1815–24			Boston Commercial Gazette
*New York, superfine.................	1815–24			New York Shipping List
*superior.............................	1825–38			U. S. Finance Report
*(not qualified)......................	1839–41			U. S. Finance Report
*state................................	1842–44			U. S. Finance Report
*Genesee.............................	1845			U. S. Finance Report
Philadelphia..........................	1830–45			Boston Daily Advertiser
west canal............................	1826–37			U. S. Finance Report
*Whiskey, domestic....................	....	gal.	1815–45	
*domestic, rye........................	1815–24			New York Shipping List
*domestic, (not qualified).............	1825–45			U. S. Finance Report
Wine.................................	....	gal.	1825–45	
Malaga, dry..........................	1825–45			New York Shipping List
port..................................	1825–45			U. S. Finance Report
*Wool................................	....	lb.	1816–45	
American full-blood, washed..........	1827–45			Boston Daily Advertiser
common..............................	1825–45			U. S. Finance Report
Saxony, clean........................	1830–37			Boston Daily Advertiser
*merino, washed......................	1815–24			New York Shipping List
*merino..............................	1825–45			U. S. Finance Report

Analysis of the series for the 1825–45 unweighted general index: The treatment of the collected series followed the well-known method devised by Professor Warren M. Persons and already utilized not only by himself but by Professors Snider and Silberling in particular investigations of price movements. Accordingly, a description here of the procedure need be but summary.[3]

The individual series were charted upon separate sheets and by use of a uniform logarithmic scale. Subsequently they were dealt with solely by number, all other marks of identification being for the moment eliminated. The graphs were then studied over a light box. Charting upon a ratio scale permitted the portrayal of relative degrees of movement among series of varying absolute values; the employment of a light box and the superimposition of charts made it possible to bring the movements of individual series into comparison with one another, while the designation of charts merely by number tended toward the elimination of personal bias.

The preliminary examination of the series im-

[3] See Professor Persons' detailed description of the method in the *Review of Economic Statistics*, Preliminary Volume I, January and April 1919, pp. 5–107, and pp. 110–212. For the applications made by Professors J. S. Snider and N. J. Silberling, see the same *Review*, vol. 6 (1924), pp. 93–118 and vol. 5 (1923), Supplement, pp. 219–62.

pressed the investigator with the great variations in the course of individual price series. Scarcely two series, unless they were economically allied, moved together over the entire period of twenty years. Closer inspection, however, began to reveal some order in the apparent diversity. It was observed that certain series not only were strikingly active but exhibited movements common to various others over a portion, sometimes over the greater portion, of the two decades. These "key" or typical series did not always turn out to be of peculiar economic significance. Indeed, they were frequently series relating to commodities of rather minor economic importance, as, for instance, oats or tallow. Perhaps such a "key" group may be looked upon as composed of series in which the price movement was particularly sensitive to changes in general business conditions. A preliminary test group was compounded of the following series.

TABLE 41. — SERIES USED IN THE CONSTRUCTION OF THE "TEST" COMMODITY-PRICE INDEX, 1825-45

Cotton, upland, New York
Cotton sheetings, brown, New York
Cotton yarn, New York
Lead, pig
Leather, hemlock
Molasses, Havana
Rum, New England
Salt, Liverpool
Tallow, American
Whiskey, domestic
Wool, American, full-blood

The development of an index number based upon this group of similarly fluctuating series was next contemplated. Admittedly such an index would probably fail to reflect the movement of prices in general — although the test of experience revealed in this case a situation somewhat contrary to the usual, sound presumption[4] — but it was thought that a preliminary index would be useful as a criterion or standard for sorting the diverse movements of the ninety-odd series collected. An index number was, therefore, constructed from these eleven series in the form of a simple arithmetic average of price relatives. This index number was adopted as a standard, and all other price series were sorted with respect to deviations from the test index.

[4] A comparison made between the movement of prices as indicated by the preliminary or test index and that shown by the general index subsequently developed, showed the course of trend and cyclical activity in the two indices to be surprisingly similar. The declination of the curve from 1825 to 1829-30 was somewhat more pronounced in the case of the test index; the amplitude of the cyclical swings was rather greater in a couple of places, e.g., the rise to 1831-32, that to the peak in 1833, and a smaller fall in 1837; but otherwise in timing and in the general character of the two indices there is little difference.

First, a considerable number of the ninety-odd series had to be discarded as too defective for use. Thus, certain wheat series were rejected, as mentioned above, because quotations in specific journals were infrequently given for the important period 1837-42. Even recourse to other sources was often unsuccessful in providing substitute or complementary series of quotations.

A large further number of price series was discarded in a second sorting because of failure to exhibit substantial variations in movement. In many instances, quotations remained constant for a year or two at a time, sometimes longer. Some of these series related to foreign commodities such as Malaga wine or Russian flax, and others related to consumers' goods, such as soap or gunpowder, for which customary prices for extended periods evidently prevailed. Whatever the explanation in the several cases, 25 series were found to reveal no considerable movement over the entire 20-year interval, and accordingly were set aside.

In addition to these two groups, certain other series were eliminated from further consideration because they displayed movements quite different from those of the test index. The two series relating to hops and tea are striking illustrations; but in two or three other cases the differences of movement, though not so conspicuous, were such as to lead us to discard the series.[5]

[5] Objection might be raised against the elimination of so many series, especially those which are set aside on the ground of their inelasticity or of their irregular movement. The defense for this action must rest on the contention that we are seeking the "typical" or "representative" course of prices, not a mere statistical measure of miscellaneous price series gathered as fortune might direct from the archives of the period. A minute investigation into the marketing of those commodities of which the price movements were peculiar either by reason of their placidity or of their individuality would probably show that no important real difference in movement existed between these cases and those of series actually retained for the index. Perhaps variations in conditions of sales made prices in effect move closely with the trends in the accepted series; or perhaps there existed special circumstances of uncertain crops or irregular supplies from abroad except for which the price movements of "irregular" series would have been more in accord with those of the "representative" series. Furthermore, it may be noted that the inclusion of "insensitive" or "irregular" series in the general index would have merely reduced the sharpness of outline in the curve as finally constructed. The major swings would not have been blotted out. Accordingly, the choice lay between a statistically complete but unresponsive index and one of which the genuineness and accuracy were guaranteed by an adequate economic diversity of individual series — though the actual number of such series would be smaller — and in which the fundamental price changes would be more clearly mirrored. No one, I imagine, would long hesitate at this choice.

Finally, the series which remained were examined for the purpose of eliminating duplicates. In case two or more sets of data were available for a single commodity, the series were again examined for imperfections in quotations, sluggishness, and peculiarity of movement; and the series which were least desirable in these respects were put aside.

The price series catalogued in Table 43, which were discarded for one reason or another and were not employed in the construction of the general index, are listed below, with the reason for their elimination.

There remained after this winnowing process a total of 38 series, representing varied economic activities, from which to construct an index number of general prices for the period 1825–45.[6]

[6] In the cases of four series — coal, Schuylkill; iron, English bar; iron, British pig; and rosin, common — the price movements do not become noteworthy until 1834 and, accordingly, they are not included in the index for the period before that date. In all four cases there is a lack of any real sensitiveness during the earlier years. The reasons for this lack are not in all cases evident. The novelty of the Schuylkill coal during the late 'twenties and early 'thirties may account for the insensitive, perhaps nominal, prices quoted for that article; while the lack of movement in both series pertaining to imported iron

TABLE 42. — SERIES USED IN THE CONSTRUCTION OF THE UNWEIGHTED WHOLESALE COMMODITY-PRICE INDEX, 1825–45

Ashes, pearl	Olive oil
Beef, prime	Pork, mess
Butter, western dairy	Rice, ordinary
Coal, Liverpool	Rosin, common
Coal, Schuylkill	Rum, New England
Coffee, Brazil	Rye, northern
Corn, northern	Rye flour, fine
Cotton, upland	Salt, Liverpool
Cotton yarn	Spirits of turpentine
Fish, bank cod	Staves, white oak
Iron, English bar	Sugar, New Orleans
Iron, British pig	Tallow, American
Lard	Tobacco, Kentucky
Lead, pig	Whale oil
Linseed oil	Wheat, Pennsylvania
Molasses, Havana	Wheat flour, superior
Molasses, New Orleans	Whiskey, domestic
Nails, assorted	Wool, American, full-blood
Oats, northern	Wool, merino

would indicate that there was something abnormal in the price conditions of that commerce. In the case of rosin no clue was found as to the reason for inactivity of price during the early years, followed by rather frequent and substantial price changes in the later period.

TABLE 43. — SERIES DISCARDED FOR USE IN THE UNWEIGHTED WHOLESALE COMMODITY-PRICE INDEX, 1825–45

Beef, mess: price movement slightly less regular than that of Beef, prime. Also, it substantially duplicated the latter commodity.

Boards, North River: insensitive. Examination of the source beyond the period for which quotations were actually secured showed that there was little movement over years at a time.

Candles, sperm: insensitive and irregular over the greater part of the period.

Coffee, Brazil: duplicate of the other coffee series included.

Cognac brandy: insensitive.

Copper, pig: both copper series proved inelastic.

Corn meal: less regular than the series for Corn, northern.

Cotton, upland: the New York series was discarded as a mere duplicate of the Boston series that was included.

Cotton sheeting: Cotton yarn was taken as representative of manufactured cotton.

Fish, dry cod: somewhat irregular and less satisfactory than Fish, bank cod.

Fish, mackerel: irregular until 1835, and in some measure a duplicate of Fish, bank cod.

Flax, American and Russian: insensitive.

Furs, beaver: both series proved insensitive.

Glass, American: insensitive.

Gunpowder, American: insensitive.

Hams, smoked: defective.

Hides: insensitive.

Hops, first sort: highly irregular.

Indigo, Bengal and Manilla: both of these series proved inelastic.

Lead, pig: one of these series proved a substantial duplicate of the other.

Leather, hemlock sole: insensitive through 1834.

Molasses, New Orleans: the Boston series proved defective.

Nails, cut: discarded in part because a duplicate of Nails, assorted, and also because less elastic than the latter.

Pork, prime: slightly less regular than Pork, mess, and besides largely a duplicate of the latter.

Rum, Jamaica: insensitive.

Sheetings, Russia, brown and white: insensitive.

Soap, American and New York: insensitive.

Sperm oil: insensitive until 1838, and rather irregular thereafter.

Steel, American: insensitive. Examination of the source beyond the point for which quotations were actually taken indicated that the series continued insensitive for much of the later period.

Tea, Young Hyson: highly irregular.

Tobacco, Bull's Eye: irregular.

Tobacco, manufactured: insensitive.

Wheat, Delaware: proved largely duplicate of Wheat, Pennsylvania; which was included.

Wheat, Genesee, North River, red, Virginia, white: defective or utilized merely to check or supplement the series finally chosen.

Wheat flour, Philadelphia and west canal: defective.

Wine, Malaga and port: insensitive.

Wool, common: less sensitive than the wool series included.

Wool, Saxony: defective.

Certain smaller groups of series, drawn chiefly from the 38 series above enumerated, were also secured, which showed diversities of movement over portions of the 21 year period under discussion. There are three of these groups, and each is composed of a sufficient number of series so that the departure of its composite movement from that of the general index may be considered other than fortuitous. Comment upon these latter groups is given in the text of this volume.

The construction of index numbers: By reason of the character of the data available for the development of index numbers and of the conditions surrounding the problem in hand, decision was made at first to employ simple arithmetic indices of relative prices. Then came the question of the most adequate base. Since these indices at the time of their original construction, were designed for use in connection with a study of the crisis of 1837, a base was desirable which would have a definite meaning with respect to that episode. Inspection of the individual price series and construction of the test index above mentioned, however, revealed the fact that one could not accurately think of the crisis of 1837 as the culmination of a brief, sharp, upward movement and the inauguration of a downward movement which in a year or two carried commodity prices to the low level from which they had departed previous to 1837. Instead of such a movement of prices immediately before and after 1837, the actual advance and decline lasted at least through the 9-year interval 1834–42. Accordingly, this 9-year period was taken as the base of the index numbers. From a technical viewpoint, it may be noted that the selection of this base insured that the most significant part of the price record, from 1834 to 1842, would not be vitiated by being far removed from the base.

With guidance derived from such conclusions, the actual monthly prices[7] for each commodity were expressed as relatives to the average price for the period 1834–42, and from these relatives were constructed unweighted arithmetic index numbers for the whole group of 38 commodities and for such sub-groups among these series (and a few others drawn in for special reasons) as were felt desirable in the interpretation of the general price movement.

Some time after the development of these unweighted indices, determination was made to construct a weighted index, and to push the period of the index back until it overlapped with that already devised by Professor Smith (and published in the *Review of Economic Statistics*, vol. 9 (1927), pp. 171–83. In pushing the index back through 1815 slight changes were made in the series used. Five series employed in the unweighted index, which either could not be carried back of 1825 or were already represented by similar commodities, were dropped from the list. These five were Schuylkill coal, British pig iron, Pennsylvania wheat, American full-blood wool, and rye flour. On the other hand, upon further consideration, two commodities were added that had not been used earlier, leather and sperm candles.

Then came the important question of proper weights. At best they could be but approximate. No data exist for this period by which accurate weights could be assigned to the various commodity series. However, with such clues as could be found in export data and census figures of production (1850), weights were chosen to express roughly the relative significance of the several commodities. The weights were arranged primarily with a view to the importance of the several commodities in determining the tone of business in the northeastern section of the country, domestic as well as foreign trade being taken into account. With the weights listed below and the relative prices on the 1834–42 base, weighted arithmetic index numbers were constructed from these thirty-five series.

---

[7] Where a spread was given in the original price data, the low figures were employed.

TABLE 44. — SERIES AND WEIGHTS USED IN THE CONSTRUCTION OF THE WEIGHTED WHOLESALE COMMODITY-PRICE INDEX, 1815–45

1	Ashes, pearl	1	Oats, northern
2	Beef, prime	1	Olive oil
1	Butter, western dairy	2	Pork, mess
1	Candles, sperm	1	Rice, ordinary
1	Coal, Liverpool	1	Rosin, common
1	Coffee, Brazil	1	Rum, New England
2	Corn, northern	1	Rye, northern
6	Cotton, upland	1	Salt, Liverpool, fine
3	Cotton yarn, 5–10–14	1	Spirits of turpentine
2	Fish, bank cod	2	Staves, white oak, hhd.
3	Iron, British bar	1	Sugar, New Orleans
1	Lard	1	Tallow, American
1	Lead, pig	3	Tobacco, Kentucky
2	Leather, hemlock sole	1	Whale oil
1	Linseed oil	4	Wheat flour, superior
1	Molasses, Havana	1	Whiskey, domestic
1	Molasses, New Orleans	3	Wool, merino
1	Nails, assorted		

TABLE 45. — WEIGHTED INDEX OF GENERAL WHOLESALE COMMODITY PRICES: MONTHLY, 1815-45[1]

(*Base: 1834-42*)

	Jan.	Feb.	March	April	May	June	July	Aug.	Sept.	Oct.	Nov.	Dec.
1815........	174	190	177	159	163	170	176	179	184	190	188	181
1816........	184	182	182	176	173	172	166	159	154	155	163	164
1817........	171	170	168	167	172	166	159	158	157	159	160	169
1818........	177	177	171	167	170	169	170	173	175	177	177	170
1819........	164	161	159	148	139	131	129	125	127	126	127	124
1820........	123	122	115	112	112	112	113	114	115	109	109	107
1821........	106	103	101	99	102	101	104	106	108	110	120	117
1822........	117	114	115	114	115	112	110	103	103	104	104	102
1823........	102	103	103	98	100	101	102	102	99	100	99	100
1824........	98	97	96	96	96	99	98	97	98	99	100	99
1825........	100	100	104	114	115	117	113	110	107	109	105	106
1826........	103	103	98	97	94	93	95	92	90	92	94	93
1827........	94	95	95	95	92	91	89	90	91	91	92	94
1828........	88	90	88	88	87	88	88	88	89	91	91	95
1829........	95	94	93	92	89	89	85	85	85	85	86	85
1830........	85	84	84	82	84	83	82	83	85	87	88	88
1831........	86	88	89	90	89	90	87	87	89	91	92	91
1832........	96	93	92	90	90	90	88	88	90	92	94	93
1833........	94	91	92	91	93	93	93	96	98	99	98	98
1834........	94	91	88	86	87	87	88	89	92	93	94	97
1835........	99	98	100	103	107	110	115	115	113	111	112	116
1836........	118	116	121	128	122	118	116	119	122	128	130	127
1837........	128	131	129	119	102	102	103	103	98	101	106	108
1838........	107	103	101	100	100	101	102	102	107	113	115	117
1839........	118	125	124	123	120	118	114	112	112	108	104	101
1840........	92	93	90	85	84	82	81	82	86	89	90	89
1841........	88	90	88	87	88	84	84	86	91	90	87	85
1842........	84	80	78	75	74	73	73	72	70	69	68	69
1843........	69	67	67	68	70	71	72	73	74	73	74	73
1844........	74	75	75	76	74	73	72	73	72	73	74	74
1845........	72	72	74	78	78	76	76	77	79	78	83	86

[1] For commodities and weights used in the construction of this index, see Table 44 above.

TABLE 46. — UNWEIGHTED INDEX OF AGRICULTURAL WHOLESALE COMMODITY PRICES: MONTHLY, 1825–45[1]
(Base: 1834–42)

	Jan.	Feb.	March	April	May	June	July	Aug.	Sept.	Oct.	Nov.	Dec.
1825	74	72	73	75	78	81	79	78	85	90	87	86
1826	88	90	85	84	83	86	88	84	83	89	90	88
1827	91	93	90	85	81	82	78	78	82	79	80	88
1828	80	77	72	73	72	74	73	73	78	83	84	88
1829	91	91	91	87	82	86	78	80	80	81	80	78
1830	79	78	77	74	76	78	76	77	82	83	81	81
1831	78	84	87	89	85	85	81	80	83	86	88	86
1832	93	89	87	80	80	85	87	88	90	90	93	92
1833	93	87	86	84	88	87	86	88	92	94	92	91
1834	87	84	77	72	74	77	78	81	85	86	87	84
1835	87	87	89	91	96	106	114	116	110	106	107	114
1836	118	117	122	130	120	113	108	114	124	133	142	137
1837	136	144	138	127	104	109	117	117	107	109	114	122
1838	115	106	105	107	109	111	109	106	117	127	127	132
1839	130	135	129	127	126	126	119	113	114	106	104	100
1840	89	92	89	83	82	81	80	86	91	95	94	88
1841	81	81	80	78	79	76	80	84	93	90	85	85
1842	82	77	76	72	73	70	69	68	64	63	63	66
1843	64	61	61	62	66	68	72	72	72	68	69	67
1844	66	68	68	69	69	66	63	65	64	67	69	68
1845	64	67	71	75	73	70	74	76	84	82	88	95

TABLE 47. — UNWEIGHTED INDEX OF INDUSTRIAL WHOLESALE COMMODITY PRICES: MONTHLY, 1825–45[1]
(Base: 1834–42)

	Jan.	Feb.	March	April	May	June	July	Aug.	Sept.	Oct.	Nov.	Dec.
1825	103	102	105	114	118	117	113	109	106	108	107	104
1826	102	102	97	97	95	93	95	93	93	93	95	96
1827	96	96	97	98	96	94	92	93	95	98	98	97
1828	96	95	93	93	92	94	92	90	91	94	92	93
1829	94	95	93	92	88	85	82	80	82	84	84	85
1830	87	85	87	83	85	82	84	84	87	92	92	95
1831	92	94	95	96	94	96	94	96	98	100	102	100
1832	101	98	99	95	94	91	91	91	93	97	97	98
1833	99	95	96	98	99	99	99	101	102	105	102	103
1834	99	96	92	89	90	88	88	90	91	93	94	98
1835	101	101	104	106	110	110	114	112	113	112	115	119
1836	122	120	124	130	127	121	118	121	124	124	129	129
1837	130	131	132	124	113	106	99	100	99	101	106	107
1838	108	104	100	99	97	97	97	100	102	108	108	108
1839	109	115	116	112	109	107	107	106	104	103	96	93
1840	91	89	88	84	83	84	81	81	85	88	90	88
1841	90	91	88	86	86	84	82	87	89	91	90	90
1842	90	85	82	80	77	78	76	76	77	78	77	79
1843	78	75	75	74	74	75	73	75	80	80	80	80
1844	82	82	81	81	80	81	81	81	81	81	82	81
1845	79	77	78	83	85	82	81	82	82	83	88	88

[1] A discussion of these indices and the commodities used are given in the text, pp. 65, 66.

COMMODITY PRICE INDICES, 1843-62

Data and their sources: For this period, too, the main reliance was put upon data compiled in the *Finance Report* already mentioned. About ninety series were transcribed largely from this source, and those others used to complement the ninety series were drawn from contemporary news-sheets. A list of these commodities, together with the periods covered and the markets to which they appertain, is presented in the accompanying Table 48.

While the list contains most items of domestic and foreign commerce which were significant during the period, the material is not without certain defects. Some important products of American manufacture are missing — wool cloth, for example, and boots and shoes. These gaps in the evidence, arising from the unavailability of data, become in some measure less momentous because of the inclusion of certain other series such as raw wool and leather — the raw stock of these manufacturing industries.

Again, series were not always complete for every month in the two hundred and forty. Gaps of a month or two were filled in by interpolation when supplementary data were not available in other sources — the change of price between known values being made to proceed by even stages — and rarely was it found necessary to improvise for longer periods. Series were discarded if they lacked data for as much as four or five months, especially when that deficiency came at a general turning point of values, such as 1847 and 1858.

A third element which might appear a defect — namely, the use of quotations taken from different markets — seems of no great real importance. An examination of price series obtained from both the Boston and New York markets shows these areas to have been so closely related that no disparity of real moment existed between the course of values in the two regions. It was possible, therefore, to bring together the series from the New York district and the few from Boston to reveal characteristic price changes in this, the most important, eastern section of the country.

TABLE 48. — SERIES OF WHOLESALE COMMODITY PRICES TRANSCRIBED, 1843–62*

In some cases, series were not transcribed in the full period for which they were available, as, for instance, when observation of quotations for a number of years indicated that the series were insensitive to changes in business conditions.

(Series used in the construction of the weighted commodity-price index are marked by an asterisk)

Commodity	Years	Unit	Total Period Covered	Source of Data
*Ashes, pearl, first sort.................	....	cwt.	1843–62	New York Shipping List
*Beef........................	....	bbl.	1843–62	
*mess, country......................	1843–44			U. S. Finance Report
*mess, (not qualified)...............	1843–50			U. S. Finance Report
mess, city.........................	1850–52			New York Shipping List
mess, country.....................	1850–52			New York Shipping List
*mess, country....................	1851–52			U. S. Finance Report
*mess, (not qualified).............	1853–62			U. S. Finance Report
prime.........................	1843–62			U. S. Finance Report
*Butter.......................	....	lb.	1843–62	
*state........................	1843–45			U. S. Finance Report
*western dairy...................	1846–50			U. S. Finance Report
*state........................	1851–62			U. S. Finance Report
Candles, sperm.................	....	lb.	1843–62	U. S. Finance Report
*Coal.........................	....		1843–62	U. S. Finance Report
anthracite, domestic...............	1843–62	ton		U. S. Finance Report
*Liverpool.................	1843–62	chaldron		U. S. Finance Report
*Coffee.................	....	lb.	1843–62	
Brazil.................	1843–62			U. S. Finance Report
*Brazil.................	1843–62			New York Shipping List
Java, white.................	1843–45			U. S. Finance Report
Java, white.................	1846–52			New York Shipping List
Java, white.................	1850–62			U. S. Finance Report
Java, green.................	1846–49			U. S. Finance Report
*Cognac brandy.................	....	gal.	1843–62	U. S. Finance Report
*Copper, pig.................	....	lb.	1843–62	
	1845–52			U. S. Finance Report
	1853–62			Boston Daily Advertiser
Copper sheathing.................	....	lb.	1843–62	U. S. Finance Report
*Corn, northern.................	....	bu.	1843–62	U. S. Finance Report
Corn meal.................	....	bbl.	1843–62	
Jersey.................	1843–44			U. S. Finance Report
northern.................	1845–52			U. S. Finance Report
(not qualified).................	1853–62			U. S. Finance Report
*Cotton, upland.................	....	lb.	1843–62	
*middling.................	1843–62			U. S. Finance Report
fair to prime.................	1843–50			Boston Daily Advertiser
fair to good.................	1851–60			Boston Daily Advertiser
middling fair.................	1861–62			Boston Daily Advertiser
*Cotton sheetings, brown.................	....	yd.	1843–62	New York Shipping List
Cotton yarn, 5–13.................	....	lb.	1843–57	New York Shipping List
*Fish.................	....		1843–62	
*bank cod and Grand Bank.............	1843–62	qtl.		Boston Daily Advertiser
dry cod.................	1843–62	cwt.		U. S. Finance Report
mackerel, No. 1.................	1843–62	bbl.		U. S. Finance Report
Flax.................	....	lb.	1843–57	
American.................	1843–57			U. S. Finance Report
Russian.................	1843–47			U. S. Finance Report
Furs, beaver, northern.................	....	lb.	1845–62	U. S. Finance Report

TABLE 48. — *Continued*

Commodity	Years	Unit	Total Period Covered	Source of Data
Gin..................................	....	gal.	1843–62	
Holland...........................	1843–46			U. S. Finance Report
Medler's Swan.....................	1847–62			U. S. Finance Report
Glass................................	....		1843–62	
American...........................	1843–44	50 ft.		U. S. Finance Report
American...........................	1847–52	box		U. S. Finance Report
American, window..................	1853–62	50 ft.		U. S. Finance Report
English crown.....................	1845–46	50 ft.		U. S. Finance Report
Gunpowder, American...............	....	25 lbs.	1843–62	
(not qualified).....................	1843–45			U. S. Finance Report
common...........................	1846–47			U. S. Finance Report
(not qualified).....................	1848			U. S. Finance Report
common...........................	1849			U. S. Finance Report
(not qualified).....................	1850			U. S. Finance Report
common...........................	1851–55			U. S. Finance Report
shipping...........................	1856–62			U. S. Finance Report
Hams, pickled.......................	....	lb.	1843–62	
	1843–51			New York Shipping List
	1852–62			U. S. Finance Report
*Hides................................	....	lb.	1843–62	
*Buenos Ayres......................	1843			U. S. Finance Report
*La Plata..........................	1844			U. S. Finance Report
*Buenos Ayres......................	1845–62			U. S. Finance Report
Hops, first sort.....................	....	lb.	1843–62	U. S. Finance Report
Indigo...............................	....	lb.	1843–62	
Bengal............................	1843–55			New York Shipping List
Bengal, middling..................	1855–62			Boston Daily Advertiser
Manilla...........................	1843–62			U. S. Finance Report
*Iron................................	....	ton	1843–62	
bar, English, common.............	1843–62			U. S. Finance Report
*pig, Scotch.......................	1843–45			U. S. Finance Report
*pig, English......................	1846–53			U. S. Finance Report
*pig, Scotch.......................	1854–62			U. S. Finance Report
*Lard................................	....	lb.	1843–62	
*(not qualified).....................	1843–62			U. S. Finance Report
Ohio, and city.....................	1843–44			New York Shipping List
Ohio...............................	1844–46			New York Shipping List
Ohio, prime.......................	1850–52			New York Shipping List
*Lead, pig...........................	....	cwt.	1843–62	
	1843–62			Boston Daily Advertiser
	*1843–62			U. S. Finance Report
*Leather, hemlock...................	....	lb.	1843–62	
*sole..............................	1843–46			U. S. Finance Report
*middling..........................	1847–52			U. S. Finance Report
*(not qualified)....................	1853–62			U. S. Finance Report
*Linseed oil.........................	....	gal.	1843–61	
*(not qualified)....................	1843–45			U. S. Finance Report
*Dutch and English................	1846			Boston Daily Advertiser
*Dutch and English................	1847–54			U. S. Finance Report
*English...........................	1855–61			U. S. Finance Report
Lumber, boards, North River, clear......	....	M ft.	1843–55	New York Shipping List
*Molasses............................	....	gal.	1843–62	
Havana............................	1843–44			U. S. Finance Report
Havana and Matanzas..............	1845			U. S. Finance Report

TABLE 48. — *Continued*

Commodity	Years	Unit	Total Period Covered	Source of Data
*Molasses (*continued*)				
Matanzas	1846–57			U. S. Finance Report
Cuba, clayed	1858–62			U. S. Finance Report
*New Orleans	1843–62			U. S. Finance Report
Nails		lb.	1843–62	
assorted sizes	1843–62			Boston Daily Advertiser
cut	1843–62			U. S. Finance Report
*Nutmeg		lb.	1843–62	U. S. Finance Report
*Oats, northern		bu.	1843–62	
*state northern	1843–45			U. S. Finance Report
*northern	1846–62			U. S. Finance Report
*Olive oil		gal.	1843–62	U. S. Finance Report
Paints, red lead		lb.	1843–62	U. S. Finance Report
*Pepper		lb.	1843–62	U. S. Finance Report
*Pork		lb.	1843–62	
mess	1843–62	lb.		U. S. Finance Report
*prime	1843–62	bbl.		U. S. Finance Report
*Rice		cwt.	1843–62	
*ordinary	1843–53			U. S. Finance Report
*fair	1854			U. S. Finance Report
*ordinary	1855–62			U. S. Finance Report
ordinary to fair	1850–53			New York Shipping List
fair	1854–55			New York Shipping List
*Rosin, common		bbl.	1843–62	
*common, (not qualified)	1843–62			U. S. Finance Report
*common, (in yards)	1851–52			New York Shipping List
*common, (delivered)	1853–62			New York Shipping List
white, (not qualified)	1851–62			U. S. Finance Report
*Rum		gal.	1843–62	
Jamaica	1843–62			U. S. Finance Report
*New England	1843–62			Boston Daily Advertiser
*Rye, northern		bu.	1843–62	U. S. Finance Report
Rye flour		bbl.	1843–62	
fine	1843–52			U. S. Finance Report
(not qualified)	1853–62			U. S. Finance Report
*Salt, Liverpool, fine		sack	1843–62	
	*1843–62			U. S. Finance Report
	1855–62			New York Shipping List
Sheetings		piece	1843–62	
Russian, brown	1843–54			U. S. Finance Report
Russian, white	1843–54			U. S. Finance Report
Soap		lb.	1843–62	
New York	1843–56			U. S. Finance Report
brown	1857–62			U. S. Finance Report
Sperm oil		gal.	1843–62	
winter, manufactured	1843–44			U. S. Finance Report
winter	1845–62			U. S. Finance Report
*Staves, white oak		M	1843–62	New York Shipping List
Steel, American		lb.	1843–48	New York Shipping List
*Sugar		lb.	1843–62	
*Havana, white, refined	1843–45			New York Shipping List
*Havana, white	1846–62			U. S. Finance Report
New Orleans	1843–62			U. S. Finance Report
Louisiana, fair	1857			New Orleans Price Current
*Tallow, American		lb.	1843–62	U. S. Finance Report

TABLE 48. — *Continued*

Commodity	Years	Unit	Total Period	Source of Data
Tea, Young Hyson.................	....	lb.	1843–62	
	1843–59			U. S. Finance Report
	1860–61			Boston Daily Advertiser
	1862			U. S. Finance Report
*Tobacco......................	....	lb.	1843–62	
*Kentucky...................	1843–62			U. S. Finance Report
manufactured, No. 1...........	1843–62			U. S. Finance Report
*Turpentine, spirits of...........	....	gal.	1843–62	U. S. Finance Report
Whalebone....................	....	lb.	1843–62	
polar......................	1843–45			U. S. Finance Report
polar, northwest coast	1846–48			U. S. Finance Report
northwest coast	1849–54			U. S. Finance Report
(not qualified)...............	1855–56			U. S. Finance Report
northwest coast	1857–62			U. S. Finance Report
slab......................	1843–44			New York Shipping List
northwest coast	1853–54			New York Shipping List
*Whale oil....................	....	gal.	1843–62	
*(not qualified)...............	1843			U. S. Finance Report
*southern...................	1844			U. S. Finance Report
*(not qualified)...............	1845–47			U. S. Finance Report
*southern...................	1848–51			U. S. Finance Report
*(not qualified)...............	1852–62			U. S. Finance Report
*Wheat, Genesee	....	bu.	1843–62	
*prime white................	1843–44			U. S. Finance Report
*(not qualified)...............	1845			U. S. Finance Report
*western...................	1846			U. S. Finance Report
*western red.................	1847			U. S. Finance Report
*mixed and red...............	1848			U. S. Finance Report
*(not qualified)...............	1849–62			U. S. Finance Report
Wheat flour..................	....		1843–62	
common				
state.....................	1843–44	bu.		U. S. Finance Report
Genesee	1845–52	bu.		U. S. Finance Report
state.....................	1855	bu.		U. S. Finance Report
(not qualified)...............	1856–62	bu.		U. S. Finance Report
Genesee, common	1843–62	qtl.		Boston Daily Advertiser
Genesee, fancy brands	1853–62	bu.		New York Shipping List
*Whiskey, domestic.............	....	gal.	1843–62	U. S. Finance Report
Wine........................	....		1843–62	
claret....................	1843–53	cask		U. S. Finance Report
Bordeaux..................	1854–62	cask		U. S. Finance Report
Malaga, dry...............	1843–55	gal.		New York Shipping List
Malaga, dry...............	1856–62	gal.		Boston Daily Advertiser
Malaga, sweet.............	1843–55	gal.		New York Shipping List
Malaga, sweet.............	1856–62	gal.		Boston Daily Advertiser
port.....................	1843–62	gal.		U. S. Finance Report
*Wool.......................	....	lb.	1843–62	
American, full-blood				
merino, washed..............	1843–62			Boston Daily Advertiser
common....................	1843–62			U. S. Finance Report
*merino....................	1843–62			U. S. Finance Report

Analysis of the series: The technique used in handling these series was the same as that used for the earlier period. The individual series were charted on a uniform ratio scale and then studied over a light box.

In the examination of the charts, the dominant purpose was the segregation of those series, the movements of which were common to a large proportion of the total number, or which fell into

remained. Like the "insensitive" items, they were considered unrepresentative. They were not lacking in variability, but their movements were highly individualistic.

Even after the elimination of insensitive and erratic series, an accurate study of the remaining charts held no small difficulties — especially for the period prior to 1852. Up to that time, commodity

TABLE 49. — SERIES DISCARDED FOR USE IN THE UNWEIGHTED WHOLESALE COMMODITY-PRICE INDEX, 1843–62

Beef, mess, varying description: defective.
Beef, prime: defective.
Candles, sperm: represented by sperm oil.
Coal, anthracite: defective and insensitive.
Coffee, Brazil (both series): irregular.
Coffee, Java, white: lack of homogeneity.
Copper sheathing: insensitive.
Corn meal: represented by Corn, northern.
Cotton, upland, varying description: discarded in favor of Cotton, middling.
Cotton yarn, 5–13: insensitive.
Cotton sheetings, brown, 4–4: insensitive.
Fish, dry cod: represented by Fish, bank cod.
Fish, mackerel, No. 1: defective.
Flax, American: defective.
Flax, Russian: insensitive and defective.
Furs, beaver, northern: insensitive.
Gin: insensitive.
Glass, American, varying description: lack of homogeneity and insensitive.
Gunpowder, American, varying description: insensitive.
Hams, pickled: represented by Pork, prime. (Included in the agricultural index.)
Hops, first sort: irregular.
Indigo, Bengal: lack of homogeneity and insensitive.
Indigo, Manilla: lack of homogeneity and insensitive.
Iron, English bar, common: represented by Iron, British pig.
Lard: represented by Pork, prime. (Included in the agricultural index.)

Lumber, boards, North River, clear: insensitive.
Molasses, Cuban, varying description: represented by Molasses, New Orleans.
Nails, assorted sizes: insensitive.
Nails, cut: defective and insensitive.
Paints, red lead: insensitive.
Pork, mess: represented by Pork, prime.
Rice, ordinary: defective.
Rum, Jamaica: represented by Rum, New England.
Rye flour, fine: represented by Rye.
Sheetings, Russian, brown: defective and insensitive.
Sheetings, Russian, white: defective and insensitive.
Soap, New York: insensitive.
Steel, American: insensitive.
Sugar, New Orleans: defective.
Tea, Young Hyson: lacking in homogeneity and insensitive.
Tobacco, manufactured, No. 1: insensitive.
Whalebone, varying description: defective.
Wheat flour, Genesee, common: represented by Wheat, Genesee.
Wheat flour, Genesee, fancy brands: lacking in homogeneity and represented by Wheat, Genesee.
Wine, claret and Bordeaux: lacking in homogeneity and insensitive.
Wine, Malaga dry: insensitive.
Wine, port: lacking in homogeneity and insensitive.
Wool, American full-blood: represented by Wool, merino.
Wool, common: represented by Wool, merino.

smaller groups exhibiting common characteristics during some significant part of the two decades. The purpose obviously was that pursued in the commodity-price investigation for the period 1815–45 — to set up major or minor groupings of the material which, over time-periods suggested by the data themselves, would reveal characteristic variations in the course of prices.

Adherence to this general aim meant putting aside once more those series which manifested no appreciable changes over relatively long portions of the time-interval. Certain other series — among them hops and Brazilian coffee — were discarded on another score. After the material as a whole had been studied, and was found to fall into certain groups based upon common price movements, a few

prices showed no single uniform or predominant general movement, with the result that groups discovered and segregated were sometimes composed of only six or eight series. The period from 1852 to 1858 was somewhat simpler in character, as if commodity-price movements were now controlled by more powerful forces than had prevailed in the earlier years; yet even for these seven years, at least two significant groups of series could be distinguished on the basis of their characteristic activities; and, although during the period 1858–61 the greater number of the selected series manifested a common movement in greater or less degree, still a cleavage was possible if the degree to which the series responded to the underlying forces then in operation was employed as a criterion.

Examination of the material, therefore, led to a formation of no less than four groups. One, containing thirteen series, extended over the years 1843–48; two, comprised of eleven and twenty-two series, respectively, spanned the decade 1849–58; and the fourth, composed of seventeen series, covered the briefer period, 1858–61. Each of these groups seemed sufficiently broad and significant to warrant the construction of an index based upon it. In addition, as a check upon these narrower indices and as a basis for gauging the general movement of all commodity prices, the aggregates of active and non-erratic series were thrown together for the construction of an all-inclusive index covering the whole twenty-year interval.

The indices to be computed, then, were:

I.   Special Index based on 13 commodities for 1843–48.
IIa. Special Index based on 11 series for 1849–58.
IIb. Special Index based on 22 series for 1849–58.
III. Special Index based on 17 series for 1858–61.
IV. General Index (unweighted) based on 33 series for 1843–62.

The series contained in the Special Indices I, IIa, IIb, and III are listed in the text;[8] while those for General Index IV are to be found in Table 50 below.

TABLE 50. — SERIES USED IN THE CONSTRUCTION OF THE UNWEIGHTED GENERAL WHOLESALE COMMODITY-PRICE INDEX (IV), 1843–62

Ashes, pearl, first sort	Rosin, common
Butter, western	Rum, New England
Coal, Liverpool	Rye, northern
Cognac brandy	Salt, Liverpool
Copper, pig	Sperm oil
Corn, northern	Spices, nutmeg
Cotton, middling	Spices, pepper
Fish, bank cod	Spirits of turpentine
Hides, Buenos Ayres	Staves, white oak, hhd.
Iron, British pig	Sugar, Havana, refined
Lead, pig	Tallow, American
Leather, hemlock sole	Tobacco, Kentucky
Linseed oil, English	Whale oil
Molasses, New Orleans	Wheat, Genesee
Oats, northern	Whiskey, domestic
Olive oil	Wool, merino
Pork, prime	

Construction of index numbers: The number and composition of the indices decided on, the form in which they were to be constructed was considered. First, an unweighted arithmetic index was determined upon — largely because this form had been previously employed in the early investigation of the

[8] See pp. 95, 96, above, and Charts 31, 32, 33. Since these indices appear on the charts mentioned above it was felt unnecessary to print the actual index numbers.

period 1825–45 — while for reasons similar to those that had prevailed in the latter case, a broad base for this index was sought. For the present investigation, the mean of monthly values over the eleven-year period, 1848–58, was chosen — an interval which appeared to comprehend the whole swing of prices which reached a peak in 1855–57. Indices constructed in this manner — simple arithmetic upon a broad base — seemed the most serviceable that could be secured under the circumstances, although admittedly they are by no means ideal and might well be inaccurate, especially at the extremes of the whole period over which they were to run.

Subsequently, a weighted index seemed worthy of construction determined by the same reasons as obtained in the case of the period 1815–45. Again, export and import data and production figures were used to assign weights which — as in the earlier weighted index — would reflect the relative importance of the commodities in the business life of the northeastern communities.

With the weights thus devised and the relative prices on the 1848–58 base, weighted arithmetic index numbers were constructed employing 37 series. Again, one series was dropped and certain others added. The series for sperm oil was eliminated by reason of the presence of that for whale oil. The series for mess beef and ordinary rice were completed by recourse to the *New York Shipping List;* and a new series for Brazilian coffee was drawn from the same source. In addition to these, it was decided to add lard and brown sheetings because of the importance of these products; even though pork and upland cotton were already included. The new list for the weighted index is given below in Table 51.

TABLE 51. — SERIES AND WEIGHTS USED IN THE CONSTRUCTION OF THE WEIGHTED WHOLESALE COMMODITY-PRICE INDEX, 1843–62

1	Ashes, pearl	1	Oats, northern
3	Beef, mess	1	Olive oil
1	Butter, western	3	Pork, prime
2	Coal, Liverpool	1	Rice, ordinary
1	Coffee, Brazil	1	Rosin, common
1	Cognac brandy	1	Rum, New England
1	Copper, pig	1	Rye, northern
2	Corn, northern	1	Salt, Liverpool
9	Cotton, middling	1	Spices, nutmeg
3	Cotton sheeting	1	Spices, pepper
2	Fish, bank cod	1	Spirits of turpentine
1	Hides, Buenos Ayres	3	Staves, white oak, hhd.
4	Iron, British pig	1	Sugar, Havana, refined
1	Lard	1	Tallow, American
1	Lead, pig	3	Tobacco, Kentucky
2	Leather, hemlock sole	2	Whale oil
1	Linseed oil, English	7	Wheat, Genesee
2	Molasses, New Orleans	1	Whiskey, domestic
		4	Wool, merino

TABLE 52. — WEIGHTED INDEX OF GENERAL WHOLESALE COMMODITY PRICES: MONTHLY, 1843–62[1]

(*Base: 1848–58*)

	Jan.	Feb.	March	April	May	June	July	Aug.	Sept.	Oct.	Nov.	Dec.
1843........	72	70	69	70	73	74	75	72	74	75	77	77
1844........	79	81	81	79	78	76	75	77	75	74	75	75
1845........	75	74	74	80	82	79	79	80	80	82	87	89
1846........	85	85	85	86	84	80	78	77	76	81	83	82
1847........	84	94	95	95	98	101	93	92	96	94	93	88
1848........	86	85	85	84	79	78	76	75	76	78	74	75
1849........	78	80	81	81	78	77	78	81	84	86	85	87
1850........	87	92	92	89	88	90	90	90	90	92	94	95
1851........	93	96	92	93	94	87	85	82	83	82	82	80
1852........	81	83	85	87	90	91	91	93	95	95	96	96
1853........	98	102	102	101	100	96	97	100	102	106	109	109
1854........	110	115	113	111	113	111	110	109	111	108	110	109
1855........	107	107	110	113	116	120	120	118	119	120	120	120
1856........	117	116	117	116	114	108	111	113	114	119	122	122
1857........	124	126	131	132	133	133	131	132	130	119	111	108
1858........	97	95	100	100	103	99	100	102	104	106	102	102
1859........	102	106	106	104	103	104	100	99	97	96	96	97
1860........	99	99	99	98	99	97	95	96	97	98	98	93
1861........	94	93	92	93	98	95	92	100	113	116	120	130
1862........	147	145	128	133	136	137	151	186	188	200	215	227

[1] For commodities and weights used in the construction of this index, see Table 51 above.

TABLE 53. — UNWEIGHTED INDEX OF AGRICULTURAL WHOLESALE COMMODITY PRICES: MONTHLY, 1843–62[1]
(*Base: 1848–58*)

	Jan.	Feb.	March	April	May	June	July	Aug.	Sept.	Oct.	Nov.	Dec.
1843	65	62	61	62	63	65	67	67	69	66	68	67
1844	64	66	68	66	64	61	59	61	60	62	63	66
1845	66	69	71	76	74	74	76	79	84	82	88	92
1846	90	86	83	82	75	69	67	65	64	78	77	77
1847	77	94	99	98	102	112	95	87	91	90	94	90
1848	84	79	82	81	80	77	73	75	76	78	76	77
1849	82	83	80	73	72	71	72	76	78	79	81	84
1850	82	84	81	76	79	85	84	81	84	83	84	91
1851	91	94	94	94	96	88	83	81	81	82	80	84
1852	89	88	90	98	95	92	93	95	96	100	103	103
1853	107	103	100	93	98	94	95	96	102	104	104	102
1854	108	115	111	102	111	113	108	104	111	104	111	115
1855	121	115	123	126	134	136	129	120	122	125	125	132
1856	123	119	115	112	103	102	106	112	114	120	121	123
1857	121	128	132	134	140	143	140	136	136	117	110	113
1858	94	92	95	99	104	97	96	104	105	108	102	104
1859	104	108	106	107	104	110	98	94	97	98	99	100
1860	101	99	99	97	95	95	94	95	98	100	101	92
1861	89	87	85	85	86	78	73	76	79	86	90	93
1862	89	92	93	90	91	82	81	95	95	109	119	124

TABLE 54. — UNWEIGHTED INDEX OF INDUSTRIAL WHOLESALE COMMODITY PRICES: MONTHLY, 1843–62[1]
(*Base: 1848–58*)

	Jan.	Feb.	March	April	May	June	July	Aug.	Sept.	Oct.	Nov.	Dec.
1843	80	78	76	77	78	76	76	76	80	80	83	82
1844	84	86	84	84	82	82	81	83	82	81	82	82
1845	80	79	78	83	86	82	81	82	81	83	88	89
1846	86	86	86	86	84	81	79	80	79	80	84	85
1847	82	87	89	89	90	87	85	89	94	92	93	88
1848	86	87	86	84	80	77	76	76	78	80	79	80
1849	80	82	82	83	79	76	78	80	83	86	85	86
1850	86	89	89	88	86	85	86	88	88	89	91	90
1851	92	92	90	89	89	86	84	84	84	83	84	82
1852	80	83	84	83	89	89	86	87	91	93	97	97
1853	100	105	105	103	101	97	97	100	102	107	114	114
1854	112	119	118	117	114	110	108	108	110	112	110	111
1855	107	105	105	105	108	108	111	114	118	119	122	121
1856	120	118	118	118	119	115	118	121	120	124	126	127
1857	128	129	132	131	130	128	127	129	127	118	110	108
1858	100	96	100	102	102	101	101	102	106	106	103	103
1859	102	107	107	106	105	105	105	102	101	101	102	103
1860	105	105	104	102	102	100	99	100	100	101	100	96
1861	93	92	92	92	98	96	95	110	121	127	130	136
1862	150	152	137	137	151	157	166	210	208	217	237	240

[1] A discussion of these indices and the commodities used are given in the text, pp. 97–99.

APPENDIX B

Data and their sources: Full particulars as to the source of data, periods covered, and description of the commodities are to be found above in Tables 40 and 48.

Construction of the indices: The lists of series used in the indices of domestic and imported commodity prices are given below in Tables 55 and 56. No deviation was made from the method customarily used, except that in these cases the indices were put on a quarterly instead of a monthly basis.

TABLE 55. — SERIES USED IN THE CONSTRUCTION OF THE UNWEIGHTED DOMESTIC WHOLESALE COMMODITY-PRICE INDEX, 1825–62

Ashes, pearl
Beef, prime
Butter, western dairy
Candles, sperm
Coal, Schuylkill
Corn, northern
Cotton, upland
Cotton yarn, 5–10
Fish, bank cod
Fish, mackerel
Lard
Lead, pig
Leather, hemlock sole
Linseed oil
Molasses, New Orleans
Nails, assorted
Oats, northern
Pork, mess
Rice, ordinary
Rosin, common
Rum, New England
Rye, northern
Spirits of turpentine
Staves, white oak, hhd.
Sugar, New Orleans
Tallow, American
Tobacco, Kentucky
Whale oil
Wheat flour, superior
Whiskey, domestic
Wool, American full-blood

TABLE 56. — SERIES USED IN THE CONSTRUCTION OF THE UNWEIGHTED FOREIGN WHOLESALE COMMODITY-PRICE INDEX, 1825–62

Coal, Liverpool
Coffee, Brazil
Hides, Buenos Ayres
Indigo, Bengal
Iron, Scotch pig
Iron, English bar
Molasses, Havana
Olive oil
Salt, Liverpool, fine
Spices, nutmeg
Tea, Young Hyson
Wine, Malaga

TABLE 57. — UNWEIGHTED INDEX OF DOMESTIC
WHOLESALE COMMODITY PRICES: QUARTERLY, 1825–62
(*Base: 1834–42*)

	January	April	July	October
1825	92	97	99	100
1826	98	94	94	94
1827	97	97	89	93
1828	93	89	87	91
1829	92	90	83	84
1830	85	81	82	88
1831	85	91	87	92
1832	97	90	88	83
1833	95	91	91	98
1834	93	82	84	89
1835	94	99	112	108
1836	119	128	112	125
1837	127	120	104	102
1838	109	102	103	116
1839	119	122	116	108
1840	93	87	84	94
1841	90	87	84	92
1842	87	76	74	72
1843	70	68	73	75
1844	76	76	73	75
1845	74	80	79	83
1846	87	83	74	81
1847	83	96	97	98
1848	88	84	76	82
1849	82	84	80	88
1850	86	85	86	91
1851	94	91	86	85
1852	86	92	94	97
1853	103	99	96	106
1854	109	109	107	112
1855	114	115	123	124
1856	128	119	116	125
1857	129	134	139	120
1858	98	102	101	109
1859	107	112	107	104
1860	106	103	101	104
1861	95	92	93	118
1862	132	125	140	176

TABLE 58. — UNWEIGHTED INDEX OF FOREIGN
WHOLESALE COMMODITY PRICES: QUARTERLY, 1825–62
(*Base: 1834–42*)

	January	April	July	October
1825	140	152	158	152
1826	143	136	132	126
1827	123	132	133	127
1828	129	122	115	116
1829	119	122	114	113
1830	110	111	110	109
1831	109	111	114	123
1832	126	113	110	116
1833	116	106	102	108
1834	102	96	91	97
1835	97	103	107	104
1836	106	114	108	113
1837	118	111	98	101
1838	110	102	101	109
1839	109	112	104	104
1840	98	91	88	93
1841	101	95	96	101
1842	95	78	75	76
1843	78	78	76	82
1844	82	84	88	88
1845	87	95	90	91
1846	89	91	88	85
1847	87	94	89	92
1848	89	86	79	79
1849	74	77	74	78
1850	81	83	79	85
1851	84	83	80	79
1852	77	77	81	88
1853	92	97	93	105
1854	110	114	108	110
1855	100	103	102	112
1856	115	116	117	119
1857	118	128	125	120
1858	100	105	103	107
1859	103	108	105	104
1860	108	110	106	108
1861	99	100	95	111
1862	124	128	126	138

APPENDIX C

SOURCES OF DATA AND STATISTICAL METHODS USED IN THE CONSTRUCTION OF MONTHLY INDICES OF SECURITY PRICES, 1795–1862

SECURITY PRICES, 1795–1820

Data and their sources: The quotations of the prices of United States three per cent "Stock" and of bank-stock prices used in this section were compiled from the *Boston Gazette* and other sources mentioned on page 144. These data were taken from the same newspapers and for the same dates as the data on commodity prices used in the earlier sections. In a table below (Table 60) are listed some of the more important security-price series which are available for the years 1795–1820. The series marked with an asterisk are those used in computing the index hereafter presented.

TABLE 59. — ACTUAL PRICES OF UNITED STATES 3% STOCK IN BOSTON: MONTHLY, 1795–1820*

(Unit: dollars per share)

Year	Jan.	Feb.	March	April	May	June	July	Aug.	Sept.	Oct.	Nov.	Dec.
1795.......	....	....	....	....	....	....	....	....	....	....	55	50⅝
1796.......	50⅝	50⅝	50⅝	50⅝	50	50	50⅞	51¼	50⅛	51¼	50⅝	49⅜
1797.......	45⅝	45⅞	46⅞	47½	49⅜	50	50	50	50⅝	50⅝	50⅝	51½
1798.......	51½	51½	51	50	49⅛	48¾	46½	45	42½	44⅜	48¾	48⅞
1799.......	50	47½	49½	49	49	47½	46¼	45	45	45	46¼	47½
1800.......	47½	47¾	49½	50	50	51⅛	51¼	51⅜	53	53	53½	55
1801.......	52½	52½	52½	52½	54	55	56¼	56⅞	56⅞	56¾	57½	59
1802.......	60	59¾	60	59	59	61⅞	65	65⅝	65½	65	62½	62
1803.......	61⅝	60	59½	59½	57½	60	57¾	58½	58¾	58	58¾	59½
1804.......	59	59	59	57¾	57¾	57¾	57½	57¾	57¾	57½	57½	57½
1805.......	56⅞	57	57	56	56½	56½	55½	54¾	56	55½	56	57½
1806.......	57	57¾	59¾	59¾	60	61¼	61½	63	63½	62¾	62¾	62¼
1807.......	61¾	62⅝	63	63¼	63¾	63¾	....	64	64¼	63¾	64½	64½
1808.......	64	63¾	64	64	64¾	64¾	64½	65¼	65½	65	65½	65½
1809.......	65	65½	65½	65¼	65¼	65¾	65¼	65¼	65¼	65¾	66	66¾
1810.......	66¼	66¼	66¼	65¾	65¾	65¾	65⅝	65⅞	66	65¼	65½	65½
1811.......	65¼	65⅜	65⅜	65⅛	65½	65½	65⅛	60	59½	58	58¼	61¼
1812.......	61¼	61¼	62½	61	60½	59½	57½	58¾	58¾	57¾	57¾	57¾
1813.......	57½	57¼	56½	52½	53¼	53¼	53½	53	53	52¾	53¾	....
1814.......	....	....	....	....	52¼	52¼	52¼	51¾	51	....	....	....
1815.......	....	....	50	50½	50¾	50¾	44½	....	....	....	....	....
1816.......	49½	50½	51½	54	53¾	54¼	55¼	54	54	56	57	60½
1817.......	62½	62	63	63	64½	65	65	65⅛	65	66	68¼	....
1818.......	....	....	71	69½	69	69	68	68	68	67	65	65
1819.......	64½	64¼	64¼	63½	62½	62	61½	64½	64½	63½	63¾	....
1820.......	65½	66	....	65	65	66	66	68¾	69	69½	69½	70

* See sources described at top of Table 34, p. 143.

Construction of indices: The index number of bank-stock prices (see Table 61) was made of the series marked with an asterisk in Table 60. Seven bank-stock prices were used — the prices of three important Boston banks as quoted in Boston, two important New York banks as quoted in New York, and two important Philadelphia banks as quoted in Philadelphia. 1802 was used as the base year. The index number is an unweighted aggregative index.

TABLE 60. — SERIES OF SECURITY PRICES TRANSCRIBED, 1795–1820*

(Series used in the construction of the bank-stock index are marked by an asterisk)

Series[1]	Period	Market	Source[2]
Government Issues			
United States 3%...................	Most of	Boston	See Boston newspapers list-
United States 6%...................	these		ed at top of Table 34, p.
United States 6% deferred...........	securities	New York	143, and sources listed
United States 8%...................	were		below.[2]
War Loan (1812)...................	listed	Philadelphia	
War Loan (1813)...................	in the		
War Loan (1814)...................	papers	Baltimore	
War Loan (1815)...................	from date		
Treasury Notes....................	of issue.		
Louisiana Stock...................			
Municipal and State Issues			
Massachusetts State Notes 5%.......	1805–20	Boston	Boston Gazette
New York State Notes 6%..........	1818–19	New York	N. Y. S. L.
City Loan (Philadelphia)...........	1809–20	Philadelphia	Hope, Scott, Grotjan
Bank Stocks			
U. S. Bank Stock (1st).............	1795–1812	All markets	Sources same as for Govern-
U. S. Bank Stock (2nd)............	1817–20	All markets	ment Issues above.
*Boston Bank....................	1803–20	Boston	Boston Gazette
Manufacturers and Mechanics Bank...	1815–20	Boston	Boston Gazette
*Massachusetts Bank................	1803–20	Boston	Boston Gazette
State Bank......................	1813–20	Boston	Boston Gazette
*Union Bank.....................	1795–1820	Boston	Boston Gazette
City Bank......................	1818–19	New York	N. Y. S. L.
Jersey Bank.....................	1806–11	New York	N. Y. P. C. & N. Y. S. L.
Mechanics Bank..................	1818–19	New York	N. Y. S. L.
Merchants Bank..................	1803–20	New York	N. Y. P. C. & N. Y. S. L.
*Manhattan Bank..................	1799–1820	New York	N. Y. P. C. & N. Y. S. L.
*New York Bank..................	1797–1820	New York	N. Y. P. C. & N. Y. S. L.
Union Bank.....................	1818–19	New York	N. Y. S. L.
Farmers and Mechanics Bank........	1808–20	Philadelphia	Hope, Scott, Grotjan
*Bank of North America............	1802–20	Philadelphia	Hope, Scott, Grotjan
Bank of Pennsylvania.............	1802–20	Philadelphia	Hope, Scott, Grotjan
*Bank of Philadelphia..............	1803–20	Philadelphia	Hope, Scott, Grotjan
The Bank of Baltimore.............	1803–20	Baltimore	B. P. C.
The Bank of Maryland.............	1803–20	Baltimore	B. P. C.
Union Bank of Maryland...........	1804–20	Baltimore	B. P. C.
Insurance Stocks			
Columbian Insurance Co...........	1801–12	New York	N. Y. P. C. & N. Y. S. L.
Marine Insurance Co..............	1807–10	New York	N. Y. P. C. & N. Y. S. L.
New York Insurance Co............	1799–1820	New York	N. Y. P. C. & N. Y. S. L.
United Insurance Co..............	1801–20	New York	N. Y. P. C. & N. Y. S. L.

TABLE 60. — *Continued*

Series	Period	Market	Source
Insurance Stocks (continued)			
Insurance Co. of Pennsylvania........	1808–20	Philadelphia	Hope, Scott, Grotjan
Insurance Co. of North America.......	1808–20	Philadelphia	Hope, Scott, Grotjan
Phoenix Insurance Co...............	1812–15	Philadelphia	Hope, Scott, Grotjan
Baltimore Insurance Co.............	1803–20	Baltimore	B. P. C.
Maryland Insurance Co.............	1803–20	Baltimore	B. P. C.
Bridge and Turnpike Shares			
Delaware Bridge Co..................	1812–17	Philadelphia	Hope, Scott, Grotjan
Germantown Turnpike Co............	1812–17	Philadelphia	Hope, Scott, Grotjan
Lancaster Turnpike Co..............	1812–17	Philadelphia	Hope, Scott, Grotjan
Schuylkill Bridge Co................	1808–20	Philadelphia	Hope, Scott, Grotjan
Fredericktown Road................	1808–20	Baltimore	B. P. C.
Miscellaneous			
New York Manufacturing Co.........	1813–17	New York	N. Y. P. C. & N. Y. S. L.
Water Loan......................	1812–14	Philadelphia	Hope, Scott, Grotjan
Water Company..................	1805–20	Baltimore	B. P. C.

[1] This list does not give all of the stock-price series that are available, nor does it indicate in every case the entire period for which the quotations are available. It is a list of the series that were transcribed. These items are given in the table in order that the record may show the extent to which stock-price quotations were given in the public press.

[2] The abbreviations used above have the following meaning: N.Y.P.C. is the *New York Price Current* (up to 1815); N.Y.S.L. the *New York Shipping and Commercial List* (1815 ff.); Hope is *Hope's Philadelphia Price-Current* (to 1813); Scott is *Scott's Philadelphia Price-Current* (1813); and Grotjan is *Grotjan's Public-Sale Report* (1813 ff.); and B.P.C. is the *Baltimore Price Current.*

TABLE 61. — INDEX OF BANK-STOCK PRICES: MONTHLY, 1802–20[1]

(*Base: 1802*)

Year	Jan.	Feb.	March	April	May	June	July	Aug.	Sept.	Oct.	Nov.	Dec.
1802........	97	98	98	98	99	99	99	100	101	102	104	104
1803........	103	101	100	99	93	94	94	94	93	94	95	94
1804........	93	92	92	91	91	92	91	91	90	90	91	90
1805........	89	89	90	89	88	87	85	85	85	84	85	86
1806........	85	86	87	87	87	88	89	89	90	90	90	90
1807........	90	89	89	88	89	90	90	91	92	92	92	94
1808........	86	87	87	88	89	90	90	91	92	92	92	94
1809........	93	93	93	93	93	95	94	94	94	94	95	95
1810........	94	94	92	93	93	94	94	94	94	94	94	93
1811........	92	92	92	92	93	93	91	89	89	86	86	86
1812........	85	85	86	85	85	85	83	83	86	86	88	89
1813........	89	90	90	89	90	89	89	89	89	89	89	90
1814........	87	87	88	85	85	86	85	84	81	79	76	75
1815........	76	78	85	84	83	83	84	84	83	83	80	80
1816........	79	80	80	77	78	78	76	76	76	76	76	78
1817........	77	78	78	79	80	81	81	83	86	87	87	87
1818........	87	87	88	87	87	88	87	88	88	87	85	84
1819........	84	84	84	83	81	80	77	78	79	77	78	79
1820........	79	80	79	79	78	80	78	79	80	80	79	79

[1] For series used in the construction of this index, see items marked with an asterisk in Table 60.

STOCK-PRICE INDICES, 1815–62.

Data and their sources: For the period before 1853, most of the quotations of stock prices were transcribed from newspapers, while after 1852 the greater part of the data was found in the *Bankers' Magazine*. The accompanying list gives the stocks for which quotations were copied, the period covered, and the markets.

Construction of indices: There are two main divisions in the construction of the stock-price indices. The first concerns the so-called "bank-stock index." It covers the years 1815–45 and was constructed from quotations of six bank stocks and one insurance stock. (The names of these stocks are marked by a double dagger in Table 63.) A simple aggregative index was found and relatives were derived based on the average monthly value for the period 1834–42.

TABLE 62. — INDEX OF BANK- AND INSURANCE-STOCK PRICES: MONTHLY, 1815–45[1]

(*Base: 1834–42*)

Year	Jan.	Feb.	March	April	May	June	July	Aug.	Sept.	Oct.	Nov.	Dec.
1815	...	100	100	98	97	98	98	99	99	100	96	95
1816	95	95	96	94	92	92	89	88	88	89	90	90
1817	91	90	94	94	93	96	96	99	101	104	103	101
1818	103	102	104	103	102	105	104	104	104	104	99	98
1819	99	98	98	97	92	91	87	90	89	88	89	89
1820	90	92	90	92	90	94	93	94	97	97	97	98
1821	98	99	101	102	102	104	105	105	105	105	106	104
1822	104	105	106	104	100	100	99	98	99	99	98	99
1823	96	97	96	96	96	96	96	97	98	99	98	99
1824	99	101	102	102	103	105	102	103	104	105	105	104
1825	105	105	104	105	104	104	102	102	100	101	100	98
1826	98	98	100	100	99	100	96	96	95	97	97	98
1827	97	97	98	97	97	98	97	97	99	99	97	95
1828	94	94	95	95	95	95	94	93	94	94	94	95
1829	93	94	94	93	92	90	90	93	93	92	93	94
1830	98	97	97	98	97	98	99	99	100	101	100	101
1831	100	102	103	102	103	105	107	105	104	105	103	104
1832	104	105	105	106	104	107	106	106	106	109	110	109
1833	108	107	108	109	110	110	109	110	108	111	108	108
1834	104	100	102	106	107	106	106	107	110	111	112	112
1835	111	109	113	113	115	116	114	116	113	113	111	112
1836	110	113	114	113	111	109	113	112	112	112	110	111
1837	113	112	109	97	83	84	93	97	98	97	101	103
1838	103	102	103	100	102	104	106	107	107	108	109	109
1839	108	106	104	104	105	106	102	100	97	91	91	94
1840	96	94	92	91	94	96	97	98	98	99	98	98
1841	95	95	90	90	93	93	94	92	92	90	87	83
1842	79	79	77	75	78	79	77	75	75	77	77	77
1843	77	82	82	84	90	91	91	92	92	93	93	97
1844	94	95	97	97	96	97	96	97	98	98	96	95
1845	95	96	98	97	96	98	97	97	98	99	98	97

[1] For list of stocks used in constructing this index see items marked with a double dagger in Table 63, below.

TABLE 63. — SERIES OF STOCK PRICES TRANSCRIBED, 1815–66

‡ *Series used in the Bank and Insurance Stock Index, 1815–45.*
* *Stocks from which were chosen the series for Railroad Index I, 1834–53.*
† *Stocks from which were chosen the series for Railroad Indices IIa, IIb, and IIc.*
Whole list of railroad stocks used for the All-inclusive Railroad Index.

Name of Company	Period Covered	Market
Bank Stocks		
Bank of America	Feb. 1815–Dec. 1845	New York
Bank of Baltimore	Jan. 1830–Dec. 1853	Baltimore
‡Bank of the Manhattan Company	Feb. 1815–April 1852	New York
‡Bank of New York	Feb. 1815–Dec. 1845	New York
Chemical Bank	Aug. 1824–Dec. 1840	New York
‡City Bank	Feb. 1815–Dec. 1845	New York
Dry Dock Bank	June 1825–Dec. 1840	New York
Farmers' Loan & Trust Company	July 1822–Dec. 1840	New York
Franklin Bank	July 1818–June 1828	New York
Girards Bank	Aug. 1832–June 1859	Philadelphia
‡Mechanics Bank	Feb. 1815–Dec. 1845	New York
‡Merchants Bank	Feb. 1815–Dec. 1845	New York
North River Bank	Oct. 1821–Dec. 1840	New York
Phenix Bank	July 1817–Dec. 1845	New York
Tradesmens Bank	May 1823–Dec. 1840	New York
‡Union Bank	Feb. 1815–Dec. 1845	New York
United States Bank	Aug. 1817–April 1845	New York and Philadelphia
Canal Stocks		
Chesapeake & Delaware	Feb. 1844–July 1853	Philadelphia
Delaware & Hudson	Jan. 1830–Dec. 1866	New York
Lehigh Coal & Navigation	Jan. 1825–Dec. 1860	Philadelphia
Morris Canal & Banking	May 1825–Dec. 1854	New York
Schuylkill Navigation	Jan. 1825–Dec. 1860	Philadelphia
Gas-Light Stocks		
Baltimore Gas	Jan. 1830–Dec. 1853	Baltimore
Manhattan Gas Light	May 1833–Dec. 1850	New York
New York Gas Light	Jan. 1825–Dec. 1845	New York
Insurance Stocks		
Aetna Fire	Aug. 1824–Dec. 1841	New York
American Marine	Feb. 1815–Feb. 1844	New York
Atlantic Marine	Mar. 1824–Dec. 1840	New York
Chatham Fire	April 1823–Oct. 1829	New York
Eagle Fire	Feb. 1815–Dec. 1840	New York
Equitable	Sept. 1823–Dec. 1841	New York
Franklin Fire	May 1818–Dec. 1835	New York
Fulton Fire	Aug. 1819–Sept. 1833	New York
Globe Fire	Feb. 1815–Dec. 1835	New York
Life Insurance & Trust	Jan. 1831–Oct. 1836	New York
Mercantile	May 1818–Nov. 1827	New York
Merchants Fire	Aug. 1819–Dec. 1840	New York
Mutual Fire	Feb. 1815–Dec. 1840	New York
National Marine	April 1817–Nov. 1835	New York
Neptune	May 1825–Dec. 1840	New York
‡New York Marine	Feb. 1815–Nov. 1845	New York
Ocean Marine	Feb. 1815–April 1843	New York
Union Marine	May 1818–Dec. 1840	New York
Washington Fire	Feb. 1815–Dec. 1835	New York

TABLE 63. — *Continued*

Name of Company	Period Covered	Market
Railroad Stocks		
*†Baltimore & Ohio	Mar. 1830–Dec. 1849	Baltimore
	Jan. 1850–Aug. 1855	Baltimore and New York
	Sept. 1855–Dec. 1866	Baltimore
*†Boston & Lowell	Jan. 1836–Dec. 1866	Boston
*†Boston & Providence	Jan. 1832–Dec. 1852	Boston
	Jan. 1853–Dec. 1866	Boston and New York
*†Boston & Worcester	Nov. 1833–Dec. 1866	Boston
*†Camden & Amboy	May 1833–Dec. 1837	New York
	Jan. 1838–Dec. 1866	Philadelphia
†Chicago & Rock Island	Jan. 1855–Dec. 1866	New York
†Chicago, Burlington & Quincy	Jan. 1858–Dec. 1866	New York
†Cleveland & Toledo	Jan. 1854–Dec. 1866	New York
*†Eastern of Massachusetts	June 1838–Dec. 1852	Boston
	Jan. 1853–Dec. 1866	Boston and New York
*†Hudson River	Jan. 1848–Dec. 1866	New York
†Illinois Central	April 1853–Dec. 1866	New York
*Long Island	June 1835–April 1857	New York
†Michigan Central	Jan. 1851–Dec. 1866	New York
†Michigan Southern	Jan. 1852–Dec. 1866	New York
*Mohawk & Hudson	Oct. 1830–April 1851	New York
*†New York & Erie	Nov. 1843–Dec. 1866	New York
*†New York & Harlem	July 1831–April 1864	New York
New York & New Haven	Dec. 1847–July 1854	New York
†New York Central	July 1853–Dec. 1866	New York
*Norwich & Worcester	Sept. 1843–Dec. 1856	New York
†Panama	Jan. 1853–Dec. 1866	New York
*Paterson	Mar. 1831–Aug. 1849	New York
*†Philadelphia & Reading	Jan. 1839–Dec. 1843	Philadelphia
	Jan. 1844–Dec. 1866	New York
*†Philadelphia, Wilmington & Baltimore	Oct. 1839–Dec. 1844	Philadelphia
	Jan. 1845–Dec. 1845	Boston
	Jan. 1846–Sept. 1850	Philadelphia
	Oct. 1850–Dec. 1866	Boston
*Providence & Stonington	April 1833–Dec. 1856	New York
*Utica & Schenectady	Aug. 1833–June 1853	New York
*†Western of Massachusetts	Aug. 1838–Dec. 1866	Boston
Miscellaneous Stocks		
Canton Company	April 1835–Dec. 1866	New York
Cumberland Coal	Jan. 1853–Dec. 1866	New York
Merchants Exchange	April 1826–Dec. 1845	New York
New York & Schuylkill Coal	Jan. 1830–Dec. 1835	New York
Pennsylvania Coal	July 1852–Nov. 1866	New York
Union Manufacturing	Jan. 1830–Oct. 1853	New York and Baltimore
Boston Bank Stocks		
Atlantic Bank	June 1834–Dec. 1843	Boston
Bank of Boston	Mar. 1815–Dec. 1824	Boston
City Bank	Sept. 1823–Dec. 1824	Boston
	Jan. 1834–Dec. 1843	Boston
Columbia Bank	Sept. 1823–Dec. 1824	Boston
Eagle Bank	Sept. 1823–Dec. 1824	Boston
Globe Bank	Mar. 1834–Sept. 1843	Boston
Manufacturers & Mechanics Bank	May 1815–Dec. 1824	Boston
Market Bank	June 1834–Nov. 1843	Boston

TABLE 63. — *Continued*

Name of Company	Period Covered	Market
Boston Bank Stocks (continued)		
Massachusetts Bank..................	Mar. 1815–Dec. 1824	Boston
	June 1834–Dec. 1843	Boston
Merchants Bank	Mar. 1834–Dec. 1843	Boston
New England Bank.................	Mar. 1815–Dec. 1824	Boston
State Bank.........................	Jan. 1816–Dec. 1824	Boston
	Jan. 1834–Dec. 1843	Boston
Suffolk Bank.......................	Jan. 1819–Dec. 1824	Boston
Traders Bank	June 1834–Nov. 1843	Boston
Tremont Bank......................	June 1834–Oct. 1843	Boston
Union Bank........................	Mar. 1815–Dec. 1824	Boston
Washington Bank...................	June 1834–July 1843	Boston

Sources:

Baltimore:	The *Baltimore Patriot.*
Boston:	The *Boston Daily Advertiser*, with the *Boston Transcript* and the *Boston Commercial Gazette.*
New York: 1815–52	The *New York Shipping & Commercial List*, with the *New York Tribune* and *New York Herald;*
1853–66	*Bankers' Magazine*, with the *American Railway Journal* and *Hunt's Merchants' Magazine.*
Philadelphia:	The *Daily National Gazette*, with the *Philadelphia Gazette, Daily Chronicle, Philadelphia Commercial List*, and the *North American & United States Gazette.*

The second part, relating mainly to railroad-stock prices from 1834 to 1862, involved more complicated procedure. After a study of the individual charts, the first conclusion was the desirability of breaking the period into two sections for separate consideration, making the break at the year 1853. For this conclusion there were three reasons: (1) only very fragmentary data could be secured for the stocks of western railroads prior to 1853, but thereafter such securities were well represented on the list of available series; (2) the stocks of a number of eastern roads were inflexible in their price fluctuations prior to 1853, so that the quotations for such securities in this period were of little value in constructing an index designed particularly to picture speculative tendencies — although after 1853 several of these series exhibited clearcut cyclical movements; and (3) in so far as any general or typical speculative movements appeared in the price fluctuations of the various stocks up to 1853, these tendencies were shared by all of the securities except such as exhibited individualistic or erratic fluctuations; while after 1853 the available series very clearly could be divided into two distinct groups, the constituents of which behaved quite differently, especially during the years 1853–61.

SELECTED LIST: RAILROAD-STOCK INDEX I, 1834–53.

After discarding certain fragmentary data,[1] it was possible to compile a list of 18 stocks for which monthly prices had been secured for all or part of the period 1834–53. (The names of these stocks have been marked with an asterisk in Table 63 above.)

A detailed examination of the charts of the monthly data for these 18 series indicated that certain of the stocks were clearly unsuited for inclusion in an index whose purpose was to measure *speculative* movements and, further, was to measure general or *typical* tendencies in such speculative movements. Six stocks were discarded for the reason that their fluctuations were highly inflexible or showed only slight or occasional response to speculative influences.[2] Furthermore, quotations for four securities were discarded in whole or in part for the reason that the fluctuations of such quotations were highly erratic and individualistic, and were quite obviously non-typical. In two of these four cases, the stocks were dropped from the list for the entire period in which they were available (up to 1853);[3] and in the

[1] Quotations for New York & New Haven, for which data had been collected only over the short interval, December 1847 to July 1854; and the fragmentary figures available for western stocks prior to 1853, i.e., quotations for Michigan Central beginning January 1851, and for Michigan Southern beginning January 1852.

[2] Boston & Lowell, Boston & Providence, Boston & Worcester, Eastern of Massachusetts, Western of Massachusetts, Utica & Schenectady.

[3] Norwich & Worcester and New York & Erie.

other two cases the stock quotations were discarded only in part.[4]

After inflexible and erratic quotations had been eliminated, there remained 10 stocks on the list of available securities. Among these 10 series there was considerable diversity as to short-time movements, and each series exhibited some individual irregularities and peculiarities. Furthermore, there were appreciable differences among the various stocks as to amplitude of fluctuation. On the other hand, however, there were certain general tendencies which were clearly apparent, and with reference to these (as well as to many of the short-time fluctuations) it is quite proper to speak of a typical movement among the 10 stocks: there was a moderate rise between 1834 and the earlier part of 1835; following this a very considerable but somewhat broken downward movement to a low point in 1842 or 1843; thereafter a sharp rise until the earlier months of 1844, followed by a slow and irregular upward tendency during the remainder of the period to 1853.

Although, as has been said, each of the 10 series showed some individual peculiarities and irregular deviations from the general tendency, nevertheless it appeared that the fluctuations of each series conformed closely enough to the typical movements described above to justify its inclusion in the index. The decision was, therefore, to base the index for 1834–53 upon these 10 series of stock prices. Some of the 10 series, however, extended over only a part of the period 1834–53; consequently, it was possible to form only 8 continuous series of price quotations, and even in these 8 cases there were some small gaps which had later to be filled by extrapolation.[5]

It will be observed that in two cases the continuous series was formed by "splicing" the prices for a pair of stocks. This practice of welding together fragmentary data is a statistical device which is probably in general one of questionable value. In the present case, however, the employment of this device seemed clearly justified by the paucity of available data and the consequent desire to take into account all of the usable evidence which could be obtained.

Another question regarding the selection of stocks to be included in the index deserves attention at this point. The procedure which was followed involved the use of discretionary judgment on the part of the persons making the selection — that is discretionary judgment in deciding just what the typical movement was and in deciding which stocks should be classified as "inflexible" or "erratic," and which should be classified as "typical."[6] However, this question has been discussed above and need not be reconsidered here.[7]

In the present study, as has already been indicated, every attempt was made to secure a fair selection of data, uninfluenced by personal bias or preconceived ideas; and it is believed unlikely that another investigator, having in mind the same object, would have arrived at results essentially different from those which have been secured and which are presented in this book. Nevertheless, as a check upon these results, there was prepared an "all-inclusive" index number based upon *all* of the price quotations which had been collected for railroad stocks, and involving therefore no arbitrary selection of data from among the series for which figures were available. Later there will appear a description of

---

[4] The quotations for Long Island, 1845–53, were excluded for the reason that such quotations fell very rapidly after 1844, at a time when the general movement was clearly upward. The prices for Philadelphia, Wilmington & Baltimore prior to 1844 were discarded for the reason that their fluctuations were much more violent than those shown by the other stocks. From these two series, one continuous series was formed by multiplying the quotations for Long Island by the ratio of the average price of Philadelphia, Wilmington & Baltimore to the average price of Long Island over the common period, January–December 1845. Similarly the two series for Paterson and for Hudson River were adjusted to form one series, using the overlapping year 1848.

[5] See Table 8, page 48, and also footnote 9 on page 179.

[6] For example, it was perhaps open to question whether New York & Harlem should be included in the "typical" or the "erratic" group. On the whole, however, it seemed better to give this security the former classification; for its quotations showed the same general tendencies as did those for the other stocks included in the index, even though the amplitude of fluctuation for this particular stock was somewhat more extreme than that for the other securities. It was decided, however, that in order to prevent the extreme fluctuations of this stock from having undue influence at certain periods, its quotations should be excluded in the making of extrapolations for missing data. (See footnote 9 on page 179.)

A test computation carried out monthly for the entire period, 1834–53, showed that the exclusion of New York & Harlem would have brought about only very slight alterations in the index; in general even the month-to-month and other short-time movements of the index would have remained practically unchanged. One possible exception might be made to this latter statement: the index including New York & Harlem showed a slightly higher figure for February 1843 than for March 1842 (Chart 9); the index excluding New York & Harlem registered a slightly lower value in February 1843 than in March 1842. The practical conclusion to be drawn from this fact is that in the interpretation of the index no particular importance should be attached to the slight difference in the relative heights of the curve as between the two dates, but that rather these two points should be thought of as standing at approximately the same level.

[7] See footnotes, 3 and 4 above.

the method by which this index was calculated, and a discussion of its validity and value.[8]

After a decision had been reached as to the series which were to be included, the index was computed by (1) averaging the 8 series month by month over the interval 1834–53, employing the unweighted geometric mean; and then (2) reducing these averages to relatives with the year 1853 as the base.[9] The geometric mean was used as being in the present case theoretically preferable to the arithmetic mean or to an index of the aggregative type, for we were interested in the average percentage of change in prices over a period of time rather than in changes in the aggregate money cost of a given set of securities; however, had the arithmetic mean been used instead of the geometric, the index obtained would not have given an essentially different picture of the

speculative movements occurring during the interval under examination.[10] The index was unweighted, since there appeared to be no reasonable basis for determining the relative values of the various stocks as indicators of speculative conditions, and in any case it would have been difficult to secure data which were sufficiently accurate to serve as measures for precise weighting; furthermore, it does not appear likely that any reasonably chosen set of weights would have yielded an essentially different index, at least so far as the broad general movements were concerned.[11] The year 1853 was selected as base, since this year was the only time-interval common to both of these periods (1834–53 and 1853–66) into which our study had previously been divided; the index, however, can readily be shifted to any chosen base within the interval 1834–53, should such shift of base be desired.

The index for 1834–53, computed by the methods just described, has been designated as Index I, and is presented in Charts 9 and 38 and Tables 64 and 65.

[8] See pp. 182, 183 below.

[9] In the computation of the index it was necessary, owing to incomplete data, to extrapolate in three series in order to fill a gap — in each case covering a comparatively short interval of time. These extrapolations were made by assuming that had the stock in question been quoted during this interval, its price would have shown the same month-to-month percentage changes as were actually exhibited by the average (unweighted geometric) of the stocks (excluding New York & Harlem, as indicated in footnote 6, p. 178 above) for which actual quotations were available during the interval.

[10] The small number of series entering the index made the use of the median obviously impracticable.

[11] For a more extended discussion of the points considered in this paragraph, see "An Index of Industrial Stock Prices" by Edwin Frickey in the *Review of Economic Statistics*, Preliminary Volume III (1921), p. 273.

TABLE 64. — RAILROAD-STOCK-PRICE INDEX I: MONTHLY, 1834–45

(Base: 1834–42)[1]

8 Selected Stocks

Year	Jan.	Feb.	March	April	May	June	July	Aug.	Sept.	Oct.	Nov.	Dec.
1834	112	103	107	122	124	119	119	125	122	128	133	137
1835	146	143	155	160	182	179	176	181	173	166	152	145
1836	148	167	163	155	154	155	143	136	128	116	110	113
1837	131	130	113	101	93	87	106	101	100	103	104	99
1838	94	91	84	82	90	96	99	103	107	96	96	87
1839	94	100	94	94	97	91	85	82	79	73	67	70
1840	73	73	70	73	72	70	72	70	73	82	81	76
1841	72	72	63	67	72	70	73	73	66	66	66	63
1842	52	48	45	46	54	55	55	51	55	51	51	51
1843	49	48	49	51	60	67	66	69	70	69	75	87
1844	87	88	94	103	112	104	104	104	107	106	99	97
1845	94	103	101	100	101	93	94	93	93	96	104	103

[1] For index numbers on the base of average values for 1853, see *Review of Economic Statistics*, vol. 10 (1928), p. 129. The base, 1834–42, for the above index was obtained by dividing the index numbers as originally constructed on 1853 as a base by the average monthly index number for the years 1834–42. To put this index again on 1853 as a base, multiply each number by the coefficient 0.67.

For the list of stocks employed in this index, see Table 8, p. 48.

TABLE 65. — RAILROAD-STOCK-PRICE INDEX I: MONTHLY, 1843–53

(Base: 1853)[1]

8 Selected Stocks

Year	Jan.	Feb.	March	April	May	June	July	Aug.	Sept.	Oct.	Nov.	Dec.
1843........	33	32	33	34	40	45	44	46	47	46	50	58
1844........	58	59	63	69	75	70	70	70	72	71	66	65
1845........	63	69	68	67	68	62	63	62	62	64	70	69
1846........	66	70	74	66	69	72	71	72	69	68	67	67
1847........	67	72	70	72	74	81	83	84	83	78	72	67
1848........	68	72	71	71	69	69	67	66	66	64	63	67
1849........	67	68	73	71	72	76	75	72	72	71	70	70
1850........	71	72	75	72	76	80	77	80	79	88	87	91
1851........	90	89	88	90	88	90	89	84	84	83	86	87
1852........	86	87	90	93	95	97	100	103	104	107	107	110
1853........	108	104	103	101	103	102	101	99	96	97	88	99

[1] For list of stocks employed in the construction of this index, see Table 8, p. 48 and footnote 4, p. 178.

SELECTED LISTS: RAILROAD-STOCK INDICES IIa, IIb, IIc, 1853–62

The methods used in the construction of indices for the period 1853–62 follow very closely those employed for the period 1834–53. As before, certain fragmentary data were discarded[12] and then there was compiled a list of stocks for which monthly prices had been secured for all or a considerable part of the period under examination. There were 20 stocks on this list. (The names of these stocks are marked with a dagger in Table 63.) The next step was, as in the preceding case, a careful study of the charts of the monthly data to determine whether there were any series which should be dropped from the list because of inflexibility or of erratic behavior. This graphic examination led to the discarding of two stocks as inflexible;[13] there were no eliminations, however, on the ground of erratic fluctuations.

The elimination of the two inflexible series reduced the list of stocks to 18. Examination of the charts of the monthly figures for these 18 series indicated that they might very definitely be divided into two groups exhibiting quite different tendencies over the interval 1853–61. It was decided, therefore, to compute separate indices for these two sets of stocks. These two groups were designated as Groups IIa and IIb, and the corresponding indices,

[12] Quotations for Utica & Schenectady, January 1853–June 1853; New York & New Haven, January 1853–July 1854; Norwich & Worcester, January 1853–December 1856; Providence & Stonington, January 1853–December 1856; Long Island, January 1853–April 1857.

[13] Boston & Worcester and Western of Massachusetts.

originally constructed to cover 1853–66, will be referred to as Indices IIa and IIb, respectively.

While the differences among the short-time fluctuations of the various stocks (in each of the two groups) during the interval 1853–66 were not nearly so marked as such differences had been in 1834–53, it was nevertheless true that for each group the constituent series exhibited certain individual peculiarities and irregular deviations from the general or typical tendencies described above. Each of the individual series, however, conformed closely enough to the typical movements for one of the two groups to justify its inclusion in the index for that group.[14]

[14] There were three stocks — New York & Harlem (entering Group IIa), and New York & Erie and Michigan Southern (entering Group IIb) — whose prices showed the same general movements as did those for the other securities included in their respective groups, but with a considerably wider range of variation. Following the practice employed in the construction of Index I (see footnote 9, p. 179), these three stocks were included in Index IIa or Index IIb, but were not used in the making of extrapolations for missing data.

Test computations showed that the exclusion of New York & Harlem from Index IIa would have had practically no effect upon that Index other than to reduce somewhat the amplitude of fluctuation. The exclusion of New York & Erie and Michigan Southern from Index IIb would have brought about little change in the Index except to raise the low point of 1859–60 to a level slightly above (instead of slightly below) that of the low points of 1857 and 1861 (cf. Chart 39). In view of this latter result, it would seem better not to attach any particular importance to the differences in the height of Index IIb at the minima of 1857, 1859–60, and 1861, but rather to think of these three low points as being at approximately the same level.

Index numbers were calculated for Groups IIa and IIb, 1853–66, following the methods which had previously been employed for Index I, 1834–53. That is, Indices IIa and IIb were computed monthly, 1853–66, each as an unweighted geometric mean of monthly prices, reduced to the base 1853 as 100. Furthermore, there was computed a combined index for the same interval, based upon the 18 series obtained by consolidating the two lists of stocks which had entered Indices IIa and IIb, respectively. This combined index (designated as Index IIc) was also an unweighted geometric mean of monthly prices, reduced to the base 1853 as 100. In interpreting the movements of this combined index, it should be remembered that its fluctuations represent an average of two divergent sets of tendencies.

TABLE 66. — RAILROAD-STOCK-PRICE INDEX IIa: MONTHLY, 1853–62[1]

(*Base: 1853*)

8 Selected Stocks

Year	Jan.	Feb.	March	April	May	June	July	Aug.	Sept.	Oct.	Nov.	Dec.
1853	109	108	106	104	106	105	104	101	99	98	94	102
1854	96	96	98	96	94	95	88	81	74	75	71	64
1855	66	73	74	73	72	72	72	70	70	67	59	58
1856	58	58	61	61	62	58	60	57	55	54	54	55
1857	56	56	58	55	56	51	50	51	47	41	42	47
1858	46	48	58	57	61	61	59	61	60	62	66	67
1859	68	68	67	67	68	65	66	66	68	68	70	72
1860	71	72	72	76	80	82	83	86	87	93	86	77
1861	76	77	79	79	68	67	66	68	66	66	73	72
1862	73	74	76	74	78	81	83	82	88	98	105	104

[1] For the list of stocks used in constructing this index, see Table 30, p. 109.

TABLE 67. — RAILROAD-STOCK-PRICE INDEX IIb: MONTHLY, 1853–62[1]

(*Base: 1853*)

10 Selected Stocks

Year	Jan.	Feb.	March	April	May	June	July	Aug.	Sept.	Oct.	Nov.	Dec.
1853	113	107	108	106	108	107	105	95	91	90	81	88
1854	89	90	95	93	90	90	81	74	69	75	71	66
1855	65	71	73	75	76	78	84	83	84	82	71	76
1856	77	76	81	81	82	80	82	84	82	84	80	86
1857	86	85	84	80	77	71	62	69	51	33	38	47
1858	48	51	61	50	53	49	46	48	47	45	46	45
1859	44	42	42	38	36	33	32	33	34	33	31	33
1860	32	31	32	38	42	44	44	52	56	60	50	41
1861	43	48	48	48	36	36	36	37	38	39	44	41
1862	43	45	49	50	50	54	56	53	59	71	77	71

[1] For the list of stocks used in constructing this index, see Table 30, p. 109.

TABLE 68. — RAILROAD-STOCK-PRICE INDEX IIc: MONTHLY, 1853-62

(Base: 1853)

18 Selected Stocks[1]

Year	Jan.	Feb.	March	April	May	June	July	Aug.	Sept.	Oct.	Nov.	Dec.
1853........	110	106	106	104	105	105	103	97	93	92	86	93
1854........	91	91	95	93	91	91	83	76	70	74	70	64
1855........	65	71	73	73	73	74	78	76	76	74	65	67
1856........	68	66	70	71	71	69	70	70	68	68	66	70
1857........	70	70	70	67	66	61	56	60	49	36	39	46
1858........	46	49	59	52	56	54	50	53	52	51	54	53
1859........	53	51	51	48	47	44	44	44	46	45	44	46
1860........	45	45	46	51	55	58	58	64	67	72	63	54
1861........	54	59	59	59	47	47	46	48	48	48	54	52
1862........	54	56	59	59	60	64	66	64	69	81	87	83

[1] Stocks included in Index IIa plus those in Index IIb (Table 30, p. 109).

THE ALL-INCLUSIVE INDEX, 1834-62.

As has been stated on an earlier page, the all-inclusive index was calculated as a check upon the selected list indices whose construction has just been described.[15] In the computation of the all-inclusive index the desire was to secure a set of relative figures which were based upon *all* of the prices which had been collected for railroad stocks, and which involved therefore no arbitrary selection of data from among the available series.

An examination of these available series (Table 63) showed that the list of stocks for which monthly quotations had been obtained, 1834-66, changed at very frequent intervals; there were in all 26 such changes scattered throughout the period, due either to the introduction of a new stock or to the disappearance of quotations for a security previously listed. Consequently, it appeared that the only feasible procedure for the construction of an index which was to be based upon *all* of the available data was to secure a chain index. The methods by which this chain index was computed will be described in succeeding paragraphs.

The first step was to obtain link indices; that is, an index was found for each month, February 1834 to December 1866, compared with the *preceding month* in each case as base. In each month-to-month comparison, there were included all the stocks for which prices had been secured for both of the two months in question.

The unweighted geometric mean was employed in

the computation of these link indices. The reasons for the use of this type of average have been set forth on a preceding page, in connection with the discussion of the fixed-base indices. In the present case, however, there was an additional argument for the selection of the geometric, as opposed to the arithmetic, mean: if an unweighted arithmetic mean be employed in the construction of a chain index, this chain index will tend to show a definite upward bias; no such bias will appear if the unweighted geometric mean be used.

The next step in the calculation was to chain together the successive link indices. The first month of the period, January 1834, was provisionally taken as the base; that is, the chain index for January 1834 was taken as 100. Next, this chain index for January 1834 (100) was multiplied by the link index for February 1834 ÷ January 1834 (93.8), thus obtaining 93.8 as the chain index for February 1834. This index was in turn multiplied by the link index for March 1834 ÷ February 1834 (103.4) giving 97.0 as the chain index for March 1834; and so on, until monthly chain indices on the base January 1834 had been secured for the entire period, January 1834–December 1866. The final step was to shift the chain index to the base 1853, in order that it might be compared conveniently with the fixed-base indices previously calculated. The all-inclusive chain index which has been computed is presented neither as a desirable form of index number nor as being, necessarily, a reliable guide in the study of speculative movements during the period under examination. The reason for its calculation, as has been indicated, was the wish to obtain an index based upon a list of stocks into whose selection, from among all of the data available, no discretionary judgment had entered, in order that this index might be compared with the indices, previously computed, based upon selected lists of securities.

In Charts 9 and 38, the all-inclusive chain-index number is compared, 1834–62, with selected list indices (Index I for 1834–52 and Index IIc for 1853–62). This comparison may be made with reference to (1) the short-time movements, (2) the general form of the longer speculative swings, and (3) the amplitude of fluctuation. With respect to (1) the short-time movements, and (2) the general form of the longer speculative swings, the all-inclusive index agrees very closely indeed with the selected list indices; there are few points of divergence, and these are of minor importance.[16] When the two curves are compared with reference to (3) amplitude of fluctuation, it appears that there is almost perfect agreement during the interval 1853–62, but that during the years 1834–52 there is a moderate difference.[17] This

discrepancy is due to a circumstance to which allusion has already been made: that is, the presence, implicitly, of variable weighting in the all-inclusive index, such variable weighting being occasioned by the fluctuations in the proportion which the number of "inflexible" stocks included bore to the total number of stocks entering the index.[18] In any event, however, the difference in amplitude of fluctuation of the two indices, 1834–52, is not a considerable one, nor does it affect in any material way the conclusions which one would form as to the nature of the speculative fluctuation occurring prior to 1853. The graphic comparison, then, indicates that — except for a moderate difference in amplitude of fluctuation during the earlier part of the period, which is ascribable to the defective weighting system implicit in the all-inclusive index — this index checks up very closely with the selected list Indices I and IIc.

[16] The two indices differ as to the exact dating of the low point of 1842–43. This fact merely confirms the conclusion previously stated (see footnote 6, p. 178) that no particular importance should be attached to the slight difference in level between the low points of 1842 and 1843, shown by Index I.

[17] From the high of 1835 to the low of 1842–43, the selected list on the base 1853 falls 92 points (from 122 to 30), while the

all-inclusive index drops 76 points (from 121 to 45); from the trough of 1842–43 to the peak of 1852, the selected list index rises 80 points (from 30 to 110), while the all-inclusive index rises 65 points (from 45 to 110). In looking at Charts 9 and 38, the reader should note the fact that these charts are drawn on a logarithmic scale; otherwise, he will obtain an exaggerated impression as to the amount of the spread between the two curves prior to 1853. (See also Table 69, footnote 2.)

[18] This proportion stood at approximately one-third in 1834–35, rose to almost one-half in 1838–39, and then fell gradually to about one-third for the years 1848–52 (Table 63).

TABLE 69. — ALL-INCLUSIVE INDEX OF RAILROAD-STOCK PRICES: MONTHLY, 1834–45[1]

(*Base: 1834–42*)[2]

Year	Jan.	Feb.	March	April	May	June	July	Aug.	Sept.	Oct.	Nov.	Dec.
1834........	101	95	97	112	113	108	106	113	112	115	119	122
1835........	128	126	135	140	155	153	151	154	146	142	131	127
1836........	129	142	141	135	135	135	127	122	117	108	104	108
1837........	118	118	108	99	95	91	104	100	100	103	103	99
1838........	96	92	87	86	92	99	97	103	105	97	97	94
1839........	99	104	99	100	103	99	95	92	90	86	81	83
1840........	87	86	83	86	85	85	85	83	86	92	91	88
1841........	86	85	78	81	85	85	86	85	81	79	81	77
1842........	64	62	59	60	65	68	65	63	65	63	60	60
1843........	58	60	60	60	69	74	73	76	77	76	81	92
1844........	91	95	96	104	113	113	110	114	115	118	114	112
1845........	106	115	114	113	115	110	110	108	109	112	118	123

[1] For list of stocks included in the construction of this index, see Table 63 above.

[2] The base 1834–42 for the above index was obtained by dividing the index numbers, originally constructed using 1853 as a base, by the average monthly index number for the years 1834–42. To put this index again on 1853 as a base, multiply each number by the coefficient 0.78.

TABLE 70. — ALL-INCLUSIVE INDEX OF RAILROAD-STOCK PRICES: MONTHLY, 1843–62[1]

(*Base: 1853*)

Year	Jan.	Feb.	March	April	May	June	July	Aug.	Sept.	Oct.	Nov.	Dec.
1843	45	47	47	47	54	58	57	59	60	59	63	72
1844	71	74	75	81	88	88	86	89	90	92	89	87
1845	83	90	89	88	90	86	86	84	85	87	92	96
1846	87	90	93	84	84	89	86	87	85	84	84	82
1847	82	87	86	87	89	95	96	97	95	91	86	83
1848	82	85	86	84	82	82	80	79	79	76	75	80
1849	80	80	83	81	83	85	84	81	81	80	80	80
1850	80	79	82	81	84	86	83	84	85	90	91	95
1851	94	95	94	96	95	96	93	87	88	89	91	92
1852	89	89	94	96	98	98	99	101	102	103	106	110
1853	105	104	103	102	105	104	103	98	96	95	89	96
1854	94	94	98	96	93	93	85	79	74	77	74	67
1855	67	74	76	76	76	77	80	79	78	75	66	68
1856	68	68	72	73	72	70	71	71	68	68	68	71
1857	71	71	71	68	68	63	58	61	52	39	42	49
1858	49	52	61	55	58	56	53	56	55	54	56	56
1859	56	54	54	51	50	47	47	48	49	48	47	50
1860	48	48	50	55	59	61	61	67	70	74	66	57
1861	58	62	62	63	50	50	50	51	51	52	58	56
1862	57	59	62	62	64	67	70	68	73	84	90	87

[1] For list of stocks included in this index, see Table 63 above.

THE INDICES FOR GEOGRAPHICAL GROUPS

The indices for the stocks of railroads situated in three geographical sections of the country (pp. 49–51 and pp. 112–14 above) were obtained by dividing the available series into three groups[19] — New England, central-Atlantic, and western — and then for these groups computing indices following the methods previously employed for Indices I, IIa, IIb, and IIc.

It should be pointed out that the index for the New England group, during the first four and one-half years for which it was computed, is based upon quite scanty data; the group comprises only two stocks during 1834–35 and only three stocks from January 1836 to the middle of 1838. Attention should also be called to the fact that the index for the western group is based upon rather fragmentary and incomplete data during the year 1853. Such deficiencies in data should be kept in mind in interpreting the movements of these two indices in the periods mentioned. (For a diagram of the movements of the three indices, see Charts 11 and 40.)

[19] There were, however, certain omissions. (1) Fragmentary quotations were, as before, eliminated. (2) Long Island, Norwich & Worcester, and Providence & Stonington were excluded. As already indicated, the first two moved erratically over the greater part of the period for which we have quotations. The third was eliminated with somewhat greater arbitrariness. By reason, apparently, of the New York connections of the Company, the railroad lying between the terminus of New York boats at Stonington, Connecticut, and the City of Providence, the course of the stock differed markedly from that typical of the New England securities as a whole. (3) Utica & Schenectady was omitted from the central-Atlantic group, for the reason that this stock (unlike the other constituent stocks falling in this geographical classification) showed very little price variation, and its inclusion would therefore have had no effect other than to reduce somewhat the range of fluctuation of the group index (see p. 177 above). (4) Three stocks — New York & Harlem, New York & Erie, and Michigan Southern — which in whole or in part had been included in Indices I, IIa or IIb, and IIc were excluded in the computation of the geographical group indices. The reason for this exclusion was that these securities, as has been previously pointed out (footnote 14, p. 180, and footnote 6, p. 178), showed fluctuations which were very violent and of considerable amplitude; and it was feared that in an index based upon a small number of series (such as these geographical group indices) the violent price fluctuation of these three stocks would have too great an influence, and would perhaps distort the movements of the indices at certain points.

APPENDIX D

QUARTERLY AND ANNUAL DATA ON PUBLIC LAND SALES, 1796–1860.

TABLE 71. — PUBLIC LAND SALES: ACRES, ANNUALLY, 1796–1860; SEMI-ANNUALLY, 1850–60*

(Unit: 1000 Acres)

TABLE 72. — PUBLIC LAND SALES: RECEIPTS BY THE UNITED STATES, QUARTERLY, 1815–60*

(Unit: $1,000)

Table 71

Calendar Year	Acres	Semi-annually		Calendar Year	Acres
Annually				*Annually*	
1796–99	1,281.9			1840	2,236.9
1800	67.8			1841	1,164.8
1801	497.9			1842	1,129.2
1802	271.1			1843	1,605.3
1803	174.2			1844	1,754.8
1804	398.2			1845	1,843.5
1805	582.0			1846	2,263.7
1806	506.0			1847	2,521.3
1807	320.9			1848	1,887.6
1808	209.2			1849	1,329.9
1809	275.0	*Semi-annually*			
1810	285.8	1st half	602.2		
1811	575.1	2nd half	803.6		
1812	386.1	———			
1813	505.6	1st half	1,043.2	1850	1,405.8
1814	1,176.1	2nd half	1,012.7		
1815	1,306.4	———		1851	2,055.9
1816	1,742.5	1st half	540.4		
1817	1,886.2	2nd half	354.4		
1818	3,491.0	———		1852	894.8
1819	2,968.4	1st half	729.1		
		2nd half	3,058.0		
1820	814.0	———		1853	3,787.1
1821	782.5	1st half	3,977.7		
1822	710.0	2nd half	9,845.3		
1823	652.1	———		1854	12,823.0
1824	737.0	1st half	5,884.2		
1825	999.0	2nd half	6,075.6		
1826	848.1	———		1855	11,959.8
1827	926.7	1st half	3,152.3		
1828	965.6	2nd half	2,094.7		
1829	1,244.9	———		1856	5,247.0
		1st half	2,048.1		
1830	1,929.7	2nd half	2,172.0		
1831	2,777.9	———		1857	4,220.1
1832	2,462.3	1st half	1,632.9		
1833	3,856.2	2nd half	2,030.7		
1834	4,658.2	———		1858	3,663.6
1835	12,564.5	1st half	1,930.9		
1836	20,074.9	2nd half	2,080.8		
1837	5,601.1	———		1859	4,011.7
1838	3,414.9	1st half	1,380.4		
1839	4,976.4	2nd half	1,163.0		
		———		1860	2,543.4

Table 72

Calendar Year	First Quarter	Second Quarter	Third Quarter	Fourth Quarter	Total
1815	....	....	....	....	2410†
1816	721	601	821	1497	3640
1817	748	1189	1957	1189	5083
1818	3970	1292	3389	4967	13619
1819	3707	3234	1514	525	8980
1820	1088	173	166	309	1736
1821	220	205	526	328	1279
1822	241	244	241	291	1017
1823	142	135	118	412	807
1824	159	315	726	300	1500
1825	376	356	198	363	1292
1826	330	205	227	368	1130
1827	383	315	304	403	1405
1828	207	191	248	574	1219
1829	311	309	873	669	2163
1830	479	351	520	1059	2409
1831	406	1029	1029	902	3366
1832	597	524	630	1052	2803
1833	608	799	768	1998	4173
1834	1054	982	955	3073	6064
1835	1990	3144	4083	6949	16165
1836	5847	8423	5859	4805	24934
1837	3479	1834	699	928	6941
1838	548	524	700	2239	4011
1839	1823	1672	1282	1710	6487
1840	950	794	468	536	2747
1841	416	313	367	416	1512
1842	253	591	263	345	1453
1843	551	388	473	638	2050
1844	497	489	525	729	2241
1845	447	531	690	794	2462
1846	630	955	665	631	2881
1847	537	860	943	931	3272
1848	729	770	506	529	2533
1849	380	381	409	573	1743
1850	451	301	341	697	1790
1851	800	517	595	680	2592
1852	502	188	428	275	1392
1853	493	608	1784	2164	5049
1854	1894	3193	2514	3901	11502
1855	1556	3390	2388	3948	11282
1856	1260	1808	786	902	4756
1857	528	1257	762	519	3066
1858	415	465	452	461	1793
1859	509	354	503	503	1869
1860	470	353	279	406	1507

* Hibbard, *History of Public Land Policies* (1924), pp. 100, 103, 106, and *Annual Reports* of the Commissioner of the General Land Office.

The above data differ from those presented by Hibbard (p. 106) for the years after 1850. At that point in his tabulation, his data shift from calendar years to fiscal years ending June 30th.

* Compiled from records in the Public Land Office in Washington, D. C.

† In a small degree estimated.

APPENDIX E

MONTHLY FINANCIAL DATA, 1795–1862; AND MONTHLY GOLD SHIPMENTS FROM CALIFORNIA, 1849–62.

DATA ON NEW YORK CITY BANKS

These data are complicated by the variety of sources from which they have been derived and also by variations of descriptions, the exact meaning of which is sometimes uncertain.

The material relating to clearings alone is simple. These figures were compiled by the New York Clearing House after its establishment in 1853, and were published on a weekly basis in the *Bankers' Magazine* for the period 1853–56 and in the Tuesday issues of the *New York Tribune* from 1856 on. There is nothing to indicate that they do not form a homogeneous series.

The data on the condition of the New York City banking institutions are ultimately of two sorts — those on a quarterly and those on a weekly basis. The former, as suggested above, extend on a fairly regular basis from 1843 to the Civil War. They are procurable from the annual reports of the New York State Bank Commissioners, although at times — especially to secure a differentiation of New York City banks from the aggregate of New York State banking institutions — it is necessary to have recourse to the statements of the New York City banks which were published in a fairly detailed form in *Hunt's Merchants' Magazine* or the *Bankers' Magazine*. The weekly data, on the other hand, became available only in the middle of 1853. Thereafter they are published sometimes in *Hunt's* and sometimes in *Bankers' Magazine*; while a transcription of certain of these series through August 1858 is to be located in J. S. Gibbons' *The Banks of New York and the Panic of 1857* (1858), pp. 330–36.

One major problem in connection with these data, especially as regards the quarterly series, was to obtain consistent, homogeneous material. The classifications employed by the Bank Commissioners were not always uniform from year to year, either with respect to loans and discounts or with respect to deposits. In the former case, the item "loans to brokers and directors" was sometimes included and sometimes not. In the latter, the situation was complicated by changing nomenclature and by the existence of a breakdown of "total deposits" into the subheadings of "due depositors," "due banks," and "due" the State and Federal Governments and the Canal Fund. Again, sometimes the report for a given quarterly interval was entirely lacking in the State Documents, and in *Hunt's* and *Bankers'* was

given in a form insufficiently detailed to be of use; and the appropriate figures had to be constructed from the returns of the individual banks of the City; while after all research had failed to produce acceptable data, reliance was occasionally necessary on judicious interpolation. In the end, however, fairly adequate data were secured, and the more satisfactory among the quarterly series, i.e., "total loans" and "due depositors," were employed in the statistical treatment the results of which are presented in Chart 41.

Another major problem pertained to the relationship of the weekly data to the quarterly. Here the identification of the two "deposits" series of weekly material proved simple. The data on "total deposits" there presented followed closely the course of "total deposits" as revealed in the quarterly material — "total deposits" in the latter being made up of the sum of "due depositors" plus "due banks;" while the curve of weekly "actual deposits" — sometimes called "net deposits" and sometimes merely "deposits" — approximated that of "due depositors" derived from the quarterly figures. Only in the periods before the middle of 1854, and from January 1858 through the middle of 1859 are there significant variations in the two latter curves.

In the first instance, acceptance of the Clearing House figures for "actual" or "net" deposits as equivalent to sums "due depositors" would give by implication a decline in this element precipitous in quality at a time when external evidence fails to yield corroboration. It was decided to give little weight to the deposit data of this period.

As to the second case, the situation is as follows: — with the commencement of 1858, the Clearing House began to report "actual" or "net" deposits as "total deposits" minus "average clearings;" and in this eighteen-month interval, the data derived from the Clearing House show a rise and fall of somewhat greater magnitude than that presented by the "due depositors" data of the quarterly reports.

With respect to the weekly series on loans and discounts, the picture corresponds in some ways with the first dubious situation regarding deposits. Unquestionably from 1855 onward the figures are identifiable as "total loans and discounts" minus "loans to brokers and directors." For the earlier eighteen-month interval — the middle of 1853 through 1854 — there is conflicting evidence. Possibly these weekly data represent "total loans" and not what

[186]

may be called "net loans." In consequence of such doubt, here as in the case of deposits, too great weight ought not to be given the data for this first eighteen-month period.

As a result of research regarding these weekly data, it seemed satisfactory to employ the figures as reported by the Clearing House. Here the curves presented in Chart 45 may be identified as "net loans" (as contrasted with "total loans" on Chart 41) and as "actual deposits" (which do not differ widely from "due depositors," the series employed in the earlier chart based on the quarterly data). As "net loans" and "total loans" moved together, there is no real loss in shifting from one series to the other; and, accordingly, the data for Charts 41 and 45 are fairly comparable with one another.

TABLE 73. — PRICES OF 60-DAY BILLS ON LONDON AT BOSTON AND NEW YORK: MONTHLY, 1795–62

The rates given below for the years 1795–1824 are drawn from the *Boston Price-Current and Marine Intelligencer*, *Russell's Gazette*, and the *Boston Gazette* for the quotation on the nearest day available to the middle of the month; for 1825–52, from *Bankers' Magazine*, v. 6 (1851–52), pp. 599–600, for the quotation at the time of the first packet each month; for 1853–61, from J. G. Martin's *History of the Boston Stock Market* (1898 ed.), pp. 22–28 and 51, for the quotation "on or about the first of the month;" and for 1862 from Martin also but referring to the high and the low for each month.

These quotations are in terms of per cent premium (advance) or discount on nominal par of $4.44 4/9 per pound sterling. After May 1834, real par was 109.75, which made the pound sterling equivalent to $4.8665. For an explanation of nominal par, see J. Q. Adams' *Report on Weights and Measures* (1821), p. 145.

(Per cent of nominal par)

	1795	1796	1797	1798
January		5½–6 dis	4 – 6 dis	3 – 4 dis
February		5 – 6 dis	2 – 3 dis	1 – 2 dis
March		3 – 4 dis	1 – 2½ ad	1 dis–par
April		5 – 5½ dis	1 – 2½ ad	1 dis–par
May		4 – 5 dis	3 – 4 ad	1 dis–par
June		1 – 2 dis	3 – 3½ ad	par
July		1 – 2 ad	2½–3 ad	1 – 2 dis
August		1 dis – par	1 dis – par	1 – 2 dis
September	par	2 – 2½ dis	2 – 2½ dis	3 dis
October	par	1 dis – par	2 – 2½ dis	3 – 5 dis
November	½ dis	par	2 – 2½ dis	3 – 5 dis
December	1½–2 dis	4 dis	2 – 3 dis	3 – 5 dis

	1799	1800	1801	1802
January	4–5 dis	2½–3 dis	1 – 2½ dis	3 dis
February	5 dis	1 dis	3 dis	2 – 3 dis
March	5–6 dis	2 dis	6 – 6½ dis	2½ dis
April	5–6 dis	2½ ad	2 – 2½ dis	2 dis
May	6–7½ dis	2 ad	½–1 dis	1 – 1½ dis
June	7–7½ dis	2½ ad	3½–4½ dis	1½–2 dis
July	9½ dis	2½–3 ad	4½–5 dis	1 dis – par
August	10 dis	par–1 ad	4 – 4½ dis	1 dis – par
September	10 dis	par	1 dis	1 dis – par
October	6–7 dis	1 – 2 ad	1½–2½ dis	1 dis – par
November	6–7 dis	2 – 2½ ad	3 – 4 dis	par
December	7–7½ dis	par–1 ad	1 – 2½ dis	½–1 ad

TABLE 73. — *Continued*

	1803	1804	1805	1806
January	1 – 1½ ad	2½–3 ad	½–1 dis	2½–3 dis
February	1 ad	2 – 2½ ad	½ dis – par	1½–2½ dis
March	1 ad	2 – 2½ ad	1 dis – par	1½–2 dis
April	1½–2 ad	3 ad	1 – 1½ dis	½ ad
May	2 ad	1 ad	1½–2½ dis	1 ad
June	3 – 3½ ad	par	3½–4 dis	½ ad
July	1 ad	par– ½ ad	5 – 6 dis	½–1 dis
August	1½–2 ad	par– ½ ad	5½–6½ dis	1½–2½ dis
September	2 ad	par– ½ ad	5 dis	½–1 dis
October	½ ad	2½–3 ad	1 dis	1 dis
November	4 – 4½ ad	2 – 2½ ad	1½–2 dis	½–1 dis
December	4 ad	½ dis	3½–4 dis	2½ dis

	1807	1808	1809	1810
January	1 – 1½ dis	4 – 4½ ad	9½–10 ad	3½–4 dis
February	½ dis-par	3 ad	7 – 7½ ad	3 – 3½ dis
March	½ dis-par	3½ ad	1½–2 ad	2½–3 dis
April	1½ dis	4½–5 ad	3 ad	3½–4 dis
May	2½–3½ dis	6 – 6½ ad	par – ½ ad	3 dis
June	2½–3½ dis	5½–6 ad	par – ½ ad	2½–3 dis
July	3½–4 dis	6 ad	1 – 1½ ad	4½ dis
August	3½–4 dis	5 – 6 ad	2 – 2½ ad	5 – 5½ dis
September	4 – 5 dis	5 ad	1 – 1½ ad	5¾–6 dis
October	2½–3 dis	4 – 4½ ad	1 ad	6¼–6¾ dis
November	1 – 1½ dis	5 ad	par	7 – 7½ dis
December	½ dis-par	8 ad	1 – 1½ dis	7½–8 dis

	1811	1812	1813	1814
January	8 – 9 dis	17¼–17½ dis	17½–18 dis	3½ – 4 dis
February	10 dis	16½–17 dis	17¾–18 dis	8 dis
March	11½–12 dis	17 – 18 dis	16½–17 dis	10½–11 dis
April	10 – 10½ dis	21 – 21½ dis	16½–16¾ dis	5½ – 6 dis
May	11 – 11½ dis	19 – 19½ dis	16 dis	10 – 10½ dis
June	13½–14 dis	20 – 21 dis	15½ dis	12½–13 dis
July	15½–16 dis	24½–25 dis	14¼–14½ dis	12½–13 dis
August	20 – 21 dis	21 – 22 dis	15 dis	12¼–12¾ dis
September	22 – 23 dis	21½–22½ dis	14¼–14½ dis	12 – 12½ dis
October	18 dis	14½–15 dis	14¼–14½ dis	15 dis
November	17 – 17½ dis	14½–15¼ dis	14 dis	15 – 16 dis
December	17½–18 dis	18 – 19 dis	12½–12¾ dis	13 dis

TALBE 73. — *Continued*

	1815	1816	1817	1818
January.............	....	2 dis	¼ ad	2¼ ad
February...........	16 – 17 dis	½ ad	½ dis-par	2 ad
March.............	8 – 9 dis	2½ ad	½–1 ad	par – ½ ad
April.............	7½ dis	3½ ad	4 ad	½ – ¾ ad
May................	6½– 6¾ dis	2½ dis	1 – 1½ ad	½–1 dis
June...............	6 dis	2 – 2½ dis	1¼–1½ ad	½ dis
July...............	12 – 12½ dis	½ dis	1¾–2 ad	¼ dis-par
August............	7½– 8 dis	½ ad	½–1 ad	¼ dis-par
September.........	1½– 2 dis	4½ ad	3 – 3¼ ad	par – ½ ad
October............	2¼– 2½ dis	4 – 4½ ad	2½ ad	½ – ¾ ad
November..........	4 – 5 dis	4½–5 ad	1½–1¾ ad	1 dis
December..........	3 dis	2½ ad	1½–1¾ ad	2 – 2¼ dis

	1819	1820	1821	1822
January.............	1½ dis	1 ad	3½ ad	11¼–11½ ad
February...........	1 dis	1 ad	4¼– 4¾ ad	13 – 13½ ad
March.............	½–1 dis	½ – ¾ ad	5½– 5¾ ad	12 ad
April.............	½ dis-par	½ dis-par	7 – 7½ ad	12½–13 ad
May................	1½ ad	½–1 dis	7½–7¾ ad	11 – 11½ ad
June...............	par	par	8¾– 9 ad	8 ad
July...............	½ dis-par	1 – 1¼ ad	8¾ ad	9½ ad
August............	2½ ad	1½–2 dis	8½–9 ad	10½–10¾ ad
September.........	2¼–2½ ad	2½ ad	8½–9 ad	11 – 11¼ ad
October............	2 ad	2 – 2¼ ad	9½–9¾ ad	12 ad
November..........	1½–2 ad	2½ ad	10 ad	12½ ad
December..........	1¾–2 ad	3 – 3¼ ad	12¼–12¾ ad	12 – 12¼ ad

	1823	1824	1825	1826
January.............	11½–12 ad	7½ ad	9½ ad	8½ ad
February...........	9½–10 ad	8½ ad	10 ad	8½ ad
March.............	..........*	9¼ ad	9¼ ad	8 ad
April.............	5½– 6 ad	9 ad	9½ ad	7½ ad
May................	4¼– 5 ad	8¾– 9 ad	8 ad	10 ad
June...............	5½– 6 ad	9½ ad	5 ad	9½ ad
July...............	6¼– 6½ ad	9 ad	5¾ ad	10¼ ad
August............	7 ad	8½– 8¾ ad	5 ad	10 ad
September.........	6¾ ad	9¾ ad	7¾ ad	11 ad
October............	7½– 7¾ ad	10¾–11 ad	10½ ad	12¾ ad
November..........	7 – 7¼ ad	10 ad	9½ ad	11½ ad
December..........	7½ ad	9¾ ad	9 ad	11½ ad

* Quotation for March given in Martin as 5 – 6 and in *Bankers' Magazine* as 11 advance.

TABLE 73. — *Continued*

	1827	1828	1829	1830
January............	11¾ ad	11 ad	8¼ ad	9½ ad
February...........	10 ad	10½ ad	8 ad	8½ ad
March............	10 ad	11¼ ad	8½ ad	8¼ ad
April.............	10¼ ad	11 ad	8¼ ad	8 ad
May..............	10¼ ad	10½ ad	9¾ ad	7 ad
June.............	11 ad	11 ad	9 ad	7 ad
July.............	10 ad	10½ ad	8½ ad	6 ad
August...........	10 ad	9¼ ad	9½ ad	6¼ ad
September.........	11 ad	10½ ad	9¾ ad	6¼ ad
October...........	11 ad	11¼ ad	9¾ ad	6 ad
November..........	11¼ ad	11 ad	9¾ ad	7 ad
December..........	11¼ ad	9¾ ad	9¾ ad	6½ ad

	1831	1832	1833	1834	1835
January............	6½ ad	10 ad	8 ad	2 ad	7 ad
February..........	6½ ad	9¾ ad	8 ad	1 dis	7¼ ad
March............	6¼ ad	9½ ad	8 ad	½ dis	7½ ad
April.............	7 ad	9¾ ad	8 ad	1 ad	8¾ ad
May.............	9¾ ad	10¼ ad	8¼ ad	3½ ad	8¾ ad
June.............	7½ ad	9¾ ad	8¾ ad	2 ad	9½ ad
July.............	10 ad	9¼ ad	8¾ ad	2½ ad	9¼ ad
August...........	10 ad	7 ad	8¼ ad	5 ad	9¾ ad
September.........	10¼ ad	8¼ ad	8¼ ad	6¾ ad	9 ad
October..........	10¾ ad	8 ad	7½ ad	7¼ ad	9½ ad
November.........	10½ ad	8 ad	7½ ad	7 ad	9¾ ad
December.........	10 ad	8½ ad	5½ ad	6 ad	9¾ ad

	1836	1837	1838	1839	1840	1841	1842
January.......	8½ ad	7½ ad	9⅞ ad	9½ ad	8 ad	8½ ad	8¾ ad
February......	10 ad	9¾ ad	9 ad	9 ad	8½ ad	8 ad	8¼ ad
March........	9¼ ad	8¾ ad	7½ ad	8¾ ad	8 ad	8 ad	8¼ ad
April.........	7¾ ad	11½ ad	4¾ ad	9½ ad	7¾ ad	7 ad	6½ ad
May.........	7 ad	11 ad	6¾ ad	8¾ ad	8 ad	7½ ad	7¼ ad
June.........	7 ad	13 ad	8 ad	9⅜ ad	7½ ad	8¼ ad	8 ad
July.........	7½ ad	18 ad	8¼ ad	9⅛ ad	7 ad	8½ ad	7½ ad
August.......	7½ ad	19¾ ad	7¼ ad	9½ ad	7 ad	8½ ad	6¼ ad
September.....	7½ ad	21 ad	9¼ ad	9 ad	7 ad	9 ad	7⅜ ad
October......	8¼ ad	14 ad	9⅞ ad	10 ad	8¼ ad	9¾ ad	8⅛ ad
November.....	8¼ ad	16 ad	9½ ad	9 ad	8¾ ad	10 ad	6¼ ad
December.....	9½ ad	14 ad	10 ad	9 ad	8¾ ad	9¼ ad	6½ ad

TABLE 73. — *Continued*

	1843	1844	1845	1846	1847	1848	1849
January	5½ ad	8½ ad	10 ad	8½ ad	5½ ad	10½ ad	9 ad
February	5⅜ ad	8½ ad	10 ad	8½ ad	6½ ad	10¼ ad	8¾ ad
March	6 ad	9 ad	9¾ ad	8½ ad	5¾ ad	10 ad	8 ad
April	5¾ ad	8½ ad	9¾ ad	10 ad	4½ ad	10 ad	6½ ad
May	7¼ ad	8 ad	9½ ad	10 ad	6½ ad	10½ ad	8½ ad
June	8½ ad	8¾ ad	9¾ ad	9¼ ad	7½ ad	10½ ad	9½ ad
July	8¾ ad	9¼ ad	10 ad	8¾ ad	6½ ad	10 ad	9¼ ad
August	9¼ ad	9½ ad	10 ad	8 ad	6¼ ad	9½ ad	9 ad
September	9¼ ad	9½ ad	9¼ ad	9¾ ad	7¼ ad	9¼ ad	10 ad
October	9¼ ad	10 ad	9¾ ad	9¼ ad	9 ad	9 ad	10 ad
November	8¼ ad	10 ad	9¼ ad	6 ad	10 ad	8¾ ad	10½ ad
December	8½ ad	10 ad	8¼ ad	6¾ ad	10¼ ad	8¾ ad	9 ad

	1850	1851	1852	1853	1854	1855	1856
January	8¼ ad	10⅜ ad	10¼ ad	9¾ ad	9¼ ad	7½ ad	8½ ad
February	9 ad	9¾ ad	10⅛ ad	9¼ ad	9⅛ ad	9 ad	8½ ad
March	8¾ ad	10⅛ ad	10⅛ ad	10⅛ ad	8¾ ad	9⅜ ad	9⅛ ad
April	8¾ ad	10⅜ ad	9¾ ad	9⅛ ad	8⅝ ad	9⅞ ad	9⅝ ad
May	9¾ ad	10⅝ ad	9 ad	9⅝ ad	9¼ ad	10 ad	9¾ ad
June	10 ad	10⅜ ad	10⅜ ad	9¾ ad	9¼ ad	10 ad	9¾ ad
July	10½ ad	10½ ad	10¼ ad	9¾ ad	9¼ ad	9¾ ad	10 ad
August	10½ ad	10⅜ ad	10¼ ad	9⅝ ad	9¼ ad	9¾ ad	9¾ ad
September	10½ ad	10¼ ad	10⅝ ad	9¼ ad	9¾ ad	9¾ ad	9¾ ad
October	10½ ad	10⅜ ad	10⅜ ad	9¼ ad	9⅞ ad	9¼ ad	9½ ad
November	10¾ ad	10½ ad	9⅞ ad	9⅝ ad	9⅝ ad	8½ ad	9¼ ad
December	9¾ ad	10½ ad	10 ad	9½ ad	9¼ ad	8¼ ad	9 ad

	1857	1858	1859	1860	1861	1862* low — high
January	8½ ad	9½ ad	9⅝ ad	9⅜ ad	3½ ad	11 –14½ ad
February	8¾ ad	9¼ ad	9½ ad	8¾ ad	6 ad	13 –15¼ ad
March	8¼ ad	9 ad	9⅝ ad	9 ad	5½ ad	11⅜–14¼ ad
April	8½ ad	9 ad‡	9¾ ad	9 ad	8½ ad	12 –13 ad
May	9¼ ad	9¼ ad	10⅛ ad	9⅜ ad	5 ad	12½–14¾ ad
June	9½ ad	9¾ ad	10 ad	9⅝ ad	5¾ ad	14⅜–21 ad
July	9¼ ad	9¼ ad	10¼ ad	9⅞ ad	6½ ad	20½–32½ ad
August	9½ ad	9⅝ ad	10⅜ ad	10 ad	7⅛ ad	24¾–29 ad
September	9 ad	9⅞ ad	9⅞ ad	9⅞ ad	7¼ ad	29 –35 ad
October	1 dis†	10 ad	10⅛ ad	9½ ad	7¼ ad	32½–51 ad
November	7½ ad	9¾ ad	10 ad	8⅜ ad	7¼ ad	42½–47¾ ad
December	9¼ ad	9¼ ad	9⅞ ad	4 ad	9 ad	42¾–48½ ad

† Good produce bills sold at 10 per cent discount.

‡ Sale on March 20 at 7 per cent advance.

* Quotations in currency, not gold.

TABLE 74. — DISCOUNT RATES ON COMMERCIAL PAPER AT BOSTON AND NEW YORK: MONTHLY, 1831–62

The rates given below for the years 1831–60 are drawn from E. B. Bigelow's *Tariff Question* (1862), Appendix 112, pp. 204–5, and are described as " 'street rates' on first calss paper in Boston and New York at the beginning, middle and end of the month;" for 1861–62 from J. G. Martin's *History of the Boston Stock Market* (1898 ed.), p. 43, for "first class three- to six-months bankable paper" indicating the high and low for each month. Martin's figures for the year 1860 run somewhat higher than do Bigelow's.

(Unit: 1 per cent)

	1830	1831	1832	1833	1834
January............		5½	7	6	15, 18, 24
February..........		5½	6½	5½	
March............		5½	6	5½	Business
April.............	*No*	5½	6½	6	unsettled
May..............	*data*	5½	7	6	
June.............		5½	6	6½	
July.............		6	6	8	Rates
August...........		6½	6	8	high and
September.........		7	6	8	variable
October...........		7	6	10	
November.........		7	6	10, 12	
December.........		7	6	12, 15	12, 10, 8

	1835	1836	1837	1838	1839
January............	5	10	16, 20, 13	11	6, 9
February..........		10	15, 21, 18	12	6, 9
March............	Rates	12	18, 20, 27	12, 18	6, 9
April.............	comparatively	12, 15	27, 26, 30	18, 12	6, 9
May..............	low	15, 18	27, 32	10, 9, 7	6, 9
June.............		15, 12	18, 9, 6	7, 6	9
July.............		15, 18	7½	6	11, 12
August...........		18, 24	7½	6, 7	12, 15
September.........		24	7½, 6½	6, 7	15, 18, 21
October...........		24, 36	6½	6, 7	21, 30
November.........		24, 30	6, 9	6, 8	20, 33, 36
December.........	8, 10	24, 30	10	7, 9, 7	18, 15, 9

TABLE 74. — *Continued*

	1840	1841	1842	1843	1844
January............	9	6, 7	9, 12	6	4
February..........	9, 12	6, 7	9, 12	6, 5	4
March............	9, 12	6, 7	9, 12	5, 6	4, 5
April.............	12, 7	6, 7	8	5	5
May..............	7	6	8	5, 4½	5
June.............	6, 8	6	8	5, 4½, 3½	5
July.............	8, 5	6	8	4	5
August...........	5, 7½	6	7¼	3¼, 4	5
September........	6, 7	6, 7	7	3½, 4	5, 5½
October..........	6, 7	6, 7½	6½, 6	3½, 4	5
November.........	6, 7	6, 9	6, 6½	3½, 4	5, 5½
December.........	6, 7	9, 12	6, 9	3½, 4	5, 5

	1845	1846	1847	1848	1849
January............	5, 6	8	8, 12	18	12
February..........	5½, 6	8, 9	8, 12	18, 15, 12	9, 12
March............	5½, 6	8, 7	8, 10	12, 15	12, 15
April.............	5½, 6	9, 12	8, 9	15	12, 15
May..............	5½, 6	8, 12	8	12, 15	9, 11
June.............	5½, 6	8, 12	7, 6	15, 18	7, 9
July.............	5¾, 6	8, 12, 9	7, 6	15, 18	8
August	6	8, 9	7, 9	12, 15	7½, 8½
September........	6	9, 6	9	12, 15	9
October..........	6, 5½	6, 8	9, 12	15, 18	9, 10
November.........	6, 5½, 8	6, 7	12, 15	18, 15	8, 10
December.........	8	6, 7	12, 18	15, 12	9½, 10½

	1850	1851	1852	1853	1854
January............	9, 10½	6, 7½	9, 8½	6, 7, 8	9, 8
February..........	9, 8	7, 8½	8½, 7½	9, 10	7, 9
March............	8, 9	7, 8½	7, 6	10, 12	9, 8, 10
April.............	8½, 9	8	6	10½, 10	10, 12
May..............	7½, 8½	7½, 6½	6	7, 8, 9	10, 12
June.............	7½, 8	7, 9	5½, 6	8, 9	9, 11
July.............	6½, 7	9, 11	5½, 6	9	10, 9
August...........	7, 8	11	5½, 6	9, 10	10, 9
September.........	7½, 9	12, 15	6, 7	10, 12	10, 12
October..........	7, 8	15, 16	6	12, 15	12, 10
November.........	7, 8	9, 12	6	15, 18, 12	10, 12
December.........	7, 8	9, 12	6	12, 10, 9	12, 18

TABLE 74. — *Continued*

	1855	1856	1857	1858	1859
January...........	15, 10	10, 12	9, 10	9, 8, 7½	5, 5, 5½
February..........	10	10, 9	8½, 9	6, 6, 5½	5½, 6, 6
March............	7, 9	10	9, 10	5½, 5½, 5	6, 5½, 5½
April.............	8, 10	9, 8	8, 9	5, 5, 4½	5½, 5½, 5½
May.............	6½, 8	7, 8	8, 7	4½, 4½, 4½	6, 6¼, 6¾
June.............	7, 6	7, 8	7, 8	4½, 4½, 4½	7, 8, 7
July.............	6, 7	7, 8	9, 10	4½, 4½, 4½	7, 6½, 7
August...........	7, 8	7, 8	9, 10	4, 4, 4	7¼, 7, 7
September.........	7, 8	8, 9	12, 24, 36	4, 4, 4	6¾, 7, 7½
October..........	7½, 9	9, 10	36, 24, 24	4½, 4½, 4½	7¼, 7½, 7½
November.........	10, 12	9, 10	24, 18, 15	4½, 4½, 5	7½, 7, 7
December.........	12, 15	10, 11	15, 12, 9	5, 5, 5	7, 8, 8

	1860	1861	1862
January.................	8, 9, 8½	15–8	6–9
February................	8, 7, 6½	9–8	9–7
March..................	6, 6, 5	8–6	7–9
April...................	5, 4¾, 4½	6–5	9–7
May....................	4½, 4½, 4½	5–6	7–4
June...................	4½, 5, 5½	5–6	3½–4*
July...................	5½, 5½, 6	5–6	4–5
August.................	6, 6, 6	5–6	5–4
September..............	6, 5½, 5½	5–6	3½–5
October................	5½, 5½, 6	5–6	4–5
November..............	6, 9, 12	5–6	4–5
December..............	15, 15, 12	5–6	4–5

* "Outside rate."

MOVEMENTS OF GOLD FROM CALIFORNIA:
SHIPMENTS TO ATLANTIC PORTS AND
RECEIPTS AT NEW YORK, 1849–1862

The data on gold movements from California are from scattered sources and not entirely satisfactory. They are offered here, however, as giving some indication of the flow of gold to New York. The figures on "gold shipped"— for the years 1849–52 and 1862 — are from ships' manifests. In 1849, however, they cover a single line, and it is doubtful whether they included all lines even in later years. The ships' manifests take no account of gold carried in pas-

senger baggage, which *Hunt's Merchants' Magazine* estimated at $500 per person. For the year 1850, *Hunt's* (vol. 24, p. 387) gives an estimate of the gold carried by passengers as 3.6 million dollars. On the other hand, "gold dust" was valued for the purposes of the ships' manifests at $16. per ounce troy, although the mint value in Philadelphia at that time was $1.50 more per ounce.

The data on gold movements given below in Table 75 are from *Hunt's Merchants' Magazine, Bankers' Magazine, De Bow's Review;* and, for 1862, from the *Report* of the New York Chamber of Commerce, 1861–62, p. 175.

TABLE 75. — MOVEMENTS OF GOLD FROM CALIFORNIA: MONTHLY, 1849–62[1]

(Unit: $1,000,000)

	1849		1850		1851		1852	
	Gold Shipped to Atlantic Coast	Gold Receipts at New York	Gold Shipped to Atlantic Coast	Gold Receipts at New York	Gold Shipped to Atlantic Coast	Gold Receipts at New York	Gold Shipped to Atlantic Coast	Gold Receipts at New York
January............			1.3	.3	2.8	2.6	2.9	2.3
February..........			.7	1.7	2.3	1.6	1.8	1.6
March............			1.1	1.1	2.1	1.8	2.2	1.8
April.............	.2		2.2	1.2	1.2		3.5	2.9
May..............	.3		1.7	.6	2.0		5.5	4.6
June.............	.3		2.8	1.2	2.5		3.6	3.0
July.............	.3		3.3	3.6	3.1		4.1	3.7
August...........	.5		3.5		3.2		3.6	3.0
September........	.6		3.2		3.5		4.1	3.5
October..........	.3		3.8		4.0		5.1	4.5
November........	1.3		3.7		4.5		5.3	4.4
December........	.7		2.8		3.4		4.1	3.7

	1853	1854	1855	1856	1857
	Receipts at New York	Receipts at New York	Receipts at New York	Receipts at New York	Receipts at New York
January............	3.7	3.5	4.4	3.3	2.7
February..........	5.3	3.8	2.9	3.7	2.6
March............	4.5	3.4	2.2	2.8	1.6
April.............	4.8	4.5	1.9	3.3	3.2
May..............	4.6	4.5	3.0	3.5	5.5
June.............	4.8	4.9	3.1	4.2	2.1
July.............	4.1	4.2	3.5	3.4	5.1
August...........	4.7	5.3	3.8	2.9	1.2
September........	4.6	4.3	2.0	3.5	2.1
October..........	5.1	3.4	5.3	3.5	5.4
November........	5.4	3.8	3.7	2.5	4.8
December........	4.8	4.4	3.8	3.5	4.8

	1858	1859	1860	1861	1862
January............	3.2	2.6	3.5	4.2	2.8
February..........	3.0	2.6	2.9	3.6	3.0
March............	2.7	1.9	2.7	2.4	2.3
April.............	2.8	3.1	2.6	3.0	2.6
May..............	3.2	3.4	2.9	2.0	3.6
June.............	3.2	3.5	2.9	2.0	2.2
July.............	2.6	3.8	2.2	2.1	4.5
August...........	3.0	4.0	2.8	4.2	4.4
September........	3.3	5.0	2.9	2.8	3.7
October..........	2.8	3.7	2.8	3.0	3.8
November........	3.5	3.3	3.2	2.6	4.5
December........	3.1	3.3	3.1	2.6	4.4

[1] For a description of the quality of these data and for sources, see p. 194.